The Man Who Rode the Tiger

Biography

Abraham Lincoln: A Press
The Fiery Trial: A Life of Lincoln

Reportage

*Dangerous Dossiers: Exposing the Secret War Against America's
    Greatest Authors*
Freedom to See: Television and the First Amendment

Literature

*Working for the Reader: A Chronicle of Culture, Literature, War, and
    Politics in Books*
Words Still Count With Me: A Chronicle of Literary Conversations

History (Editor)

Civilians Under Arms: The Stars and Stripes, Civil War to Korea
The Letters of Carl Sandburg
Washington, D.C., in Lincoln's Time
America at Random: Topics of the Times
Spectator of America

Novels

The Return
Get These Men Out of the Hot Sun
The Montauk Fault
Kings in the Counting House

Plays

Mister Lincoln
Knight Errant

THE MAN WHO RODE THE TIGER

The Life and Times
of Judge Samuel Seabury

by

HERBERT MITGANG

with a new introduction
by the author

Fordham University Press
New York
1996

Library of Congress Cataloging-in Publication Data

Mitgang, Herbert.
    The Man who rode the tiger : the life and times of
Judge Samuel Seabury / by Herbert Mitgang
    Originally published: Philadelphia : Lippincott, 1963.
With new intro.
    Includes bibliographical references and index.
    ISBN 0-8232-1721-3 (hardcover); ISBN 0-82320-1722-1
(paperback)
    1. Seabury, Samuel, 1873–1958.   Judges—New York
(State)—New York—Biography.   3. Political corruption—New
York (State)—New York—History.   4. New York (N.Y.) Politics
and government—1898–1951.   I. Title

KF373.S4M58   1996
347.747'014'092—dc20
[B]
[347.470714092]
[B]   96-24906
                                                   CIP

Printed in the United States of America

To my brother, Leo Mitgang, 1916–1944

Contents

List of Illustrations

The following illustrations appear as a group after page 172

Acknowledgments

MILLIONS of words of minutes and reports of the three Seabury investigations are on the official record. The library of The Association of the Bar of the City of New York is especially helpful in this respect. Still more voluminous are the newspaper accounts and editorial comments. *The New York Times* and *New York Herald Tribune* ran full texts of some of the testimony and most of the reports, and such bright and perceptive journalists as Doris Fleeson of the *New York Daily News* and Heywood Broun of the *New York World-Telegram* wrote about the investigations.

The Seabury family provided essential information about the man. I especially want to thank Judge Seabury's three nephews—Andrew Oliver, John B. Northrop, and William B. Northrop—for opening up family records, showing me around the former Seabury lands and homes, and telling me about incidents connected with and reactions to family and public events. Mrs. William Marston Seabury, Judge Seabury's sister-in-law; Louis Seabury Weeks and Henry S. Parker, Judge Seabury's cousins and boyhood friends, gave their recollections and candid views.

The Seabury staff members are part of the drama of the investigation; their feats are mentioned in the book. Interviews with these Seabury "boys," distinguished lawyers and public servants, afforded a rare look behind the scenes at the investigation and the Judge's personal and political life. George Trosk of Judge Seabury's law office served as his chief of staff; others who served as Seabury counsel to whom I am indebted are John Kirkland Clark, Irving Ben Cooper, Robert M. Davidson, James H. Goodier, Harry D. Guthrie, Jr., Philip W. Haberman, Jr., Carroll Hayes,

Oren C. Herwitz, Herbert Levien, George B. Levy, Joseph G. Miller, J. G. Louis Molloy, William B. Moore, Robert Morris, William G. Mulligan, William B. Northrop, Andrew Oliver, John C. Walsh.

For information, interviews or correspondence, many individuals— some of whom crossed the Judge's path at various times—provided essential material. In most cases their affiliations indicate in what respect they helped in the research. I want to thank: Robert O. Anthony, curator of the Walter Lippmann papers at Yale; Mrs. Amy O. Bassford, librarian of the Long Island Collection, East Hampton Free Library; Saul Benison, Oral History Research Office, Columbia University; Adolf A. Berle, Jr., former chamberlain of New York City and, with Judge Seabury, special counsel to the Board of Estimate on transit; John E. Berry, executive secretary, New York State Bar Association; the Reverend Robert S. Bosher, General Theological Seminary; Ernest M. Breuer, law librarian, New York State Library; William M. Chadbourne, former Fusion leader and Bull Mooser; Arthur A. Charpentier, librarian, the Association of the Bar of the City of New York; Robert Clancy, the Henry George School of Social Science; Samuel C. Coleman, justice of the New York State Supreme Court; Edward Corsi, former La Guardia associate and commissioner of immigration; Desmond L. Crawford, comptroller of the Corporation of Trinity Church; Frank P. Davidson, who, with his brother Robert M. Davidson, a Seabury staff counsel, provided information about their father, Maurice P. Davidson, reformer and a La Guardia commissioner; the Reverend Samuel Davis, rector, St. Luke's Church, East Hampton; Thomas E. Dewey, former district attorney, governor, and presidential candidate; Frederick H. Ecker, honorary chairman of the board, Metropolitan Life Insurance Company, a personal client of Seabury's; William Dean Embree, former president of the New York County Lawyers Association and chairman of The William Nelson Cromwell Foundation; Edward R. Finch, former presiding justice of the appellate division First Department, New York, who appointed Seabury referee of the magistrates' courts investigation; Felix Frankfurter, former Justice of the U.S. Supreme Court, who explained his role in the Walker removal; Anthony Grech, assistant reference librarian, Association of the Bar of the City of New York; Edward H. Green, of Sullivan and Cromwell, and the Cromwell Foundation; the late Judge Learned Hand of the United States Court of Appeals; Roy W. Howard, publisher of the Scripps-Howard newspapers; Robert L. Jacoby of the Franklin D. Roosevelt Library, Hyde Park; Herman Kahn of the National Archives, Washington, D.C., formerly director of the Roosevelt Library, Hyde Park; Mrs. Fiorello H. La Guardia; Reuben A. Lazarus, consultant on municipal affairs to the New

York State Assembly and formerly on Mayor Walker's legal staff; Walter Lippmann, who explained his political friendship with Seabury; Nicholas Livingston of East Hampton, once Seabury's chauffeur; Joseph L. Maged, executive director, New York County Lawyers Association; Lee McCanliss, of McCanliss & Early, who shared various cases with Seabury; David C. Mearns, chief of the manuscript division, the Library of Congress; Benjamin and Florence Mitgang, the author's parents, for recollections of Congressman La Guardia, trade unionism and politics in East Harlem, and encouragement over the years; Raymond Moley, contributing editor, *Newsweek* magazine and former professor of public law, Columbia; Robert Moses, former Republican candidate for Governor of New York; Allan Nevins of the Huntington Library, California, for guidance to sources at the Oral History Research Office, Columbia; Edgar B. Nixon, acting director, Roosevelt Library, Hyde Park; V. G. Peterson, executive secretary, Schalkenbach Foundation to Promote the Economics of Henry George; Hamilton F. Potter, former assemblyman and vice chairman of the Joint Legislative Committee investigating New York City, whose scrapbooks and recollections were of great help during the research; Joseph M. Proskauer, former justice of the New York State Supreme Court and Cromwell trustee; Jeanette E. Rattray, publisher of the *East Hampton Star,* who opened personal files on the Seaburys; Stewart Richardson, Phyllis Croissant, and Bernhard Kendler of J. B. Lippincott Company; W. Bernard Richland, authority on municipal law, who recalled his service as clerk and lawyer in Judge Seabury's office with humor and insight; Mrs. Franklin D. Roosevelt, for her appraisal of the President's attitude on Judge Seabury; Samuel I. Rosenman, former counsel to Governor Roosevelt and state supreme court justice; Catherine Snelling, private secretary to Sir Winston Churchill; Louis M. Starr, director, Oral History Research Office, Columbia; George Stevens, managing editor, J. B. Lippincott Company, for editorial warmth without weight; Floyd W. Tomkins, Jr., who served as a lawyer in Judge Seabury's last law office; Bethuel M. Webster, former president of The Association of the Bar of the City of New York, a most gentle and inspiring mentor for the Cromwell Foundation during the whole course of this book; Mrs. John F. W. Whitbeck, for many years Judge Seabury's secretary; Paul Windels, former corporation counsel of New York City.

Introduction to the Fordham Edition

IN HIS "Notes on Virginia," written in the years between the Declaration of Independence and the Constitution, Thomas Jefferson cautioned his countrymen about the two worst dangers that could confront the governance of the Republic: "The time to guard against *corruption* and *tyranny* is before they shall have gotten hold of us. It is better to keep the wolf out of the fold than to trust to drawing his teeth and talons after he shall have entered."

As the United States heads toward a new millennium, it continues to be the most revered democratic government in the world. After slumberingslam-bang open primaries and conventions, a hush falls over the land on Election Day and a President is elected, or re-elected. Just before and during World War II, Franklin D. Roosevelt was the only President to gain a third and fourth term. Thereafter, the Twenty-second Amendment to the Constitution was approved, limiting a President to two terms. No matter how kingly the incumbent or how dangerous the crisis facing the nation, that cannot change.

In the first two American centuries, there have been forty-two Presidents: a few scoundrels, a large number of mediocrities, a handful of quite goods, and several truly greats. Regardless of who occupied the Oval Office, no monarchical coat-of-arms or dictatorial cross-and-bones was ever raised over the White House. We have come close once or twice—only one President, Richard M. Nixon, resigned rather than face impeachment—but banana republic-style tyranny, supported by an armed palace guard, has never ruled in the United States.

"There is nothing more difficult to carry out, nor more doubtful of success, nor dangerous to handle, than to initiate a new order of things," Machiavelli wrote in *The Prince*. "For the reformer has enemies in all these who profit by the old order, and only lukewarm defenders in all those who would profit by the new order."

Remarkably, the new order has survived without *tyranny* in this country. One reason why is that reformers in the press, in academia, in citizens' organizations, and in legislative bodies serve as watchdogs for the public, alerting them to the dangers of dictatorship. *Corruption*, however, has been rampant in many Administrations—federal, state, and city. Time and again, the wolves that Jefferson mentioned in his telling metaphor have been at the gates or entered the folds of government.

The word corruption standing alone does not appear in the Constitution; the closest word to it is bribery, an impeachable offense. Now as well as in the past, bribery of public officials assumes familiar forms in business, in elections, and in government. All three are interrelated. Influence in the form of tax breaks and subsidies for privileged people and businesses are bought by big givers in campaigns. At the same time, efforts at campaign reform languish.

In 1996 alone, a number of distinguished United States Senators and Congressmen in both parties decided not to run for re-election, mainly because they would have had to beg for millions of dollars to mount campaigns. The higher the office, the more humiliating the game. Everyone knows that fundraising incurs obligations to donors and hobbles the legislative process, yet it is as American as . . . corruption.

There are solutions, but they may be as tough to change as getting the automobile manufacturers to approve seat belts and air bags—until one private citizen, Ralph Nader, mounted a personal campaign that, over the years, has saved hundreds of thousands of lives. Can it happen in political broadcasting? Television is one of the most costly items in running a campaign. In the original language of the Federal Communications Commission, the agency that regulates radio and television, the airwaves are licensed "in the public interest, convenience and necessity."

Beginning on the national level, if a certain amount of free time were given to eligible candidates, there would be greater willingness to run by dedicated men and women, fewer dropouts in the Senate and House, and fewer corrupting influences. Why should candidates seeking *public* office have to buy commercial time to be heard over the *public* airwaves?

Reformers are often ridiculed. They go up against power and power brokers who have been around for a long time. If Americans were prevented from receiving royal titles from foreign powers, at least we could boast of having our very own Robber Barons. The nineteenth-century industrialist William Vanderbilt put it cynically: "When I want to buy up any politician, I always find the anti-monopolists the most purchasable—they don't come so high."

The term Robber Barons was used to describe industrial leaders and corporations—such as Andrew Carnegie and Henry Clay Frick in steel, John D. Rockefeller in oil, Jay Gould and J. Pierpont Morgan in high finance, Cornelius and William Vanderbilt in railroads. Many of them displayed their wealth ostentatiously; hence, the derogatory term. They were criticized for setting up monopolies and trusts, often with the help of anti-labor private armies of Pinkertons. The Robber Barons and their twentieth-century successors were first exposed by journalistic "muckrakers" and then attacked by President Theodore Roosevelt, whom cartoonists liked to show carrying a big stick as a "trust buster." A few generations later, President Franklin D. Roosevelt attacked certain businessmen, repeating the first Roosevelt's phrase, as "malefactors of great wealth" who stood in the way of his New Deal measures to combat the Depression.

Times have changed; some of the heirs of the Robber Barons have proved to be educable. Now several of the formerly derided names are linked to benevolent foundations, educational institutions, libraries, and museums that are among the glories of our civilization.

Judge Samuel Seabury set an example for future reformers by his ethical investigations of corruption in the 1930s. The courageous investigator rode the Tammany Hall tiger without ending up inside, exposed corruption on every level of city government, forced Mayor James J. Walker to resign, and caused Fiorello H. La Guardia to become the most effective and popular Mayor in New York history.

In contrast to the Seabury investigations, later efforts were made to turn special prosecutors into political lackeys. The notorious Watergate affair—in which President Nixon and his aides conspired to sabotage the Democratic National Committee's headquarters in the Watergate apartment complex in Washington— brought down the Republican President. In 1973, Nixon was forced to name a special prosecutor, Archibald Cox, while he and his cronies were trying to impede the Senate select committee's investigation. Several months later, Nixon ordered Cox fired, because he had tried to subpoena secret recordings of presidential meetings and conversations. Rather than carry out the order, the two highest officials in the Justice Department resigned. After public outrage at what became known as the "Saturday night massacre," a new special prosecutor, Leon Jaworski, was named, and he resumed the effort to obtain the devastating tapes. Because Nixon corrupted the electoral process and sought to expand presidential powers beyond constitutional limits, he came close to impeachment. His resignation under fire showed the country the importance of investigations of public officials who violated their oaths of office.

Corruption is much smoother and more difficult to recognize today. It is disguised behind platoons of lobbyists parading in the corridors of power—in city halls, in state houses, and in Congress. It can be found in wealthy individuals and political action committees who find ways to circumvent the law and hide millions of dollars in campaign contributions. In return they receive a quid pro quo from bought legislators. Who is more influential in Washington than the National Rifle Association in shooting down the most reasonable efforts at gun control? What is true of the gunslingers in the Capitol also applies to lobbying associations in other fields—from anti-environmentalists to those who oppose a na-

tional health program to defense contractors seeking to sell out-
moded weapons to fight old cold wars.

Historically, the Seabury investigations in the early 1930s underscored the central point that the renowned journalist Lincoln Steffens made in *The Shame of the Cities* in 1904: "Politics is business—
that's what's the matter with it. The corruption that shocks us in
public affairs we practice ourselves in our private concerns." He
found that corruption was not merely political. "It was financial,
commercial, social; the ramifications of boodle were so complex,
various and far-reaching that one mind could hardly grasp them."
Steffens saw a system where corruption existed in banks and labor
unions and dummy corporations as well as in political machines.

In recent years, major cities all over the United States have had
their share of corrupt officials and scandals. New York City isn't
the worst; it's just the biggest. The Empire City has witnessed
parking-meter exposés, indictments of taxi and limousine commissioners, resignations of chairmen in the Health and Hospital Corporation, borough presidents using their offices to give themselves
and their friends franchises, public school contractors ripping off
the city with high bids and incomplete work, attempts to take the
smell out of the Fulton Fish Market, long controlled by gangster
elements.

The parallels of corruption then and now are apparent. Tammany is hardly mentioned in Democratic circles today. Once it was
an instrument of bribery and skullduggery. Democratic reform elements are stronger in Manhattan—and more influential in Washington—than some of the clubhouse bosses in other boroughs who
still control their fiefdoms through concessions to the changing
demographics and ethnic patterns in the city. But Republican officials in towns and cities just as often use their positions for private
enrichment in land deals and public contracts—adjacent Nassau
and Suffolk Counties on Long Island have had their share of scandals involving Republican leaders and judges. When it comes to
corruption, both major parties can include equal-opportunity
felons.

The Seabury investigations can be studied profitably (better
strike out that word) by current students of city and state govern-

ment. Judge Samuel Seabury (1873–1958) was an anti-Tammany Democrat and Progressive party reformer who served on the Court of Appeals, then returned to private practice and became an affluent lawyer in the 1920s. He once owned a mansion in the East Sixties and a large farm property with hundreds of acres in East Hampton.

As a longtime "goo-goo" (good government) reformer, when Seabury was summoned to look into municipal corruption, he could not resist. For nearly three years, he practically shut down his private practice and concentrated all his energies on saving the city. As a result, there were three Seabury investigations between 1930 and 1933—the first, into corruption in the magistrates' courts; the second, into the District Attorney's office; and the third, into all the departments and affairs of the City of New York. It was this inquiry that led into Mayor Jimmy Walker's office.

Initially, Judge Seabury was named a referee to examine the magistrates by the presiding justice of the State Department's Appellate Division, after consultation with Governor Roosevelt. Then FDR himself named Judge Seabury as commissioner to study the conduct of the Manhattan District Attorney. Finally, a joint state legislative committee was created to look into citywide corruption, with Judge Seabury as its counsel.

It was a boozy time between the World Wars when Tammany clubhouse leaders had divvied up the city and every service had a price—$50 to make a cut in a sidewalk for a gasoline station, $10,000 and up for a seat on the bench, $50,000 to lease a pier to berth an ocean liner on the Hudson River.

The magistrates were the center of a system of political payoffs, quashing of indictments, bribery, and false imprisonment. Judge Seabury found that, as mayoral appointees, the magistrates "delivered" when called to do so by their patrons—the county political bosses who had arranged for their positions in the first place.

The Manhattan District Attorney, Thomas C. T. Crain, was then punished for his puerile investigation of the magistrates and inability to halt unscrupulous bail bondsmen and police officers, some of whom were on the take during Prohibition and the running-board, getaway-car gangster era.

Judge Seabury and his investigative staff, made up of two dozen lawyers whose average age was 28, began to dig deeply into city records. They turned up the case of Dr. William (Horse Doctor) Doyle, who gave up his veterinary practice to become a lobbyist for builders, contractors, and landlords in cases before the Board of Standards and Appeals. He split fees with public officials. The board had the discretionary power to permit building variances—a power providing a rich source of graft.

The department-by-department investigation of the Walker Administration remains a casebook for other investigations of municipal corruption. Judge Seabury faced the grand sachems of Tammany Hall who protected their public-trough-feeding roles by holding down jobs as sheriffs and county clerks.

Eight-five district leaders received salaries of about $7,000 each for no-show positions as keepers of various seals and records. Beneath the leaders were clubhouse fixers who killed traffic tickets, served as the links to corrupt city departments and, of course, got out the vote for Tammany candidates.

The Seabury investigations were not devoid of public entertainment. Long afterward, they would lead to the musical *Fiorello!* and a hit tune about "little tin boxes." The subject of greatest ridicule was the Sheriff of New York County, the Honorable Thomas A. Farley, who testified during the citywide investigation. On a salary of $8,500 a year, the sheriff had managed to accumulate nearly $400,000 in six years. Judge Seabury personally cross-examined him and elicited this testimony:

SEABURY: Where did you keep those moneys you had saved?
FARLEY: In a safe-deposit box at home in my house.
SEABURY: Whereabouts at home in the house did you keep this money that you had saved?
FARLEY: In the safe.
SEABURY: In a little box in a safe?
FARLEY: A big safe.
SEABURY: But a little box in a big safe?
FARLEY: In a big box in a big safe.
SEABURY: Was the box crowded or very full?
FARLEY: Well, it was full and plenty in it.
SEABURY: Now, Sheriff, was this big box that was safely kept in the big safe a tin box or a wooden box?

FARLEY: A tin box.

SEABURY: Giving you the benefit of every doubt on sums from your official vocation, the $83,000 extra you deposited in 1929 came from the same source that the other money came from?

FARLEY: It did. Same tin box.

SEABURY: Kind of a magical box?

FARLEY: It was a wonderful box.

SEABURY: A wonderful box. What did you have to do—rub the lock with a little gold, and open it to find more money?

FARLEY: I wish I could.

At the beginning of the investigations, Governor Roosevelt remained aloof, knowing that what happened in the New York County courthouse could affect his chances for the Presidential nomination in 1932. His advisers told him that he needed Tammany Hall and other big-city machines. At the same time, they were aware that he could not give the appearance of being soft on corruption.

Governor Roosevelt personally presided as judge at the removal proceedings against Mayor Walker in Albany. Although he had limited experience as a lawyer and none as a jurist, FDR surprised and impressed the country. Future voters for the presidency admired the impartial and intelligent way he conducted the trial of Jimmy Walker, the most prominent and popular Tammany mayor.

Records unearthed by Judge Seabury's staff showed that a slush fund was maintained for Walker by a group of politicians and businessmen; a $10,000 letter of credit in his name for a European trip was discovered; a brokerage account for him was found, bearing the initials J.J.W., to which he contributed nothing.

Using Seabury's evidence, Governor Roosevelt deftly exposed Walker's secret accounts and business ties. The glib mayor complained that he was being "transported back to Russia." Walker's mentor, Alfred E. Smith, onetime Governor of New York and former Democratic nominee for President, tried to save the mayor but finally asked him to resign for the good of the party. When Mayor Walker did so, Franklin P. Adams cracked in his newspaper column, "The old gay Mayor, he ain't what he used to be." Roosevelt went on to win the nomination and the White House.

After the investigations, Judge Seabury emerged as a national personality. There was talk of his running for President; privately, he dreamed of capturing the Democratic nomination for himself—in effect, stealing it from Roosevelt. But lightning did not strike. He declined invitations to run for mayor himself and insisted that the candidate be a fiery reformer on a Fusion ticket who despised Tammany as much as he did—Fiorello H. La Guardia, the Little Flower.

Corruptio optimi pessima—the greatest evil is the good corrupted.

That is the lesson behind the Seabury investigations of corruption in New York City. The meaning should not be limited to the obvious modern examples of collusion between racketeers and politicians, to ordinary shakedowns and handouts, or even to the pervasive influence of organized crime.

It is the *legitimized corruption* that has become the most alarming in the United States. For example, during its heyday, the Nixon Administration approved subsidies to the oil industry that cost the American consumer and taxpayer about sixty billion dollars. By contrast, the Teapot Dome oil giveaway during the Harding Administration amounted to mere hundreds of millions. Teapot Dome is studied as a scandal because of overt bribery, but subsidies to the oil industry are considered perfectly legitimate.

The whole field of conflicts of interest, outside hidden income and loans, franchises of public facilities, partnerships and stock ownership in private industry, environmental intrusions on national lands, fixing violations for major lobbyists and campaign fund donors, engineering special-interest tax exemptions and laws favoring the few—these are the greater evils.

An ethics code does exist for the Senate and House and employees of the Executive branch, but it lacks strong enforcement provisions. Everyone in the Federal Government is admonished "never to discriminate unfairly by the dispensing of special favors or privileges to anyone whether for remuneration or not; and never to accept, for himself or his family, favors or benefits under circumstances which might be construed by reasonable persons as influencing the performance of his governmental duties." Persons on the Federal payroll are told to engage in "no business with the Government, either directly or indirectly, which is inconsistent with the conscientious performance of governmental duties." These are worthwhile statements of principle but they are often honored in the breach.

Conscience—the exercise of a private, unwritten code of ethics—can be found in the life of such public servants as Judge Samuel Seabury, the fighting reformer for a civilized city. In the end, to overcome tyranny, public ethics must be guarded; to prevent corruption, private ethics must be lived.

HERBERT MITGANG
1996

But do you not admire, I said, the coolness and dexterity of these ready ministers of political corruption? Yes, he said, I do; but not all of them, for there are some whom the applause of the multitude has deluded into the belief that they are really statesmen, and these are not much to be admired.

Plato, The Republic.

I'd have my son know Seabury instead of Cicero.

Heywood Broun, The World-Telegram.

BOOK I

The Making of a Reformer

1873-1930

Politics is business: that's what's the matter with it. The corruption that shocks us in public affairs we practice ourselves in our private concerns.

Lincoln Steffens, *The Shame of the Cities*

CHAPTER 1

A Bishop Looks Over His Shoulder

BEFORE the close of the Victorian era of well-mannered privilege and the advent of the twentieth century of occasional human progress, a newly minted attorney named Samuel Seabury was confronted with a case involving the ancient doctrine of eminent domain—the right of the state to force a property owner to sell land needed for public use. The case was relatively unimportant in the City of New York; but because it brought the larger social conflicts of the moment into an extremely personal focus for the young lawyer, its lesson stayed with him for the rest of his life.

His law firm, Morgan & Seabury, was maintained as counsel by the Corporation of Trinity Church, the historic Protestant Episcopal parish at Broadway and Wall Street. The Tammany commissioner of public buildings, an ex-alderman and lumber dealer named William Walker, who owed his allegiance to the infamous "Boss" Richard Croker, had decided to condemn St. John's Burying Ground, on Hudson Street in Greenwich Village, near the North River. The graveyard belonged to Trinity Church; in it rested the forefathers of many venerable New Yorkers. Now the "Irish Democrats" who lived in the neighborhood agreed that a small park would be more pleasant than a Protestant graveyard. It so happened that Commissioner Walker owned the house at No. 6 St. Luke's Place, diagonally across from the cemetery that devalued his property. With typical

Tammany altruism, he decided to improve the block, provide a play area for the neighborhood children (whose parents had elected him to public office) and—incidentally, of course—increase the land value in the area, including the property at No. 6.

Since the condemnation was a Tammany project, it could hardly be viewed as disinterested. There was, indeed, reason to wonder at the concern of the Tammany building commissioner for the children of Greenwich Village, for, since the sensational Lexow committee investigation in the middle of the 1890's, it had been common knowledge that many minors were being diverted not into public parks but into houses of prostitution, with the collusion of headquarters police and district leaders. Seabury approached the problem as a lawyer. He found that public condemnation was a well-established right, which the city had exercised many times in the past. Furthermore, it was clear to him that Commissioner Walker had not only the law on his side, but also the controlled courts. Seabury accordingly could only recommend that the Corporation of Trinity Church sell St. John's Burying Ground to the city and transfer the graves to the parish's larger cemetery on the northern end of Manhattan. Commissioner Walker triumphantly called upon the famous architect Stanford White to draw the plans for the new Hudson Park.

Meanwhile, Samuel Seabury and his father, the Reverend Dr. William Jones Seabury, professor of canon law at the General Theological Seminary, and former rector of the Church of the Annunciation on West 14th Street, were among the Episcopalians who disinterred their ancestors and carted the headstones and remains to the cemetery at 155th Street and Broadway. Two of their distant kin, Maria and Edward Seabury, had been buried at St. John's for three-quarters of a century. Both father and son were aware that the paws of the Tammany Tiger had now reached even to where the dead lay buried. And thus the son, at the very beginning of his legal career, ran up against Tammany personally. He did not yet know that in years to come the son of that same Building Commissioner Walker, James J. Walker, who had as a boy played among the St. John's tombstones of Seabury's ancestors, would be Mayor of New York; or that his and Walker's paths would cross briefly during the summer of 1932, when citizen Seabury would cross-examine Mayor

Walker, as the climax of the greatest investigation of municipal corruption in the history of the United States. . . .

All his life, Samuel Seabury bore the Protestant ethic and the
Anglo-Saxon legal traditions of his ancestors, not as a burden but as
an escutcheon. Nothing interested him more than his family's genealogy, although he tried to keep this interest secret during the peak
of his civic power for fear that Tammany enemies might make political capital of it. He was proud that he carried the famous name of
his great-great-grandfather, Samuel Seabury, the First Episcopal
bishop in the United States.

In his father's library and later in his own, the portrait of the
Bishop literally looked over his shoulder, as did the stern and patrician portraits of his other ancestors. Bewigged, bearded, mus-
tached, in the vestments of the church or the robes of bench and bar,
they hung by the dozen in ornate, gilded frames. They included
governors, lawyers and clergymen—the intellectual aristocrats of a
New World who made up a nobility of their own. Among them
hung portraits of their loyal wives, white-collared, laced, or sometimes rebelliously frilled—portraits at once austere and elegant, hanging above mahogany shelves that held books of legal proceedings
from Temples and Inns, genealogical tables of the families of the
West Country of England, heraldry, history and political science,
from the dreams of the first civilizations to the dreams of the twentieth century.

Above the great fireplace in his own library was the portrait of
the Bishop, done in three-quarter length. He is garbed in black, with
billowing sleeves of white ruffled at the wrists, and on his round face
is an enigmatic look that could be either a half-smile or half-frown
or both. Sam Seabury was always pleased, in later years, when a
visitor remarked on the striking resemblance of facial expression
between the Bishop and his great-great-grandson.

There was, indeed, good reason for him to take pleasure in the
comparison. The Bishop was a remarkable man, as well as a famous
one. It required tenacity to live up to the Latin motto on the Seabury
crest—*Supera Alta Tenere* (Hold to the Most High). And he
could be tenacious, even when on the wrong side of a popular cause,
as he was when he opposed the American Revolution. But his char-

acter was so balanced by prudence and integrity, that, as a colonial churchman, he was able to attain the highest rank of the Episcopal Church in the new nation.

Often, in the library of his father, young Sam Seabury would read of the lordly shadow cast by the Bishop. The old sermons were carefully bound and preserved in tan cloth and gold-stamped leather, commemoratives and declarations by and about him neatly catalogued, including discourses delivered by the Bishop in Trinity Church, New York. Encouraged by his father, who set aside a small desk in his own study for the boy, Sam Seabury probed deeply into the family's origins and achievements. And he discovered at least one parallel between the Bishop's early life and his own. Both youths were the sons of clergymen and grew up in modest, and sometimes poor, circumstances.

The first Samuel Seabury was born on November 30, 1729, in Groton, Connecticut, and was educated first at home and later at Yale, graduating before he was nineteen. When his family moved to Hempstead, Long Island, he helped his father by acting as a lay reader in Huntington. He went abroad to study medicine for a year at the University of Edinburgh because his father stressed the need for a knowledge of "physic and anatomy." However, he was drawn to the church and, proceeding to London in 1753, he was ordained by the Church of England. Returning to the colonies, he was thirty years a preacher, both on horseback and during permanent assignments on Staten Island, Long Island, and in Westchester County and New Jersey. For ten years he was in charge of a mission in East Chester, and occasionally he had to combat the influence of such itinerant evangelists as George Whitefield, who brought about the "great awakening" in New England. At the same time he devoted himself patiently to winning back many lapsed communicants to the Church of England.

The young clergyman, in spite of his own colonial ancestry, was a servant of the Established Church and a missionary for the Society for the Propagation of the Gospel in Foreign Parts (the "Foreign Parts" including the American colonies). "Faithful and true" to the church and the king to whom he had sworn allegiance when ordained, he would not omit any portion of the Liturgy, such as the prayers for the royal family of England. The despised George III had no more faithful adherent; Seabury's sense of loyalty kept him an out-and-out Tory. As a result, he achieved a distinction attained by no other Seabury in the New World—he was thrown into jail for six weeks by a band of American patriots.

The patriots who put him in a New Haven jail did so, from their point of view, for good reason. Over the signature of A. W. Farmer (short for "A Westchester Farmer"), he wrote a series of pamphlets vigorously denouncing the revolutionaries, defending the mother country, and equating the rights of the Church of England with the rights of the King of England. The "farmer" letters, presenting the Tory view, were answered by an eighteen-year-old firebrand named Alexander Hamilton, then a college student, and for months the pamphlet controversy raged in New York.

Hamilton's letter, "A Full Vindication of the Measures of the [Continental] Congress from the Calumnies of Their Enemies," chided the pseudonymous "farmer" for his "strong language." To which "farmer" Seabury replied, "You give me a hint about swearing. I have profited by it. I intend never to swear more. I wish you would take a hint about fibbing. It is rather a meaner quality than that of rapping out a little now and then." Seabury allowed himself such an occasional flash of humor; and in the twentieth century, those who listened closely when his namesake cross-examined witnesses detected similar brief moments of biting wit and sarcasm.

"Tell me not of Delegates, Congresses, Committees, Riots, Mobs, Insurrections, Associations—a plague on them all," said "farmer" Seabury. "Give me the steady, uniform, unbiased influence of the courts of Justice. I have been happy under its protection and I pray God I shall be so again." He wanted legal government; and what most infuriated the patriots was that he used his ministerial position in what had become a political controversy. But speak out he did, courageously denouncing the agreements adopted by the Philadelphia Congress and warning that revolutionary regulations would bring an unwarranted invasion of the people's privacy.

Open your doors to them. Let them examine your tea canister and molasses-jugs, and your wives' and daughters' petticoats. Bear and cringe, and tremble and quake—fall down and worship our sovereign lord, the Mob. But I repeat it, by Heaven, I will not. No, my house is my castle;

as such I will defend it while I have breath. No King's officer shall ever enter it without permission unless supported by a warrant from a magistrate; and shall my house be entered, and my mode of living enquired into by a domineering committeeman? Before I submit I will die; live you, and be slaves!

This devotion to principle—especially a principle rooted in the common law of Great Britain—became a firm Seabury characteristic. Stubbornness in the face of popular opinion could also be associated with the Seabury name. In years to come, when reviewing the deeds of their Tory ancestor, Sam Seabury and his father, sitting in their study, spoke admiringly of the way the Bishop followed his conscience.

Sam Seabury read of Bishop Seabury's ordeal in the Bishop's own words, addressed to the "Lords Commissioners of Your Majesty's Treasury":

> Your Memorialist soon became suspected of writing in support of legal government, & on that account & on account of his having acted openly in support in the County of Westchester, he became one of the first objects of revenge. . . . That after some time your Memorialist, hearing of no further threat, returned home, & continued unmolested, though occasionally reviled by particular people for not paying obedience to the order of Congress enjoining fast days &c; until the 19th day of Novr. 1775 when an armed force of 100 horsemen came from Connecticut to his house & not finding him at home they beat his children to oblige them to tell where their father was—which not succeeding they searched the neighborhood & took him from his school & with much abusive language carried him in great triumph to New Haven, 70 miles distant, where he was paraded through most of the principal streets, & their success celebrated by the firing of cannon &c; that at New Haven he was confined under a military guard & keepers for six weeks, during which time they endeavored to fix the publication of A. W. Farmer's pamphlets on him; which failing, & some of the principal people in that country disapproving their conduct your Memorialist was finally permitted to return home. . . .

After his release, Seabury resided in New York, practicing medicine and occasionally taking on a church duty. His loyalty to the Church of England remained; he received the degree of Doctor of

Divinity from the University of Oxford during the Revolution, and he continued to serve the king. Sir Henry Clinton, commander in chief in North America, appointed him chaplain of the king's American regiment. As chaplain he watched in anguish as the British were defeated. He saw the church fall into disrepute and many of its members flee to Nova Scotia and back to England. But Seabury did not think of retreating; he considered himself an American, even though he still respected his pledge to church and crown.

When Seabury returned to New Haven, the place of his imprisonment, it was as the first bishop of the Protestant Episcopal Church. That he was a devout and sympathetic pastor had been proved by his long and impoverished years of service to his parishioners. Now, by vote of his colleagues in Connecticut in March, 1783, he was named bishop. This was a mixed blessing. In the northern colonies, especially in New England, the antichurch movement was especially strong; many of the early colonists had left England to avoid worshiping according to the Anglican ritual and to rid themselves of hated bishops. For years no clergyman who remained linked with the church was allowed to establish himself. No bishop had ever come to the colonies; the Bishop of London supervised the Anglicans in New York and New England. Under these odd circumstances, the Reverend Dr. Seabury sailed for England, armed with letters and credentials from the clergy, to be consecrated.

Dr. Seabury spent fourteen months in London trying to persuade the Archbishop of Canterbury to allow his consecration as Bishop of Connecticut. His Tory connections were of no avail. Canterbury procrastinated. His main objection was that an oath of allegiance to the British crown was an essential part of the ceremony, but since the Revolution, no such allegiance, in fact, could be exacted. When Seabury finally realized that it would take an act of parliament to allow the omission of this oath, a highly unlikely concession, he turned northward, to the disestablished Episcopal Church in Scotland. Almost a hundred years before, the Scottish bishops, loyal to the House of Stuart, had refused an oath of allegiance to William and Mary, causing a schism between the Church of England and the Church of Scotland. The Scottish bishops scrutinized Seabury's credentials and concluded that it was their sacred duty to consecrate him. On Sunday morning, November 14, 1784, in a makeshift chapel

on the upper floor of a house in Longacre, Aberdeen, Bishops Kil-
gour, Petrie, and Skinner laid their hands upon Samuel Seabury's
head and consecrated him as bishop.

All the details of this notable event in the Seabury family history
—and in the history of American Protestantism—were traced in
detail, again and again, by the young attorney Sam Seabury, and by
his father, during the genealogical researches that occupied them,
off and on, all their lives. Sam Seabury felt a special closeness to the
old church in Aberdeen, often visiting Scotland, and in turn serving
as host to the Bishop of Aberdeen whenever he visited the United
States.

The Seabury ancestors could be traced even beyond the famous
Bishop. And nothing delighted Sam Seabury more than doing so.
He often stood before the portraits and described each ancestor's
lineage, characteristics, and contributions. (Later, with his brother-in-
law, William H. P. Oliver, he helped to found an organization to
trace the origins of all the first settlers who came to the American
colonies.)

The Seabury side went back to that wistful Plymouth Colony
poetic triangle of John, Miles, and Priscilla. After Priscilla had sup-
posedly told John to speak for himself, the John Aldens had eleven
children, including David, whose daughter, Elizabeth, married John
Seabury. John was the son of the original Samuel Seabury, a physician and surgeon, whose father, John, had come to the New World
in 1639. The second Samuel Seabury was a clergyman, who was converted from Congregationalism to Anglicanism. And the third
Samuel Seabury, who carried on the missionary and parish work of
his father, became the Bishop.

Complementing the prominent clergymen in Sam Seabury's gallery
of paternal ancestors, there was a distinguished legal forebear. This
was Samuel Jones, "the Father of the New York Bar," according to
Chancellor James Kent. Judge Jones was a member of the New York
State Legislature, and he helped to draft the bill that adopted the
Constitution of the United States. Together with James Varick, later
Mayor of New York, he compiled the state's official Revised Statutes.
After serving as recorder of New York County, he resigned when
his law-school classmate, Governor De Witt Clinton, appointed him
comptroller of the State of New York. Judge Jones and his colonial

ancestors stood firmly on the side of the American revolutionists. Sam Seabury's forebears included fighters against authority, too.

In 1835, the fourth Samuel Seabury, a grandson of the Tory bishop, married a granddaughter of the post-revolutionary judge. The Reverend Samuel Seabury, from 1838 to 1868, was rector of the Church of the Annunciation, and he also served as a professor at the General Theological Seminary. The tradition was carried on by his son, William Jones Seabury, Sam Seabury's father. William Jones Seabury wavered between the church and the law. He was admitted to the New York Bar and practiced for several years until shortly after the Civil War, when he was ordained, and succeeded his father first as rector of the Church of the Annunciation, a post he held for thirty years, and later as a seminary professor.

There was another side, of course, to Sam Seabury's ancestry. It was hardly known to the public, which, sometimes affectionately, sometimes derogatorily, referred to the attorney as "the Bishop." But as the years of his own life passed, Sam Seabury became more and more fascinated by his mother's adventurous ancestors, the Beares— and by that part of his own nature that was more adventuresome. All his life, it seemed, the conservatism of the Seaburys kept overshadowing the daring of the Beares.

At the height of his political and legal career, Sam Seabury took time to compile the story of his mother's side—a volume, privately printed, entitled *Captain Henry Martin Beare, 1760–1828, Life, Ancestry and Descendants.* It was dedicated to Sam's mother, Alice Van Wyck Beare Seabury, "in affectionate memory." The captain and the captain's second wife, who were Sam Seabury's great-grandparents, looked, and were, different from the clergymen and lawyers of the Bishop's line. Their smaller pictures hung apart on one side in the Seabury library, but something in their lively expressions—a curl of the lip, a twinkle in the eyes—gave them a humanity that refused to be confined in varnished oils and gilded frames. That Sam Seabury saw this was evident; he devoted precious time in his maturity to costly researches here and abroad tracking down the background of the captain and his lady. And in his later, reflective years, in the quiet of his study, where he spent much time alone after midnight, he might have pondered on the attractive romantics who had failed to transmit their lively personalities to him.

Captain Beare left Devon, England, at age twelve to go to sea. He was wounded at the Battle of Ushant in 1778, taken prisoner by the French, held for thirteen months in Brittany, and then released in an exchange of prisoners. Retiring from the British Navy, Henry Beare entered the service of the East India Company and soon commanded his own ships sailing from the Isle of France to China. He married the niece of the American consul in 1793 and, a few years later, purchased his own vessel, the *Cleopatra,* sailing for New York with a rich cargo. The $100,000 cargo became the subject of a famous law suit, which Sam Seabury studied in all its details, as if it were one of his own important cases on appeal.

The case was notable chiefly for the eminence of the counsel on both sides: Aaron Burr and Alexander Hamilton representing Louis LeGuen, plaintiff and part owner of the *Cleopatra*'s cargo of cotton, sugar and indigo; and Gouverneur Morris and Brockholst Livingston representing the commission merchants Gouverneur & Kemble. The nature of contracts, agency, sales, fraud, and other legal issues were all involved in the case, which was finally decided for the plaintiff in the New York Court of Errors in 1800.*

The captain's marriage to Charlotte Young in 1802, after the death of his first wife abroad, brought him to New York City permanently and led him to take American citizenship. He was forty-two when he married the seventeen-year-old daughter of a prominent merchant. He alternated making trips to the East Indies with tending his prosperous business on Lower Broadway. The Beares' domestic life centered around Trinity Church, where their children were baptized. One of their sons, Henry Martin Beare, became a clergyman; another, Thomas Marston Beare, a businessman. (The latter was Samuel Seabury's grandfather.) Now, the histories of the Seaburys and Beares in the New York of the early and middle nineteenth century began to resemble each other. The wandering captain was interred in the same St. John's Burying Ground on Hudson Street that was to mean so much to his great-grandson.

It seemed altogether fitting that, with such a distinguished roll call of colonial forebears, Sam Seabury should be born on Washington's Birthday, 1873. The fifth Samuel in the line was born in the

* *1 Johnson's Cases 437.*

rectory of the Church of the Annunciation on West 14th Street. In the early dawn of that twenty-second of February, the anxious Dr. Seabury diverted himself until the arrival of his first son by preparing a sermon on George Washington. A part of Sam Seabury's life was spent escaping not only from the bounds and strictures of his own class, but also from the life of his parents.

His father, Dr. Seabury, was an unusually well educated man—even more so than his son. He had received his bachelor's and master's degrees at Columbia College. Then he was admitted to the New York Bar in 1858 and engaged in practice for six years. But the pull of the church on him was stronger than that of the courts. He entered the General Theological Seminary in 1864 and was ordained a deacon and priest two years later. While serving as rector of the Church of the Annunciation, he received his doctorate from Hobart College in 1874. After his children had grown up, Dr. Seabury became professor of canon law at the General Theological Seminary—a post he held until his death. The fact that he had persuaded the vestry of his church to establish a special chair in this subject, and immediately occupied it himself at the seminary, was cause for amusement for his son.

His mother, a descendant of New England's governing Saltonstalls as well as of the adventuresome Beares, was the devoted hostess of a seminary household, a woman of warmth and compassion. While his father was essentially a teacher, who taught his children by his own quiet example, his mother assumed the task of regulating the household and disciplining the children. "She was more than equal to the task," her son said in later years. Visitors to the house recalled that her dinner table was often set for a dozen guests—professors, students, cousins from Long Island, and friends. The emphasis in the Seabury household was upon hospitality as well as familial closeness.

The Seaburys lived in modest circumstances. To some of their more affluent cousins, visiting from the North Shore of Long Island, they seemed to be poor. "Each needy church was left quite free/to stay as poor as poor could be." So Dr. Seabury wrote in a poem called "The Redundancy of Rectors," which included truths about his own parish. Twice or more Dr. Seabury tried to resign as rector of the Church of the Annunciation, in order to let another man try to retrieve the fortunes of the parish, but the vestry had declined his offer.

All during young Sam's boyhood, his father struggled along on the small salary of a rector of a church that had to be maintained by private donations. Finally the church was overmortgaged, and its land was disposed of. The genteel poverty of Dr. Seabury's calling, however, did not deprive his family of the basic necessities. It had the beneficial effect, moreover, of causing Seabury to begin his son's education personally instead of sending him to costly schools.

"My father had a study attached to the Church of the Annunciation, which consisted of a large room holding a considerable part of his extensive library," Sam Seabury recalled. "At an early age he gave me a desk in that room so that I could have a place in which to read and study. I have always regarded it as true that a large part of what I call my education was received in that room, where I had the constant companionship of my father, and in which we discussed all questions that arose. My father encouraged this questioning habit, and would answer the questions which I propounded. I would often undertake to look up a question in the library and, with his assistance, usually found the correct answer. The closest companionship existed between us, and as long as he lived I would often stop in to see him and spend the evening discussing some of the subjects in which I was interested."

His formal education began at a small private school in the neighborhood, which was attended by many of the youngsters living "uptown" on 14th Street. Family tradition caused him to transfer to Trinity School, where his father served as trustee (as had his grandfather). Sam Seabury's impression was that Trinity was "a very old but not a good school," and he left after two years.

His father had taken him out of school briefly to attend an event that left a deep impression on the eleven-year-old boy—and was an education in itself. The year 1884 marked the one hundredth anniversary of the consecration of Bishop Seabury in Scotland. Dr. Seabury was invited to attend the special services in London and Aberdeen, and he took along his son. They sat in St. Paul's Cathedral together and listened to the Archbishop of Canterbury deliver a sermon about another Samuel Seabury—"a simple, grand, conciliatory, uncompromising man." Dr. Seabury himself was given the honor of reading the Gospel on that Sunday in November, 1884.

Later, in Aberdeen and Edinburgh, honors of church and state were heaped upon the name of Bishop Seabury—and the young boy was introduced to church dignitaries and embassy officials as the namesake of the first American Episcopal leader. But there was more to the trip than sitting in old churches and being patted on the head by bewhiskered grownups. Before they returned home on the trans-Atlantic steamer *Germanic,* Dr. Seabury took his son all around London. They visited the House of Lords and heard Lord Salisbury speak to the right honorable members. They saw the Temples and Inns of court, and they took a trip to the Shakespeare country. These were imperishable memories for Sam Seabury, who later made annual trips to England and Scotland during his great years as attorney, judge, and investigator.

When Sam was going on fifteen, his father presented him with a tiny leather pocket diary. On the dedication page, Dr. Seabury inscribed it, "From an affectionate father to his son," and added beneath his own signature—more, it seemed, as a reminder than as a warning—a phrase in quotes: "Remember always thine end, and how that time lost never returns." During the year 1888 Sam penciled in, in the back of the diary, simple slogans and aphorisms—pep talks by a teen-ager to himself that incorporated the old-fashioned virtues and wisdom picked up from lectures, conversations, and books:

A good name is better than riches.
There is no rose without a thorn.
Out of sight, out of mind.
The pot can't call the kettle black.
Pennywise and pound-foolish.
When you are among the Romans, you must do as Romans do.
Strike while the iron is hot.
He laughs best who laughs last. (Rira bien qui rira le dernier.)
A man is known by the company he keeps.
He that will not when he may, when he will he shall have nay.
He that is born to be hanged will never be drowned.
Hunger will break through stone walls.
Give the devil his due.

The proverbs, haphazardly put down during that year, were in keeping with his father's warning that lost time never returned. Young Sam seemed so busy pursuing knowledge that he hardly had time to inscribe his day's activities beyond Wednesday, February 22, when he wrote: "Was my birthday. I am fifteen years old today."

But the entries for days earlier in that year reveal what a serious youth in New York did in the winter of 1888. "I got up at 6 A.M. and went to church at 7 A.M.," he wrote on a Sunday morning. "Went to the usual amount of services," he wrote most Sundays; or, "I was late for the early services but I went to the other two"; or, "Went to all three services today." On school days, he prepared his lessons the night before, "as usual." After returning home from school in the afternoon, "played chess." One day's lessons in school he found "well worth recording." Some afternoons he "exercised" or "trained." One afternoon at the school gymnasium, he weighed in at 133 pounds, then "ran ½ mile in 4 minutes." And sometimes he wandered around the city with a friend or cousin. "We walked to 65th St. in the park." "Went down to the foot of the 42nd St. Ferry." "The great six-day walking race at Madison Square Garden commences."

A few times that winter, he went to the theater to see the acts at the Lyceum and once attended a performance of *Romeo and Juliet;* most evenings he stayed home, studying his lessons and playing chess. The days were happy ones, but there was little time spent on tomfoolery. A touch or two of humor did creep into his diary. "Once he noted that "Pie-faced Kate Patterson came to dinner." On another occasion, a schoolteacher asked him about a mythological Greek god's parentage, and he noted his reply: "He was a son of a gun." But the light touches were rare for this youth whose father had told him to remember always "thine end."

He attended the Wilson & Kellogg School, a small private high school for boys, which was run by the two scholarly men who gave the institution its name. "It was an excellent school because they were ceaseless in their efforts to arouse the students," he recalled. He also plunged into afterschool activities, editing the school paper, debating in the literary society, and acting in the dramatic club, doing a part in a play called *Freezing a Mother-in-Law.* As "counsel for the defense" in a mock trial of one John Most (who actually had been convicted by the New York courts in 1888 for "inciting to riot"), young Seabury ended his summing up with a stirring appeal: "In the words of Voltaire, I don't agree with a word you say, but I will die for your right to say it!" He got his man freed.

By the time he graduated from Wilson & Kellogg's in 1890, he had already decided to become a lawyer. The courts of London had left an indelible mark on his mind, and ever since his trip to England he had talked law. His father and three sisters and younger brother all recognized his ability to argue a cause in the parlor. Even Frau Wortman, who served for a time as the family's governess, told him that eventually he would become president of the association of lawyers, because, she reasoned, "You will outargue them all."

One thing became certain: Sam Seabury was going to be a lawyer.

But Dr. Seabury did not have the money to send his son to college or law school. The clergyman and professor of theology was an intellectual patrician, and the Seabury name was highly thought of among old New Yorkers, but a fine reputation could not pay the tuition. Father and son knew this well. Furthermore, considerateness counted between them. "My father was very anxious that I should take a college course," Sam Seabury later said, "and he was willing to make the sacrifices which would have been involved. But I felt strongly that it would be too great a burden on him."

They arrived at a sensible interim solution: the seventeen-year-old youth would get a job in a law office; then, perhaps, college or law school would follow a little more easily. Dr. Seabury went to the law office of Stephen P. Nash, a prominent Manhattan lawyer and one-time president of the Association of the Bar of the City of New York. Before turning to the church, Dr. Seabury had worked as a lawyer in Nash's firm. The distinguished attorney looked over the applicant and then told his father that, yes, there was a place in his office for the young man—filing papers, researching in the county clerk's office, carrying his employer's briefcase, sometimes sitting next to him during trials.

All this he did for a year, getting the feel of a law office and learning the procedures of the courts. He felt that Mr. Nash was "a great lawyer," and he studied his behavior during trials. One case brought home to him the fact of professional life that sometimes a lawyer had to uphold the cause of a client in spite of personal reservations about its validity. Mr. Nash represented Trinity Church Corporation, the owner of vast real-estate holdings in New York City dating back to grants from the crown, in a contest over a New York tenement-house law requiring a bathroom in all dwellings of five rooms and over. At the time, many large families resided in small apartments in ratty tenements—and some of these apartments were without bathrooms. The court held that the landlord had to provide improved toilet facilities. Seabury was not out of sympathy with the decision, even if his "side" had lost: large social forces were stirring in Manhattan, and the spirit of the times was beginning to be reflected in the decisions of the courts.

Although employed full time in Mr. Nash's law office, Sam Seabury needed another job. His clerkship alone did not pay enough to provide for law school. One day he discovered that law-book publishers needed digests of current cases. Laboring far into the night after a full day's work for Mr. Nash, Seabury earned forty cents an hour for summarizing cases that were being heard in the courts he visited. In his later years on the bench and in private practice, he retained this habit of staying up after midnight to read and write.

He was able to enter the new New York Law School in 1891. He had to leave Mr. Nash's law office but kept his other outside job, while acquiring still another source of income. He began to tutor. A close friend and classmate, Henry M. Stevenson, recalled that Sam Seabury's capacity for working and studying was almost superhuman. "He worked until three in the morning, digesting court cases and reading law. At seven he was up and at his studies again. Many times he came to class without any sleep, his eyes red from study." Seabury never mentioned it later, but during this time he contributed a part of his earnings to help support his parents' household.

Graduating from law school in June, 1893, with a fine academic record, he received an honorable mention but not one of the top prizes in the class. What he remembered most vividly from the graduation ceremony was a quotation from de Tocqueville uttered by Whitelaw Reid, president of the Board of Regents, as he handed out the diplomas: "The authority entrusted in America to members of the legal profession and the influence they exercise in the government are the most powerful existing security against excesses." When he attained his own prominent position in the New York Bar, he quoted that statement on more than one occasion.

Not yet twenty-one and thus too young to take the bar examination, Seabury decided to take postgraduate courses. "I had the pleasure of hearing the lectures of both Woodrow Wilson and Charles E. Hughes, subsequently rival candidates for the Presidency," he said. "Professor Wilson of Princeton lectured on constitutional law, standing up during his talks and speaking without a single note. He was eloquent and convincing." For a brief period, he served as assistant secretary of the New York Law School, studying, digesting, tutoring, and holding down an administrative post all at the same time.

In the month he turned twenty-one, February of 1894, he published his first law work and made his first real money. The work was a thirty-six-page pamphlet, *Law Syllabus on Corporation Law,* which outlined the subject for students preparing for the degree of Bachelor of Laws. It was a dry, straightforward presentation of definitions and case citations written in collaboration with another young graduate, S. Sherman Pickford. The law school publication, *The Counsellor,* gave it an editorial plug: "It is the work of Messrs. Seabury and Pickford, of the third-year class, and these gentlemen have evidently spared no pains in its compilation, as the result shows." The pamphlet had a brisk sale among students preparing for the bar, and the two authors divided some $3,000. "In those days," Seabury later said, "we both found that sum to be of great assistance in the effort to make our way in life."

He was admitted to the bar on March 16, 1894, and almost at once began law practice as a member of the firm of Seabury & Pickford. Before doing so, he had unsuccessfully applied to a large law firm for a job as a clerk; possibly he was turned down because he asked too much: seven dollars a week. The partners planned a series of pamphlets for bar candidates on subjects other than corporation law; but their legal and publishing collaboration was brief, for Seabury soon struck out on his own. He had two different cards printed. The first said simply:

Samuel Seabury,
Attorney and Counsellor at Law,
120 Broadway,
New York.

The second card, which was handed out liberally at the New York Law School, located in the same old Equitable Building where the new attorney had declared himself in business, read:

DOWN TOWN COACHING SCHOOL.

———

Equitable Building, 120 Broadway.

———

LAW QUIZZES
by
Samuel Seabury, LL. B., Member of N. Y. Bar.

———

Quizzes throughout the year on Junior and Senior Subjects
in preparation for the LL. B. and Bar Examinations.
Special Quizzes when desired.
Special Examination Reviews after May 1.

Clearly, Samuel Seabury, Esq., at twenty-one, was not anticipating a multitude of clients beating down the door of his new office at 120 Broadway. He hoped that the coaching could bring in enough income to pay for the office expenses and his contribution to his father's household.

Meanwhile, in another household in Greenwich Village, another father, William Walker, was about to start his fourth term as a city alderman, and, as a faithful servant of the Tammany machine, would in due course be promoted to the post of commissioner of public buildings. "Every Irishman wants his children to be better off than he was," the future commissioner told his son, voicing the hope of every immigrant. "It's law school for you, my boy." His dreams for his son, Jimmy, included a political career: had not the beneficence of Tammany politics provided the good life for him? There would be no problem about paying the tuition, and some years later, the song-writing James J. Walker would be enrolled, against his will, in the same New York Law School.

But young Seabury, just starting out, had no political connections, nor had he reason to expect favors from Tammany Hall. Indeed, the new attorney and his clergyman father were already beginning to take aim upon the tough armor of Tammany.

CHAPTER 2

The Eager Lawyer Discovers the People

ALMOST immediately after his admission to the bar, Samuel Seabury realized that coaching students, digesting cases for publishers, and holding on to small jobs around the law school was merely a postponement of the terrifying realities of legal and political life. The courts of New York, at the time, were an instrument of machine politics. Justice was frequently meted out by the Tammany clubhouse, through its lawyers and judges. Although the poor might receive a bucket of coal and a basket of food from Tammany at Christmastime in return for their votes, they were often, through the alliance between politician and judge, deprived of a fair day in court. The municipal and magistrates' courts especially were adjuncts of Tammany rule in the years before the turn of the century. But Seabury had nothing to lose by backing unfashionable causes or pleading unpopular cases. Having no patronage, he could help those who were—in the phrase he once copied and knew well himself—"as poor as church mice."

One evening in the fall of 1894, he took the ferryboat across the East River to Brooklyn Heights, where a political rally was scheduled. In November there was to be a gubernatorial election, in which the independent Democrats were opposing not only the Republicans but the regular Tammany-supported state Democratic ticket. Speakers were needed in Kings County, and Seabury, who had never actively campaigned before joining the Good Government Club a few months earlier, volunteered. On the Brooklyn side of the East River, a horse-drawn truck decorated with political banners met Seabury and transported him and other independents to the rally at Bergen Street and Classon Avenue. A hostile crowd, assembled by the "Ring Democrats" from the local district clubs, was waiting when the truck pulled up. Seabury mounted the body of the truck and, with cospeaker Joseph F. Darling, began to plead the cause of independent voting on election day, when there was a commotion in the crowd below him. He tried to raise his voice over the grumbling and shouting, but looking down, he saw a group of bullyboys angrily shaking their fists at him. Suddenly, a stone flew through the air, landing on the body of the truck. Another struck the speaker's foot, and the rally turned into a brawl. Still Seabury and Darling talked on as the stones flew. Then several hooligans tried to cut the truck horses' harness, but, before they could, the driver whipped the animals toward the river again, with the guests from Manhattan hanging on as best they could.

His introduction to partisan fervor made Seabury fully aware of the divisions within the Democratic party. (These typical Tammany campaign tactics, however, were often borrowed by the Republicans.)

Tammany Hall itself, a post–Civil War building, was certainly geographically close to Seabury. This center of power for the New York County Democratic organization was located on East 14th Street, a short walk past Union Square from the rectory of the Church of the Annunciation. Here the sachems of old still flourished their club badges as they had in the great days of the Tweed Ring. But the famous solid-gold $2,000 honorary badge—in the form of a tiger's head, with a pair of rubies for eyes, set in a belt of blue enamel and crowned with three diamonds—was a mere gewgaw compared to the booty stuffed into the pockets of the district leaders and the black knights of 14th Street.

Tammany had its ancestors, too. Before the founding, in 1789, of the Society of St. Tammany, there had been the "Sons of Liberty" and the "Sons of St. Tammany," groups that had originally helped the cause of American independence. Noble ideals perished quickly, however, and spoils corrupted and scandals pursued Tammany leadership in the nineteenth century. Diversion of revenue; acquisition through bribery of valuable public land in the heart of the city; extortion for business licenses of any sort; graft from street paving, and from sewer construction and repair; sales to the city at huge prices and purchases from the city at cost—all became routine maneuvers for Tammany. Leaders of Tammany were scorned by Manhattan's organization Democrats not when they were involved in shady dealings but only when they were stupid enough to be caught.

The king of subterranean ward politics and the greatest spoilsman of Tammany, William M. Tweed, established his absolute monarchy after the Civil War. Tweed was a Cherry Street boy who became a volunteer fire fighter when that position was a rung on the political ladder, leading the lads by blowing his silver trumpet. When he was made a sachem of the Tammany Society and elected to the Board of Supervisors, he formed what became known as his "Ring," whose purpose was to lobby in support of bills for unnecessary supplies. As soon as he climbed to the top of Tammany, he increased the "tax" of those supplying materials to the city from the "normal" 10 per cent to 35 per cent. Every position from janitor to judge had a price tag. "Ring" nominations for such a lucrative office as county clerk cost $40,000, for example. One of Tweed's frequent practices was to create a fictitious public institution, establish several of his friends as its officers, and then set aside hundreds of thousands of dollars in payoff funds to "run" the nonexistent institution.

But independent political reform groups inevitably arose. Some brave Democrats and journalists spoke up. *The New York Times* published evidence that blew the Tweed Ring wide open, detailing the theft from the city of $10,000,000. Nearly $3,000,000 of the money had been charged to the *Transcript,* an official city organ, for printing expenses. The best cover for appropriations was the new county courthouse, on which enough money was spent to build at least six courthouses. One friendly firm alone received nearly $6,000,000 in two years "for supplying furniture and carpets." All told, Tweed's take was estimated to be about $75,000,000. After being indicted, tried, and convicted, Tweed uttered an unforgettable line on entering prison. When the warden of Blackwell's Island Penitentiary asked his occupation, Tweed drew himself up and said, "Statesman!"

Times had changed when Sam Seabury took to the street corners in the 1890's. Nearly a quarter of a century had passed, and Tammany had undergone several so-called reforms. Ordinary thieves and plunderers still existed, to be sure. Now, however, there were signs of what was to be known as "honest graft." The internal reformers who appeared from time to time tended to prefix their names with the word "honest"—there were such stalwart sachems as "Honest John" Kelly and "Honest John" O'Neill, whose sobriquets did not prevent them from taking bribes or save them from periodically spending time in jail.

"Honest" graft was different. One of Tammany Hall's philosophers, a district leader named George Washington Plunkett, once defined the difference between business and larceny in clear terms:

> The politician who steals is worse than a thief. He is a fool. With the grand opportunities all around for the man with a political pull there's no excuse for stealing a cent. It makes me tired to hear of old codgers boasting that they retired from politics without a dollar except what they earned in their profession or private business. If they lived today they would be just the same as the rest of us. There ain't any more honest people in the world just now than the convicts in Sing Sing. Not one of them steals anything. Why? Because they can't, my boy, because they can't. As for me, I see my opportunities and I take them. Honest graft.

Some "honest" politicians became partners in equipment firms that magically knew the lowest bids on city contracts down to the last dollar. When a new school or public park was to be erected, the insiders, knowing where it would be located, bought the land to sell to the city for ten times the price regularly paid in a condemnation. From government printing to sewer construction and the supply and repair of thousands of items, district leaders with interests in the right companies could share in the legal booty. In the event of litigation, there were Tammany judges (and sometimes Republican judges), with bipartisan political support who would act to legitimatize the deals, franchises, and condemnations because of their own heavy obligations to the machine.

At the time that Sam Seabury stepped into politics as a member of the Good Government Club, the leader of Tammany Hall was Boss Richard Croker, a former fistfighter and head of the "Fourth Avenue Tunnel Gang" who had occupied two profitable positions during his rise to power—superintendent of market fees and rents, and coroner. (No one could die or rent a pushcart in Manhattan without a fee being paid.) It would have demeaned Croker's talents to prefix his name with the word "honest." If Tweed was a "statesman," Croker was an aristocrat, raising the tone of Tammany socially, if not morally, by racing his stable in England—especially during periods when exposure threatened him in New York. And at the moment exposure was threatening him from the city's pulpit. The Reverend Dr. Seabury and other members of the clergy took up the cry first raised by the Reverend Charles H. Parkhurst of the Madison Square Presbyterian Church.

Dr. Parkhurst, dressed in loudly checked black-and-white trousers and red flannel tie, toured the dens of vice for weeks: the ten-cent-whiskey saloons frequented by children; opium dens; "tight houses," so called because the ladies cavorted there in tights; five-cent-lodging houses, from which derelicts emerged on Election Day as Tammany voters; and, most famous of all, Hattie Adams' brothel, where a celebrated "dance of nature" was performed by five playful ladies. It was here that the famous "leapfrog" episode occurred, with naked young ladies jumping over Dr. Parkhurst's guide while Parkhurst himself slowly sipped his beer and took notes. Hattie herself pulled on Dr. Parkhurst's whiskers, but he bristled so that she did not attempt further familiarities. Yet Dr. Parkhurst demanded, "Show me something worse!" and, after resolutely downing a drink of Cherry Hill whiskey, he visited the Golden Rule Pleasure Club on West Third Street, where the proprietress, "Scotch Ann," escorted him to a row of cubicles. "In each room sat a youth whose face was painted, eyebrows blackened, and whose airs were those of a young girl. Each person talked in a high falsetto voice, and called the others by women's names," reported Charles Gardner, the private detective showing the city's pleasures to Dr. Parkhurst. After the detective explained this mystifying sight to Parkhurst, the clergyman decided he had seen enough. "Why, I wouldn't stay in that house for all the money in the world," he declared, and fled past "Scotch Ann" into the fresh air.

When Dr. Parkhurst spoke out against the vice purveyors of Manhattan, he described them and their Tammany protectors as "a lying, perjured, rum-soaked and libidinous lot." Again and again he told his ever-growing congregation, "Anyone who, with all the easily ascertainable facts in view, denies that drunkenness, gambling and licentiousness in this town are municipally protected, is either a knave or a fool." He further characterized Tammany as "a commercial corporation, organized in the interest of making the most possible out of its official opportunities" to exploit vice. In 1894, a legislative committee, headed by State Senator Clarence Lexow, began an official investigation of the conditions revealed by Dr. Parkhurst, and a group of young reformers in the city joined in the effort to once again clean up the municipal government. Among them of course, was Sam Seabury.

But the young attorney was not interested merely in reform. He wanted a deeper view into the causes of corruption, and with it a philosophy to guide him.

It happens, once in a great while, that a book so influences a man's thought that one may properly characterize it as a turning point in his life. So it was for Samuel Seabury. "My cousin, Charles Seabury Bell, handed me a copy of Henry George's *Progress and Poverty*," he said. "I read it carefully and it made a profound impression on my mind. As a result of the conviction born of reading that book, I joined the Manhattan Single Tax Club in September, 1894." But reading such a book was not enough for Sam Seabury: he must meet the man who wrote it. So late one afternoon, he went down to the waterfront and took a ferryboat to Fort Hamilton, Brooklyn. There he visited Henry George in his study, which overlooked lower New York Bay and the Narrows. They discussed the basic theory behind the single tax: that all men have equal right to use the land; that it is unfair for a few to have great wealth through the accident of owning land which yields valuable natural resources; that all taxation should be on the land.

"Suppose that a caravan is crossing a desert," said the American economist to his future disciple, by way of illustration. "The water supply becomes exhausted. Some members of the caravan, blessed with stronger endurance, run ahead to an oasis and return with water. No one will deny their right to a just profit for their labor. They have served all. But suppose, on the other hand, they do not bring the water to those suffering in the desert. Instead they build a wall, and when the thirsty travelers arrive they are informed that they cannot drink without paying tribute. Then there is no justification for their demand. They have usurped rights which Nature placed in the earth for the benefit of all."

George applied this parable to his beliefs. The land was symbolized by the well, the private landowners by those who built the surrounding wall, and the workers, who create the true value of the land by their labors, by the thirsty travelers. Young Seabury was captivated, and he left carrying copies of George's latest pamphlets, which he urged upon his friends. What stirred him was not merely the controversial single-tax idea but its broader implications. To him, George's theory of economics was merely part of a social philosophy that, if put into practice, would provide the good things in life for everyone in America. He saw George as a visionary who applied the philosophy of freedom to human relations, who saw the state as an instrument for serving the people. Seabury later explained George's principles, as he understood them, in campaign documents:

First, that men have equal rights in natural resources, and that these rights may find recognition in a system which gives effect to the distinction between what is justly private property because it has relation to individual initiative and is the creation of labor and capital, and what is public property because it is either a part of the natural resources of the country, whose value is created by the presence of the community, or is founded upon some governmental privilege or franchise. Monopoly should be abolished as a means of private profit. The substitution of state monopoly for private monopoly will not better the situation. It ignores the fact that even where a utility is a natural monopoly which must be operated in the public interest, it should be operated as a result of co-operation between labor, capital and consumers, and not by the politicians who control the political state.

The second principle is freedom of trade among the nations—not free trade introduced overnight, but freedom of trade as an end toward which the nations should move. There are two ways by which the people of one nation can acquire the property or goods of the people of another nation. These are by war and by trade. There are no other methods. The present tendency among civilized people to outlaw trade must drive the states which prescribe such outlawry to acquire the property and goods of other peoples by war. Early in man's struggle for existence the resort to war was the common method adopted. With the advancement of civilization men resorted to trade as a practical substitute for war. The masses of men wish to trade with each other, but the state alone prevents them from so doing. A dictator may, by reducing the standard of living and regimenting the people, run all industry within the state over which he rules; but a democracy, which if it is to be true to itself, must preserve individual initiative, cannot do so without transforming itself into a dictatorship.

The third great principle is the necessity for government, especially in democracies, to free its processes from the influence of corruption. A relentless warfare must be waged upon the corruption of both the Democratic and Republican parties in the cities.

Samuel Seabury came away from his visits with Henry George fired with enthusiasm, and he spent many hours in the evenings discussing these new ideas with his father in their study on Chelsea Square and with Henry Stevenson in Battery Park. He began to write about the movement in letters to the editors of the New York newspapers and in the publications of the Single Tax Clubs. Internecine arguments broke out about theory and interpretation in the light of practical politics in Manhattan. George's ideas, on first consideration, seemed misty, but Samuel Seabury saw no reason not to have faith in their underlying purpose.

"The objection is that the single tax would be the means of placing in the hands of the dishonest men who administer government large sums of money which would afford increased opportunities for political corruption," he noted in a small broadside in *The Single-Tax Courier* in the fall of 1894. But, he argued, "This supposes that as long as politicians are corrupt, society cannot be bettered or its condition improved. The single tax will bring about equality in the distribution of wealth, by removing artificial impediments to its distribution and by giving to all men equal opportunities to produce wealth. The inference that increased intelligence and honesty would not follow a more substantial equality in the distribution of wealth is unreasonable." In his attack on those who disputed these ideas Seabury quoted George: "We have no right to assume that men would be as grasping and dishonest in a social state, where the poorest could get an abundant living, as they are in the present social state, when the fear of poverty begets insane greed." And he revealed his own youthful idealism in a sweeping conclusion about single-tax legislation: "It would tend to purify government in two ways—first, by the betterment of the social conditions on which purity in government depends and, second, by the simplification of administration."

Henry George began to call Sam Seabury and Oscar H. Geiger, who later founded the Henry George School of Social Science, "the babies of the movement." But there were others active in George's behalf, including Hamlin Garland, Lawson Purdy, Joseph Dana Miller, Walter Rauschenbusch and many writers, theologians, college professors, and students of the unfinished American dream— all participating in the impulse toward reform growing in the American populace. The labor unions, including the Knights of Labor, were reaching out to organize in new industries; sympathy toward the workingmen and reaction against monopolistic trusts coincided. Single taxers, Socialists, and reform-minded Protestants especially sought Utopian measures to replace the businessman's society with some roseate ideal.

Seabury worked actively in both the Good Government Club and the Manhattan Single Tax Club. It was in one of the nonpartisan Good Government Clubs where the idea first came to him of a Fusion movement (so called because several parties united behind the same candidate) to defeat Tammany forces and win New York's mayoralty. And, indeed, nearly forty years later, during the Fusion campaign to elect Fiorello H. La Guardia as mayor, which was led by Seabury, the same arguments for and against a Fusion tie with Republicans were made.

In the fall of 1895, the Good Government Clubs, in convention, determined to support the Republican ticket. The public was aroused as it had not been since the Tweed Ring exposures; now the mayoralty campaign centered on the revelations of the Lexow committee. A Committee of Seventy, representing all reform elements, was formed, and proposed William L. Strong, a Republican, for mayor. After floundering for several months, Tammany picked Hugh J. Grant, the only Tammany member on the board of aldermen unsmirched by "boodle" scandals. The problem for Seabury and other reform-minded people in the city was to weigh the equities of working against the Democrats against working for an honest Republican whose party was against any progressive economic programs. There was no La Guardia around to tip the scales with his personality.

The Good Government Clubs' support of the Republican ticket aroused widespread opposition in Seabury's own club, Club F, half of whose members wanted to condemn the action of the convention of the Good Government Clubs. Seabury attempted to arbitrate, pointing out that the real enemy was bossism and corruption in both parties. He set forth this idea in a letter to *The New York Times* on October 10, 1895, headlined "Faithful to Principle," which said:

> To one who believes in the principles of nonpartisanship, Republican "Boss" Thomas Platt is just as much an enemy as Democratic "Boss" Richard Croker. Both Platt and Croker are representatives of the spoils system; both are absolutely opposed to nonpartisanship in municipal affairs; both believe that this city is a rich field to be harvested only by party spoilsmen; both represent a gang of plunderers who seek to prey upon the prosperity of the city. It was in the *North American Review* that "Boss" Croker said, "All the employees of the city government, from the Mayor to the porter who makes the fire in his office, should be members of the Tammany organization." And "Boss" Platt's similar view was expressed at the Republican convention, "We will now leave the register with his thirty or forty employees to consider the candidate for county clerk, who will have 160 employees, every one of whom will be Republican."

In the campaign Seabury supported the Republican candidate, who was elected. On January 1, 1896, Strong became the reform Mayor of New York City, proving that Fusion could work to defeat Tammany when the people were aroused. It was a lesson to be recalled more than once in New York politics during the twentieth century.

Reform and single tax went hand in glove, and in 1897 Samuel Seabury was elected president of the Manhattan Single Tax Club. He now took the ferry to George's Fort Hamilton cottage regularly, together with other bright young men of the day, to discuss economic theory and its application to the city scene. As president of the club, he was constantly on the go. A campaign was being waged in Delaware, and Seabury went off every week to speak at meetings there. At one notable gathering he led a discussion on religion and reform, in which a number of Protestant Episcopal clergymen spoke on the relevance of the Christian ethic to clean progressive politics. One evening, before an overflow crowd, Seabury himself made an important address on "Municipal Gas and the Public Franchise." In it he called attention to the large tax payments made by Paris gas companies to that city. He declared that Boss Croker's great wealth explained why the New York utility companies paid the city nothing for similar privileges. The speech was greeted with cheers, and Seabury's name got into the newspapers. A few weeks later he was asked to repeat the speech before the Citizens Union.

Seabury continued to fight against private ownership of public utilities with their resulting monopolistic practices, as, forty years later, he was to fight for the reorganization of the New York transit system. He favored this idea of municipally owned utilities throughout his life, and his "socialistic" credo on this subject often caused his more conservative clients and friends to raise their eyebrows.

R. Fulton Cutting, leader of the Citizens Union, admired Seabury's earnestness. He asked him to help rally voters in his home district. When the Citizens Union decided to enter its own ticket in the mayoralty campaign of 1897, Seabury was named to his first place on a ballot—candidate for the Ninth Assembly District's seat on New York City's board of aldermen—traditionally the home of the big boodle and the Tammany rubber stamp. Sam Seabury, aged twenty-four, accepted the nomination and prepared to plunge into the campaign with his usual enthusiasm. But, suddenly, another candidate entered the lists—Henry George himself, running for the top spot on the reform ticket, Mayor of New York. Seabury decided to throw all his energies into George's campaign. The only way he could do so, he decided, was to withdraw his own candidacy. Out of loyalty to the Citizens Union, he obtained George's endorsement for the candidate named to succeed him; later, Seabury's successor was elected alderman.

Seabury worked at George's side throughout the mayoralty campaign, one of the weirdest ever held in the city. The anti-Tammany forces had unlearned their Fusion lesson all too quickly. Boss Croker, who had enjoyed himself at the English race courses during the Lexow investigation, returned home in September, 1897, just before the meeting of the Democratic nominating convention. He hand-picked Robert C. Van Wyck, although the organization did not care

for him. The Citizens Union, the single taxers, and the Republicans
went their separate ways. The Union nominated Seth Low, former
Mayor of Brooklyn; the single taxers and labor groups, under the
Jeffersonian Democratic banner, backed Henry George; Boss Platt
picked Benjamin F. Tracy for the Republicans, who refused to co-
operate with either reform group. The conclusion of this divided race
could almost be predicted. Nevertheless, Sam Seabury persevered in
the battle for Henry George and "Jeffersonian Democracy." The
candidate was in poor health and had been warned by his physician
that the campaign would probably cost him his life. At Cooper
Union a month before the election, George lashed out at "the trusts,
the rings and money power"; he deplored the triumph of the "aris-
tocracy and despotism"; he promised to revivify "the imperial city"
and spread the gospel of democracy to the far corners of the country
and the world. When George finished, Seabury was the first to shake
his hand on the platform. "Your speech was an inspiration to all of
us," he said. In private memoirs, Seabury recalled that years later,
on rereading George's speech he still thrilled to its soaring language
and ideals.

Not everyone was moved by idealism in Manhattan, however.
When Alfred Henry Lewis wrote in the *New York Journal,* "I'd
trust George till the end of time but not with the city, not surrounded
by sharps and wheedlers and thieves and bunco men who would
deceive him and he would never know it—one might as well elect
the Ten Commandments to be mayor," Seabury called the article
"the meanest and most unscrupulous attack [of the campaign]."
Meanwhile, George was starting to pick up support in the city. He
spoke to packed meetings. His supporters felt he stood a good chance
—that the populace might indeed vote for the Ten Commandments.
But the campaign unfortunately, was, drawing to a close.

"On the last night of active campaigning, less than a week before the election," Seabury related, "he spoke at Flushing, White-
stone and College Point, in Queens. I was among those who started
with him on the journey. It was my job to go to one of the meetings
ahead of time and help to keep it going until Henry George arrived.
I got on the platform and spoke in all these places. That day we all
went over to Long Island City by the ferryboat that ran from East
Thirty-fourth Street. At the final meeting in Queens, he delivered a

strong attack against the machine government of both Boss Croker and Boss Platt. He promised to put the Tammany chieftain in jail and return the franchises to the people that had been sold by the city to the utility magnates."

After a stirring day of electioneering, George complained of pain. Seabury accompanied him back to the Union Square Hotel, discussed plans for the next day's itinerary and went home. The next morning, as Seabury was on the way to his law office, a man came up to him, pointed at the Henry George campaign button on his coat, and said, "Your candidate is dead." At first Seabury thought that the man meant politically dead, and he responded resentfully to the remark. "Oh, no," the man said, "I'm a Henry George supporter myself. But he died last night in his hotel. If you'll step into the nearest saloon you can see it on the news ticker." Seabury then learned that George had indeed died.

George's funeral procession was one of the largest and most eerie New York had ever witnessed. The saddened young lawyer took part in it as the marshal of the first division of fourteen groups of marchers. Mounted on a horse, as were all the marshals, he rode in the cortege through streets, lined with half a million citizens. At dusk the casket was brought out of Grand Central Palace and placed on a lofty black catafalque, which was trimmed with white roses and bore on one side a small black block inscribed "Progress and Poverty." As the procession reached the first of the great crowd waiting at Lexington Avenue and 42nd Street, word went through the crowd, "Uncover, uncover." For years Seabury saved an aged clipping from the *New York Sun,* dated November 1, 1897: "The densely packed streets, the silence of the vast multitude of bystanders, the solemn black-clad line of men without the glint of a single uniform, moving along the dim streets behind that lofty catafalque, while a crescent moon, half hidden behind gauzy clouds, shed its uncertain light, made up such an event as the New York of today will tell to its children, and they to their children, until it has become history more living and more vivid than any historian can write into his pages." And Seabury summed up his own feelings in a marginal note: "All respected him and paid tribute to him as a sincere and great teacher of mankind."

There would be poverty but little progress politically for years to

come in New York. Seabury and the other Manhattan Single Tax
Club leaders of the "Jeffersonian Democracy" got together and nomi-
nated Henry George, Jr., as a substitute for his father on the ballot.
But the division of reform forces had assured victory for Boss
Croker's Tammany candidate, who won a plurality of the vote,
polling 233,997, against Low's 151,540 and Tracy's 101,863, with a
token vote for George, Jr., of 21,693. "The election of Mayor Van
Wyck," Seabury announced to his friends at the Manhattan Single
Tax Club, "brings Croker back as the ruler of New York." Seabury
was right. The Van Wyck administration was both corrupt and
incompetent, typically Tammany.

While Sam Seabury spent his evenings at the reform clubs, making
speeches and writing letters to the editors of New York newspapers
about single-tax economics and anti-Tammany politics, Samuel Seabury, Esq., attorney and counselor at law, devoted his energies in the
daytime to trying to build up a practice. All of his life, in fact, he
tried to balance his professional interest in the law against his fascination with politics.

There was no one big client, unfortunately, to cover his office
expenses; indeed, there was not even a small paying client at first.
His only recourse was to hang around the courts, observe judges and
lawyers in action, and perhaps receive some assignments from the
bench. The court of general sessions, where felonies were tried in
Manhattan, seemed a logical place to go. And no sooner did he go
there than he became acquainted with a remarkable woman, Mrs.
Rebecca Salome Foster, whose benevolent work around the Manhattan city prison had earned her the admiring name "the Tombs'
Angel."

In the 1890's, there was no effective probation system to reclaim
offenders before they turned into hardened criminals. Mrs. Foster
contributed her services to protect and aid the unfortunates who
found their way into the criminal courts. She had neither wealth
nor influence, but her selflessness had its effect on judges, jailers and
attorneys, and they gave her what assistance they could. The help
she gave young girls and boys was immeasurable. When Seabury
had followed several cases as a spectator, Mrs. Foster came up to him
one day and asked him if he would act as counsel for some of her
nonpaying clients.

"I at once accepted her invitation," Seabury told his father and sisters that evening at dinner. Thereafter, he threw himself enthusiastically into the cases that she recommended. "She was kindly, sympathetic and humane and so great was my respect for her that there was no case that she asked me to defend that I refused," Seabury said. "These cases gave me a chance to acquire experience. There was no need to wait for causes and clients to come to me now. Mrs. Foster saw to it that I was well supplied. I did an unlimited amount of work, much to the annoyance of the assistant district attorneys prosecuting cases in general sessions. I filed demurrers, made motions to inspect grand jury minutes, and asserted every legal right for my clients—who were criminals of every description."

In one of these defenses, he appeared before John W. Goff, the recorder, sitting at the trial of a young stable hand accused of breaking and entering a stable and stealing a harness. The assistant district attorney put the boy on the stand and repeatedly asked him if he had locked the stable the night before the alleged entry, a point that had to be established by the prosecution in order to substantiate a charge of burglary. The boy was so frightened by the prosecutor's barrage that he could barely speak above a whisper. The assistant district attorney continued to press his point, shouting at him to speak up. Recorder Goff, too, ordered the witness to answer. Terrified the youth stammered almost inaudibly. "Witness," said Recorder Goff, "you have deliberately refused to answer questions though repeatedly instructed to do so by the Court. I hold you in contempt and order you incarcerated in Tombs Prison." Seabury jumped to his feet, declaring that the youth was frightened and unable to speak. He made a formal motion for dismissal, but the motion was not accepted. "I would like to have the opportunity to examine the accused," Seabury said. "He has given some testimony and I have a right to cross-examine him on what is in the record. In spite of the fact that the assistant district attorney has frightened him into silence, I believe I can persuade him to talk." Again Recorder Goff denied Seabury's request, and the boy was led away. Later that week, accompanied by Mrs. Foster, Seabury visited the boy, who had recovered his voice, in jail and promised to do his best to free him.

When the case went to the jury, Seabury moved that the Court declare a mistrial because the accused had not had a chance to speak up, nor had his attorney had the right of cross-examination. The motion was denied. At this point, Seabury decided that it would be best to keep his client off the stand. He rested his case without calling a single witness. After the assistant district attorney presented his evidence, Seabury arose and spoke to the jury. He called for sympathy for the witness held in contempt because he could not speak, complained that he had not had an opportunity to cross-examine him, and that there was no evidence offered of the youth's breaking and entering for the purpose of burglary. The jury deliberated for twenty minutes, and returned a verdict of "not guilty." Recorder Goff had no alternative but to discharge the stable boy. Mrs. Foster and attorney Seabury were jubilant.

"However," Seabury wryly recalled in his memoirs, "two weeks later I was in another part of general sessions and whom should I see but my late 'client' the stable boy pleading guilty, this time to another crime, and being led away to jail."

Every lawyer is an "officer of the court," but not every lawyer always remembers his primary obligation to justice when pleading a client's cause. Many attorneys, however, do retain the concept of justice for its own sake, even extending their obligation outside the courts. Attorney Seabury was one of these. Once he saw from a window of the family home two policemen clubbing a youth. A crowd had gathered, but no one spoke out against the brutality of the policemen. Seabury ran up, identified himself as a lawyer, and demanded that the policemen stop the beating and take the youth to the station house and charge him. When they had stopped swinging their clubs, Seabury learned the boy's name and promised to see him at the station house. The policemen made insolent remarks to the lawyer as they led the sixteen-year-old boy away.

Twenty minutes later Seabury was at the police station, but the prisoner had been taken to Jefferson Market Court. When Seabury arrived breathlessly at the court, he was informed that the case had already been disposed of and the youth was behind bars for "interfering with an arrest, assaulting the police most grievously, and resisting arrest." Seabury immediately went up to the magistrate and asked that the case be reopened. He said that he had witnessed the arrest himself, that the police had treated the prisoner brutally, and that the boy had submitted without the slightest struggle. The pris-

oner was brought forward again, together with the arresting policemen, who feared that they themselves would be hauled up on charges
if they did not bring in the youth. He had been one of a crowd that
had gathered to taunt the policemen while they were trying to arrest
another youth. The policemen needed a prisoner. After Seabury uncovered the facts, the magistrate freed the youth. Thus Seabury won
another "case" for a nonpaying client.

General sessions provided a cross section of criminal activity in
Manhattan. From cases involving petty larceny to those involving
murder, Seabury served as attorney for the defense—free, if requested
to do so by the "Tombs' Angel," for a fee when appointed by the
court. He prepared all of his cases carefully, and it soon became evident to those on both sides of the bar that, win or lose, he would put
up a strong scrap.

He defended a jeweler accused of unlawful possession of stolen
silverware. Seabury produced character witnesses for the jeweler and
put the defendant on the stand to establish that he had no knowledge
at the time he bought the goods that they had been stolen. The jury
thought otherwise and convicted him in spite of Seabury's moving
plea. Furthermore, Seabury's motion for a new trial was denied. In
another case, he defended a robber and managed to get the charge
reduced from first- to third-degree robbery, and a new trial ordered
when the jury disagreed over technicalities.

His first big criminal case came when, at twenty-five, he was appointed by the court to defend Lorenzo Priori, charged with first-de-
gree murder. He found himself defending a man with a criminal
record. Priori had been playing cards in a drug store, where he served
as a clerk, with Vincenzo Garagusi, a prosperous banker, when Garagusi taunted him, asking if he disliked his beer, and why he did not
drink it more quickly. Priori resented his questions and sulked when
the other card players laughed at him. When the game broke up,
Garagusi walked home alone. Just as he stepped into the doorway of
his home on Broome Street, a figure emerged from the shadows and
pumped three bullets into him. At the inquest, the dead man's eight-
year-old daughter testified that she had seen Priori kill her father.
Seabury visited the accused in jail, in an attempt to gain some helpful
information, and received little but denials of guilt. He decided to
visit the scene of the crime; day after day, he searched the crowded

streets and tenements of the Little Italy section of the Lower East Side, trying to discover witnesses to the shooting, or at least, some character witnesses for Priori. But none came forward—the old code of silence was obviously at work here—and Seabury prepared his case unaided.

The trial lasted a week in the criminal part of the supreme court before Justice James Fitzgerald. The assistant district attorney was an aggressive prosecutor and was determined to get a conviction. Seabury repeatedly rose to object to the manner in which the evidence was being presented. The assistant district attorney just as repeatedly usurped the role of judge by stating the law on the question of deliberation and premeditation. Although the judge sustained most of Seabury's objections, the assistant district attorney managed to get his points across to the jury, not only introducing questions of law, but using the defendant's Italian nationality to prejudice the jury against him.

Seabury thus objected vehemently after the assistant district attorney delivered his summation: "The law of the defendant's native country is different. These people are impulsive. Upon the slightest provocation human life is sacrificed. Without desiring to prejudice you against him because of his race—and I beg you not to be prejudiced against him because of that—yet that regard for human life is not with them as it is with us. Here when the divine command 'Thou shalt do no murder' is transgressed, a life must be expiated for a life, but in the kingdom from whence the defendant comes, to murder there simply means a penalty of twenty years in prison." Judge Fitzgerald upheld Seabury's objections and directed the jury to disregard the prosecutor's words of anti-Italian prejudice. Nevertheless, the experienced assistant district attorney had reached the jury. They returned a verdict of guilty, and Judge Fitzgerald sentenced Priori to death.

Seabury was incensed. Again he surveyed the neighborhood where the murder had been committed, searching for new evidence, for a friendly witness. Finally, he located one such witness and obtained an affidavit from him, which he submitted to Judge Fitzgerald, together with a plea for a new trial on the ground of newly discovered evidence. The plea was refused. Seabury decided to appeal to the highest court to save Priori's life. Legal opinion was divided as to whether the appeal could go directly to the court of appeals in Albany. Seabury argued his right to appeal in the highest court in New York state; the district attorney moved to dismiss the appeal because it would establish a new legal precedent: the right to insure a correct record in a criminal case by direct appeal from a trial court to the court of appeals. The high court upheld Seabury. It was only a temporary victory, however. Although Seabury was allowed to insert his new evidence into the record, together with a motion for a new trial, the appeals court finally held: "There is not only ample proof of circumstances tending to show that the decedent was killed by the defendant, but there is direct proof to the same effect." As the date set for the execution neared, Priori communicated with the Governor that he had a confession to make which would disclose the real name of Garagusi's murderer. Seabury visited his doomed client in the death house, but the only confession he had to make was that he had not committed the crime. In due course he was executed.

Soon clients other than criminals began coming to Seabury. He had acquired many friends in the reform clubs. Seabury's post–law-school affiliation with his classmate S. Sherman Pickford ended, and in 1898, he joined with onetime judge Bankson T. Morgan to form the firm of Morgan & Seabury. Also in the firm was Samuel's younger brother, William Marston Seabury, who had graduated from the New York Law School in June, 1898. From offices at 43 Cedar Street they conducted a general law practice.

Seabury found himself involved in all sorts of litigation. Inevitably, less of it was charity work for the "Tombs' Angel" and her troubled general sessions clientele. He represented a physician in a contested divorce suit against his wife and won "an absolute divorce" for him in the state supreme court. He represented another client, who had been led into making a mortgage by fraudulent representations, in the Westchester County Supreme Court, and proved that the mortgage was invalid. He argued for plaintiffs and defendants all over metropolitan New York. His clients' names were Brown, Dougherty, Goldstein, Ruttenberg, Bloodgood, Cameron—people of Chelsea, of the Lower East Side, of the uptown business community—and for all of them he fought hard, usually as a trial-and-appeals lawyer. His knowledge and his skill were growing.

At the same time that his law practice was finding roots, he continued to devote much of his almost unlimited energy to the Manhattan Single Tax Club and the Citizens Union. There were nightly meetings to attend, speeches to deliver, letters to write to the editors of the New York press. And there was, too, the thrill of politicking for causes he deemed worthwhile.

In 1899, Tammany was firmly entrenched. Boss Croker was in England racing his horses while governing New York City through a former court clerk, who, in turn, passed on orders to Mayor Van Wyck. The Mayor was the owner of 5,000 shares of ice trust stock, worth $500,000, for which he had paid nothing. The ice trust compelled the people to pay sixty cents for a hundred pounds of ice, and by stopping the sale of five-cent pieces, cut off the supply to very poor people. When charges were brought before Governor Theodore Roosevelt, he investigated them but in the end did not act against the Mayor. Three decades later, Samuel Seabury brought charges against another mayor before Governor Franklin D. Roosevelt, with more positive results.

In November, 1899, there was to be an election for various judicial offices in New York. Here was a chance to wipe the slate clean and enter the new century with a group of reform justices who would not pay the "standard fees" to Croker ($10,000 for lower courts, $25,000 for the supreme court) for judicial nominations. In the lists, nominated by the Independent Labor party for justice of the city court, was Samuel Seabury.

In September, Seabury appeared before the Independent Labor party, at a mass meeting at Cooper Union, to make his first speech of the campaign. He was applauded loudly when he denounced the attempted Ramapo water swindle, in which Tammany politicians had schemed to steal $5,000,000 annually for supplying the city with water from a private company, only to be exposed and frustrated. He struck at the Republican state administration, too, for failing to improve the situation of laborers.

"The law provides that corporations having franchises in cities of the first class shall not work their men longer than ten hours a day. Why doesn't the Governor enforce the law?" he demanded.

The union men in the vast basement auditorium of the historic hall applauded and yelled, "Right!"

"The political offices in this city are governed and occupied——"

"By thieves!" shouted back the crowd.

According to the report in the *New York World*, "The speaker severely scored the Mayor and the Governor for not enforcing the labor laws, and was greeted with a chorus of cheers when he mentioned the name of John P. Altgeld."

A few evenings later, Seabury addressed a meeting at the Grand Central Palace under the auspices of the Manhattan Single Tax Club. On the platform with him as he called the meeting to order was John N. Parsons, a leader of the Knights of Labor. Speaking of Henry George, Seabury said: "He believed in the principles of Thomas Jefferson and endeavored to apply them to modern conditions. Only twenty years ago he wrote *Progress and Poverty,* which gave rise to a new crusade that is yet destined to make men free."

Still another mass meeting was held outdoors, sponsored by the Independent Labor party. Seabury addressed the crowd and made a big point of advocating municipal ownership of the street railways. The Laborites and the Socialists applauded him vigorously.

Now his every speech was being reported fully in the New York press—and he was sensitive to any misquotations. He immediately addressed himself to the editor of *The New York Times* after one such error, and, on September 6, 1899, *The Times* printed a letter from him in which he defined his "radical" views:

> Permit me to say in your columns that I did not say that "private property is a greater crime than slavery." I compared the institution of private property in land with the institution of chattel slavery, and stated that the crime of private property in land was greater than chattel slavery. This I believe to be true. Land is the gift of the Creator to all mankind in common, and no one individual has the right to make special to himself that which belongs to all, unless he shall pay to all the value of this special privilege.

And at another meeting held at Cooper Union, under the auspices of a printers' union, Seabury asked why it was that a rapid-transit system had never been established even though the people had voted for one. He reminded the audience that the political bosses always favored the construction of such a system just before election and forgot about it immediately afterward. He predicted that municipal ownership would eventually bring free transportation to the people of the city, and cited the Brooklyn Bridge as a shining example of what municipal ownership could accomplish. And he closed with strong words against the Democratic and Republican bosses: "We will not have rapid transit if we trust to the Crokers, the Platts, and the Whitneys. The attitude of Platt and Croker in the Ramapo water-franchise-grabbing affair makes that certain. We have got to urge the people to wake up and give Platt and Croker notice that the citizens of this great city are able to administer their own affairs without their interference or advice."

When Seabury ran on the Independent Labor party ticket for the city court in 1899, the Republican party endorsed him and all but one of the Labor candidates. The Citizens Union and various Fusion groups backed the Labor party candidates, and it seemed that a real anti-Tammany movement existed.

The support of the Association of the Bar of the City of New York was of great importance to a candidate and, indeed, an endorsement by this group still carries great prestige today. Its judiciary committee reported that "Samuel Seabury has been admitted to practice only a few years, but the result of your committee's inquiries has been to the effect that he is otherwise well qualified for the position."

The press was uncertain. The *New York Tribune* remained on the fence with an editorial comment that "Samuel Seabury is a young lawyer who has not been a voter himself for many years. . . . He has been classed as a Henry George Democrat." A *New York Sun* editorial on the anti-Tammany ticket singled out Seabury as a strange candidate to carry Republican approval, since he repudiated everything that that party stood for. *The Sun* noted that Seabury was "a single taxer of the single taxers, and a [William Jennings] Bryanite of the Bryanites," and that "he has fits over 'plutocracy.'"

The Citizens Union, made a strong reply to *The Sun* a few weeks before Election Day:

> Samuel Seabury has had the rare good fortune to incur the hostility of the *New York Sun*. This staunch upholder of monopoly, privilege, government by injunction and other perquisites of plutocracy sees all the horrors of Georgeism, socialism, anarchy, etc., following the election of this rising young Wendell Phillips, who in his youth has taken up the

cause of the underdog in the fight. The accusation of *The Sun*, strange to say, is truthful. Every enemy of *The Sun*, therefore, should vote for Seabury on general principles; those who know Seabury will vote for him anyway.

The Fusion forces lacked the spark of a popular personality at the top of their ticket. The Republicans, while endorsing the Independent Labor candidates, bickered over one or two of the judicial positions: they were plainly not thrilled at the idea of seating justices holding radical ideas of reform. The campaign was comparatively dull, and on Election Day, the Fusion candidates were defeated.

The twenty-six-year-old lawyer's campaign had not been costly; his expenses had amounted to less than forty dollars. Among his souvenirs of the election was the label "radical"—a label that would still be with him when he ran for Governor of the State of New York.

Sitting at home in Chelsea, he told his father that there was nothing to do but concentrate on his own law office and plan for the next campaign in 1901, assured of the support of labor because of his many statements and legal fights on its behalf. Dr. Seabury agreed that his son's law practice and politics were vitally important to him—but that a rounded life included other things as well.

CHAPTER 3

Reformer Takes a Wife

THE Seaburys lived at 8 Chelsea Square; the Richeys lived at 5 Chelsea Square. That was the beginning of it. Dr. William J. Seabury and Dr. Thomas Richey were both professors at the General Theological Seminary, and they were close friends as well as colleagues. Both had children, boys and girls, who visited back and forth and played together on the seminary grounds. Sam Seabury was the same age as Frank Richey, and the two were good friends. But involvement in law, politics, and social reform movements left Seabury hardly any time to notice that Dr. Richey's youngest daughter, Josephine Maud, was growing up.

The seminary professors lived with their families in an intimate little world of their own. They spent their days lecturing, churchgoing, visiting and receiving parishioners, students, church dignitaries, and studying church publications that treated the role of the church and religion in a changing community. The general atmosphere was much like that of a small college town, except that the sounds and sentiments of Manhattan constantly intervened. The professors, who could not help but be aware of the intolerable living conditions of the working classes of Chelsea, made up, with other Protestant clergymen, one of the more active reform groups in the city.

The progressivism of the professors notwithstanding, behind the walls of the seminary on West 20th Street, tradition ruled. Although the professors' incomes were modest, a seminary education like that afforded by expensive private schools placed heavy emphasis upon the art of being a gentleman and the graces of being a lady. The training of the seminarians' offspring differed in one respect, however, from that of the children of New York's plutocrats. Uptown, class distinctions were perpetuated, and so-called gentlemen were measured primarily by the soundness of their financial statements and the size of their stables. This was not true at the seminary.

Besides their being neighbors and owning a common heritage, there were other links between the Seaburys and Richeys. When, in 1895, the Church of the Annunciation on 14th Street, established by Dr. Seabury's father, was auctioned, Dr. Richey had come to the aid of Dr. Seabury. There had been a controversy in the Episcopal diocese of New York about what to do with the funds remaining after the mortgage claims had been paid. The members of the corporation of the Church of the Annunciation proposed to use these funds to endow a chair in the General Theological Seminary for Dr. Seabury, who, like his father, had served as rector of the church, and to erect a dwelling for Dr. Seabury on the seminary grounds. The parish did so over the opposition of the Episcopal Bishop of New York, as a reward for the nearly thirty years Dr. Seabury had devoted to keeping the church's doors open.

Dr. Richey boldly supported Dr. Seabury in a letter to the editor of *The Churchman,* which said in part:

> The neighborhood in which the church is situated has undergone a complete change, and the services have had to be maintained at the expense of the very few families left. Notwithstanding the insufficiency of support, Professor Seabury has, summer and winter, kept up the daily services and maintained the weekly Eucharist almost single-handed, ever since his father's death. No one will question the corporate right of the vestry to dispose of the property to pay off the indebtedness, nor the lawfulness of their obligation to apply what remains to the honorable retirement of the rector during his life. This is in accordance both with the law and the equity in the case. I may be permitted to add that I have never spoken to the Reverend Dr. Seabury on the subject in question.

That the Seaburys appreciated the support of a colleague at the seminary in these trying times was beyond doubt. Dr. Richey was aware that it was a catastrophe for the family to lose its home on 14th Street.

There was yet another tie, albeit sentimental, between the two families. The Richeys lived in "Christmas House"—the only remaining building from the old Moore farm that had become the seminary's property. Here, in 1822, Dr. Clement Clarke Moore of the seminary faculty had written "A Visit from St. Nicholas." The Reverend Samuel Seabury, grandfather of the young attorney, had once lived in "Christmas House" while serving as dean of the General Theological Seminary. Now, as the two professors—Seabury of canon law, Richey of church history—lived side by side in Chelsea Square, their families grew closer, too.

Josephine Maud Richey was a gentle young lady, with firm ideas of family life and with more of an interest in church affairs than Sam Seabury, who by now had broken from many of the church formalities. She had attended St. John's, an Episcopal school in the Stuyvesant Square area. At school and at home on the seminary grounds, her friends included Lydia and Muriel Seabury, Sam's younger sisters, and Katharine Hovey, the daughter of a New Hampshire clergyman who had first met his wife in the home of Sam's father. They had a full day, what with school, helping to cook and sew and clean the house, and acquiring ways of gentility. The steady though not lavish entertaining around the seminary kept all the ladies busy.

On some holidays, the families gathered around the piano in the Richey home for an evening of singing hymns and patriotic songs. Maud's mother, the former Emma Cecelia Bacot, had come to the United States from France to begin a career as a professional pianist, but she was sidetracked into marriage after she met the young clergyman, who was an immigrant from Ireland. Maud was born on January 22, 1878, in the small town of Faribault, Minnesota, where her parents had continued to live for several years, until her father's appointment to the staff of the seminary had brought the family to New York. Like her mother, Maud played the piano, tried her hand at painting, took pleasure in the arts.

One evening, Sam was prevailed upon to take a respite from his law work and join the rest of the Seaburys at the Richey home.

While Mrs. Richey played the piano, Maud sang some solos for the group—and Sam noticed her gentleness and grace for the first time.

"Why don't you join in, Sam?" she teased.

"I'm a better listener," he confessed, somewhat embarrassed.

"There must be some songs you like," she said. "Mother can try anything you wish. Isn't there some favorite song you'd like her to play?"

"Well," he said, "I'll join in if everybody else sings *John Brown's Body* and *The Battle Hymn of the Republic*." That was his speed; and he liked the sentiments in the lyrics.

Mrs. Richey began to play, but it was not until she came to "His truth goes marching on," that Sam's voice came in. Maud and his sisters encouraged him, and he bellowed forth "Glory, glory, halle-lujah!" as if John Brown, truth, and a Higher Being were all stand-ing at his shoulder.

For the rest of that evening, he sang energetically, if off-key.

Maud had the light touch; Sam was more somber. Encouraged by his younger sisters, Sam began paying court to Dr. Richey's daughter. She told him not to call her Josephine; Maud was more casual. In 1899, when she was twenty-one and he tweny-six, they became en-gaged. Both families were pleased. Years before, Dr. Richey had said to Dr. Seabury, "Young Sam is a fine boy. He'll be a great man some day." Now, it seemed, Sam not only was actively working toward public recognition; he wanted recognition from Maud, too. Through-out his life, this was to be so.

At the corner of Tenth Avenue and 20th Street, an Italian vendor often stood with a wagon full of cut flowers and potted plants. On the way home from his office, Sam stopped to buy a bouquet and delivered it, quite romantically, to Maud. Before Dr. Richey's daugh-ter came into his life, he spent his evenings playing chess with a law associate or debating the need for public ownership of private utili-ties with his father in their study. Now, after dinner, he would dis-appear, but only to call upon the girl next door. On Sunday evenings, there was something of a ritual. Cousins from Oyster Bay and else-where on Long Island where Seabury relatives thrived were fre-quently house guests in Manhattan. Maud joined these Seabury family gatherings.

They were married on June 6, 1900, in the Chapel of the Good

Shepherd at the General Theological Seminary, in a ceremony performed by their fathers and the Reverend J. Nevett Steele of Trinity Church. The grounds of the seminary were bursting with blossoms, and the newspapers reported that it was a "small but picturesque wedding." The *New York Sun* reporter added touches of color: "It was a field-daisy wedding, as the bridesmaids wore gowns of pale green organdy with large hats to match, which were profusely trimmed with that most fascinating wild flower, and they carried large bouquets of the same." Walking serenely past this bower of bridesmaids in organdy and rustling chiffon came the bride, on the arm of her brother, the Reverend Alban Richey. She wore a gown of white crepe de Chine, trimmed with old-point lace and orange blossoms.

They lived first in an inexpensive rented house, near the Hudson River, on 145th Street which was almost open country at that time. Every morning before breakfast, Sam exercised by riding a horse, cantering around the upper Manhattan slopes and along the river bank. Then he took the elevated railway that ran on Ninth Avenue, swung east on 53rd Street, and went down Sixth Avenue. His law office was at 43 Cedar Street. Els, trolleys, and horse carriages were the Manhattan transportation of the day.

Family life in Chelsea flourished in spite of the couple's move uptown. All the Seabury children were married within several years of one another—to clergymen, doctors, or lawyers. Samuel's brother, William Marston Seabury, carried on the tradition by marrying Katharine Hovey, with Dr. Seabury going to Portsmouth to perform the ceremony.

At this time, a colleague of Dr. Seabury's asked him, "Aren't you sorry that your two sons are both lawyers, instead of carrying on the Seabury tradition as clergymen?" Dr. Seabury replied, in a remark that became a family joke, "Not at all. The Seaburys have saved souls for everybody else. It's time the family did something for itself."

That summer Sam and Maud began to spend their week ends in East Hampton, the beautiful village on the southeastern shore of Long Island that was to be their home and voting residence for almost half a century. The Long Island Railroad made the nearly hundred-mile run in a leisurely four hours, chugging past woods filled with deer and small game, past fields of potatoes and vegetables, which thrived in the loamy soil of Suffolk County. Here in the Hamptons, closer to the Atlantic Ocean than to Long Island Sound, life centered around the individuality of villages that had no ambition to become cities. The Indians who had once roamed here still maintained their own pace on the Shinnecock reservation, and blended into the working life of the communities. A local historian before the turn of the century gave the village the name "Rest Hampton" with good cause.

The newly married couple stayed at "Dune Cottage," Dr. Richey's small but comfortable, weather-beaten, shingled house in the Divinity Hill section of Georgica Road. The section was so called because a number of clergymen, with long vacations but short incomes, had established their summer residences here, where life was simple and inexpensive. Artists, writers, and actors discovered the same charms. Dr. Richey's cottage, built in 1894, was within the circle of dunes facing the Atlantic Ocean. Sam enjoyed the ocean and the near-by golf links. At "Dune Cottage," Maud cultivated her gardens. She and Sam walked arm in arm for miles along the dirt roads adjacent to the ocean, explored old tombstones and church records in St. Luke's, dropped in at farmhouses, strolled in the dusk along the grassy borders of the town pond that idled beneath overhanging tree branches on the single unpaved street that bisected East Hampton Village.

Life was peaceful, the pace slow and even on these week ends at "Dune Cottage." Sam Seabury required just such a place to relax after his hectic schedule in Manhattan. Maud stood by loyally, adjusting her life to his, as he sought new dragons to slay.

Sam Seabury's prolabor speeches and reform positions in various political and social clubs brought him to the attention of the unions. They recognized in him a man who not only believed in their cause but would fight for them with every legal weapon at his command. The tough longshoremen on the West Side docks of Chelsea found a champion in the lawyer who did not condescend, but who talked of their rights, sought recognition for their leaders, and understood the needs of the rank and file.

When a thousand longshoremen assembled at a mass meeting at the foot of West 24th Street, the two main speakers were Edward McHugh, president of the American Longshoremen's Union, and

Samuel Seabury. Sam helped to form the stirring resolution adopted that night by the cheering men at the dock:

> This meeting of longshoremen, called under the auspices of the American Longshoremen's Union, desires to put on record its hearty detestation of the cold-blooded murder of unarmed Pennsylvania miners and urges laboring men to band themselves together to secure the restoration of their God-given rights to the use of land and the ownership and control of the produce of their labor, and as a means to this end this meeting further urges a tax to be imposed upon the value of unused and all other land in use, whether rented or not by so-called owners.

The unions were fighting for their rights—including the rights of peaceful assembly and free speech in the streets. One particular case, watched by labor unions all over the United States, occupied Samuel Seabury day and night. Frank J. Devlin, secretary of the longshoremen's union, had been arrested for making a public speech and arraigned in magistrates' court on a charge of "disorderly conduct." He was fined five dollars for violating a city ordinance that forbade the assemblage of people in the Battery, parks, markets, and other public places. The longshoremen came running when their secretary was arrested. Seabury accompanied Devlin to magistrates' court and paid his fine—under protest. He decided to contend that the city ordinance was unconstitutional. Having received the right to appeal, he appeared before Judge McMahon of the court of general sessions. Seabury, backed up by militant members of the union, argued that Devlin and his longshoremen were not interfering with anyone's rights, that their open-air meeting was an act of citizens exercising their right of freedom of speech. He spoke bluntly: "This arrest grew out of a desire to prevent an American labor union from perfecting its organization among the longshoremen."

Judge McMahon, following his own upside-down antilibertarian reasoning, quoted from the United States Constitution, Article I, Sections 8 and 9, and said: "There is nothing in either of these sections which deprives the government of the power of preserving the public places and keeping them free for the common use of the people at large. The people may peaceably assemble for the purposes indicated, but not in such a manner as to deprive other people of the free and proper use of the streets, parks, markets and public places."

Seabury had made his point on principle; his socially progressive ideas were a little ahead of their time for the average judge to comprehend—the Hughes, Brandeis, and Cardozo social philosophy was still to be expounded for lesser courts to appreciate. Four decades later, looking back on the case, Seabury said, "We have made great progress since that time, and I do not believe that such rulings would be made in any case which occurred today."

Meanwhile, Seabury was learning the power of an aroused public as a counterforce to police and legal inertia. The moment that the unfavorable decision came down from the court of general sessions, he and the officers of the American Longshoremen's Union assembled in an open-air meeting on a farm at the foot of Fulton Street. The police were there again, but this time the laborers technically were not in a "public place." The press was there, too, with reporters waiting for another arrest. A resolution was passed, protesting the interruption of orderly meetings by the police and, going further, insisting that the police were obliged to protect the right of free speech at such meetings. As attorney for the union, Seabury invited the press to report what they saw and heard. He thereby learned to make use of the press early in his career; it was a lesson that would serve him well.

He carried his fight for the longshoremen's union into other areas of the city in order to arouse sympathy and support for the workingmen. As the main speaker at a meeting of the Social Reform Club, he upheld the principle of freedom of public speech and denounced regulations that required the permission of the chief of police before one could speak at street gatherings. The point he made was that "the police power might regulate, but should not prohibit, public assemblages." As a result of his speech, the Social Reform Club appointed a committee of lawyers and laborers to work for the repeal of the city ordinance, and Seabury followed up his address with letters to the editors of *The Daily News* and *The Evening Journal.*

Another "radical" notion of the trade unionists that Seabury supported was the eight-hour day. In an era when the working day was at least twelve hours, this was indeed revolutionary. At the request of the Central Federated Union and several other representatives of organized labor, Seabury made the presentation of the first test case of the eight-hour law that Governor Theodore Roosevelt had signed. The Governor himself had sent the pen that he used to sign the law to John Henry, secretary of the Central Federated Union, "as a token of fidelity to the noble and holy cause of labor." The eight-hour day was upheld.

Typographical Union No. 6 of New York selected Seabury as its main speaker in a meeting held at Cooper Union. Here, he spoke on two of his favorite subjects: he took Tammany to task and came out strongly for municipal ownership of a rapid-transit system for the city—a project he promoted for many years until, finally, in the mid-1930's, he succeeded in bringing about the unification of New York City's transit system. On another evening, Seabury took the platform to propose a toast to Edward McHugh, the president of the American Longshoremen's Union, on the occasion of his departure for England.

"I have no doubt but that he will carry back to darker England, where the people are not in such a state of political enlightenment as exists in our country, and still submit to the rule of a Queen, rather than assert their independence and allow a political boss to select a President for them, much useful knowledge as to the constitutional right which our citizens enjoy." And Seabury rubbed it in again on the point of peaceful assembly and speech when he said sarcastically, "In the short time that Mr. McHugh has been with us, he has enjoyed a liberal education as to our American institutions. He has been afforded ample opportunity of appreciating all that American liberty, as it exists today in the United States, really means. I have heard him tell how he witnessed the Constitution of the United States overruled by a policeman doing duty along shore, in order to prevent a man being guilty of 'disorderly conduct' while making a speech." Yet in future years, as a result of efforts by Seabury and other street spokesmen, the right to speak freely was upheld and the reformers, Socialists, and workingmen had their meetings and their say in the open.

As a labor lawyer, Seabury worked for enactment of legislation recognizing the responsibility of employers for the welfare and protection of their workingmen during the time they were on the job —a new concept. Seabury went into the legal validity of, and precedents for, labor legislation. As he was to do on many occasions, he referred to examples and decisions from British jurisprudence. In an article in the old *New York Daily News,* he wrote:

> When the labor unions of England first demanded that Parliament pass the Employers' Liability Act, they were met with loud denunciations on the part of some employers, and the argument was made that if the act became a law, employers would soon become bankrupt. The operation of the law for a period of several years has shown that it is not only just in theory, but that it is entirely fair in practice. The law today in New York State holds that an employer is not responsible to one of his employees for the negligence of a fellow employee. This rule acts with special hardship upon workingmen, and tends to make employers careless of the qualifications of the workmen they employ. Frequently employees are injured or lose their lives because of the negligence of someone employed with them, and yet unless they or their next of kin can prove that the employer knew the person to be grossly negligent, no recovery of damages can be held. Workmen are thus left remediless, because such negligence is very difficult to prove.
>
> Justice and common sense demand that the law of this state be changed. No radical change is asked. What is sought is merely that this great state shall show itself as considerate of the right of the producers of its wealth as the British Parliament and the legislatures of many of our states have shown themselves [to be] in protecting the rights of workingmen. If the force of organized labor would put its shoulder to the wheel, a little pressure would make it move. A refusal on the part of the workingmen to vote for candidates who would not pledge themselves to the carrying out of this reasonable measure of reform in our law would certainly have the desired effect.

Here were arguments for the broad concept of a workmen's compensation act. These matters were being hammered out by the Federal Government and in state legislatures. It was to encourage the enactment of such a law that Seabury declared himself openly for labor education and labor lobbying:

> The labor unions of this country have done much to benefit workingmen. Presenting a concentrated pressure upon the legislatures, they have often been rewarded by legislative action friendly to their interests. Workingmen thus counteract the pressure of the concentrated power of wealth. To accomplish their purpose and to protect themselves, they

must consolidate. The United States Labor Bureaus and similar departments in most of the states, factory laws, laws relating to the inspection
of machinery and providing for decent and fit places to work in, are
achievements of which organized labor may justly be proud. They are
the direct result of the action of labor unions. But above all the labor
unions of this country have been the centers of education. They are the
universities which have not only educated the toiler, but have instructed
professional and businessmen.

Now Seabury pursued his campaign tenaciously. In half a dozen
other publications—daily newspapers, legal periodicals, Bryan Democratic magazines—he called for enactment of labor laws protecting
the workingmen. Phrases of a fired-up reformer leaped out of the
pages: "City employees forced to work on Sundays without pay . . .
Laws are grossly violated in the interest of corporations . . . Public
officials purposely violate the law . . . Resort to the ballot is the remaining weapon in the hands of labor."

City employees, too, had begun to find their way to the law office
of Samuel Seabury, Esq. The laws in 1900 permitted a ten-hour day
with a half an hour for lunch, but many city departments were forced
to put in longer working days. Street cleaners came to Seabury; they
complained of having to work on Sundays without extra pay. He
denounced the practice as "a gross outrage" and immediately wrote
a letter of protest to the Department of Sanitation and the press.
Policemen came to Seabury; they complained that they could not
bring a legal proceeding against the police commissioner for a
grievance without making an application, long and involved,
through their local commanding officer. Seabury saw this for what
it was: a means whereby those having claims were intimidated by
the threat of reprisal. Again he voiced his disapproval publicly.

Having taken on the state legislature, Seabury proceeded to carry
his fight for labor's rights into the courts. He began to fire broadsides
at the Federal judiciary, contending that they were not as concerned
about the rights of workingmen as they were about the privileges of
monopolists. He deplored the granting of injunctions to restrain
laborers and their unions. He cited numerous cases in Federal district
courts across the country that showed a pattern of "government by
injunction." In each instance, it was the employees who were en-

joined and restrained from striking. The legal point he made—and his strength in these speeches and communications was that he sought a judicial underpinning for his position—was that the Federal courts had become virtually a lawmaking body.

"The most extreme case of judicial usurpation and tyranny yet perpetrated was the case of the United States v. Debs," he declared in the *National Single Taxer*. Eugene V. Debs was the union leader and Socialist who in the 1890's had helped to form the American Railway Union. During a railway strike, when the A.R.U. had ordered a boycott on the moving of Pullman cars, President Grover Cleveland had summoned Federal troops to remove the mails, and Debs was later sentenced to a six-month jail term for "conspiracy to obstruct the mails." Seabury said that to issue an injunction in the Debs case, it was necessary to twist the antitrust law out of shape so that it applied to labor unions. The single taxers, labor unions, and Socialist clubs at the time were envisioning a great independent-labor-reform movement—the roots of what would grow into City Fusion.

Seabury was a very busy man. On many of the evenings when he was invited to speak as a representative of the Manhattan Single Tax Club or as an independent with a strongly prolabor outlook, Maud accompanied him. She sat in the rear of the clubrooms and auditoriums, taking no part in the meeting, but nevertheless making her presence known. Often, club leaders were invited to the Seabury home for dinner before a meeting; afterward, with Sam still going full steam, a guest or two would return home with them. Maud prepared the refreshments but retired before midnight, while Sam, who required much less than eight hours of sleep, would debate points of law and reform politics until two or three in the morning.

Together, Maud and Sam went to a conference on "Practical Sociology" held at the Social Reform Club on University Place. There Socialists and single taxers listened as Seabury spoke in behalf of "farmers and wage workers." On another occasion, when he was counsel for the Association for Public Control of Franchises, Maud accompanied him to Albany and heard him speak before a senate committee in favor of a bill to tax franchises. The point he emphasized was that "corporations engage in a swearing-off process to such an extent that they often do not pay a tax on their personal property

—and that they would if these franchises were regarded as real estate." She joined him at many late-evening rallies of the labor unions he represented. And when he sat up at his desk after midnight to write articles for the organization publications, she was there, reading or listening as he tried out the sound of his sentences.

Speaking out on controversial issues inevitably brought him personal attacks. He crossed the Hudson one evening to Passaic and addressed an audience on "The Declaration of Independence," taking the occasion to make a strong anti-imperialist speech against President William McKinley. He emphasized that the Declaration was an absolute statement of the rights of man—one that applied to Filipinos and Puerto Ricans as well as to North Americans. Two days later, he obtained a copy of the *Passaic Daily News,* a Republican newspaper, and read in it an editorial entitled "That Seabury!" The editor attacked him, attempting to prove by some twisted logic that in opposing McKinley's policies the lawyer was against the Negro franchise as well as the Declaration of Independence. Seabury immediately replied by letter to the editor, making no attempt at conciliation. That he spoke as neither Democrat nor Republican but as an Independent Laborite with single-tax ideas emerged in his letter: "I consider the action of the so-called Democrats of the South both unjust and unconstitutional and in direct violation of the principles of the Declaration. The principles of the Declaration are of universal application, and include both the Negro in the United States and the people in the Philippines. It is certainly a shame that politicians, both in the Republican and Democratic party, do not protest against the disfranchisement of the Negro."

In the summer of 1901, he shaped all his speeches and writings about labor's rights into a monograph. He went to E. R. Mantz, printer, on Cooper Square, and had it printed as a fifty-three-page pamphlet with the title *A Review of the Labor Laws Relative to the Rates of Wages and the Hours of Labor in the State of New York.* The author was identified as "Samuel Seabury, Member of the New York Bar." The purpose of this tract, a pioneering document in its time, was to bring enforcement of the labor laws; the unions in the city found that in it their own position was summarized for the first time.

"A labor law regulating the wages and hours of work of laborers employed by cities and by contractors upon public work was passed by the people of the state," he wrote in the pamphlet. "It was enacted largely, if not solely, as a result of the intelligent agitation conducted by the organized labor of the state. When it was first enacted it was ignored by those public officials whose duty it was to enforce it. When it was no longer safe for these public officials to ignore the law, they and the courts so construed the law as to strip it of its true meaning, thereby rendering the law almost worthless."

This labor law had had a dismal history. It had been ignored at first, and then misconstrued. Labor, through its own pressures upon the Albany legislators, added amendments. Then the constitutionality of the law was attacked by big corporations; they said that the legislature had exceeded its powers by interfering in private business. When a test case came up to the court of appeals, the law was declared unconstitutional, even though a minority of the justices pointed out the public benefits that would accrue from its enforcement. Seabury quoted in his pamphlet a favorable judicial opinion from the court of appeals: "There is no expressed or implied restriction to be found in the Constitution upon the power of the Legislature to fix and declare the rate of compensation to be paid for labor or services performed upon the public work of the state." Shorter hours had been introduced on public jobs; now the problem was to get decent wages.

Seabury accused the nation's monopolies of controlling economic opportunity. "Laborers may wrap themselves in the flag and boast loudly that they are free men, but they are in reality actually slaves," he wrote. "They are in no position to participate with the owner of a monopoly in fixing the terms of a contract for employment. A man or woman who is offered the alternative of agreeing to work fourteen or sixteen hours a day or starvation, either for himself or herself, or those who are near and dear to them, cannot be said to be free in assenting to the terms of the work contract."

Seabury offered the most basic legal and humanitarian reasons for shorter hours and improved wages, arguing that in many cases men who worked unreasonably long hours endangered not only their own health but that of others. He gave as an example a motorman of an electric car who, exhausted by a twelve-hour shift, represented a threat to the safety of his passengers. In enforcing the labor law, he declared, the state would merely be exercising its police power. Another argument he put forward for the labor law was that it would tend to preserve the public peace. "The disputes between large quasi-public corporations, such as railways," he said, "that have resulted in strikes, lockouts and loss of life and property would in most cases not have resulted if fair wages and just and reasonable hours had been allowed the employees."

In reprimanding public officials and the courts for failure to enforce the labor law, he cited experiences of his own clients. He noted the enforced Sunday work of the street cleaners. He mentioned the men employed at cut rates by the police department and denied recourse to the machinery of appeal. And he considered the decision of the court of appeals that the labor law violated the city's right to home rule. "Why is it not a 'city purpose' to pay its laborers, if it is a city purpose to pay its contractors?" he asked. "Why does this legislation become class legislation when the large class of employees receive the money and not class legislation when a few contractors are enabled to apply this money to their own personal use? These are questions which the prevailing opinions of the court do not answer, but which disclose the injustice of this decision."

Concluding his pamphlet, Seabury declared that mere denunciations of the courts and judges would accomplish nothing; that organized labor must map out a definite plan of action, because it had an issue that could sway public opinion at the ballot box; that since the selection of judges was made by the political bosses, little help could come immediately for labor from the bench. Instead, he proposed the idea of a constitutional amendment that would give the state legislature the right to fix the wages and the hours of labor of city employees and of subcontractors engaged in public works. He called upon a united labor front to support such an amendment. And, in a peroration at the end of his pamphlet, he made a somewhat unusual remark: "It is much to be regretted that the judges of our courts are not more in touch with the people and with the progressive tendency of the present day. . . ."

Political leaders and friends in the labor movement interpreted this remark just as Sam Seabury had intended them to—as a statement of availability. Surely *he* was in touch with the people; and *he* was in the vanguard of the progressive movement. For at the age of twenty-eight he was ready for public office. Tammany was in power; Fusion was in the air. Another municipal election in New York was about to test the rule of Boss Croker and his City Hall straw men. One obvious issue in the fall of 1901 was the same one that had led to Dr. Parkhurst's underworld tour of the fancy houses and the Lexow committee investigation: vice and the corruption of young girls. The Women's Municipal League issued a pamphlet, widely circulated by the City Club, called *Facts for New York Parents.* The facts were drawn from court records and revealed the same merry-go-round of police and district leader collusion with the vice kings and queens. As Special Sessions Justice William Travers Jerome (with whom Sam Seabury would soon be feuding) wrote in *The New York Times:*

> People are simply ignorant of conditions on the East Side. If those conditions existed in some other communities there would be a vigilance committee speedily organized, and somebody would get lynched. The continued greed and extortion of the police captains who charge five hundred dollars for a disorderly resort to open in their precinct, and then collect fifty to a hundred dollars per month, has, however, made even vice unprofitable. Details, I know, are revolting and not nice to read, but yet the people ought to know about them. Just yesterday I sentenced to six months in the penitentiary the keepers of one of the most depraved houses of the East Side. I firmly believe that they were merely the agents of the man who owns not one but many of such places. He is well known as a politician in a certain notorious district. That house is but one of hundreds within a radius of one mile of this building [the criminal courthouse] where criminals are sometimes brought to justice. I will stake my reputation that there are scores within less than that distance from here in which there are an average of ten or twelve children from thirteen to eighteen years old.

There was another issue born of scandal that was central in Seabury's campaign. This was the need for public ownership of city transportation facilities. Here, corruption was nonpartisan. Both Democratic and Republican legislators were coerced by agents of the Metropolitan Street Railway Company. The stockholders of this private company had been bilked of more than $10,000,000 by the businessmen who manipulated Boss Croker and secured franchises and privileges of enormous value. The "disorderly resorts," as *The Times* quaintly called them, brought in mere pin money for the local politicians and police; the street railway brought in fortunes for the bosses themselves.

To defeat Tammany, it was necessary for the diverse elements in the reform groups to negotiate with the Republicans for the fall, 1901, municipal campaign. The Citizens Union was the pivot power for Fusion, bringing together single taxers, the "Greater New York Democracy," Republicans, and labor elements. After much acrimony, a Fusion ticket was assembled, with Seth Low, a Republican, who had been president of Columbia University, as candidate for mayor; William Travers Jerome, a Democrat, for district attorney; Jacob A. Cantor, a Democrat, for Manhattan borough president. Also on the ticket were other Republicans and reform Democrats, chosen—as was the custom in minority-oriented Manhattan politics—with an awareness of religious and racial origin. For justice of the city court, Samuel Seabury was nominated. His political affiliation was simply listed as Citizens Union.

This time the Bar Association openly endorsed his candidacy:

> In the report of your committee in 1899, the judicial standard of the city court was severely criticized and a change for the better in its personnel was recommended. Attention was called to a lack of ability, learning, and judicial dignity, and your committee finds that there are still complaints by many members of the bar. . . . In respect to the candidacy of Samuel Seabury for judge of the city court, your committee desires to call attention to the language of its report in 1899 regarding his candidacy for a similar position. It then stated that he and another candidate were not of such prominence at the bar as to make it easy to pass upon their merits, that he had been but a short time admitted to practice, but that he was otherwise well qualified for the position as far as the committee could learn. Your committee is of the opinion that, with his qualifications and his additional experience at the bar, his candidacy should now receive the approval of the Association.

The brunt of the campaign was carried by William Travers Jerome, who lashed out at both red-light-district and transit scandals.

"You are calling a spade a spade," Seabury told him, during one of their campaign meetings. "The moral sentiment of the community is being aroused. Even the cynical among the wealthy classes are being stirred."

Jerome assured Seabury that as a prosecuting district attorney he would press for an investigation of vice and corruption. Seabury, who had not been for Seth Low's candidacy on their ticket, was aware that Jerome's crusade could carry the whole Fusion slate. In his own campaign speeches, he followed a line similar to that developed more strongly by Jerome.

"If I am elected," Jerome had said in a widely quoted speech, reported in the *New York Herald,* "I shall make it my business to follow the trail of wrongdoing and corruption not only when they lead into tenement houses, but I shall follow them even if they lead into the office of the Metropolitan Street Railway Company. I am arraying myself against the most dangerous, the most vindictive and the most powerful influences at work in this community."

Boss Croker struck back with an old Tammany trick—reform from within. He appointed his own "Anti-Vice Committee," with personal orders to clean up the red-light district. But the people of the City of New York, enlightened by a series of revelations in the newspapers, would not be fooled this time. Given the choice of Tammany or the Fusion ticket, they voted for reform all across the line.

The Sunday after the election, the Seabury and the Richey families gathered for a victory dinner in Chelsea Square. Maud had brought along congratulatory letters and telegrams from the labor unions, the single taxers and other reform groups. The Episcopal Bishop of New York, who during the campaign had described vice as "a burning shame to any decent and civilized community," offered his good wishes to the Reverend Dr. Seabury, who proudly read aloud an editorial from *The Times* while Maud beamed and the others gently teased the twenty-eight-year-old "Judge."

Samuel Seabury, who was elected judge of the city court of New York on Tuesday, as the candidate of the Citizens Union party, is the first single taxer to be selected by the people of this part of the country for an important office, and the event (for such it is) has attracted the attention of those who are observing the development of new men and new ideas in the first year of the new century.

Judge Seabury was placed on the Fusion ticket because he was a single taxer and one of the leaders in this state of those Democrats who believe in the party creed. It is fortunate that this distinguished recognition has been bestowed upon one so peculiarly worthy. A descendant of one of the most honored families in the land (another Samuel Seabury was the first Episcopal bishop in America), he has steadily demonstrated the sterling stock that is in his line, and added further lustre to his name.

Defeat has had no terrors for Judge Seabury. At the age of 25 he was defeated by a 50,000 majority for the same office to which he has been elected three years later. When but a little more than 21 he was president of the Manhattan Single Tax Club, founded by Henry George; later he was a stanch advocate of the election of Mr. Bryan to the Presidency, and today is an unswerving opponent of the plan of the reactionaries to "reorganize" the Democratic party on the lines of conservatism. Judge Seabury believes in the dignity of labor, and his address in this city two years ago on "Government by Injunction" will be recalled.

In the course of events he has come to be known as a "radical," and there is no doubt whatever that he believes in municipal ownership and some other things that the corporations and the very rich either don't, can't or won't understand. The youngest judge in the metropolis has principles and sticks to them, and his is the reward.

The office of city court judge is for ten years, and the salary is $10,000 a year. The jurisdiction is similar to our county court, except that the city court is entirely civil, no criminal business coming before it.

What Dr. Seabury was thinking as he read the editorial was not expressed; he could have been recalling the year when there was not enough money in the family to send his son to law school. Now, seven years after being admitted to practice, Sam was about to go on the bench. Dr. Seabury, a former lawyer himself, knew what that meant. After dinner that Sunday, they all trooped next door, across the seminary grounds, to the Richey home, where they sang around the piano. Then Sam and Maud took the train uptown to their rented house on West 145th Street.

There was still another dinner—this one more formal, given by the single taxers for the judge-elect, at the Hotel Marlborough. A few weeks before January 1, 1902, the Seaburys feasted on blue points, filet mignon and redhead duck. It was a notable event—at least, to Dr. Seabury, who saved the menu in a scrapbook that was beginning to fill up with mementos of the events in his son's life. At the dinner cards were passed out that read:

Morgan & Seabury,
43 Cedar Street

> We beg to announce the withdrawal of Samuel Seabury from the firm of Morgan & Seabury, owing to his election as Judge of the City Court of the City of New York. On and after December 1st, 1901, the undersigned will engage in the general practice of the law under the firm name of Morgan and Seabury.

The card was signed with the names of his former partners, Bankson T. Morgan, William M. Seabury, Townsend Morgan.

For the rest of his life, Sam was known as "Judge Seabury," or "the Judge." A very few close friends called him by his first name; and the future Mayor Fiorello H. La Guardia called him (but not to his face) "the Bishop," affectionately.

On New Year's Day, 1902, when Judge Seabury was sworn into office, a newspaperman asked him what he was politically, and he replied, "I'm an Independent Democrat." So he was, but sometimes the Independent and the Democrat went off in different directions.

Family life occupied the Seaburys at the end of the business day. It was now almost a year and a half since he and Maud had married. They had no children; nor would they ever have any. His ascent to the bench marked a turning point in their lives, an end to their financial struggles. Their marriage was a good one. Few outsiders, regarding the Judge as dignified to a fault or courtly in the extreme, could imagine the depth of his feelings for Maud. In the twilight of their lives, the gray-haired reformer inscribed, for the family records he treasured, these words:

> On June 6, 1900, it was my good fortune to marry Maud Richey, the youngest child of the Rev. Thomas and Cecelia (Bacot) Richey, D.D. We were married in the Chapel of the General Theological Seminary in

New York City by the Rev. Thomas Richey, D.D., the Rev. William Jones Seabury, D.D., and the Rev. Nevett Steele, D.D. The lines recorded within her wedding ring were "Our way one way." As I look back, I realize how much happiness we have both had together, and from my standpoint it was the wisest act of my life, which has been proven not only in our daily relations, but in all the great problems which must be met in the journey through life.

CHAPTER 4

The Youngest Judge in New York

SEEING people from the pedestal of the bench left its mark on the young judge. His cousin and contemporary, Louis Seabury Weeks, once remarked candidly: "Fundamentally, Sam was a very human individual, but he was a little hard to kid—it was that judicial mien he acquired so early. When we were young men, at the beginning of the century, there were definitely class distinctions. It was one of the major facts of life. The gentlemen with wealth were supposed to have all the virtues while the common folk were crude and dull. But very soon, as a politician in the streets, Sam discovered that these distinctions were completely false. This awareness is what made him a good judge—and fit him for his investigative role later."

The cases that came before Judge Seabury in the city court were not only an index of the people's economic and legal difficulties but also of the growing conflict between the individual and the corporation. There were claims and counterclaims of bewildered litigants usually in court for the first time in their lives. Within the jurisdiction of the city court, original trials began and ended, with the raw material of life visible.

In spite of a Fusion victory, Tammany's presence was still felt on the bench—as Seabury soon discovered—and elsewhere in the city. Boss Croker attempted to continue his rule from the paddocks of English race courses but he soon found that his trans-Atlantic puppet system did not work. He was replaced first by a triumvirate and then by a new boss, Charles Francis Murphy, a gentleman from the "Gas House District," who bore the nickname "Silent Charlie." In the four saloons owned by Murphy, decorum was the rule and no women were allowed. The new leader of Tammany Hall had made his million dollars in the 1890's during his tenure as dock commissioner of the busy Port of New York. Boss Murphy could be accused of none of the usual vices, such as smoking or drinking. He had a democratic touch, and often kept office hours under a street lamp on Second Avenue and 20th Street, rather than appearing at the Hall itself.

But occasionally Murphy and some of the other Tammany leaders had to resort to the courts when they could not protect their interests solely in the clubhouses. Once, when the large calendar began to back up in the city court, Judge Seabury noticed that one justice, J. Henry McCarthy, was not writing his share of the opinions. The outspoken and zealous Seabury made a startling offer. "I told Mc-Carthy that if he wished, I would write his opinions," Seabury later recalled, "and he could file them under his own name. He said that was a very generous offer and he was delighted to accept it."

Judge Seabury set about writing opinions—his own and Judge McCarthy's—and worked long past midnight. Nevertheless, he was on the bench promptly at ten every morning. In a few days he returned all the unfinished cases with opinions "signed" by McCarthy, Justice, City Court. The latter looked them over and expressed his gratitude. Later that afternoon, he entered Seabury's chambers. "These are wonderful opinions," he said. "I've read them all and I am amazed at their clarity and logic. I agree with every conclusion you have reached."

"I am very pleased that you do," Seabury said. "If you wish, I can see that they are filed."

In those days the city court justices had no secretaries and not only wrote their own opinions but recorded them.

McCarthy said that he would take care of that small detail himself, and again thanked his ambitious colleague profusely.

Several days elapsed and Seabury noticed that the decisions had not yet been recorded. He walked into McCarthy's chambers to ask why.

"I don't want to retract a word I said about your opinions," McCarthy said. "It's just that I'm troubled by this one case, Bailey v. Kraus. All your facts and citations are sound, but you went wrong on your conclusion. I'm going to use the precedents you cite, but put in a 'however' and change your conclusion."

Seabury was puzzled, and then shocked as he became aware of the reason behind the switch in the decision. He realized that in the case, a bankruptcy proceeding, George J. Kraus, was an intimate friend and supporter of "Big Tim" Sullivan. "Big Tim," also known by his earlier nickname, "Dry Dollar" (from his habit, in the days when he was a saloonkeeper, of carefully wiping the bar before placing money on it), was the Tammany sovereign who controlled the East Side below 14th Street—second only to "Silent Charlie" Murphy in power. "Big Tim" was a leader who took care of his constituents and judges. He was considered a friend of the poor because he gave away Thanksgiving Day turkeys and Christmas dinners.

Seabury warned his colleague that he would file a dissenting opinion if the defendant was discharged of his obligation. When McCarthy filed his decision, retaining all of Seabury's work but merely changing the ending, Seabury dissented. Thus the same precedents were cited—and Seabury wrote both the prevailing and dissenting opinions! *

"It was circumstances of this nature which profoundly disgusted me with the conditions which then prevailed in the city court," Seabury declared. "The absence of legal merit was sufficient to convince me that the influence of 'Big Tim' Sullivan extended into the decisions in the court."

Nevertheless, Seabury continued to defy political pressures in his decisions. In civil suits involving false arrest, in cases involving the abuse of injunctions, in cases concerning the rights of unions to organize and expand their influence, Seabury wrote strong opinions in support of personal liberty and the rights of labor. His decisions in the social field especially were responsible for his name being mentioned more and more frequently by the progressive press.

In the case of a deceased cigar maker who had belonged to an independent and to an international union, a question arose as to which union would pay death benefits to his widow. The local had

* Bailey v. Kraus, 39 Misc. 845.

consolidated with the International Cigar Makers' Union before the cigar maker's death, and the widow claimed the increased benefits accruing since the merger. Judge Seabury had decided in favor of the widow in this case. However, he allowed a motion for reargument by the union attorney, who introduced certain evidence of practices in the field applicable to members' benefits. As a result, Judge Seabury sustained the union attorney's arguments and reversed his own stand.

The conservative *New York Sun* had its editorial needle handy whenever Seabury decided a case against "the business community." It repeatedly complained that he was carrying politics into the courtroom. One editorial, written in Seabury's first year on the city court bench, chided him sarcastically: "Judge Seabury, the boy judge of the city court and also of the Henry George Society, does not act on the theory that persons holding judicial office should either be reticent or inactive in political matters."

But he also had his support from the rank and file. A labor newspaper, *The Union,* retorted to *The Sun*'s editorial in a friendly tone: "Justice Seabury of the city court enjoys quite a career on the bench and the popular good will and wishes of the bar and the lay as well; and the people say he is as honest as the day is long and an intelligent and fair-minded man from the word go, which fact is unmistakably shown by his up-to-date and progressive rulings which are unusual characteristics for judges of the city court and more so of this age."

One of the most important cases decided by Judge Seabury showed his great ability to grasp a complex situation and follow through to a sound legal conclusion—an ability that later made him one of the outstanding appeals lawyers in the 1920's and enabled him to probe the many departments of the government of New York City in the 1930's.

This was a case * that started out in his court, and where his ruling was upheld not only through the state's higher courts but up to the Supreme Court of the United States †—an unusual journey for a city court case.

The situation was complicated. A jury had been waived and the

---

* Johnson v. Mutual Reserve Life Insurance, 43 Misc. 251.
† Mutual Reserve Life Insurance v. Birch, 200 U.S. 612.

entire decision rested on Seabury's opinion. The case concerned the rights of out-of-state policyholders in dealing with an insurance company chartered in New York. The plaintiff, Johnson, was the assignee of various nonresident individuals; the defendant was a large and powerful life insurance company. The company had at one time signed up many individuals in North Carolina, then left that state, and now maintained that it could not be reached legally anywhere but in New York. Company attorneys even had an appellate division precedent upholding their position. It would have been simple for Seabury to decide the case for the company, and console the insured individuals with a few well-chosen words of regret.

Seabury did no such thing. He reviewed every question of law and fact involved, and reached a conclusion directly opposed to that previously held by the appellate division. In concluding his opinion, he said: "The courts of this state have no right to arrogate to themselves the function of determining as to the wisdom or justice of legislation enacted in another state." He ruled that an insurance company could not run out on its interstate obligations by hiding behind the jurisdiction of the state where it had been chartered. The result was that the plaintiffs recovered their money, the defendant was forced out of business by the exposure of its fraudulent methods, an erroneous rule of law was annulled, and a just one set up in its place to control similar insurance cases in the future.

Courage was not always a conspicuous attribute of the judges. Seabury was one of the few who did not condone the shabby practices of the clerks, the careless handling of fees, and the special court privileges afforded to the attorneys of the big private utilities. There was a common suspicion that juries were being bribed right under the noses of some city court judges.

One morning, while presiding at a trial term of the court, Seabury noticed a friend on the jury. For some time he had suspected that the city court clerks were not paying the jurors their legal fee of one dollar for each case. He asked his friend how much he had received. Since two cases were being tried together before Seabury at the same time, the juror was entitled to two dollars but he had received only one dollar. When Seabury questioned the clerk about the money, he received a defiant answer. Privately he began an investigation of each of the five city court clerks, only to discover that they were stealing sheriffs' as well as jurors' fees. The practice had continued so long that it had become routine. Seabury asked each clerk to produce his books; all refused to do so.

One of the clerks complained to a Tammany judge that his "rights" were being abused.

"Has Judge Seabury a right to order my books from your court into his private chambers for examination?" the clerk asked.

"Well, I don't know what is the exact legal status," the judge replied. "But if there is nothing to conceal, why not help him examine your books?"

"He says he doesn't need any help—he's going to examine all the books himself," the clerk said.

"All right," the judge said. "You better let that reformer have his way or there will be hell to pay."

As a result of Seabury's private investigation, charges were brought against all five city court clerks. At first, the chief justice of the city court defended the clerks, saying, "I do not think there is really anything in these charges. It is more the fault of the lawyers than the clerks." Nevertheless, Seabury pressed their superior, the chief clerk, to discharge them. The difficulty here was that the chief clerk, Thomas F. Smith, was secretary of Tammany Hall and a friend of Boss Murphy's. When no action was taken against the clerks, Seabury let it be known to the press. The chief clerk's hand was forced, and all five clerks were removed and others appointed.

Much more serious than the discovery of this petty larceny was the revelation of a system for bribing jurors devised by the Metropolitan Street Railways Company. Men of great wealth and influence controlled this privately owned public utility, and for a thirty-year-old city court judge to challenge their practices required either courage or foolhardiness. But in Seabury's own mind, the reason for taking up the challenge was simple: "It was a scandal and a disgrace," he explained later, "that such practices had taken place in a court of justice. I felt that the burden rested upon me to make an investigation of the facts."

The facts appeared incriminating. Whenever the Metropolitan Street Railways Company was being sued by some individual in an accident case, Judge Seabury noticed that the jury verdicts followed a pattern favorable to the company. Examining the pattern a little more closely, he found that at least one floating juror sat in the trials repeatedly. This "civic-minded" stooge, William H. Tillinghast, was actually a night watchman employed by the company, who managed to spend most of his days slipping onto juries with the connivance of a court clerk. Once he was sworn to a jury, usually under the name of a juror who had been excused from the panel, he either tried to swing the verdict for the company or, at least, hold down the amount of the recovery for the plaintiff. In addition, a member of the company's legal department, Stanley S. Bagg, bribed the jurors. To do so, he had vouchers for payments of bribes approved by the company's legal department—clear evidence that the company lawyers were guilty of collusion.

Seabury directed the district attorney, William Travers Jerome, to bring the Company's admitted briber, Bagg (he had been named by Tillinghast), before him. Although usually only concerned with civil suits, Seabury sat as a committing magistrate. He asked Henry M. Stevenson to serve as attorney for one of the company investigators who was willing to co-operate in exposing the bribes. Jerome, who had a reputation as a forceful personality in his own right, was chagrined to find that Seabury dominated the prosecution of the case.

As the cross-examination by the court and district attorney began, it soon developed that Jerome was not pressing the prosecution of James L. Quackenbush, general counsel for the Metropolitan Street Railways. While Seabury kept demanding that the payment vouchers for the jury bribes be produced, Quackenbush insisted that they had been destroyed.

Bagg was called to the witness stand and suddenly announced that he was going to tell "the whole truth," as he put it. This time he denied ever having had anything to do with the bribes.

Whereupon Jerome refused to continue examining him, saying he could never bring such a self-confessed liar before the grand jury.

"What you will or will not do is a matter for yourself to determine, Mr. Jerome," said Seabury. "This testimony may be corroborated, and I shall examine Tillinghast in connection with it and everyone else connected with it."

Quackenbush suddenly arose and protested against the entire proceeding. He said that Judge Seabury had no jurisdiction in criminal cases.

"I again rule that you have no standing in this court and overrule your protest," Seabury replied.

"I think that I can straighten out this matter by a few words," Jerome intervened. "As to Your Honor's jurisdiction, you are a magistrate sitting here on information furnished to my office and as such have full jurisdiction to hear all the evidence and to issue any warrant for which you find foundation, but as to the matter of an independent criminal charge against the corporation, that is another matter."

"But if the Metropolitan was involved in any jury fixing I think it ought to come out," Seabury replied.

"Certainly, if any warrant has been issued," said Jerome.

"But no warrants have been issued at all," said Seabury.

"In that case I don't know where I'm at," said Jerome.

Again, the company's general counsel challenged Seabury's right to run a criminal case, and once again Seabury warned him that he had no place in the court. Now, strangely, Jerome found himself defending the "honor" of Quackenbush, in a farcical exchange.

"Your Honor has been informed by me," said Jerome, "that we have held an investigation and are satisfied that the vouchers have been destroyed."

"But do you know, Mr. Jerome," said Judge Seabury, "that there is not one scintilla of testimony concerning this destruction; that we don't know that the vouchers have been destroyed at all?"

"Then the district attorney withdraws from this case," Jerome replied, his face flushed. "I have heretofore tried to take the proper means and here you have the public challenge of a gentleman, and his word will always be taken, and he gives you his word that they have been destroyed. In all my experience I never saw such a proceeding."

"I know of no precept in law which accepts the word of a gentleman in substitution for legal evidence," said Seabury, his face turning scarlet. "The Court does not care to be lectured by you, Mr. Jerome, and if you care to withdraw you are at liberty to do so."

"Nor do I care to be lectured by you," the district attorney answered, picking up his coat, making a bow, and leaving the courtroom quickly.

At the end of the hearing, Quackenbush caused a commotion

outside the courtroom. "This man Seabury is a disgrace to the bench," he declared loudly. "He is unfit to be a judge. When I say unfit, I speak advisedly. Mark that. Steps should be taken to impeach him and remove him from office."

The jury-bribing case did not result in a prosecution, because the bribery charges were not sustained. Yet Seabury, reading the *New York World* aloud to Maud the next evening, was pleased with the editorial: "There was the district attorney's office with 200 employees and the Metropolitan's law department with 300 employees on the other side; but Judge Seabury did what he could and the people will not forget that."

Later Seabury said, "I think the purpose of the court hearing was accomplished, at least for a considerable period of time. The people were put on notice that jury bribing did and could exist. I have no doubt that if New York County had had a district attorney who intended to expose the facts, the results would have been far-reaching."

Several years later, when Jerome himself was arraigned on charges of misconduct before a governor's commission, Seabury was called as a witness. Jerome asked Seabury, "Mr. Justice, will you be good enough to express your honest opinion of me?" Seabury said, "Do you really want my honest opinion?" Jerome replied, "I do." Then Seabury rendered the special insult that he kept for rare occasions. "I find it impossible to raise you to the level of my contempt," he declared.

The city court occupied Seabury's working time, but he still kept politically active. His off-bench utterances again brought down upon him the label "radical." (Mildness in speech was never one of his outstanding characteristics.) Part of his time outside city court he spent writing "opinions" of a partisan political nature for various publications. In an article in *The Liberal Democrat* entitled "Public Operation of Public Utilities a Function of Government," he wrote:

The modern monopolists and millionaires, such as Morgan, Rockefeller, Vanderbilt, *et al.,* have been and are still performing a useful mission for society. They are as useful to future society as were the feudal lords and barons of an earlier time to our own day. In feudal times the lords rendered valuable services in return for the labor of the mass of

men which they appropriated. While they used their serfs and depend-
ents to fight their wars and win more lands for them, they kept the
peace and preserved order within their own dominions. Today the great
railroads of the nation, the great telegraph and telephone systems, and in
the cities of the country the street railroads, gas and electric lighting
plants are in the hands of the private corporations. Upon the fair and
proper operation of these public services, which these private companies
are permitted to perform, depends the health and sometimes the lives of
our citizens.

Our captains of industry, as they proudly term themselves, have demonstrated beyond question that the rendering of these public services,
depending as they do upon governmental grants of franchises, are natural monopolies. Having demonstrated that these public services can be
brought under one control, it now only remains for the people to substitute their own government for the Vanderbilts, Morgans and others,
who now use their privileges as a means of plundering all the people.
The operation of these natural monopolies is a function of government.
The exercise of this function by government is not socialism, but is absolutely necessary to preserve the individual rights of each citizen.

This article, like a number of others he wrote for the independent
Democratic periodical, was not signed by Seabury. However, Dr.
Seabury, who had a sense of destiny about his son, kept a scrapbook,
in which he pasted a copy of each article, signing his son's initials at
its conclusion. Perhaps he had a premonition that some day a historian would be using the scrapbook.

Of course, the young judge did not confine his crusading to the
printed page. He served as chairman for many public meetings of
the reform element called the "Liberal Democracy" and advised the
anti-Tammany Democrats about positions on the executive committee concerned with nominating candidates in state and local campaigns. "We are fundamentally opposed to the present unjust
distribution of wealth that creates a system of society in which the
few get without working, while the many work without getting,"
he stated at one meeting. "This condition is due to the monopoly of
natural opportunities and the creation of special privileges by law."

His remarks did not go unheeded, especially in *The Sun,* where
the editorials were explosive whenever Seabury attacked the business
"captains." After one especially fiery meeting of the Liberal Democ-

racy, *The Sun* said: "Is the Samuel Seabury who presided at a public meeting last night the Samuel Seabury who was elected to the bench as representing the single taxers? The city pays him a large salary as a judge, and, considering his extreme youth, he ought to reconcile himself to keeping out of politics for the time being, as he is not a candidate for anything."

While the reform elements in New York and the independent political movements beyond the Hudson were firing the imaginations of workers and farmers, big-business lawyers were not idle. In high state and Federal courts, they counterattacked to preserve monopoly and discredit the trust busters. Spreading strikes raised a number of side questions that had never before been legally resolved. In cases growing out of labor's right to organize and strike, especially against large industries and public utilities, there were, besides Seabury, few men on the bench who were sympathetic to the unions or capable of viewing acts of downright defiance on labor's part as the expression of a constitutional American dream of freedom. On the contrary, many judges began to find new uses for the power of injunction—to break strikes and labor unions. Among those who spoke out against this abuse of injunction was Clarence Darrow, who had been a member of the counsel for Eugene V. Debs when the Socialist leader was indicted for conspiracy in the railroad union case. At the time when Seabury was on the city court, Darrow was chief counsel for the labor interests in the anthracite strike arbitration proceedings at Scranton in 1903. Timing his attack to coincide with that arbitration, which was being watched by unions all over the country, Seabury in several legal publications published an article called "The Abuses of Injunction."

Here, he reached back deep into the English chancery courts to cite many precedents against the use of injunctions when other remedies at law existed. He found that the use of injunction in labor disputes flourished in American courts, but not in British courts. He cited two extreme examples of abuse: "The famous 'starvation' injunction issued last summer prohibiting workmen from giving food and assistance to their associates during a strike has been followed by a recent injunction prohibiting a payment of benefit moneys by a labor union to its members pending a strike." Such injunctions, he said, violated fundamental rights. He criticized the Debs case,* in which there had been granted a sweeping injunction against all the members of the American Railway Union—an injunction that Seabury called a "police proclamation putting the community in general under peril of punishment for contempt." He concluded his article by declaring that the rights of free speech and trial by jury, prohibited by these injunctions, were won only after men had suffered imprisonment, the thumbscrew, and the rack. "Are we to be deprived of them now by pieces of paper signed by judges of courts of equity?" Fearlessly, he was willing to oppose the actions of the highest state and Federal judges.

Although the Manhattan Single Tax Club still attracted the ideological attention of Seabury, the single taxers, after the death of Henry George, lacked a figurehead, a spokesman for their rigid economic philosophy. Now there were more immediate outlets for Seabury's energy and attention. He turned to the Municipal Ownership League of Greater New York. In this organization he could devote himself to forwarding one of his favorite causes: public ownership of utilities and, especially, of the city's transit system.

During a state legislative session in 1904, Seabury went to Albany with his friend, attorney Melvin G. Palliser, and spoke on behalf of half a dozen bills advocated by the Municipal Ownership League. One bill conferred on the City of New York the right to own and operate all public utilities and take private property by condemnation after just compensation; another empowered the city to build and operate its own electric lighting plant, not only to supply light on public streets and in parks but actually to provide light to every inhabitant in private dwellings; another called for a major investigation of the gas trust by the state legislature. These bills were advocated as remedies for the evils perpetrated by the Consolidated Gas Company and the New York Edison Company. Judge Seabury, according to *The World*, said that "both of these corporations exist in violation of the law and enjoy absolute monopolies in the necessaries of life; both have violated the law of the state; both have made false reports to avoid the payment of their just taxes, and both have entered into a close and friendly alliance with public officers whose

* 158 U.S. 564.

duty required that they should protect the public from extortion."

Samuel Seabury, justice, could also talk like Samuel Seabury, citizen. During the 1930's, his manner of saying privately but openly what he could not say officially irritated Governor Franklin D. Roosevelt.

He addressed an open letter "To the Board of Rapid Transit Railroad Commissioners." (Although presumably it was printed with no official affiliation, it bore the emblem of the printers' union large beneath his signature.) "I understand that the board is about to act upon some nineteen routes which it has already laid out, and that bids for franchises in these routes are to be invited. The franchises to be granted are of very great value and have been estimated to be worth about $500,000,000." Aware that the "Metropolitan interests" and the "Belmont interests" were attempting to obtain these franchises without paying taxes on the land, he made clear to the board— and by sending copies to the newspapers, the whole city—the opposition of the Municipal Ownership League to a suspected steal. "A due regard to the welfare of the city will require that these grants be made only for short terms, upon adequate compensation, and to preserve to the city and state the right of taxation," he declared.

All his off-bench speeches and articles he collected in a 200-page booklet, *Municipal Ownership and Operation of Public Utilities in New York City,* signed "By Samuel Seabury." He was described as "one of the Justices of the City Court of the City of New York." The booklet borrowed liberally from *The History of Public Franchises* by Gustavus Myers, eminent muckraker and historian of Tammany Hall, but made a major contribution of its own. It described some of the public franchises owned in New York by private corporations, pointed out the abuses existing under their managements, and argued for public ownership as the only way to achieve efficient operation without graft.

The booklet's real value was that it set forth clearly the facts about the gas and electric companies, the methods and practices of the lighting trusts, the street railway monopoly, and even the financial histories of the bridges across the East River. Obviously, the joke about selling the Brooklyn Bridge had at one time a basis in fact. Seabury suggested legal methods by which the city could acquire public utilities, citing pertinent provisions of the Greater New York

Charter. Finally, he said that "municipal ownership is essentially a business matter, the advantages of which are capable of being demonstrated to hard-headed business men. Those who fight for municipal ownership and operation of public utilities fight for the right. It is inevitable."

The Seabury booklet served to arouse many citizens. All the newspapers commented on it, most of them praising the presentation of the facts and of the legal background. But at least one voice expressed disappointment in the booklet and its author. Writing in *The American,* a latter-day Loyalist named Leonard Tuttle commented: "Judge Samuel Seabury's time might better be employed in protecting the rights of property rather than in an attempt to destroy them. He should emulate his namesake, Bishop Seabury of Connecticut, who stood firmly and loyally for established conditions against a revolutionary mob. The men who made this country what it is did not use their time and talents in exciting discontent among the working men, or in fostering unions or strikes or closed shops, or other seditious socialistic agitations which are now keeping the country in a ferment."

The booklet that struck some readers as "socialistic" had one fascinating result, which was to change the course of Seabury's political career several times: it got him a meeting with William Randolph Hearst.

Seabury met Hearst during the publisher's progressive period, when he was a leader in the movement for municipal ownership. Among those who praised Hearst as a champion of the people because of some of his worthwhile crusades were Lincoln Steffens and Clarence Darrow. The politically ambitious young publisher had real newspapers to play with, presented to him by his father, the former United States Senator George Hearst, a California mine operator. And, as long as circulation was good, Hearst followed the muckraking style of *McClure's, Collier's, Munsey's, The Independent,* and other national magazines.

Hearst was taken with Seabury's *Municipal Ownership and Operation of Public Utilities in New York City.* He asked to meet privately with the outspoken city court justice who not only supported trust busting but favored public ownership. A mayoralty campaign was in the offing in the fall of 1905, and clearly the problems of constructing and operating a utilities system for the city would be a major issue. Charles Evans Hughes, chief counsel of the State Insurance Investigating Committee, had exposed the management of the gas trust and the large life insurance companies, establishing himself in the process as a potential candidate for governor. Hughes had been able to serve as counsel because Hearst, Seabury, State Senator John Ford, Clarence J. Shearn, and others in the Municipal Ownership League had persuaded the state legislature to investigate conditions in New York City and, inevitably, the links between Tammany and the trusts.

Before the meeting of Hearst and Seabury, Hearst's *New York American* printed a story saying that "both Judge Seabury and Senator Ford have warm admirers" among those considered as Fusion mayoralty candidates. "Judge Seabury is one of the best judges on the local bench," the story said. "To promote him to the mayor's chair would be a substantial loss to the judiciary; but he is a very worthy and well-equipped man for the mayoralty. His character is unimpeachable. He is young, vigorous and if elected would help put an end to the vicious granting of franchises beyond the recall of the people." The Hearst newspapers, as well as others, played up Senator Ford and Judge Seabury. Hearst was also discussed, though the Citizens Union retained doubts about the newspaper publisher's motives. Finally, it was determined that Hearst, Arthur Brisbane, managing editor of Hearst's *Evening Journal,* and Seabury would meet to decide what course Fusion should take and who would carry the mayoralty standard.

Seabury titled his private notes of that meeting: "Hearst's Plan to Nominate Me. How I Changed the Plan." He described the historic meeting for his own record in these words:

On the afternoon of October 5, 1905, I had an interview with Hearst and Brisbane. The interview lasted about two hours and they both expressed the idea that I should become the candidate of the Municipal Ownership League. I told Hearst that it was a subject that I had given a good deal of thought to and I had decided that I did not want the nomination for mayor on an independent ticket, and could not see my way clear to accepting it. I told him frankly that if I should be nominated, I would be put in a position where I would necessarily be dependent upon him.

Both Hearst and Brisbane disputed this and assured me that I could be just as independent of Hearst as I saw fit, and urged me to take the nomination. I told them it was not as simple as they seemed to suppose. It cost money to run a campaign. That I might go into the campaign and Mr. Hearst and I might disagree as to the course to be followed. That he might cease to contribute to the campaign and that since I did not have the necessary money, I would be put in a position where I would be entirely dependent upon him in the expression of my views. That was a position I was unwilling to occupy. Moreover, I told them I much preferred going on the supreme court bench.

I told Hearst that the growth of the municipal ownership idea had been due largely to his advocacy of it—and that I was quite sure that he would be a stronger candidate than any other person. Before I left, I had Hearst's personal assurance that he would make no attempt to stampede the meeting for my nomination. Hearst said he must have some time in which to consider whether it was wise for him to take the nomination. I told him that it was—but it should be definitely understood that under no circumstances was I to be nominated for mayor, and that I had their assurances that no such attempt would be made on my behalf.

That evening, the Municipal League convention took place. When Seabury arrived a few minutes before eight o'clock at the Grand Central Plaza, he met some of his close friends. They held out their hands and congratulated him. Seabury wondered at this.

"They're all set to nominate you on the first ballot," one of his friends whispered, and added that he was delighted and would do everything to help insure the nomination.

"But the agreement is that I should not be nominated!" Seabury said, in great agitation.

He realized, however, that he would have to move quickly to prevent the convention from sweeping him into the mayoralty nomination. Looking over the enormous crowd, he immediately went from group to group and gathered a dozen of his friends together in a corner. He selected Simon Levy, an old friend of his from the single-tax movement, with whom he had worked during the campaign when Henry George was candidate for mayor. Levy asked Seabury what he wanted done.

"If Hearst in his speech gives any indication that I should be the candidate," Seabury said, "I want you to get up on the floor and nominate Hearst for mayor. I suspect that he will try to stampede the meeting."

Levy and the small group of friends agreed to help to block the nomination, which Seabury felt he could not campaign for freely as his own man.

Now the Municipal Ownership League meeting was called to order. The huge crowd was ready to come to a decision. Before any of the Seabury group spoke, Hearst was summoned to step forward to the podium. He spoke of the corporation grafting schemes, of the dangers that awaited the city with the re-election of Mayor George B. McClellan, who was influenced by Tammany's leaders, of the new subways to be built with "a billion dollars hanging as the prize to the corrupt ring." Then Hearst closed with a stirring peroration:

> I am not here to flatter you, or other voters of this city. You know what kind of government this city has. Now, whose fault is it? It isn't the fault of the corporations. It isn't the fault of Charles Murphy or Benjamin Odell. It isn't the fault of Murphy's puppet or Odell's puppet. It's your fault. You are like a sleeping giant pillaged by pygmies. Wake up! Nominate honest and independent men like Judge Seabury or Senator Ford, who I am sure will lead you to victory, and elect them. And restore to this city a government of the people, by the people, and for the people.

The mention of Seabury's name drew great applause. As soon as it had died down, Simon Levy made his move. He forced the chairman to recognize him. A moment later he was swaying the convention with an impassioned argument against the grafting politicians and corporations. By the time he finished speaking, the crowd yelled for a candidate. "I nominate William Randolph Hearst!" he cried, and thousands of flags fluttered in response, delegates stood on chairs and cheered, and the cymbals of the Seventy-first Regiment Band crashed.

While this demonstration was going on, Hearst turned away from the crowd, trembling. He edged his way toward Seabury on the platform, and said, "Judge, will you not stop this?" Seabury replied, "This is the nomination they want, and this is what they are going to get." Now from the floor came the voice of Simon Levy. "I move that the nominations be closed," he declared. Instead of putting the motion, the chairman recognized Seabury. When the crowd quieted down, Seabury spoke:

> Mr. Chairman, ladies and gentlemen, I did not come here to make a speech. If you people by this time do not understand that the public service corporations of this town own both political parties, nothing that I can say can make you realize that fact. [Applause.] Gas trusts and traction run this town. They set the Republicans and Democrats fighting each other. No matter which one loses, they always win. They own both parties and they send their representatives to the state legislature. When we wanted to pass a bill in Albany which gave the City of New York the right to run its own subway railroad, they formed an alliance of Democrats and Republicans to assassinate that bill. When there was a proposition to give New York City cheaper gas, Republicans united with Democrats to defeat that bill. Why, gentlemen, you are electing to the state senate men that you should be sending to the state prison. The thing to do now is to act—to nominate a ticket free and clear of all other political parties and machines, and the man to nominate to head that ticket is William Randolph Hearst! [Applause.] Now, I move, if a motion is in order, Mr. Chairman, that a committee be appointed to carry out the will expressed by this convention.

The motion was unanimously adopted, Hearst was nominated by acclamation, and Seabury had gracefully eluded a candidacy he did not want. The Municipal Ownership League shortly thereafter nominated Seabury for justice of the supreme court—a judicial advancement he coveted.

The 1905 mayoralty campaign was a rough-and-tumble affair. In the three weeks between nomination and Election Day, the Hearst press laid down a heavy barrage against Tammany. In a famous cartoon, Boss Murphy, the Tammany leader and backer of Mayor McClellan, was drawn wearing prison stripes, over the caption "Look out, Murphy! It's a short lockstep from Delmonico's to Sing Sing." (Murphy, having graduated from the street light on Second Avenue, now conducted his affairs at Delmonico's Restaurant on Union Square.) So effective were Hearst's printed attacks on Tammany that Mayor McClellan promised to pursue an independent course. The

Republican nominee, William M. Ivins, was discounted from the start. Seabury and the Municipal Ownership League gave Hearst their full support. It looked as if he could defeat Tammany and carry out the radical schemes proposed in Seabury's booklet on public ownership of utilities.

On the day before the election, editorials in the Hearst newspapers called on the Irish to vote as Robert Emmet would have voted; on the Jews to vote as Maimonides; on the Poles to vote as Kosciusko; on the Italians to vote as Garibaldi; on the Hungarians to vote as Kossuth. Whom did that omit? Just to be safe, the "Americans" were called on to vote as "Jefferson and Lincoln would vote." Obviously, the editorial indicated, all these sterling patriots were for William Randolph Hearst. The publisher enlisted the Reverend Charles H. Parkhurst on his side, to write about public morals, home, mother, and the good life. Brisbane gave a benediction to Anthony Comstock, and all bases were touched. The citizenry was aroused.

On Election Day, Tammany bullyboys were out in full force. The prison-stripe cartoon had cut Murphy to the quick, and his lieutenants had been ordered to slug out a victory, if necessary. This they did, in a classic Gas House maneuver, with men registering from vacant lots, votes cast in the names of cats and dogs, floaters imported from Philadelphia, and ballots dumped in the East River. One Hearst supporter set out in a rowboat and scooped up a mess of filthy, water-soaked ballot boxes. Pistol shots rang out during the night and city hospitals were filled with bruised voters. When the ballots were counted—this was before the days of voting machines—McClellan was hurriedly announced as the victor by a close margin. Fraud was charged, a recount demanded, fresh ballots turned up to replace the dumped ones, and all were magically marked with McClellan crosses. The final official recount gave McClellan victory by a mere 3,500 votes out of 600,000 cast for the three candidates. Seabury was defeated in the judicial election by a margin of 20,000 votes.

With the campaign behind him, Seabury turned his attention to personal matters. He and Maud had moved back to 8 Chelsea Square from 145th Street when his mother had died, in order to keep house for Dr. Seabury. They were again close to the Richey home and the seminary enclave. Going downtown to the city court was easier from this location. Later, they rented their own house at 8 West Tenth Street, still not far from the family. On week ends, far into the fall, they went to East Hampton. They acquired the Richey summer cottage on Divinity Hill and stored many possessions there, especially their growing collection of books.

Judge Seabury still found time in the evenings to work with the reform organizations in New York. The Municipal Ownership League's name was changed to the Independence League—a title better suited to attract the voters in upstate New York. Another election was coming up in 1906, this one for the governorship, and already there were stirrings. Seabury went out as a scout, to see how the farmers and townspeople in Oswego, Madison, and other counties would respond to the Hearst name. At the annual outing of the Central New York Hop-Growers, he was the only speaker before 25,000 people. Each time he mentioned Hearst's name, the response of the picnickers was enthusiastic. Reporting to Hearst and Brisbane in the city, Seabury said the prospects looked good. But Hearst had learned that he needed the support of one of the regular parties, in addition to that of the Independents, to win an election. At the same time, Boss Murphy, licking his wounded pride, decided that it would be better to win with Hearst than to lose to a Republican. Hearst permitted himself to be nominated for governor by the Democrats at Buffalo, one of the fastest turnabouts in the history of political opportunism. It was rumored later that Hearst's arrangement with Murphy was on a straight business basis—half a million dollars to the Tammany leader for the nomination and victory, though only part as a down payment. The stakes here went beyond Albany. Hearst and his friends saw a chance at the White House in 1908 from the springboard of New York state's executive mansion.

During the gubernatorial contest in 1906, ten justices of the supreme court for the First Judicial District were to be nominated. Among those named by the Independence League were Samuel Seabury and John W. Goff, both of whom had been vigorous in their anti-Tammany statements. But under the strange alliance between Hearst and Murphy, Seabury, Goff, and other anti-Tammanyites received the Democratic nomination as well. The recognition of Hearst's consistently liberal stands against the trusts and for municipal ownership, and the hope that with him as governor reforms could be put into effect, were responsible for the Independents' continued support of the publisher. Nevertheless, later in his career, Seabury was reminded more than once that he had made the supreme court race with Boss Murphy's Democrats.

During the campaign, the attacks were particularly strong against Goff and Seabury. The latter did not allow them to go unanswered. At the Harlem Casino, Seabury denounced the Republican gubernatorial candidate, Charles Evans Hughes, and spoke up strongly for Hearst, who shared the platform with him. He also struck out at the Republicans running for the supreme court. Seabury's politicking while on the bench, and his closeness to Hearst, caused one of his judicial opponents to declare:

> I do not believe that Judge Seabury would do a dishonest act, but with his judicial robes upon him, he has for years, three or four, done nothing but in the most abject manner served the political objects of his boss and master, a certain newspaper proprietor. Now, it may be that Judge Seabury knows all that a judge ought to know about law, it may be that Samuel Seabury knows all that a judge ought to know of private morality as between man and man; but one thing is dead sure, and that is he has not the first inkling of public morality that should exist between the judge and the people whose judge he is.

A few days before the election, President Theodore Roosevelt, fearing that Hearst might defeat Hughes and thereafter pose a challenge for the Presidency, dispatched Secretary of State Elihu Root to New York to campaign. In a speech in Utica, the Secretary of State declared: "With the President's authority, I say to you that he greatly desires the election of Mr. Hughes; I say to you that he regards Mr. Hearst as wholly unfit to be governor; as an insincere, self-seeking demagogue who is trying to deceive the workingmen of New York by false statements and false promises." It was feared that this intervention from the White House would have a strong effect on the electorate. Seabury answered Root at a mass rally in Carnegie Hall; even William Jennings Bryan mounted the platform and endorsed Hearst without qualification.

On Election Day, the usual pattern of strong Republican votes upstate and strong Democratic voting in New York City was soon apparent. However, many Tammany district leaders, smarting under Hearst's attacks upon them in the past, had not gotten behind Boss Murphy's new friend during the campaign. As a result, Hughes was elected governor, but he was the only Republican elected to state office. In New York City, the combined Democratic party–Independence League triumphed. The ticket on which Seabury ran was elected by a plurality ranging from 90,000 to 100,000 votes. At the age of thirty-three, City Court Justice Seabury now became Supreme Court Justice Seabury.

He had things to do that Christmas before going on the higher court on January 1, 1907. During the holidays, he finished a huge book into which he put what he had learned during his tenure on the city court. He called the book *The Law and Practice of the City Court of the City of New York,* signing it, "By Samuel Seabury, one of the Justices of the Supreme Court of the State of New York, formerly one of the Justices of the City Court." In this book he set forth the sections of the Code of Civil Procedure, interpreting their provisions. Published by Baker, Voorhis, the 1,317-page volume, known simply as "Seabury's City Court Practice," was for years a standard work for judges and lawyers.

His performance of one act before taking the bench indicated that the Judge's social conscience and philosophy would not be altered by his court elevation. A young English boilermaker, William Bishop, had been ordered deported by the Immigration authorities, ostensibly because he was "a pauper," in reality because he admitted to being a Socialist. Somehow, the matter came to Seabury's attention, though it had nothing to do with his court. Indeed, it was none of his business—but he made it so. In a letter to Victor H. Metcalf, United States Secretary of Commerce and Labor, he wrote:

Although I differ from the Socialists in their ideas of government, I recognize that as a class they are law-abiding citizens, who seek to effect changes in the laws by peaceable and lawful methods and who are as much entitled to their opinions as I am to mine. The exclusion of young Bishop because of his belief in Socialism would be an insult to many hundreds of thousands of loyal citizens who profess to believe in Socialism. It would also place our own government in an exceedingly narrow, bigoted and illiberal position. If government officials may exclude a person because he is a Socialist, they may exclude one because he is a Prohibitionist, or a Democrat, or because of his race or religion.

Secretary Metcalf thanked Seabury for calling attention to the case and informed him that, as a result of his letter, the deportation order had been revoked.

CHAPTER 5

Radical in Supreme Court Robes

ON the day before he was sworn in as a justice of the New York State Supreme Court, Samuel Seabury stopped at a stationer's on Lower Broadway and purchased the most expensive diary in the shop. It was an impressive book, bound in red leather, trimmed with gold scrolls, with a stout brass lock. The pages were ruled and marbled on the edges. It was clearly the purchase of a man very much aware of a turning point in his life; what he wrote in the diary might record the making of history.

Once before, on January 1, 1888, he had begun a diary. His father had written his name on the title page of that tan leather pocket diary with the admonition "Remember always thine end, and how that time lost never returns." Now, on January 1, 1907, Sam wrote his own name, the date, and the word "Personal," underscored. Not many years separated the two Januaries. He had lost little time between his admission to practice before the supreme court and his elevation to its bench. Dr. Seabury's son was remembering his end.

On the day Seabury was sworn in, he made the following entry in his quick, angular hand:

Today I became a justice of the Supreme Court of the State of New York. I took the oath on Saturday morning in the old county courthouse with John J. Brady, before Judge Davis. The oath was administered first

to me and then to Brady. I sent it at once to be filed in the office of the
Secretary of State at Albany. I met several of the newly elected justices
and we discussed the appointments of court attendants that are to be
made from the civil service list. Civil service regulations are probably
beneficial but as at present applied they are absurd. They compel the
selection of men who are inferior to those whom the justices would appoint if not bound by such regulations. I selected one man as court
attendant who had been connected with the city court and its law journal; he is at present second on the list. The one who stands first is first
merely because he is a veteran. Under the law, no appointment can
be made from the list until the veteran is "taken care of." I appointed
John Lair as my secretary. I called in Judge Patterson and the order
fixing his salary at $2,500 per annum was signed by him and sent to a
majority of the justices and signed by them, and John was sworn in. He
is much elated by his appointment and promises to do well. Time will
tell.

About five o'clock I went to William Randolph Hearst's house to pay
him a call and wish him a happy New Year. He had gone out. Examined and digested some cases bearing upon the powers of the appellate
division to deprive judges of an opportunity to perform their function,
by making arbitrary designations as to terms of the court and the justices assigned to them.

Although I have commenced the year making this entry today, I have
no intention of making daily entries in this book. The only rule I shall
adhere to is that whenever I desire to make an entry I shall do it. The
abandonment of all attempts at regularity and order in the keeping of a
journal has, I believe, the sanction of the precedents established by the
examples of both Byron and Scott. If I had kept such a journal during
the last two years I might have presented an account of some political
occurrences of great interest. Such a record would have told the true
story of the great municipal campaign of 1905 and the state campaign of
1906. Certainly these were two of the most remarkable campaigns that
have occurred in the history of this state.

At about the same time that Judge Seabury went on the bench,
two men then unknown to him, whose public careers would cross
his intimately, were engaging in unusual, if far less significant, activities. James J. Walker, after much prodding by his father, had finally finished his courses at the New York Law School but had
failed to take the bar examinations, claiming a need for "postgradu-

ate work." His only studies were made in the vicinity of Tin Pan Alley, where he was writing such songs as *There's Music in the Rustle of a Skirt, After They Gather the Hay,* and *In the Valley Where My Sally Said Good-bye.* Not until 1912, ten years after his first year in law school, was he admitted to practice. Another future Mayor of New York, Fiorello H. La Guardia, after three years in the consular service, had returned to New York to work and study. He became an interpreter at Ellis Island for $1,200 a year, and, after a full day's work, took the ferry to attend evening classes at New York University Law School. He was admitted to the bar soon after graduating and almost immediately embarked on a career as a lawyer specializing in labor-union–defense work.

Seabury kept up the entries in the red leather book only until April 20 of that year. Although he marked the diary "Personal," most of his entries are discreet, with only an occasional burst of sarcastic humor. They reveal the broad range of his interests: the court system, the cases before him, the reform movement and politics, his reading, and chess.

What he wrote, and what he refrained from writing, disclose a cold-eyed view of the justices: "Met the judges at the supreme court this morning," he wrote on January 3. Immediately two of them had pre-empted the best rooms in the newer quarters, and could not be blasted out. With eight rooms left for the newly elected judges, they decided to draw lots—the justices of the supreme court ironically relying on luck to dispense justice among themselves. "Eight numbers were written on slips of paper and given to Justice O'Gorman, who, having his high hat on his head and a long black cigar in his mouth, put the slips into the very small hat which Justice Erlanger uses to cover *his* head, and each judge drew one slip. The drawing took place alphabetically and resulted in the last slip going to me. But as the 'last shall be first' I secured slip No. 1, and chose the next best room—the only private room left that had a full window. Justice Platzek, with characteristic modesty, conveyed sundry hints that he would like the room I picked, but I did not respond to his delicate suggestions."

When he took his seat on the supreme court bench for the first time, many of his friends from the Manhattan Single Tax Club and other reform organizations sent him flowers—which he made sure did not get into the courtroom. He found the silk gown "warm and an infernal nuisance," but he found some of his colleagues even more nettlesome. At a dinner at the Manhattan Club given by the justices for Judge Patterson, Seabury noted that "several of the speeches praised the court, one another and themselves." Nor was he impressed with Presiding Justice Patterson. "Patterson was insistent upon the need to exalt the office. I suppose this means obedience to the maxim that it is the function of a good judge to extend his jurisdiction. Patterson thought the justices possessed the attributes of the deity Himself. After dinner, several of these Godlike creatures got around a table, blessed poker, and otherwise refreshed themselves. The whole thing was a contemptible and absurd affair."

The newly elected justices met late one afternoon in February and decided to give a dinner for the senior justices. Seabury commented, "This is nonsense, but all agreed that it should be done and I have agreed to it, also." At this dinner, which he describes, probably in derision, as "a magnificent affair," all the judges made speeches. Presiding Justice Patterson made his usual speech, calling upon his colleagues to "exalt" the office. The others made "boring" speeches. As for himself "I made a boring speech, too," Seabury said. After the dinner, several of the judges "played their usual game of poker." His entries betray his belief that he was superior to the average political hack on the bench. Subtlety was not one of his characteristics, and he rarely concealed his feelings; consequently, he came to number several colleagues on the supreme court among his foes.

His fascination with politics continued unabated. Although many people were already suspicious of Hearst the reformer, Seabury stuck by him. Again and again, his diary reveals, he paid calls at the publisher's house to discuss politics. "In the afternoon, went to Hearst's house and had a conference as to devising ways and means of promoting principles of the Independence League." And again, "Had a long talk with Hearst about traction matters and urged that he sign and send petition I wrote on this subject to the Board of Estimate." After lunching with a group of reform Democrats, he came away saying, "All these men distrust Hearst and even deny him a fair amount of credit for what he has done." On one visit to Hearst's office, Seabury had a long talk with Arthur Brisbane. In the middle of a conversation on new subways, Brisbane suddenly turned to his own work. "I was much amused watching him in action," Seabury noted. "He talks all his editorials into an Edison Phonograph [an early Dictaphone] and then gives them to a typewriter [stenographer] who immediately writes them out, while Brisbane writes another editorial. He strikes back at enemies in this way. 'If you will excuse me for a few moments, I will give the scoundrel a few punches while I feel like it,' he said. Then he turned to the phonograph and for three minutes poured into it a scathing editorial."

In his conversations with Hearst, Seabury talked not as a supreme court justice but as a politician hatching plots. In Hearst, he met his equal in political maneuvering. "Called on Hearst and spent over an hour talking over political matters," Seabury recorded. "He is convinced that the only hope of reform lies in the formation of a new party, entirely free of monopoly control. The formation of a new party or the preservation of the Independence League organization is comparatively easy, but the difficulty is to prevent the same forces that dominate the old parties from exerting control over the new party. Hearst is keenly sensitive to this danger—and feels that the organization must be kept in his control or in the control of his friends until such time as direct nominations are possible. Hearst has in mind the formation of Independence Leagues in other states and contemplates a meeting of representatives of state organizations to form a national organization." As for Hearst's plan, Seabury noted: "If the organization of the party is made democratic, unprincipled men, wholly out of sympathy with its original aims, can secure control; if the organization is autocratic, many good men, in sympathy with its aims, will have nothing to do with it. It is a very serious problem."

Court in the morning and afternoon, dinner with friends and Maud, an occasional political reform meeting in the evening, then study and reading past midnight—this was the supreme court justice's routine as he turned thirty-four on Washington's Birthday, 1907.

His diary is a record of the cases and his frank reactions as a jurist: a suit against a liability company ("exceedingly dry and boring"); an adjustment of a claim against the New York Life Insurance Company ("the defendant's position was crazy—it was miserably tried by the counsel"); a suit for a broker's commission for the sale of stock ("very dry"); a case where the plaintiff sought to recover his deposit on a contract for sale of real estate ("I directed a verdict for plaintiff"); a legal motion involving two conflicting court orders ("the case illustrates the small and tricky practices some lawyers will sometimes resort to"); a suit by a receiver against the president and treasurer of a railroad corporation ("the officers of these railroads are corrupt and ruthless and regard their companies as private chattels"). His view of the law was at a reformer's eye-level.

He took a personal interest in each case. Preparing himself for a complex suit involving the principles of bills and notes, he studied the textbooks and casebooks—especially the English precedents—far into the night. "Worked on these cases until one-thirty before retiring" is a frequent entry in the diary. The pace of his work was incredible by modern judicial standards. Sitting in the appellate term branch on a temporary basis only months after joining the supreme court, in one day he wrote eleven opinions. The work was performed, alone, starting in the court chambers and ending between dusk and dawn in his library at home.

"Whatever Sam did was all right with Maud," according to a close associate of Sam's during those formative years. She stood by quietly in the background. For weeks at a time, the diary shows, they were without company in the library after dinner. "Played chess with Maud in the evening and worked in the library till late." Automobile rides were rare, for good reason—"got stuck in the mud," he noted, while visiting in White Plains. Most Sundays were devoted to exploratory walks, from Chelsea all the way to the northern reaches of Central Park. Sometimes, they stopped for dinner at Delmonico's, Holland House, or the Breslin Hotel. On free evenings, once or twice a month, they went to the theater. They enjoyed seeing Ellen Terry in *The Good Hope* at the Empire Theater. Seabury liked *The Lion and the Mouse* at the Sycamore Theater so much that he summarized its plot: "It portrayed the modern monopolist as a factor in corrupt American politics. The play centers around the attempt of this dominant figure to have the U.S. Senate impeach a judge who on the bench has protected the public rights against the monopolist and his friends. The monopolist's heart is softened by the daughter of the judge, and he relents and the judge's daughter marries the monopolist's son."

At this time, whenever he found a spare moment on the bench or at home, he did research on a growing interest—the study of the struggle of the laborer in early English history. "I worked at the court until late, writing. I am endeavoring to describe the conditions of the laborer under Anglo-Saxon rule. It is not easy to find information about the workingmen. The doings of Kings and Queens, Knights and Monks, are all recorded, but little do our historians say of the laborer. The acts of the useful members of society are forgotten and the acts of the worthless creatures whom they carried on their backs are recorded. But the day of the laborer is coming, and I hope it is not too far distant."

Seeing the lines drawn between the poor and the rich, Seabury was in the front rank of those speaking up for labor unions, trust busting, and the still undefined goals of the common American man. He kept adding to his library and his personal fund of knowledge. Of Peck's *Twenty Years of Commerce* he said, "This is a very interesting and well-written book, although it is written from an aristocratic viewpoint." Reading, studying, and writing down his philosophy of the nobility of labor, he showed his pro–trade-union stripes on the bench and at meetings. He made no attempt in the name of judicial dignity to conceal where he stood personally. To the business and insurance hangers-on around the supreme court, he was "that hard-headed radical."

Maud was concerned about his pace and attempted to slow him down. "She thinks I am going at it too hard and put on my mantelpiece a card with Goethe's lines upon it: 'Rest is not quitting/ This busy career,/ Rest is the fitting/ of Life to its sphere.'" Later entries indicate that Judge Seabury did not take this admonition to heart. What he could not finish before two in the morning he picked up again before the start of the court session at ten.

The final entry in the diary was made on April 20, when, after working on court matters, he decided to write a poem. It summed up, in rather stiff cadence, the mixture of progressivism and judicialism that he was making peculiarly his own on the supreme court bench in Manhattan. He called his poem "Voltaire." It went:

Mocker, scoffer, sceptic thou!
Would to God, we had thee now.
Whose every facile epigram
Hurled a shaft against some sham.
Ancient frauds and old abuses
Themes for thy wit, served new uses.
And what reason could not teach
Thy keen-edged wit would surely reach.
Friend to liberty and progress thou!
Would to God, we had thee now.

If his poetry could be faulted, at least his aspirations were high. His idealism was apparent in a number of important judicial decisions. Not that the quality of his opinions suffered; he dug deeply into legislative intent and English and American precedents in his decisions. Nevertheless, as the customs of the market place and the lives of the politically awakening people changed, he applied his own social and libertarian philosophy in interpreting the law.

For example, a motion was made by a private boxing club in New York to stop the police from breaking in on their meetings. In this case,* Seabury declared that the police would violate the law themselves if they proceeded without a warrant. He said that police officers possess no right of search on mere suspicion of a misdemeanor, that it is an essential characteristic of free government that every official is himself subject to the law and none are above it. He quoted from a decision by Lord Camden to show that his own decision was not arbitrary: "To invade a man's house by virtue of a nameless warrant in order to procure evidence is worse than the Spanish Inquisition; a law under which no Englishman would wish to live an hour. It was a most daring public attack made upon the liberty of the subject." Seabury concluded by saying that at common law the king had no right to enter without warrant the house of his humblest subject on the mere suspicion that the subject had committed a crime—and what was right for a king was good enough for a police commissioner.

In another case involving the city, Seabury came to the conclusion that even nonresident landlords had to install proper fire prevention

* Fairmont Athletic Club of Greater New York v. Bingham, 113 N.Y. Supp. 905.

equipment in their buildings.* In the dense tenement districts on the
Lower East Side, fires left a pall of death among the poor. Seabury,
unwilling to stick to technicalities here, overturned previous lower
court rulings, to the chagrin of hundreds of building owners. He was
pleased when Fire Commissioner Adamson wrote him: "It was your
opinion which upheld the right of the fire commissioner to order
sprinklers installed in buildings and thus protect the lives of workers all over the city. This decision rendered in 1907 in a large way
paved the way for the development of fire prevention in this city.
Everyone owes to you a debt of gratitude."

When he sat in the appellate term of the supreme court, his efforts
to maintain a consistent position on matters he deemed important
often placed him in a minority. He was no judicial trader. In fighting for something as small as the right of New Yorkers to be able
to get streetcar transfers at cross-points, he displayed his tenacity. Upholding the position of the individuals who sued the private streetcar
companies,† he said that public convenience required that the various railways be considered "as a single railroad with a single rate of
fare." He held that the same plaintiff could bring as many actions
as he was denied transfers, and to recover penalties each time. Seabury's was a dissenting opinion, but when the railroad law was
changed and the regulation of fares was placed under the Public
Service Commission, a more favorable system of free transfers was
worked out.

One of his famous cases involved the firing of a married school
teacher in New York City because she was pregnant. The concept
was not as obvious then as it seems today. The law gave the Board
of Education the right to discharge teachers for "neglect of duty"
(though having a baby was not specifically listed as a negligent act
against the city). Nevertheless, a teacher was fired by the head of
the school system because she had been absent for several months
"for the purpose of having a child." When the case ‡ came before
Judge Seabury, he immediately ordered Mrs. Peixotto reinstated to
duty as a teacher in the Bronx public schools. His decision had the

* Lantry v. Hoffmann, 105 N.Y. Supp. 355.
† McCarthy v. N.Y. City Railway Co., 55 Misc. 208.
‡ People ex rel Peixotto v. Board of Education, 144 N.Y. Supp. 87.

social tinge with which such United States Supreme Court Justices as Brandeis and Cardozo would be identified in later years:

> The policy of our laws favors marriage and the birth of children, and I know of no provision of our statute law or any principle of the common law which justifies the inference that a public policy which concededly sanctions the employment of married women as teachers treats as ground for expulsion the act of a married woman in giving birth to a child. . . . The fact is that the legislature has sanctioned the employment of married women as teachers. Married women being lawfully employed as teachers and excusable for absence caused by personal illness, the idea that because the illness is the result of maternity and it therefore becomes "neglect of duty" is repugnant to law and good morals. As maternity cannot be attributed to the fault or wrongdoing of the relator [Mrs. Peixotto], and as her absence is due solely to that cause, such an absence cannot be held to be neglect of duty.

Judge Seabury's decision, while greeted warmly in editorials, was reversed by a unanimous decision of the supreme court's appellate division. The case divided the court of appeals, the majority holding that it was merely a matter of school discipline and not subject to review. However, all ended well when the case later was referred back to Dr. John H. Finley, commissioner of education, who took the same humane view of the law as Judge Seabury. He reinstated the teacher.

The supreme court did not hear only important cases; its daily routine also included cases involving small family matters that called for a human understanding. Under headlines such as "Mother Love Wins Over Law's Decree," the newspapers in November, 1913, reported the case of Mrs. Elizabeth C. Hirsch, whose fourteen-year-old son had run away from the St. Christopher's Home for Boys. She was brought before the court by the sheriff of New York County and threatened with a jail sentence for failing to produce her son in court on a writ of habeas corpus sworn out by the lawyer for the Home. She refused to give up her son. The sheriff was unwilling to let her be taken away to Ludlow Street Jail, which would have left her other children uncared for. Judge Seabury spoke to the counsel for the Home privately. As the newspapers reported it: "Justice Seabury saw no reason to break up the family and deprive it of their necessary support. He paroled the fourteen-year-old boy in the custody of his mother. The Court even refused to punish her for her defiance of the court order."

In an action for assault brought by a woman when a man attempted to kiss her against her will, could evidence be admitted that the man had been divorced and had been named a corespondent in the past? No, said Judge Seabury,* since "these questions were asked solely to prejudice the defendant in the eyes of the jury—and a verdict won by such means is not fairly won." In a criminal appeal from a conviction for manslaughter,† the defense lawyer, Max D. Steuer, moved for a certificate of reasonable doubt. Seabury granted it on the grounds that the trial judge was unfair, because "his frequent remarks, elaborate discussions and charge to the jury tended to prejudice the jury against the defendant." Could an author's real name be used without his consent by a publisher when his stories were published under a nom de plume? No, said Seabury, ‡ granting an injunction protecting the writer's right of privacy. Leases, marriage contracts and breaches of promise, criminal trials and complicated corporate proceedings—all came before Justice Seabury.

The long evenings in his father's and his own library served him well when he was called upon, while sitting in the appellate term, to make a ruling on the writings of Voltaire. The case § involved an action by a publishing firm to recover $200 which the defendant was to have paid for a forty-two-volume set of the works of Voltaire. The defendant had come up with a unique theory to avoid paying—he said that the books were "obscene, lascivious and not fit reading for defendant's family." A lower court had agreed with the defendant, and the publisher now appealed the case. In concluding that the defendant would have to pay for the set of Voltaire's works under his written contract, Judge Seabury declared—citing evidence going back to Chaucer—that many books had been considered "obscene or immoral" in their time, yet could be literature.

The judgment which the learned court below delivered is not the first

* Rothschild v. Weingreen, 121 N.Y. Supp. 234.
† People v. Heineman, 142 N.Y. Supp. 833.
‡ Ellis v. Hurst, 121 N.Y. Supp. 438.
§ St. Hubert Guild v. Quinn, 118 N.Y. Supp. 582.

judicial determination which has condemned *The Philosophical Dictionary.* The last time it was condemned, so far as I know, was in France in 1766, when, together with a youth who was suspected of an act of malicious mischief, and in whose possession a copy of the book was found, it was publicly burned in the streets of Paris. The other work complained of, *The Maid of Orléans,* had a history less tragic, although sufficiently exciting to have given even the careless Voltaire many moments of anxiety for his own safety on account of it. *The Philosophical Dictionary* is a collection of articles dealing with romance, history, science and religion, many of which were originally contributed to the great Encyclopédie of which Diderot, D'Alembert and Voltaire were the inspiration. It is not only a reservoir of sarcasm and wit, but it has exerted a profound influence in favor of the humane and rational administration of the law.

Censorship ran counter to his ideas of liberty of expression; indeed, had he not inscribed in his own diary his allegiance to Voltaire as a "scoffer and sceptic"? He would not tolerate intolerance of ideas— nor would he tolerate intolerance toward racial or religious groups. Before World War I, in the private clubs, in the restricted professions and schools, it was fashionable to sneer at minorities or to ignore discrimination. In later years when Seabury was investigating Mayor Walker and Tammany hacks and crooks, he was accused of conducting an inquisition against the Irish Catholics in high office. The whole record of Seabury's personal dealings and decisions showed otherwise—showed, in fact, that he was in the forefront of those fighting prejudice.

Privately, Seabury was proud of his role in the "Morris Quasha matter." Publicly, he made no reference to it, lest someone think he was trying to gain attention or approval by his stand. Morris Quasha, a Jew, was a law-school graduate who had passed his bar examinations. However, the "character committee" had turned him down. The appellate division of the supreme court supervised admission to the bar; the committee had allowed a year and a half to pass without admitting Quasha. Because Seabury was considered the most liberal-minded judge on the bench in New York, the matter was brought to his attention. First, he complained to Presiding Justice George L. Ingraham (who was considered in general disagreement with Judge Seabury's social philosophy) about the character committee's lack of evidence, and then he minced no words about what he considered outright bias. Second, he wrote the character committee members a letter denouncing them as agents unworthy of the supreme court and demanding that they either produce evidence against Quasha or immediately pass upon his qualifications. The letter read, in part:

> The committee has failed to file any report of its investigation of his moral record, nor have its members disputed his good character nor the testimonials of thirty of his friends, in any direct way.
>
> If the committee act capriciously, they act not only unjustly but unlawfully. If the committee's refusal to act is for cause, then I submit that it is a requirement of justice that the cause shall be made known to the applicant and that he should be accorded an opportunity to answer it. If this is not so, then it is evident that if the Committee on Character choose to indulge a prejudice against an applicant because of his race, his religion or his politics, they do so with impunity.
>
> Yet we know that such cannot be the case because the legislature has distinctly enacted that "race shall constitute no cause for refusing any person examination or admission to practice." The fact that your committee has assumed a position which leaves it open to this imputation impairs its usefulness as a committee representing the court.

Seabury's blast produced immediate action, and Morris Quasha was admitted to practice before the supreme court.

This was behind the scenes. But Seabury came forward more and more in the public eye. Now a case arose that rocked Tammany Hall, shocked the city and country, and was instrumental in the Fusion victory in New York's next mayoralty election. The cast of characters was nothing less than brilliant; no novelist would have dared to invent such *noms de crime*. Furthermore, the "Becker case" was not a simple trial. The law had been openly defied. A police lieutenant, Charles Becker, ordered four hoodlums—"Lefty Louie," "Gyp the Blood," "Whitey Louis," and "Dago Frank"—to murder the gambler Herman Rosenthal the day before he was scheduled to give testimony to the New York County grand jury about Becker's "partnership" in his gambling establishment. The four gunmen poured bullets into the gambler's head as he lit a cigar in the doorway of the Hotel Metropole, on 43rd Street between Broadway and

Sixth Avenue, and roared off in a long gray getaway car up Fifth Avenue at two in the morning on July 16, 1912. The people of the city were startled and aroused when they read about it later that day.

It took two Becker trials to send the police lieutenant to the chair. John W. Goff, who had directed the Lexow investigation into police corruption in 1894, presided at the first trial. The conviction was reversed in the court of appeals because the evidence linking the murder plot to the defendant was insufficient and uncorroborated. The appellate division then assigned Judge Seabury to preside at the second trial. The legal talent in the case was formidable. Max D. Steuer, representing "Bridgie" Webber, negotiated a deal with the district attorney whereby Webber confessed the plot to kill Rosenthal but said that Becker had forced him and the others to do so. The law firm of Cockran & Manton was hired for the defense. W. Bourke Cockran, a noted orator and a leader of the anti-Bryan Democrats, appropriately had served his apprenticeship as counsel to the Tammany sheriff of New York County. Martin T. Manton was to become the infamous United States Circuit Court of Appeals judge who was convicted of selling justice and sent to the penitentiary; in legal circles he came to be known as "Preying Manton."

Seabury was designated to conduct the second trial because of his reputation for fairness and firmness. The trial lasted seventeen days. Seabury sat throughout the case, according to the *New York World*, "as if his face had been carved out of stone," giving no indication of his feelings. So tense was the atmosphere, said the reporter for *The World*, that "even a shrug of the judge's shoulders during the testimony or a smile of incredulity or a lifting of the eyebrows would have swung the case."

His personal notes of the trial relate the sequence of events as he saw them unfold from his position on the bench:

At the beginning, Cockran came into court and charged the district attorney was responsible for the creation of an atmosphere prejudicial to the defendant, making it impossible for a fair trial to be had, and he moved that the trial be discontinued until another date, and that a change of venue be granted and that all the talesmen be dismissed and a new trial ordered, and, finally, that District Attorney Whitman be punished for contempt of court for having uttered, or having caused to be uttered, statements to the press damaging to the interests of Becker. I denied the motion and Mr. Cockran withdrew from the case and did not return. In the course of the Becker case, there was a publication of District Attorney Whitman's opening address to the jury made before its delivery. Mr. Manton, counsel for Becker, moved at the opening of court for the withdrawal of a juror and to have the case declared a mistrial. I denied the motion, as no one who had seen the address in the newspapers would be called on the jury. I charged the jury in the case on May 22, 1914.

That day, all New York was aware of the forty-one-year-old judge. Entering the jammed criminal branch of the supreme court, he moved firmly from his chambers to the high-backed leather chair. His prematurely white hair, neatly parted in the center, contrasted with his ruddy complexion and flowing black silk robes. No gavel was necessary; his mien alone served to silence the courtroom. He looked at his notes and began a two-hour charge to the jury. Reviewing the facts and interpreting the law, he revealed himself to the spectators as an impartial trial judge with a deep respect for the law. His language became a model for future criminal trials in New York state:

A reasonable doubt is not a mere whim or surmise, nor is it a subterfuge to which resort may be had in order to avoid doing a disagreeable thing. It is such a doubt as reasonable men may entertain, after a careful and honest review and consideration of all the evidence in the case. . . . While it may be true that crime is never committed without a motive, yet motive is not an essential ingredient of the crime of murder. The crime of murder may be proved without any proof at all of motive. . . . I make no intimations upon any of these questions of fact, but I leave them on this summary of the evidence fairly and squarely for you to determine as a question of fact. Did this defendant direct the killing of Rosenthal? That is the most important issue in the case for you to determine. If he did not, if you entertain a reasonable doubt as to that, acquit the defendant. If you are satisfied beyond a reasonable doubt that he did, then this defendant at the bar is legally responsible for the murder.

The jury found Becker guilty for a second time. This time the highest court in the state affirmed the conviction and declared that the defendant had received a fair trial. Becker was executed on October 30, 1915.

In his scrapbooks, Judge Seabury saved several of the editorials about his conduct of the trial. *The World* said that he was "dignified and stern-faced" and that he "ably presided." *The Sun* said that "Mr. Justice Seabury and District Attorney Whitman have both earned public gratitude by their conduct of this case."

The voting public would soon have an opportunity to reward the prosecutor and the judge. The graft and corruption that lay behind the murder stirred mass meetings of citizens. A citizens' committee, made up of various reform and independent groups friendly to Seabury, reported after a meeting at the Cooper Union: "The sums collected by the police excite the greed of certain politicians who demand their shares, and in their turn they protect the criminal breaches of the law. The presence of politics brings strength to the system and makes it harder to break up. The city, we believe, is convinced that it is time for more radical efforts at improvement."

Seabury was at that time an unhappy Democrat. His leanings were to the Progressive movement; yet he knew that in city politics the reform groups had to merge with one of the major parties in order to win an election. Over just such an issue he had finally broken with Hearst. In the 1909 mayoralty election, Seabury had been instrumental in the nomination of William J. Gaynor. But Hearst refused to support an Independent party candidate backed by the Democrats. Seabury, siding with the Independents, rapped the powerful New York publisher in a campaign speech: "It is not so long ago that Mr. Hearst saw no impropriety in accepting for himself a Democratic endorsement. But now, when he himself is not a candidate, he will tolerate no endorsement—unless it comes from the Republican machine." Mayor Gaynor was elected and served from 1909 to 1913. Hearst's personal ambitions had overtaken his early radicalism; his newspapers were being used as a private soapbox. Commenting on Hearst's sincerity, Seabury wrote a political associate: "He is now completely exposed."

In the fall of 1913, the Progressive party nominated United States District Court Judge Learned Hand for chief judge and Supreme Court Judge Samuel Seabury for associate judge of New York's highest court, the court of appeals. The party was dominated by Theodore Roosevelt, but he was in Brazil during most of the campaign. A series of antilabor decisions had been made by the court of appeals. This gave Seabury reason to run. Judge Hand was unwilling to run, but, nevertheless, felt that he could not flinch. Seabury and Hand had a private talk in which Seabury suggested that they speak out against the reactionary elements in the court of appeals. Hand refused to do so. "I was already on the bench and the thought of haranguing the electorate was more than I could bear," Hand recalled long afterward. Seabury was irritated, saying that both had an obligation to define the issues, otherwise the votes they received would have no significance. In retrospect, Hand, talking about his failure to campaign, said, "I think, perhaps, he was right."

Seabury determined to issue one loud blast that would make clear the real grounds for his—and Hand's—candidacy. He did so in spite of the fact that running on an independent ticket with no major-party support offered little chance of success. He did so in spite of the fact that his own supreme court decisions would be subject to review, and possible reversal, by the court of appeals. He did so, in the face of accusations of radicalism, because he had to.

"The efforts for social reform can amount to nothing unless the judicial department of the government shall cease to be the bulwark of privilege and private monopoly," he said, anticipating by a quarter of a century the ideas of President Franklin D. Roosevelt.

> The reactionary decisions of the court of appeals judges are the natural results of their mental attitude and the class bias which unconsciously dominates them. In reference to the "fellow-servant rule," "assumption of risk," "contributory negligence," "details of the work" and all such other defenses which the courts have conferred upon the employer, it is competent for the legislature to change them. The court of appeals declared the Workmen's Compensation Law invalid, not because it offended any provision of the Constitution, but because they disapproved of the policy of such legislation. If nothing more is accomplished by the candidacy of Judge Hand and myself than to emphasize a protest against that decision, our candidacy will not have been in vain.

The press was less than enthusiastic about this bold speech, though several newspapers, the *New York Globe* among them, commented that "Judge Seabury does the bench something of a service by discarding false reserve and discussing the subjects of the day frankly." The *Albany Journal* saw his speech as a "clear example of progressive propaganda." The *New York Post* introduced a little propaganda of its own into the campaign by printing a picture of Judge Seabury together with Tammany's Boss Murphy, embellishing the caption by saying that Seabury had called upon the Democratic leader at his home and implying that something shady was going on. Actually, as *The Post* explained in a retraction later, the picture was not taken at Murphy's home but at the National Golf Links, near Southampton. Seabury had been playing with his friend Judge Edward E. McCall of the New York State Supreme Court. McCall had stopped for a moment to speak to Murphy, and a photographer had snapped the picture at that time. *The Post*'s retraction was not printed, however, until after the election.

The results would not have differed, in any event, since this was a futile campaign for the Progressives. A Democrat, Willard Bartlett, was elected chief judge, and a Republican, Frank Hiscock, elected associate judge. However, Seabury surprised the professional politicians in both parties by receiving 190,000 votes; Boss Murphy noted that no Progressive had gained this many votes while he controlled the city's Democratic machine. It was a lesson Tammany remembered in the gubernatorial campaign in 1916. For his part, Seabury was satisfied that he had presented the issues to the public. Putting down his thoughts later, he wrote: "My speech, I think, struck the nail on the head."

Early in January, 1914, one vacancy had to be filled on the court of appeals. Now a comedy not of errors but of vacillation occurred. The two outstanding supreme court jurists were Benjamin N. Cardozo and Samuel Seabury. Both were New Yorkers, friends, and had similar social awareness of the law. Governor Martin Glynn had to pick one of them to bolster his own shaky position—but he could not make up his mind. The Progressives were pushing Seabury; Cardozo, also an anti-Tammany man, was a less controversial figure. Seabury had preceded Cardozo on the supreme court. Once, when Cardozo had appeared as an attorney in a case before him, he had made a reasoned, legalistic appeal without histrionics which Seabury admired because it did not have what he called "hurrah features." Now they were friendly rivals for the vacancy. Glynn told Seabury to "clear your desk" because he intended to name him to the court of appeals. A week later, Glynn told Cardozo to clear *his* desk—for the same job.

Grumbling against Seabury was heard from the high bench in Albany. The judges remembered all too well his speech of the previous year castigating their antilabor decisions. Seabury, still willing to stand for what he believed in even if it meant not getting the promotion, wrote to the Governor:

> Since I heard from you on the 3rd of January as to the proposal to designate me to the court of appeals, I have been informed that the members of the court, or some of them, have opposed my designation. I have been given to understand that their opposition is based upon the speech which I made in accepting the nomination of the National Progressive party for the office of associate judge. I take the liberty of enclosing a copy of this speech. I desire to add that the sentiments expressed in that speech embody my sincere convictions, and that if those sentiments are deemed by you inconsistent with my designation to the court of appeals, I hope you will not consider my name further in this connection.

Several more weeks elapsed. Then, once again, Glynn called Seabury and told him that his appointment was getting closer. Seabury reported this to his colleague, Cardozo, who thereupon related that Glynn had said the same thing to him. "This situation continued for more than a month," Seabury later recalled, "and it was the occasion for much amusement between Judge Cardozo and myself. One day I would say to Judge Cardozo, 'You are out, as I have just heard from the Governor.' The next week Judge Cardozo would come into my chambers and say, 'You are out, as I have just heard from the Governor.' Finally, Governor Glynn designated Justice Cardozo." When Seabury heard this, he walked into Cardozo's chambers, shook his hand, and declared, "No better selection could have been made."

Later that year, Seabury joined Cardozo on the court of appeals. In the early fall of 1914, the Progressives, this time with the Democrats, nominated Judge Seabury for the high court. The Democrats hoped that he would help the rest of the ticket upstate. However, Governor Glynn and the other Democratic state candidates were defeated; Judge Seabury's plurality was 58,000. In the same election,

Charles Whitman, the prosecutor of Police Lieutenant Becker, became the Republican governor of the state. Seabury's fourteen-year term on the court of appeals was to start January 1, 1915, but outgoing Governor Glynn prevailed upon him to begin sitting a month earlier to fill a vacancy. The state supreme court radical now took his robes to Albany.

As the only member of the state's highest court who had been elected as a Progressive party nominee, Seabury sensed prejudice against himself. He thought little of his ultraconservative colleagues. Of Chief Judge Willard Bartlett, who had once been among the counsel for William M. Tweed of that most famous of Tammany rings, he noted privately, "I understate his attitude when I say that he was a seasoned ultraconservative who slavishly retarded social growth." The words he reserved for nearly all the others ranged from "conservative" to "reactionary." The judge he most admired was Cardozo.

"He was a man of deep learning and great gentleness of character, with a charming literary style which added much to the great reputation he attained," he commented about the future United States Supreme Court judge. "I do not think his convictions were strong, or if they were his inherent tact led him to be very cautious in discussing them. He was indefatigable in his industry. The cautious manner in which he expressed his views, especially in the early days of his service in the court, aroused no antagonism. He was personally friendly to me, and very tactful in his arguments and discussions, and in consultation, rarely taking an uncompromising position on any subject." Afterwards, when Cardozo had become chief judge of the court of appeals, Seabury sometimes would call him "my chief."

In the year and a half that he sat in Albany, Seabury wrote thirty-six opinions for the court plus three concurring opinions and fourteen dissents. A number of these opinions underscored legal principles; several had important effects.

In a case involving enforcement of the Civil Service Law,* Seabury wrote the unanimous opinion, reversing the appellate division, and restoring the job of a clerk who had been removed because he had failed to make a political contribution. "The purpose sought to be accomplished by the Civil Service Law is now a matter of common

* People ex rel Somerville v. Williams, 217 N.Y. 40.

knowledge," he wrote. "That purpose was to require all appointments within the law to be based solely on merit and not to be made as a reward for political and partisan services. . . . If the object of the law is to be attained, it is essential not only that appointments to office that are within the law shall not be governed by political and partisan considerations, but also that those who have been appointed as a result of competitive examinations shall not be subject to removal upon these grounds." The decision was considered at the time a body blow to the spoils system.

In a case upholding the state's right to decide who could work on public projects,* Seabury's decision underscored a principle and caused the law to be changed. The Alien Labor Law provided that only United States citizens could be employed on public works. The defendant had employed aliens to build sewers. In support of the law, Seabury wrote: "The legislature has the right to prescribe who shall work on its public property. This regulation and control is a part of the police power of the state. . . . Just as the individual may, generally speaking, do what he will with his own, so the state may exercise a like control over public property. . . . The state denies to the individual the right to intrude within its social sphere of action and insist that he has a right to be employed upon its works. The right of the state control springs from the public or social character of the work." After Seabury upheld the constitutionality of the law, the legislature took his hint and amended it, permitting aliens to be employed on public works and merely stating that preference be given citizens. In later years, on United States Government contracts, the same principle upheld by Seabury was used by the Federal courts to prevent discriminatory hiring practices against Negroes.

An important dissenting opinion he wrote helped to put workmen's compensation cases in a separate category, so that there was no need to show where fault lay, as in ordinary accident cases. The decision in the case,† which involved the widow of an iceman accidentally killed on the job, hinged on whether a liberal or a strict interpretation of the laws of evidence applied. Seabury's dissent declared, "The Workmen's Compensation Law is a new step in the field of social legislation. We should interpret it in accordance with

---

* People v. Crane, 214 N.Y. 155.
† In re Carroll v. Knickerbocker Ice Company, 218 N.Y. 435.

the spirit which called it into existence. Our reverence for the traditional rules of our common law system should not lead us to restrict it by subjecting it to the operation of these rules. This court is under no obligation to see to it that laws enacted to remedy abuses arising from new industrial and social conditions shall be made to square with ancient conceptions of the principles of the common law." Later, fault or contributory negligence did not prevent victims of industrial accidents from receiving compensation. The Seabury dissent left its mark on the legislature and Workmen's Compensation Board.

The only thing he did not like about sitting on the state's highest court was that it separated him during the week from Maud. He would stay at the Hotel Ten Eyck when the court convened and return to New York or East Hampton for week ends. On their wedding anniversary in June, 1916, he found himself in Albany, but he could not concentrate on the appeals before him that day. "Dearest," he wrote to her, "While a tiresome lawyer is talking upon a very dry case, I want to start this letter in your direction, carrying my wish for many happy returns and telling you how much I love you. I hope our next anniversary we will be able to spend together." The letter ended abruptly, "The lawyer that is talking is getting very noisy and I will close and write you again later. Good-bye, sweetheart." It was a letter that Maud cherished all her life.

While on the bench in Albany, he continued to address himself to the national conscience. When President Wilson nominated Louis D. Brandeis for the United States Supreme Court in 1916, the appointment was bitterly contested in the Senate. Once before, in the Morris Quasha matter, Judge Seabury had astonished his stiff-necked colleagues. Now he did so again. In praising strongly and openly Wilson's appointment of Brandeis, he attacked by implication the reactionaries and bigots in the Senate and the country.

This man Seabury refused to sit still. "There was much scandal," said Oswald Garrison Villard, in the *New York Post,* "as to the books which Justice Seabury was caught reading when not actually sitting on the bench. They said he read all the latest books on Socialism and social reform of every kind." He was growing restless—even in the state's highest judicial robes.

CHAPTER

Futile Dreamer, I: The Almost Governor

ON July 9, 1914, former President Theodore Roosevelt, Progressive and reluctant Republican, wrote one of his bully-for-you notes to Judge Samuel Seabury, Progressive and reluctant Democrat, after they had had dinner at Oyster Bay. It was the most important letter Seabury had ever received; it encouraged him to dream of high elective offices. He framed that letter and saved it for years, at first proudly, and then later as a mocking example of the ways of politics.

> My dear Judge Seabury:
> That's a *fine* address of yours. By George, it does me good to come in contact with a man who is not afraid, and whose blows count! I am really greatly obliged to you for having given me the chance to look over that address.
> I need hardly say how much I enjoyed having you at dinner the other night.

After signing the note, "Faithfully yours," Roosevelt appended a P.S. in his own hand: "I want you on the Court of Appeals, or as Senator, or as Governor!"

It was a measure of Roosevelt's vainglory that he believed he could designate others for elected offices. He did, indeed, hold a peculiar power, but it was more often a power to defeat than to elect. When he became dissatisfied with the policies of President Taft, although

Taft's nomination was one he had successfully maneuvered, he organized the Progressive party and became its candidate for the Presidency in 1912. The result was a defeat for both Republican Taft and Progressive Roosevelt and a victory for Democrat Woodrow Wilson. Seabury succeeded in balancing his pro-Wilson and pro-Roosevelt sympathies. In 1914 he was the only judge to be nominated, and elected, on the Democratic and Progressive party tickets to the court of appeals. Roosevelt's Progressive backing had indeed helped in the 1914 election; now Seabury allowed himself the privilege to dream.

When Seabury had dinner at Oyster Bay, he and Roosevelt talked over the whole political situation. The only other person present was George W. Perkins, a partner of J. P. Morgan's. Perkins had momentarily deserted the Republicans, and was making heavy financial contributions to the Progressive party. Roosevelt denounced Governor Whitman, accusing him of being unable to stand up to the machine politicians. "The truth is not in Whitman," Roosevelt said, adding that under no circumstances would he support him for re-election. He expressed his admiration for the prolabor tone of Seabury's acceptance speech for the court of appeals race. And he went on to encourage Seabury to resign, in due time, from the court and run for governor.

But Seabury forthrightly raised some questions.

"I do not see how you could support me, since I would support Wilson again for President," he said.

"I will support the Republican candidate for the Presidency," Roosevelt replied, "but that will in no way interfere with my giving you my support for the governorship."

Seabury said that, in all probability, Charles Evans Hughes would be nominated for President on the Republican ticket, and he did not see how Roosevelt at the same time could support him to succeed Hughes as governor.

"I have considered the whole problem from every angle," Roosevelt reassured his guest. "If you accept the Progressive and Democratic nominations for governor, I would support Hughes for the Presidency, but that would not interfere with my open and aggressive support of you for governor. If you secure the Democratic nomination, my support will insure your election."

Seabury (as he later recalled in his private notes of the conversation) said he believed that to be true. He accepted Roosevelt's offer of support as the Progressive candidate. Roosevelt, continuing to denounce Whitman's weakness, praised Seabury's anti-Tammany attitude and independence.

Elated at the prospect of Roosevelt's support, Seabury told Maud about the conversation, and, that evening, made a record of the meeting.

Roosevelt's offer seemed sincere. Indeed, he told others how much he respected Seabury. To George L. Record, a New Jersey Progressive party leader who had been in the Henry George movement, Roosevelt wrote: "As for the ticket, if for instance some such man as Judge Seabury, who as I understand it is a very bitter opponent of mine but who does sympathize with our platform (although he voted for Wilson) and who may stand on such a platform locally as this of which I am speaking, is found to be the choice of the bulk of the plain people who are against Tammany, why I don't feel that we would have any right to fail to rally with other good citizens to his support. I mention Judge Seabury merely as an example; I'll take any good man who will stand on the right kind of platform, and one we think we can elect." To Hiram Warren Johnson, Governor of California, he stressed again the need for someone of the caliber of Seabury to run for either governor or United States Senator.

There was at least one difficulty, however, for any Progressive party nominee—and that was the party structure itself. The people behind it were high-minded, but the organization was built on aspiration rather than on clubhouses with grubstake politicians. By 1916 the Progressive party was a conglomeration of free-lance idealists, major-party mavericks, and Roosevelt's personal followers. The unifying force was T.R. himself, but he was speaking softly and carrying a very small antitrust stick. Wilson, with his reform doctrines, had stolen much of the Bull Moose's thunder. Progressive-minded citizens were still devoted to Roosevelt, but they found it difficult to disagree with Wilson's program "for the application of Jefferson's principles to our present-day America." Whether Roosevelt could bring about the election of a candidate other than himself remained to be seen.

In the meantime, Seabury decided to enter the race, although fully aware of the political traps strewn along the course. From Albany he wrote Maud, "The news is that Roosevelt will back down to the Republicans and Hughes will get the presidential nomination. If this is done, it will mean a very hard and bitter fight for Governor of New York. It is only a question of bluff between Roosevelt and the so-called Old Guard. But it looks as if the Old Guard will be successful in bluffing Roosevelt." In a later letter to Maud, he wrote, "I hear reports that the Democratic leaders think the independent support coming to me is positive proof that I cannot be counted on as a strict party man. I have been advised to discourage my independent supporters. But if the independent support is considered an objection, I mean to tell the Democrats to give their nomination to someone else." As an afterthought, he wrote, "When I started out, I did not intend to write you a political letter. I miss you very much, sweetheart. . . ."

The Democratic party's nomination was the vital one. The prelude to nomination was the endorsement of primary candidates by a state party convention; endorsement insured formal nomination. In the middle of August, 1916, the leaders met in Saratoga, a convenient place, since a number of politicians were there for the racing season. Boss Murphy's men were certainly there. It was common talk that "Tammany does not want Seabury," but Murphy kept silent. On the opening day of the convention, only moments before post time for the first race, the keynote speaker and presiding officer, John F. Fitzgerald, suddenly developed a sore throat, and the meeting was adjourned for the afternoon. After the eighth race, the condition of the speaker's throat magically improved, and the convention opened that evening.

A Democratic Roosevelt was present at the gathering in Saratoga. Several letters written by Franklin D. Roosevelt, then Assistant Secretary of the Navy, to his wife and Louis Howe, neatly trace the undercurrent of resentment against Seabury on the part of Tammany and the overwhelming feeling for him on the part of the delegates. The letters also reveal that the delegate from Hyde Park had been approached as a possible gubernatorial nominee himself.

Writing to Howe from Washington, Franklin Roosevelt said that he had heard that there was "much apparent opposition to Seabury by Tammany." He added that he could not make out "whether it is the real goods or not." To his wife, Eleanor, he wrote, "I had an intimation that the New York organization would like to use me to beat Seabury out of the nomination for governor, but I declined to flirt and the six votes of Dutchess County will be for Seabury if it comes to a head." After Seabury's nomination, Roosevelt wrote to his wife at Campobello: "I helped to put Seabury across."

Seabury gained the strong support of leaders from every county at the convention. Even Boss Murphy tolerated Seabury's nomination, recognizing that to do otherwise would be to put himself in a vetoing position. However, Murphy kept a watchful eye on events, and the slate for the convention was drawn up in his hotel room.

Accepting the designation by the Democratic leaders in Saratoga, Seabury attacked the reactionary Democrats as well as the Republicans—an attack that did not endear him to those present and voting. "So far as Governor Whitman stands for anything except re-election," he told the leaders at Convention Hall, "he stands for the application of reactionary principles to the government of this state. That has been conclusively shown by his advocacy of the proposed constitution, which was submitted to the people a year ago, and overwhelmingly repudiated by them. The constitution was framed by the most distinguished advocates of reaction that could be found in the State of New York. Not only were the foremost reactionaries of the Republican party selected to sit in that convention, but they had the active co-operation of the leading reactionaries of the Democratic party." Boss Murphy and his men listened to the speech, but they did not applaud.

Hearst and Seabury were now implacable foes. The day after the Saratoga meeting, Hearst ordered his editors to assail Seabury. The Hearst editorial writers in New York began to call Seabury "chameleonic" and suddenly discovered virtue in Governor Whitman. Disregarding Seabury's long anti-Tammany record, the Hearst papers referred to him as "the tool of Murphy." At the same time, voters in New York could read just the opposite in *The World:* "The real opposition to Judge Seabury on Fourteenth Street [Tammany headquarters] is that he is independent and resolute and the knowledge that his would not be a machine administration. . . . The conference designated one of the ablest candidates for governor the people of New York have had a chance to vote for in a generation. He is one of the original leaders of that new American democracy which is more concerned with human rights than property. Added to this is a genuine talent for government and an intimate knowledge of state affairs."

Within weeks after the Saratoga conference, on August 30, 1916, Seabury met a great personal loss, the death of his father and friend, Dr. William Jones Seabury. He died in East Hampton, where he had been staying at Judge Seabury's home, and he was buried in the Trinity Church cemetery grounds in upper Manhattan.

But Seabury put aside personal considerations and devoted himself to the campaign. He resigned from the court of appeals upon receiving the Democratic nomination for governor. He spoke in the up-state counties, and his prospects for election were conceded to be strong. He gradually made his way toward New York City, speaking half a dozen times a night to political and labor groups. All that seemed necessary to insure the victory was the Progressive party's endorsement. In the light of Roosevelt's promises, that seemed but a formality.

It was not so simple, however. In a private memorandum Seabury wrote: "I stopped to speak at a meeting in Westchester, and when I finished my address a newspaper reporter handed me an evening paper and asked for my reaction." He was stunned. The story reported that, although Seabury had been the choice of most of the delegates at the Progressive party convention, Whitman had been endorsed. The Democratic candidate's shock could not be concealed as he read Roosevelt's statement: "Judge Seabury is supporting Mr. Wilson and running on the same ticket with Mr. Wilson, and therefore doing all in his power to bring about the re-election of Mr. Wilson. I believe this would be a disastrous calamity to the country and therefore no Progressive should vote for Mr. Seabury."

Melvin G. Palliser, Seabury's campaign manager, became agitated. "I can't believe it," he said.

"I can," replied Seabury. "There isn't a bad word against me or a good word for Whitman in this statement."

Palliser telephoned some of the Progressive party supporters in New York to confirm the newspaper report. There had been no mistake. The state gubernatorial election had become entangled with the national election. The larger objective was the defeat of Wilson, and accordingly Roosevelt capitulated.

The Judge decided to see Roosevelt at Oyster Bay. Only hours after getting the bad news, Seabury stormed up Sagamore Hill. When he confronted Roosevelt, he berated him for his treachery. He reminded Roosevelt of the promises made by him and by his emissaries. He took from his pocket the letter that Roosevelt had written to him and read aloud Roosevelt's sentence, "I want you on the Court of Appeals, or as Senator, or as Governor!" Roosevelt started to say something, but Seabury interrupted. "Mr. President, you are a blatherskite!" Then he stalked out. For once, Roosevelt was speechless, according to Seabury's nephews, who were told the story often.

Seabury reminded his family and friends that Roosevelt long ago had remarked to him, "The truth is not in Whitman." Now Seabury paraphrased that. "The truth is not in Roosevelt."

Not all the Progressives, however, were fooled by Roosevelt's repudiation of Seabury. From Amos Pinchot, one of the leaders of the party, came reassuring words:

> I confess that I was not particularly surprised to read Colonel Roosevelt's advice to the Progressives to vote against you and for Whitman. The fact is, the Colonel is merely running true to recent form. You stand squarely for the things the Progressive party has stood for in the past; about as squarely as Whitman stands against them. I do not think that anybody would question this, not even the Colonel. But, for quite a good while, it has been fairly clear to the majority of us that Roosevelt, Perkins and the steel trust, the Old Guard group around them, have not been interested in the things which the Progressive party stood for. In fact, they have effectually thrown all liberalism and democracy overboard and are now playing pure, old-fashioned Republican politics.

In the campaign, Seabury aligned his state campaign with Wilson's. When he made his acceptance speech in October before the Democratic State Committee, he said, "The country is to be congratulated upon the achievements of the President of the United States. Due to his self-control and statesmanship this nation is at peace with the world, and prosperous. I have entered this fight to aid in promoting the fundamental principles of democracy. The contest now about to open is only a battle in the long war which the people are waging against privilege. I do not ask election to the governorship upon the record of the national Administration. There are great issues before the people of this state, and they should be determined upon their own merits."

The Seabury campaign moved upstate, from county to county, by special train and limousine. Seabury raised issues of state-wide concern, from prison reform to equitable taxation. In Albany, he said, "Taxation falls most heavily upon those least able to pay, and to a large extent exempts those enjoying special privileges." In Elmira, he found fault with the state's conscription law, pointing out that it was designed not as a measure for military preparedness, but to provide the Governor with "an instrument which in times of industrial strife he could use to serve the beneficiaries of privilege." In the Genesee Valley, he told the farmers that they should be closer to the consumers and that they were discriminated against, while "great organizations of middle men secured a preference" under existing state laws. On a street corner in downtown Brooklyn, not far from the place where he once was stoned during the campaign for Henry George, he returned to a favorite subject—the Workmen's Compensation Law. He attacked the amendment that allowed for direct settlement, because it favored "the insurance companies and the Republican Old Guard." Phrases recurred in all the speeches: "the forces of privilege," "those who prey upon society," "a need for social justice."

He managed to get in a few licks at the Progressives, now on the Republican side. "A few Bull Moose have returned to Republican captivity—dehorned—but they lack their old-time spirit. They do not sing *Onward Christian Soldiers,* but pledge themselves to follow the Republican Old Guard." He was especially bitter in his comments about George Perkins, Roosevelt's strongest follower, and said that he had "assassinated the Progressive party and was determined to deliver the corpse to a Republican undertaker." *The New York Times,* during the campaign, agreed with Seabury about the odd behavior of Roosevelt, at one point remarking: "The Bull Moose led his loyal followers into the wilderness—and there deserted them."

Whitman challenged Seabury to support the charges that his administration had been "extravagant and incompetent," and Seabury produced nineteen allegations—charges of padding the court system

with lawyers and judges; charges of nepotism; charges of graft. The
Governor took them seriously enough to write a twenty-eight-page
reply. Seabury countercharged that Whitman's reply was "of such
a character as to prevent its being read generally by the people."
Whitman publicly asked Seabury if he would put Henry George's
tax theories to work in the State of New York. Name calling and
preposterous accusations obscured the issues, and a fickle electorate
made the outcome of the election unpredictable.

Much depended on Tammany's support, but Boss Murphy chose
to play the statesman instead of the vote getter. Tammany was sulk-
ing in 1916. The Wilson Administration had not given Tammany
patronage in New York. Furthermore, Wilson's obvious sympathy
with the Allied cause made him unpopular with the German and
Irish voters, on whom Tammany depended. A small complication
was the fact that William F. McCombs, running for Senator on the
Democratic ticket, had broken with Wilson when the President did
not put him in the Cabinet. McCombs, campaign manager for Wilson in 1912, was Boss Murphy's man in 1916. Seabury and McCombs
argued about how to conduct the state campaign. McCombs wanted
to ignore the national election altogether and merely fight the state
Republicans, but Seabury insisted that they support the national
ticket. He told McCombs he would not ride with him on the campaign train unless he came out for Wilson. McCombs gave in, and
both candidates endorsed the Wilson Administration publicly.

Wilson and Seabury respected each other. Seabury received a presidential summons during the campaign to come to Shadow Lawn,
Wilson's hotel-like cottage on the Jersey shore near Long Branch.
Before dinner, Seabury reminded Wilson that he had heard him
speak while a student in the 1890's at the New York Law School.
Through dinner and into the night they talked politics. New York's
electoral votes were needed badly, and Wilson was worried. He recalled that Murphy, during the 1912 Democratic national convention, had announced, "The boys don't want him," and, at a crucial
moment in the balloting, had thrown his delegation to Champ
Clark. The Tammany sachems were still afraid of Wilson, and they
were not reassured by the anti-Tammany position Seabury had taken
in the past. It was true that Tammany was going through the
motions for Wilson and Seabury and other candidates. Indeed, Sheriff

Alfred E. Smith had marched as Grand Marshal of a parade in the President's honor when he came to New York the first week in November, and a dignified row of bemedaled sachems strode behind him. But on Election Day they would drag their feet.

The odds quoted on Wall Street were 3½ to 1 on Whitman to win, with one brokerage firm offering to bet $7,000 against Seabury. There were no takers. Tammany Hall predicted a plurality of 100,000 votes for the Democrats in New York City. In a speech upstate, Whitman called Seabury the "Tammany candidate," but Wilson and Seabury agreed at Shadow Lawn that they would not change their behavior to appease 14th Street. After their meeting President Wilson endorsed Judge Seabury's candidacy, and Seabury returned the compliment at dozens of Democratic rallies.

The Sunday before November 7, *The New York Times* ran an editorial called "The One Issue Between Seabury and Whitman." It picked up a theme that Seabury had stressed all along. "The structural weakness in Governor Whitman's administration, the irrefutable argument against his re-election, is his lack of ability and willingness to check extravagance in state expenditures. He has not the talent, the courage, nor strong desire for financial reform. This want of political courage, the willingness to please the party leaders and advance his political fortunes at the expense of the state, is unfortunately the characteristic of Governor Whitman. Is this extravagance to go on? That is the one issue between Samuel Seabury and Charles S. Whitman." While *The Times* and the Democratic press backed Wilson and Seabury, the Hearst newspapers hammered away at Seabury's radicalism and Tammany backing.

Seabury campaigned at full stride, regardless of what he secretly believed the result would be on Election Day. At the Church of the Ascension, in the last hours of the campaign, he spoke on abstract principles of politics. He said that both parties had elements of special privilege, but he hoped that the Democratic party stood for democratic principles. Under the auspices of the Wilson–Seabury League, he toured Brooklyn and Manhattan on election eve, speaking at fourteen meetings. "I close the campaign confident of success," he told a street corner crowd at Avenue C and Third Street. "I have toured the state from Montauk to Buffalo. I am supported by a Democratic party absolutely united. By all Progressives who remain loyally progressive and are not seeking revenue or office. By scores of thousands of intelligent Republicans. I will receive the solid independent vote because the independent voters know that I am independent." The laborers in the crowd cheered. They had known Seabury as a young attorney battling for their right of assembly on these streets.

On Election Day, pleasant weather brought out large crowds. The 4,500 policemen at the polls had only a small number of drunks to control. There was no trickery reported from the precincts. The voters had a choice of Seabury on the Democratic line, Whitman on the Republican, Independence League, Progressive or American party lines. There were also Prohibition, Socialist, and Socialist Labor candidates. The story went around that Whitman, though hardly a teetotaler, was sure of the Prohibitionists' vote because once, when he was a magistrate, he had passed a saloon and decided to drop in for a drink. A small fight was in progress at the bar, so he held a court session then and there, sending the combatants off to jail before quietly ordering a drink. The first half of the story appeared in newspapers at the time, and the Prohibitionists chose to think he was one of them, militant.

Sam and Maud Seabury arose early, voted before breakfast, and then drove around the various precincts before going to election headquarters at the Hotel Breslin to check the incoming results. The first reports in the early evening showed good returns for the Democrats from upstate cities, and if New York came through strongly, there seemed to be hope for Seabury. Hughes had a margin of 187,-000 votes by the time reports came in from the Bronx, with the votes for Whitman running slightly behind. However, as key precincts from the five boroughs reported in, it became apparent that Tammany had not delivered enough of the city vote, for either Wilson or Seabury, to offset the upstate Republican lead. Wilson had a scant 40,000 plurality in the city, while Seabury's lead was only 21,000. Hughes ran ahead of Wilson in New York. Seabury was defeated by 154,000 votes, but rolled up 79,000 more votes than his running mate, McCombs.

Late that evening, Seabury went to dinner at the home of his younger brother, William Marston Seabury, on East Ninth Street. There, periodic bulletins were delivered to him, and political leaders and reporters checked in. When he openly admitted that he no longer stood a chance of election, his sister-in-law was surprised by his equanimity. No look of anger or surprise crossed his face. "Why don't you wait for all the results to come in from upstate before conceding, Sam?" she asked him. But he replied, "No, when you don't pick up certain districts in the city you are out of the race. Whitman's lead cannot be overcome."

The next day, Murphy was silent. He was not in to callers at Tammany Hall. The talk in the city was that the machine had "knifed" Wilson and Seabury. But some Tammany district leaders did volunteer explanations. They claimed that hyphenated New Yorkers—the German-Americans and Irish-Americans—did not support the Democratic ticket because of the Wilson Administration's support of France and England in the war. One Tammany leader conceded that a charge of organization treachery could be made in the case of Seabury. The general Democratic voter had nothing against Seabury, said this leader, but "he has brought down upon his head the ill-feeling of Murphy's resentment." Seabury had been too vigorous in his denial of the stories that he had been personally intimate with Murphy which resulted from the accidental photograph taken in the golfing group in Southampton. Furthermore, the hostility of Hearst's newspapers contributed to his defeat.

Long afterward, Seabury confessed that he knew he was in a losing battle from the beginning. "When I carried the Democratic primary but lost the Progressives, I knew that result would insure my defeat. But I went through the campaign and made the best fight I could. I knew that I had resigned from the court of appeals because of Roosevelt's promise, and I knew also that the breach of that promise spelled my defeat for the governorship. I was also aware of the treacherous character of the Democratic leaders and that they could not be depended upon. However, I had no other alternative but to make the fight with Wilson. For myself, I had no misgivings as to the result."

Seabury never forgot that Roosevelt and Tammany, in combination, had stopped him from becoming Governor of New York state. His spectacular career had suddenly come to a halt. But events would show that he could be a patient enemy, with a long memory.

CHAPTER 7

Samuel Seabury, Esq., Again

AT the age of forty-three, Samuel Seabury had to make a new beginning as a lawyer. He noted for himself:

> After my defeat I immediately gave my attention to the arrangements for practicing law. I had been away all the years in judicial office from the time I took office as a justice of the city court in January, 1903, until I resigned from the court of appeals in September, 1916. I had been on the bench performing judicial services for almost fourteen years—in the city court, the supreme court and the court of appeals. I had enjoyed every minute of that service, and I had given it every energy which I possessed. I determined to devote myself to private practice; not, however, losing sight of the necessity for giving some attention to public affairs.

He had no other choice. As when he had begun in the 1890's, there was no independent income or family business to fall back on. Although Maud and Sam had no children of their own, they assumed part of the obligation of educating John and William Northrop, Mrs. Seabury's nephews; Bill Northrop lived with them for many years. They owned a brownstone on East 11th Street and a cottage and farm acreage in East Hampton. Living simply but well, as a former public official affiliated with many organizations, could be expensive.

Seabury's image as a reformer and prolabor judge was established. There was some question, in spite of his great experience on the bench, whether the business community would now turn to him for counsel. Anyone who thought he would change his stripes was mistaken. He was still outspoken. Commenting on the appointment of Brandeis to the United States Supreme Court, an appointment which was opposed bitterly in the Senate and in some legal circles, he declared, "If the heads of the American Bar Association turn down Louis Brandeis, it does not reflect on him at all—only on them." Brandeis and Seabury held similar views on social change and legislation. There was some talk that President Wilson might name Seabury to the Supreme Court or to some other high government post, but Tammany's coolness toward him and the need for a semblance of Democratic unity in the state thwarted any Federal appointment.

At about the same time, two others whose names were now known to Seabury were being heard from.

Jimmy Walker, who had written *Will You Love Me in December as You Do in May?*, composed a series of flop tunes. Then, with the help of his politically well-fixed father and uncle, he had asked for, and received, the Tammany nomination for state assemblyman from his Greenwich Village district. Several years later, he had finally passed his bar examinations in Albany, and at the age of thirty-five, he was becoming known as a glib legislator who could be trusted by the Democratic machine. Walker knew how to exploit his position in Albany to supplement his income as an attorney practicing in the New York City courts.

Fiorello H. La Guardia, with the nomination of the Progressive party and the Republican party for United States Representative, carried on a successful campaign in the same year that Seabury was defeated by Whitman. La Guardia, age thirty-four, and the darling of the labor unions, made it by a narrow margin—the first time a Republican had been elected to Congress from any district below 14th Street since the founding of the party.

La Guardia and Walker became acquainted a year or so before the election that sent La Guardia to Congress. Previously La Guardia had held a job in Governor Whitman's administration as a deputy attorney general in New York City. One day, he found himself prosecuting a case in which State Senator Walker, in his role as a private attorney, appeared on behalf of the defendant, a meat-packing association accused of falsifying weights on labels. Walker himself had helped to write the Weights and Measures Law—and now La Guardia was shocked to see Walker accepting a fee to argue against his own law. A Tammany judge was sitting, and he soon decided in favor of Senator Walker's client. Afterward, La Guardia recalled in his memoirs that he had asked Walker how he could possibly appear in the case. Walker winked it off. "Fiorello," he said, "when are you going to get wise? Why are you in the attorney general's office? You're not going to stay there all your life. You make your connections now, and later on you can pick up a lot of dough defending cases you are now prosecuting. What are you in politics for, for love?"

Once again, Seabury formed a short-lived partnership. Once again, announcement cards were printed and sent out to a wide circle of friends and business acquaintances. Seabury, Massey & Lowe, Counsellors at Law, 120 Broadway, New York. Before he was elected to the city court, Seabury had been a partner of a retired judge, Bankson Morgan; now *he* was the retired judge in a partnership. His younger brother, William, an expert in the new field of motion-picture law, was also a partner. Albert Massey and John Z. Lowe, well-known lawyers in their own right, had formed the original partnership, but they put Judge Seabury's name at the head of the firm. Lowe, who was distantly related to Mrs. Seabury, had served as Judge Seabury's law secretary. More important, he was an excellent chess player—and Seabury dearly loved to match wits across the chessboard.

One more man was to join the firm, not as a partner but as the chief attorney in the office. No one realized that, when George Trosk joined the firm on January 2, 1917, he would become Seabury's legal right arm—a brilliant behind-the-scenes attorney who shaped the briefs and fashioned the arguments during all the great appeals and investigative years. After attending City College, Trosk studied law, passed his bar examinations before he was twenty-one, and became a law clerk in the office of Edward M. Shepard, president of the Board of Trustees of City College. One day, Trosk appeared on behalf of a client in the supreme court while Judge Seabury was on the bench.

"I had never seen him before," Trosk explained in later years. "I heard a rap on the side door and the Judge entered quickly and sat down. His mere presence silenced the courtroom. He was imposing and handsome—a Greek god in judicial robes. He was courteous to me and the other young clerks before him. There was perfect decorum in his court, which he achieved without raising his voice. I felt that here was the embodiment of the law in all its dignity. When I left the court later that day, I said to myself, 'What can I do to be like that man?' As a starter, I began to part my hair in the middle!"

Some time later, Trosk displayed his legal acumen by causing a complaint, brought by a client of the Seabury firm, to be dismissed. A month later, William Marston Seabury telephoned to commend him on his handling of the brief and to offer him a job with Seabury, Massey & Lowe. Trosk accepted, and soon found himself working almost exclusively for Judge Seabury. When the United States entered the world war, Trosk enlisted and became personnel adjutant and judge advocate at Fort Slocum. When he could get into the city, he often dined with Judge Seabury. After the war the members of Seabury, Massey & Lowe went their separate ways. Seabury privately explained to his nephews later that he was pulling most of the weight in the firm and preferred to practice independently.

Now Seabury became, and would stay throughout the investigation of the 1930's, simply: Samuel Seabury, counselor at law, located at 120 Broadway, cable address, "SASEAB NEW YORK." With him as chief attorney—his hair still parted in the middle—remained George Trosk. Others in the office included Henry J. A. Collins and William Northrop.

Seabury began to build a reputation as a lawyer's lawyer. He practiced as a barrister in the English tradition, although the American legal system makes no distinction between barrister and solicitor. Seabury also adhered to the English tradition in his style of living. His office reflected his manorial tastes. In the reception room there were long, straight-backed black benches, which made some visitors feel that they had stumbled into a church. The atmosphere was similar in the Judge's room. He sat in a heavy leather chair, behind an enormous mahogany desk with huge legs. The walls were hung with pictures of English legal lords. His new secretary, Dorothy Benner, carried herself with proper dignity. She had come to work, on the recommendation of a friend of Bill Northrop's, only after the Judge had assured her that it was perfectly ladylike to ride alone in the subways.

Most of the time, Seabury was called upon to handle appeals. An attorney in a case would come to his office and ask him to assist by serving "of counsel." He listened to the facts of the case, weighed them as if rendering a decision, and then decided if the legal merits were sufficient for him to take on the appeal. Sometimes, if the facts were clouded, he assigned Trosk, Collins, or his nephew to investigate the case. Trosk once spent two months examining the record of a case before reporting to the Judge that there was no legal validity for an appeal. The Judge declined to take the case, thereby losing a large retainer. With few exceptions, the appeals handled by the Seabury office concerned trusts and estates, corporation law, and various business matters, generally involving large sums of money. He avoided negligence, matrimonial, and criminal cases. His appeals were handled on a straight-fee, rather than a contingency, basis; it did not matter, as far as payment was concerned, if he won or lost. A fee of several thousand dollars—and sometimes many times that— for preparing the briefs and personally appealing a case was not at all unusual for Judge Seabury.

In the preparation of cases for appeal, Seabury displayed what seemed to his associates a fantastic memory for doctrines, concepts, and precedents. Once, when an appeal was brought to him involving a question of agency, Seabury listened carefully and then said, "I suggest you look at Paterson v. Gandesqui, an 1812 case decided by Lord Ellenborough at London Sittings. I think it can be found in *Smith's Leading Cases.*" Amazed by this ability to cite not only the case but the book where it could be found, the lawyer asked Seabury how he remembered it. "From law school," Seabury replied, amused. Actually, he had done his homework well in the years he sat on the bench, researching and writing his own opinions. That gave him a background in many fields of law.

In actual practice, he relied on Trosk's analytical briefs. When Seabury was trying a case, the facts and citations were assembled for him. He believed strongly in giving those he trusted full responsibility and full credit for their labors. This policy paid off handsomely when he later hired his staff of young lawyers during the investigation of the City of New York. Appearing before the appellate division or the court of appeals, Seabury used a memorandum that set forth his line of argument in a succession of catch lines. In New York, he and Trosk ate at the Manhattan Club near the appellate division when they were trying a case there; in Albany, they usually lunched at the DeWitt Clinton Hotel. All through the meal they discussed the presentation of the case. Then Seabury made his argument before the judges by resorting to the catch lines instead of the printed brief. He had listened to many dry readings by lawyers when he sat on the bench, and he knew that judges, too, could become bored.

He was Edwardian in his manner, especially with his office employees. Rarely would he order one of his lawyers to perform a job. He would call him in for a "discussion." When he wanted something done, the phrase he used was "I would suggest." When he insisted that it be done, the tone of command took the mild form of "I think it might be done this way." Nor did he avoid at the luncheon or dinner table those with whom he had labored in his office; frequently he invited his lawyers to join him for his usual roast beef and cigar at the Bankers Club in their office building. When a case carried over into the evening, the Judge and his colleague went home to dine with Maud. Dinner was usually preceded by one rather small cocktail.

When the time came to hire an office boy, fifteen-year-old W. Bernard Richland, who had just arrived in this country from England, applied for the job. "I told the Judge that I had not completed my schooling," recalled Richland, who became an attorney and remained with Seabury into the early 1940's. "He asked me why I had not continued my education and I replied that, out of necessity, I had gone to work in a factory which manufactured American flags. He found this amusing, and was pleased when I told him that I had been a British Boy Scout. He tried me out for the job. The first week a clerk from another law office came in to serve a paper. I went into the Judge's room and announced, 'Mr. Lewis's *clark* is here to see Judge Seabury.' He raised his eyebrows quizzically at my pronunciation. At the end of the week, he told me that I could consider my trial period over. I think he liked hearing my accent around the office because of his family links with Britain and interest in their legal traditions."

The Judge advised his office boy to continue his schooling after work, recalling that he himself had been unable to go directly to law school because of financial strain. "I went to night high school," Richland said, in retrospect. "Sometimes my crusty friends would meet me, and I would get disapproving looks from the others in the office. One night, three of them dropped into the office to pick me up. I wasn't ready, so they sat impatiently on the hard black benches, being stared down by the secretaries. The Judge happened to come out of his room—and asked to be introduced to my cronies. Then he had me send out for sandwiches for all of us. Somehow, afterwards, I got the impression that he had handled an office situation diplomatically, and that it really wasn't right to bring around the boys. I never did again."

Young Richland went on to become a law clerk, doing research and discovering fresh approaches for cases handled in the office. He read law in Judge Seabury's office, attended New York Law School as a nonmatriculated student, and then asked the Judge to file a certificate of clerkship for him so that he could take the bar examinations. He became one of the few lawyers in the 1930's in New York to do so without graduating from a law school. Nevertheless, he acquired the scholarly approach that prevailed in Judge Seabury's office. One day, when researching a knotty problem, he brought a copy of the *Harvard Law Review* to the Judge, who, to Richland's surprise, declared, "Don't bring me these schoolboy magazines." The Judge preferred the weight of principles backed by precedents.

The law practice flourished. At first there were assignments to act as referee in state accountings in the supreme court—appointments given by other judges to one who had been one of their own. But Seabury's sense of propriety made him feel uncomfortable about receiving court patronage. When he went to Albany to appear before his former colleagues in the court of appeals, he avoided any social mingling that might be interpreted wrongly. Occasionally, as a matter of convenience, a case of his might be advanced or set back on the calendar to fit his schedule, but this was done for many other attorneys, too.

His fees grew large because many of the cases involved major suits.

He was retained as counsel to help straighten out the affairs of the Pittsburgh Life & Trust Company and other concerns which had been involved with a group of financial adventurers in questionable multimillion-dollar deals; a conference in his office effected a settlement, and litigation was avoided. He represented the defendant, the Fisher Body Corporation, in a $2,000,000 suit brought by the Perfect Window Regulator Company for an accounting. In Federal District Court, he served as counsel for the Italian Vineyard Company to restrain Federal authorities from attempting to enforce the provisions of a wartime Prohibition law. He represented no less than three thousand tort claimants seeking to recover more than $2,000,000 from the Brooklyn Rapid Transit Company for injuries resulting from a tunnel accident. "I am surprised at those who have urged all along that these poor victims should be paid," he told the court, "and now appear in an attempt to block payments to these unfortunate people." The case echoed his old interest in the city's transit situation, its inequities as a result of private ownership, and the need for a unified system, which, eventually, he helped to put into effect.

He could indulge himself by taking cases involving free and untrammeled expression. When a play called *The God of Vengeance* was shut down and the producer and cast fined for "tending to corrupt public morals," Judge Seabury fought the district attorney of New York County up to the court of appeals. There, Judge Irving Lehman reversed the supreme court decision and found that the lower court had erred in convicting and fining the producer, Harry Weinberger, and the leading players, Rudolph Schildkraut and Virginia McFadden. In another case, he represented Florenz Ziegfeld against Elizabeth Hines, an actress who had been hoping to be starred in *Show Boat*. When it was decided to arbitrate this suit for breach of contract, Judge Seabury, aware that theater people lived and conducted their affairs by a looser code than the rest of the community, agreed to arbitration only on the condition that the arbitrator was broad-minded and familiar with that tenuous field of operations known as show business.

By far his biggest case was the Jay Gould trusteeship litigation, which exposed the sordidness behind the handling of the $93,000,000 estate of the great American financial manipulator. For a dramatic cast of characters, for an example of the dissipation of the heirs of

the very rich, and for sheer weight of legal precedent and obfusca-
tion it resembled nothing so much as the endless chancery suit of
Dickens's *Bleak House,* Jarndyce and Jarndyce. "Innumerable children have been born into the cause; innumerable young people have
married into it; innumerable old people have died out of it," Dickens
wrote. "Scores of persons have deliriously found themselves made
parties, without knowing how or why; whole families have inherited
legendary hatreds with the suit. The little plaintiff or defendant, who
was promised a new rocking-horse when Jarndyce and Jarndyce
should be settled, has grown up, possessed himself of a real horse,
and trotted away into the other world."

The litigation over the Gould estate involved the heir of a business
buccaneer of the type Seabury despised. Jay Gould, in association
with Jim Fisk, had struggled against Cornelius Vanderbilt for the
Erie Railroad; looted the Erie's treasury; caused the Black Friday
panic by attempting to corner gold; extended his domain from the
Missouri Pacific to the New York Elevated Railways. Tweed's Tammany Ring and Gould's board of directors for the Erie Railroad were
interlocking; Tweed had been placed on the board of directors of
the Erie Railroad at Gould's behest.

Several years before Seabury entered the case, *McClure's* magazine,
in a lead article, hinted at what had been happening to the Gould
fortune: "One of the most significant phases of the present railroad
situation is the extent to which the children of Jay Gould are losing
control of the family properties. Of the dozen railroad lines that
make up what is commonly known as the Gould system, only one
is now paying dividends. The Goulds are losing control of their
ancestral domain because, like the Vanderbilts, they have attempted
to do two incompatible things—live lives of idleness and luxury, and
at the same time control great enterprises."

The description applied with particular aptness to Seabury's client,
Frank Jay Gould, the pirate's youngest son, a *bon vivant* who maintained a lively interest in horses, gambling houses, and dancers in the
Folies Bergère. From his home at Juan-les-Pins, the Riviera resort he
virtually created and owned, he indulged in the voluptuous pleasures of a French Sybarite, returning to the United States only to
acquire a railroad or two in the South. He had inherited a talent for
railroad finance and was known as the "traction king" of Virginia.

His ability to make money was balanced by his ability to spend it. He had filled a need in the world by founding the Palais de la Méditerranée at Nice, a monumental gambling casino. At its opening, he declared, "This is a place the Caesars could not have built." In fairness to the Caesars, none had a seat on the stock exchange or a $10,000,000 inheritance from Jay Gould.

If Seabury had any conscientious doubts about either his client's high life or the source of his wealth, he kept them to himself. He mentioned neither in recalling the circumstances of the case for his personal records:

> My firm had not been long in existence before my old friend Walter B. Walker, whom I had known well ever since he was a boy, called on me and said he needed my help in the Gould case. Bert Walker used to visit me in East Hampton and we discussed his entry into the legal profession. Besides being a good lawyer, he became a remarkable and skillful accountant. In 1917, he telephoned for an interview, and I invited him to lunch with me at the old Hardware Club on Broadway. He explained that he had been devoting himself to the accounts of the trustees of the Gould estate, he was about to commence an action, and he wanted my assistance as counsel. He said he thought the case would take years —and he was right.
>
> From his study of the case, he had no doubt that the trustees had acted in a very high-handed and illegal manner. They had disregarded all the rules which governed the fiduciary relationship. I agreed to look at all the facts before assuming an attitude on the case. I devoted a great deal of time to studying the records. The deeper I got into the case, the more I was astounded at the latitude which the trustees had taken. For many months Walker and I worked on the case. There were many interests, parties, executors and trustees involved. I believe there were more than forty lawyers representing the different interests.

When Jay Gould died in 1892, he left his fortune to his executors in trust, with a provision that the estate was to be divided into six parts—a part for each of his children. There were four sons and two daughters—George, Edwin, Howard, Frank, Helen (Mrs. Finley Shepard), and Anna (the Duchesse de Talleyrand). George, the oldest son, was the "villain." He had worked closely with his father and gradually gained active control of the railroad empire. After his

father's death, George prevailed upon his brothers and sisters to disregard the direction to divide the trust fund and, instead, to com-
mingle everyone's shares. This was done. He then invested the fund
in speculative securities, made loans of as high as $50,000,000, and
sold trust securities for his own gain in an effort to retain control of
the "Gould or Southwestern System" railroads. In addition, he collected commissions for himself on invested trust funds and actually
converted funds from the trust to his own accounts. No accounting
had been made of the Gould estate for nearly thirty years, and, as
one might expect, there had been births, marriages, divorces, and
children, legitimate and illegitimate. At the same time, vast changes
had taken place in the railroad securities which formed the bulk of
the estate. At this stage, Seabury, having decided on the legal merits
of the case, spoke up for the new client by saying to Bert Walker, "In
a case such as this the way to defend is to attack."

Many notable members of the New York Bar took part in the
battle over the disputed millions. Among the lawyers were a former
and a future Democratic candidate for President, Alton B. Parker
and John W. Davis, plus such other distinguished counsel as William
Nelson Cromwell, John B. Stanchfield, J. Du Pratt White, William
Dean Embree, and Winthrop W. Aldrich. These teams of attorneys,
representing the various heirs and the secondary trusts, came from
the major law firms in the city. In a sense, Seabury, a newcomer to
private practice, was taking some of them on. Before he finished,
there were 14,600 pages of testimony presented before three different
referees, two of whom died during the progress of the case.

Seabury noted in his own records of the case:

> As a first step, I obtained an order for the examination of George
> Gould before trial. The lawyers in the case were asked to meet in the
> offices of Alton B. Parker to discuss the situation. Judge Parker wanted
> to see if the matters could not be amicably arranged. I told him that
> there could be no amicable arrangement until we knew the facts; that
> ever since the death of Jay Gould the trustees had been managing the
> properties and estates, and that we did not know what the actual facts
> were. Judge Parker then said he thought he could vacate my order for
> examining George Gould before trial. I told him I differed with his
> assumption—and that I was quite ready to meet his challenge. I added

that any move on their part to vacate the order for examination would be taken by the public and the profession as an admission of their guilt.

Parker and the attorneys for the various factions conferred privately, then conceded the point to Seabury. Seabury maintained that he was interested in the facts first, and asked that they be obtained in full. Sullivan and Cromwell, representing children and grandchildren of the Duchesse de Talleyrand (she had been one of the first American heiresses to marry a titled European), agreed with Seabury that an accounting of the activities of George Gould, as trustee of the estate, should be given. Now Seabury and Bert Walker prepared to examine the man who had managed the great American fortune. They agreed on a plan between themselves: Seabury would question Gould only on his general methods of handling the estate; Walker would deal with the particulars.

"George Gould was not only utterly unscrupulous," Judge Seabury noted, "but since the death of his father had dominated the family and dictated what should be done in estate affairs. Edwin was a weak character, Howard paid no attention to his trustee duties, and Helen had no understanding of the trusteeship arrangement, not wanting to hurt any of her brothers. Both Frank and Anna had at all times been excluded from management or even knowledge of the estate that George ruled. The statements made by him in the examination before trial by us showed maladministration, misappropriation, gross misconduct and neglect, and a motion was made to remove him as trustee."

The removal proceedings was hard-fought. John W. Davis, springing to the defense of his client, George Gould, chided Seabury, saying, "If declamation and personal abuse were to take the place of proof, we would consider the case as closed." Nevertheless, Seabury and Walker, together with the attorneys for the Duchesse de Talleyrand and her children, had amassed the evidence. In 1922, the appellate division upheld the order removing George Gould as a trustee. A year later, he died in his villa in France. "Death Holds Up Litigation with Family Over His Father's Estate" was the headline in *The Times;* "Fifty Lawyers Open Court Fight Over Gould's Millions," the one in *The World*.

The quibbling and accounting dragged on in the courts well into

1927. "We had to draw up new papers all the time," Edward Green, of Sullivan & Cromwell, recalled. "Every time we had one set prepared, a new heir would be born." Furthermore, it was difficult to keep the personal lives of the litigants from complicating the already complex court procedures.

One sensational event involved none other than Seabury's client, the *bon vivant,* and, for once, Seabury had to accommodate a high-paying client by taking on a matrimonial case.

After Frank Gould's first marriage ended in divorce in 1910, he married Edith M. Kelly, a young lady from Brooklyn who was a singer in London's music halls. The second Mrs. Gould accused him of repeated cruelties to her "due to intoxication and unfaithfulness with Parisian women," the phrase used by her lawyers and gleefully adopted by part of the New York press. Thereupon, Gould left her, and in 1919, in Paris, obtained a divorce. It was the validity of this foreign divorce that Judge Seabury was called upon to defend in the supreme court in New York in 1921, the appellate division in 1922, and the court of appeals in 1923.

Mrs. Gould, having acquired the extravagant tastes of her ex-husband, spent money with style. When she sued for support, one of her smaller bills was for "70 pairs of silk stockings." Seabury told the court that the Paris divorce decree was based chiefly on Mrs. Gould's confession that she had lived with a person other than her husband, a gentleman named "Cassasus." Furthermore, Seabury maintained, Frank Gould was no longer her husband, the French decree was in accord with the laws of the State of New York, and the decree had to be recognized under the comity of nations. The court agreed, and, using a gambling casino term that few could appreciate as much as Frank Gould, Supreme Court Justice Mullen declared that his former wife "wants to play the red and the black, too." The former Mrs. Gould was denied further support because she was no longer his wife, and the French divorce decree was recognized in New York.

At last the main Gould case drew to a close. Former United States Senator James A. O'Gorman, sitting as referee, heard Seabury's two-day summation, which included "a psychoanalysis of the disintegration of the character of the late George J. Gould." Seabury called him "a daring Wall Street speculator" who used money belonging to the estate for his own profits and destroyed all the books when he realized that an accounting would have to be made. He absolved Frank, Anna, and Helen, who had believed that the trustees were acting in a responsible fashion, and he demanded that the trustees be surcharged, so that "any profits that might have accrued should be paid to those children having no part in the mismanagement." As a final touch, he excoriated the high-powered attorneys who excused the misbehavior of the trustees they represented.

Referee O'Gorman, working with the facts unearthed by Walker and argued by Seabury, was asked to restore more than $40,000,000 to the original estate, but this was lowered to $20,000,000 when the trustees indicated a willingness to wind up the family affair. Frank Gould's interest in this surcharge was about $5,000,000, which, added to the approximate $9,000,000 in his personal trust, enabled him to get by quite nicely on the French Riviera.

Seabury's legal fees for the ten years the case was in his office amounted to about $1,000,000. During this time, he received half a million dollars in periodic payments, and when the estate was finally settled he was paid another half-million. Bill Northrop recalls walking to the bank and depositing that half-million-dollar check with a feeling of awe. That night, he, the Judge, and "Aunt Maud" celebrated by going out and buying the best grand piano they could find, a Mason & Hamlin costing $4,500.

"When the case was closed," Bert Walker told Walter Chambers, a reporter for the *New York World-Telegram,* "Judge Seabury had lost none of his friends who had opposed him in the litigation. Those who met him there for the first time became his steadfast friends." Once during the Gould case hearing, Justice Edward G. Whitaker turned to Seabury and said, "Judge, you handle figures like an expert accountant." He would do so again to unravel the fiscal scandals of the City of New York.

There was one case he especially enjoyed handling because it gave him an opportunity to put William Randolph Hearst on the griddle. When a clerk asked where to serve Hearst, Seabury innocently said, "Why not try Marion Davies' apartment?" The enmity between the two had deepened since their political break. The same antagonists and attorneys seemed to crop up repeatedly in Judge Seabury's career. In William Randolph Hearst v. Dexter Sulphite Pulp and Paper Company, Hearst was represented by the bright and famous Max D. Steuer, a Tammany lawyer, and Clarence J. Shearn, longtime Hearst attorney; Seabury and former Governor Nathan Miller defended the case. It concerned a newsprint mill which Hearst had bought through an agent, with a large down payment in cash, so that he could get paper during the world war shortage, and afterward. When the bottom dropped out of the newsprint market in the early 1920's, Hearst refused to make additional payments to the mill owners, claiming that his agent had been bribed and displaying an amazing vagueness about his own newspaper operations.

Seabury put Hearst on the stand for three hours in the $3,500,000 suit. The undercurrent of bitterness between the two broke the dam of judicial politeness. "In attacking Hearst, Seabury stepped in front of the editor and shook a finger in his face to emphasize his caustic remarks," the *New York Daily News* reported. "If Hearst was surprised at the bitterness of one of his political protégés in the days of the Independence League, he did not show it but simply grinned." The examination was interrupted by frequent clashes of counsel. Seabury's line of questioning was designed to show that if Hearst's agent, Charles F. Zittel, was corrupt, it was on behalf of, and not contrary to, Hearst's interests. Obviously, Hearst knew what Seabury was trying to do, for, time and again, he couldn't remember.

Seabury, pressing his points, said, "What would your best recollection be?" Hearst replied, "When I don't remember, how would you define my best recollection?" Seabury answered, "Well, you may not have a clear memory on a subject, yet you may have a best impression. At least, we lawyers go on that assumption. Anyway, as I understand it, when you say you don't remember, that means you have no memory on the subject?" Hearst replied, "It means I don't remember." Seabury retorted sarcastically, "You mean your mind is a blank on that subject?" Hearst answered, "I would hate to say my mind is a blank on any subject." They had a few more exchanges on the subject of Hearst's memory, with Hearst using such phrases as "I am not certain" and "I am not sure." Finally, at the end of the interrogation, Hearst said, "Here again, I don't want to be definite." Seabury, turning his back on Hearst, answered for the benefit of the court, "I don't think there is any danger of that, Mr. Hearst."

After several such sessions at the library of the New York Law

Institute at 120 Broadway, where the supreme court examination before trial took place, it became apparent that Hearst was either
deeply implicated in the activities of his agent or an extremely naïve
man. Seabury had proved his point. An adjournment was followed
by a settlement of the case favorable to the defendants represented
by Judge Seabury and Governor Miller.

Seabury again seemed impassioned—as he had been when fighting
for union rights in the 1890's—in his defense of Sidney Hillman,
president, and the Amalgamated Clothing Workers Union of America. The members were fighting for their union lives through the
bitter winter of 1920–21. To the clothing industry and to the workingmen in New York and the United States, the Amalgamated strike
and lockout was a last stand. It meant union growth or union death.

A series of injunctions had been directed against the union by the
Clothing Manufacturer's Association, which was represented by Max
D. Steuer. The union had picketed a retail shop which had also been
a factory; the shop had decided to stop manufacturing, and the employees were thrown out of work. When an injunction was granted
against further picketing, *The New York Times,* in the language and
spirit of 1920, commented editorially: "So the Bolshevist purpose declared in the constitution of the clothing workers is abandoned."
Such was the attitude of a segment of the press and public that Judge
Seabury was called upon to combat in the courts. Injunctions against
public demonstrations by the union members had been granted rap-
idly by various supreme court justices in New York and Brooklyn.

The next step by the manufacturers was to try to break the union
itself. In J. Friedman & Co., Inc. v. Sidney Hillman, a motion was
made by Steuer, speaking on behalf of one large clothing manufacturer, for the dissolution of the Amalgamated. Steuer sketched the
history of the New York clothing industry and told the supreme
court that its annual business was $200,000,000, that agreements
between the manufacturers and union had expired, and that a down-
ward business trend was sweeping the country. He said the manufacturers were for a piecework system instead of a "life tenure of
office" for employees; that they would no longer abide closed shops,
business agents, and other union practices. His legal peroration
blamed the union's activities on radicals and Socialists and called the

Amalgamated "a mob banded together to throw the Constitution on the scrap heap."

Seabury found himself not merely fighting the antiunion manufacturers but a clever Tammany-oriented attorney raising false issues of "Bolshevism" against the predominantly Jewish and Italian cutters and tailors and operators. Seabury struck back indignantly—he knew what it meant to be called a dangerous radical:

> If Mr. Steuer's argument were stripped down to mere facts, there would be none. If his speech had been delivered in the political arena, it would be branded as demagoguery. . . . The purpose of the union is to improve conditions in the clothing industry and to secure for the workers an American standard of living. After years of working with the union, the manufacturers have just discovered the preamble to the union's constitution. During the years of prosperity, when the manufacturers were making money, the preamble meant nothing to them. The manufacturers are seeking to return to the sweatshop system. Their aim is to curtail production, maintain the price of clothing and get rid of surplus stock. The Amalgamated stands for arbitration of differences, but the plaintiff will not agree to any such proposition. They don't want peace in the industry. Their purpose is to destroy the union.

Steuer called the Amalgamated a revolutionary body, ready to take upon itself the work of "handling" the government. The union's preamble had used the phrase "class consciousness," and Seabury was asked by Justice John M. Tierney to define what that meant. "The framers thought that at some time they might obtain ideal conditions which would benefit their particular class," he explained. "There are other classes, as you know from your work in this court, who also think they are entitled to some special privileges. My Americanism is second to none, but my adversary is waving the Red flag to make it appear as if it were the flag of the Amalgamated."

The New York State Supreme Court set aside the antiunion injunctions, and the way was paved for a settlement. After six months of strikes and lockouts, an agreement was signed in June, 1921, providing for an impartial chairman for the industry, a joint committee to determine wage scales, a 15-per-cent wage reduction for all classes except cutters, a forty-four-hour work week, and the recognition of the union as the bargaining agent. Seabury's arguments on behalf of

Hillman and the Amalgamated had accomplished their main aims. An editorial in *The New York Times* the day after the agreement said: "The Amalgamated Clothing Workers of America hail the settlement as a victory. In one sense it is. The principle of the union shop is to prevail and the week is limited to forty-four hours."

Seabury championed others in minority political positions. There were pacifists and Socialists, like Scott Nearing of the Rand School and Morris Hillquit, the international secretary of the American Socialist party, who found themselves under steady attack from United States Attorney General A. Mitchell Palmer's raiders. The Federal Government's vigilantes had their counterparts in some state governments. In New York, Senator Clayton Lusk headed a legislative committee investigating "seditious activities." When the Lusk committee caused the suspension of five Socialist assemblymen at the opening session of the legislature, Seabury and other attorneys volunteered their services for the defense.

The Citizens Union, the City Club, and the Association of the Bar of the City of New York condemned the legislature for failing to seat the elected Socialists. The Bar Association, by a vote of 174 to 117, adopted a resolution of support for seating them. It was introduced by Charles E. Hughes, and a special committee behind the resolution included such legal leaders as Morgan J. O'Brien, Louis Marshall, Joseph M. Proskauer, and Ogden L. Mills. Seabury was in the forefront of the legal fight to seat the Socialists.

For the editorial section of *The World,* one of the newspapers which nearly always supported him, he wrote a long article on January 18, 1920, called "A Political Party Cannot Legally Be Proscribed." It was signed by Samuel Seabury, "a former judge of the Court of Appeals of New York," and the editors of the newspaper pulled his gubernatorial campaign picture from their files and ran it with the article.

The action of the Assembly of New York excluding five duly elected members of the Socialist party, not because of personal disqualification, but because they were elected on the Socialist platform, is the culmination of a series of recent acts directed against freedom of speech and of press and the fundamental principles of representative government. A startling illustration of the low level to which our representative as-

semblies have sunk is the fact that, with two exceptions, all the legislators, Republican and Democrat, voted for the resolution condemning
them. The pleas put forth by the speaker and the assembly that the Socialist members were excluded because they would follow the wishes of
an outside organization is too shallow to deceive even the most ignorant.
Such a plea, coming from the members of the Republican machine and
Tammany Hall, is too ridiculous for serious comment.

He went on to cite legal precedents, going back to Lord Chatham
and the House of Lords, the history of other abuses in contested elections, the sections in the state constitution that covered elections, the
weight of judicial proceedings, and pertinent literary-legal allusions
from Samuel Johnson and Thomas Erskine. He called upon all the
people of the state to make their voices heard in Albany. He pointed
out that the Socialists were a legal political party that had polled
over 2,000,000 votes at the last national election, a party that was organized to make changes in an orderly way under the constitution
and the laws. He concluded:

If the speaker and his associates were really panic-stricken by imagi-
nary dangers besetting the commonwealth, we might condone their hasty
action as that of men who take counsel of their fears; but it passes all
patience to see our precious constitutional rights, which have been secured through ages of travail and persecution, overridden and denied
by a group of politicians seeking personal advantage by appealing to
the fear of a populace whose minds have been poisoned by a panic-
mongering press. In this time of unrest and lawlessness, even on the
part of legislators, the clarion call has gone forth that New York state
shall be loyal to its past record, and vindicate again the principles of
constitutional government.

With Governor Alfred E. Smith, the Bar Association, and many
clergymen also defending the Socialists, the movement to exclude
them was not pressed. Somehow the free enterprise system was not
torn down in Albany's legislative halls and lobbies, then or later,
and law prevailed over political injustice.

Through the 1920's, Judge Seabury continued publicly to defend
unpopular persons and causes, sometimes at his own expense. He
willingly acted to maintain the liberties he believed in.

CHAPTER 🔳

The Affluent Barrister, But—

ON a summer's day in the mid-1920's, Seabury stood on the porch of his large farmhouse and looked out across the flat potato fields and woodland toward the dunes of East Hampton. Only a few saltboxes and cottages interrupted the landscape then. When his sister Lydia's son, Andrew Oliver, who was visiting for the week end, called, "good morning, Uncle Sam," he acknowledged the greeting with a wave of his pipe. Then he turned to his nephew and, not boastfully but baronially, declared, "Drew, all the land you can see in every direction belongs to me."

Thirty years earlier, young Sam Seabury had sat at the feet of Henry George in his modest cottage in Brooklyn. "Land is a permanent and fixed quantity," the economist told him. "Humanly speaking, capital is neither. To take possession of land, the only possible method is to take the land now in existence, but there is not the same compulsion to take existing capital." Now, many years later, the affluent attorney acquired as much land as he could in the area where his father and Maud's father and the other seminary professors who could not afford expensive summer places had settled. To a disciple of Henry George's, land meant more than capital. Indeed, he seemed uninterested in acquiring a big bankroll, or investing his income in stocks, or even purchasing real estate in order to rent it to strangers. He spent almost all he earned. He was exceedingly generous, lavishing attention on all the Seaburys and Richeys, concerning himself with the welfare of those he employed in the city and East Hampton, and not caring very much about what would be left in hard cash at the end of the year.

Seabury had an image of himself, and he lived in style—but without ostentation. The style was one of boundless grace and a gentleman's dignity.

When he paused to put down his personal thoughts, his words emerged as straightforward and idealistic. What if others later considered them unsophisticated and rather old-fashioned? A man's tone counted more than the polish of his epigrams. On the first day of January, 1923, he wrote "Rags and Tatters" on the title page of one of the small diaries distributed by banks. For the next twenty days, he put in scraps of poems and inspirational comments, for his own eyes only. "Life is an opportunity to mar or aid the welfare of mankind," he wrote in one poem. "While here, our lives brighten or sadden the lives of others," he stated unoriginally in another. Although he was not motivated by religious convictions—some in his family even thought him an agnostic—nevertheless he wrote a prose statement entitled "Caesar and Jesus," in which he said: "There are two plans of government, only two: One is based on force, one is based on love. Caesar or Jesus, choose." Under the title "Progress," in unfettered prose he wrote: "Up! Up! Through the distant years the climb has been slow and weary. On! On! The distance lengthens as we go: the path is easier. The village beneath more beautiful, the sky above clearer."

His chivalrous attitude toward all women—he was the first to offer chairs, open doors, and remove his hat in their presence—was inspired by his courtly manner with Maud, whom he worshiped. Their letters, some of which Maud saved, revealed the maturity and understanding of a happily married couple. They were open and warm, never prudish or distant. There was a depth of human feeling that belied any suggestion of coldness about Sam Seabury. The judge with the patrician air who could silence a supreme court room filled with hundreds of spectators merely with a look of disdain was a different man with his wife, his family, and even with strangers in the normal amenities apart from official obligations. This quality seldom penetrated to outsiders.

East Hampton represented home, voting residence, and week-end place. He had first lived with Maud in the small "Dune Cottage." When he was on the bench, he began to buy "all that certain tract, piece or parcel of land" that he could afford. His holdings reached a peak of about 600 acres. "Wyandanch Farm" and "Hardscrabble Farm" were part of his acreage. The main house, called simply "the farm," was located on the Sag Harbor Road. When he applied for a mortgage, he described the property this way: "The dwelling house is a large frame building with a large fireproof library. There is a garage, a large barn, a dairy, and other farm buildings, on the premises. These structures are insured for $77,600, exclusive of their contents. Approximately forty acres are rented to a potato grower on a yearly basis. The property is unencumbered."

The library that Judge Seabury built on the farm was worthy of one who had grown up in Dr. Seabury's library. He called upon his cousin, Louis Seabury Weeks, an architect, to design it to his specifications. Weeks watched as Sam and Maud measured off forty by sixty feet. "He wanted it to be fireproof and to look like an addition to a Long Island farmhouse," his cousin later recalled. "Sam had a deep regard for the fitness of things. The wooden-looking beams made the library come out more or less English, but they were actually of reinforced concrete. A balcony with additional stack space encircled the second floor of the library. Sam was not interested in the cost of the library; in fact, he was never upset about the costs of any architectural changes on the farm. The library was his pride and joy. It was a real working library, and he knew every one of the seven thousand books in it. He put every book away himself, and there was a logical arrangement—bound volumes of English and American trials, genealogical records, economics, religion and political philosophy. When an argument took place, he would make a point of reaching for the right book, turning to the exact page and pointing to the evidence."

The comfortable old farmhouse was meticulously preserved. Only a few improvements were made, but none to change the eastern Long Island look of the place. Inside were many antiques—old American pewter, dark and rather somber furniture picked up in England and France, and shipped home during summer visits. The portraits of the Seabury ancestors hung in the library, in the center of which was a huge fireplace. In one corner stood the lectern actually used by Bishop Seabury; on it was the prayer book showing the alterations in the services that were necessary for American Episcopalians. A wooden carving—a historical scene showing Anne Boleyn being led to her execution—was nailed over the entranceway of the library door leading out to the garden.

The farm itself was divided arbitrarily, according to John Northrop, between "Uncle Sam's and Aunt Maud's side." Where the trees and gardens were richly cultivated Aunt Maud held sway; on the back patio, the Judge sat in a wicker chair, reading, playing chess with one of his nephews, or just relaxing. Barrie and Lassie, the collies, rounded out the country scene.

Nick Livingston, whom Judge Seabury always called "Nicholas," drove the Seaburys back and forth every week end. Seabury simply could not drive himself, and his work kept him constantly on the move. "He wasn't even interested in the car itself," Livingston later remembered. "I would go out and buy a new car for him every four or five years. Usually we had dark green cars—Lincolns. But no whitewalled tires. He was very conservative that way. He didn't care what color the car was or what kind, as long as it wasn't loud. The same with the license plate. I had a friend who was politically connected, and he said he could get the Judge a real low license plate—maybe SS–1. When I gave the Judge the form to sign, he refused, saying it was too conspicuous. On my own, though, I got him a low number—SS–19—and that remained the Judge's license."

The farm was run by a general handy man named Adam O'Fee; appropriately, he was married to a woman named Eve, who served the family as cook. There was also a gardener, Tony Flower. For a while, the Judge visualized himself as a gentleman farmer. A lengthy headline in the quaint *East Hampton Star,* attributing to him a middle initial, noted: "Samuel A. Seabury Buys 170-Acre Hardscrabble Dairy Farm Here. R. J. Dayton to Re-Lease Farm & Dairy and Will Continue in Dairy Business; One of Largest Single Tracts Sold Here in Years; Property Held at $1,000 an Acre." The dairy, incidentally, was equipped with a cow barn, sizable enough to produce a large share of the milk supply for East Hampton and Sag Harbor. There was a flaw in Seabury's self-image: he was not the farming type. He was a product of the streets of Manhattan. "If he touched a wheelbarrow," one of his nephews said, "the wheel would fall off. He was a most unhandy man."

On some week ends, he played golf with his nephews and friends. One was Henry James, a lawyer, who was a nephew of the famous novelist. Former Governor Miller of New York was another golfing companion. Seabury usually played at the National Golf Links at Southampton or at the Maidstone Club in East Hampton, a rather exclusive establishment; he served as president of the Maidstone for a year and then declined renomination. Every Election Day he drove to Rye and played a round of golf with Judge Edward McCall, who had succeeded him in the supreme court. As a golfer, he was deadly serious. In getting ready to putt, he studied the green, weighed the possibilities with judicial care, and then hit the ball. Sometimes it went in.

His analytical mind was better suited to chess. He was such an avid player that he would wake up his nephews or guests after midnight to play. He even played chess while sailing. A chess board was used that held the pieces in place in a rolling sea. One summer he chartered the *Idalis,* a large yacht, and relaxed on deck with Maud while it sailed around Long Island Sound. But sailing it required a crew of three or four, and when some of the crew steered off course after a Saturday night of Prohibition drinking, he got rid of the *Idalis.* Thereafter he bought his own thirty-two-foot sailboat and christened it the *Maud S.* It was anchored off Sag Harbor, and on good week ends he had a local captain sail it around Shelter Island.

He was always available for any service the Village of East Hampton might require of him. He made speeches on the village green on patriotic and commemorative occasions. He served on the Free Library's advisory board and Maud was a more active board member. Both were active in the East Hampton Historical Society. When East Hampton celebrated its 275th anniversary in 1924, Judge Seabury wrote a short history of the community, *275 Years of East Hampton.* The profits from the sale of the book went to the library and district nursing association.

Samuel Seabury, Esq., was now one of the few leading counsels in New York. He was practicing the way he wanted—as a barrister—

and living the way he wanted—as a gentleman. A serene life in East Hampton and an assured substantial income from appeals work would have satisfied most men of middle age. But Judge Seabury was a political creature. He was fascinated by the policies and conduct of public authority, and he always had a strong sense of mission. He seemed to vindicate the prophetic utterance of de Tocqueville: "I cannot believe that a republic could subsist at the present time if the influence of lawyers in public business did not increase in proportion to the power of the people."

He became very active in the New York County Lawyers Association (at that time regarded as more democratic than the "Uptown" Bar Association), and in the years 1925–27 he served as its president. The distinguished vice presidents during that period were Henry W. Taft, Charles A. Boston, and William Nelson Cromwell. So impressed with Seabury was Cromwell that when he established a foundation several years later—"For research of the law and legal history of the colonial period of the United States of America; a museum and other matters of a legal nature"—he appointed Seabury his first trustee.

The Henry George School still interested Seabury, though he was no longer active in promoting its policies. When Robert Schalkenbach, who had been in the printing business, died, he left the residue of his estate to further the economic principles of Henry George. Seabury was named to the board of directors in the will but declined to serve, because, he informed the officials of the George School, he "made it a rule not to accept board membership." It was more likely that he had moved forward from the theories of Progress and Poverty, though, as he later declared, "I found inspiration in his [Henry George's] ideals."

Politics kindled him. As a former gubernatorial candidate, his voice was listened to. As a Democrat from Republican Suffolk County, he had little trouble finding a platform to speak on. And as an anti-Tammany fighter in a Tammany-dominated city and state, he found enough enemies to attack. At the same time that he was reentering the practice of law at the end of World War I, he was called upon for aid by the Bryan Democrats and then the Wilson Democrats. When "The Commoner" passed through New York City while lecturing on the Chautauqua circuit, he often stayed with the Seaburys. Bill Northrop remembers former Secretary of State Bryan's working habits: "He got up at five in the morning to go down to the library and sat around in his long underwear, drinking cup after cup of black coffee with saccharine, and writing his speeches. He wore a black silk Jewish *yomulka* on his head, covering his bald spot. Once in a while, he would read a phrase or sentence aloud to test its effect. He still had a fine voice."

Seabury was convinced that he had been knifed by the Tammany machine and that the blade had been twisted by the Hearst press during the gubernatorial campaign. He was on call for Democratic insurgents all over the city and outside it. "Because of the New York City influence," he said at a dinner of the Westchester Democratic Club, "the Democratic State Committee has ceased to be a useful instrument for creating Democratic sentiment in the state. These two causes, lack of sympathy with progressive Democratic principles and an inefficient sectionally controlled party organization, are largely responsible for the present demoralized condition of the Democrats."

When Seabury ascertained that both his enemies, Tammany and Hearst, were about to team up at the Democratic state convention at Saratoga in 1918, he put aside for the moment his growing practice and made a plan to destroy the alliance. Everyone knew that Boss Murphy had made a deal to nominate Hearst for Governor of New York state. The thought so aroused Seabury that it sent him, officially, back into the political bear pit.

I determined to use every effort in my power to defeat Hearst for Governor, yet there was no doubt that Murphy controlled the overwhelming majority in the conference. The question was, How could I best accomplish my purpose? My first step was to get named as a delegate from Suffolk County. The local leaders readily granted my request, and I was duly elected as a delegate. After much thought, and realizing that I controlled only my own vote, I decided that I must accomplish my aim by introducing a resolution which would eliminate Hearst. The resolution would be offered in the early stages of the convention before Hearst's name was brought before it. Hearst would not be named in the resolution, yet the resolution would make it unmistakably clear that the only person to whom it could refer was Hearst.

When Seabury arrived in Saratoga, Hearst had already engaged twenty-seven rooms in various hotels to accommodate his followers. All the Hearst political leaders were there in force. Former Governor Martin H. Glynn was prepared to place Hearst in nomination. Judge Joseph A. Kellogg, the temporary chairman, called the convention to order. No sooner had the chairman finished his tedious address than Judge Seabury arose from the middle of the hall and asked to be recognized. He strode to the front of the hall waving a sheet of paper. Before the delegates knew what was happening, Judge Seabury turned to speak to them and the chair at the same time.

"Mr. Chairman and gentlemen of the convention," he said quickly. "In this crisis of our country's affairs I beg the indulgence of the convention while I read a resolution."

Chairman Kellogg interrupted. "Under the rules," he declared, "you may only offer your resolution which must go for reading to the Committee on Resolutions."

"But there are no rules. We have not adopted any, and I am in order if the convention chooses to hear me."

The delegates began to hoot and boo. Boss Murphy turned to his circle of Tammany runners and whispered, "Look out for that resolution—it's loaded." Shouts went up from all over the hall directed against Seabury: "Sit down!" "You're out of order!" "Put him out!"

Charles Weiss, the sergeant at arms, silently paced behind Seabury as he strode up and down the aisle in front of the presiding officer. As Seabury angrily pressed his request to read his resolution, Weiss, a very gentle political constable, ventured to place his hand softly on Seabury's arm, urging him to take his seat. Seabury shook him off contemptuously. "Take your hands off me!" he shouted. "I won't have a sergeant at arms following me around! Give me room, I tell you!" But the chairman refused to let him speak.

At this point, a tactical motion was made by two anti-Tammany delegates who proposed that the rules of the state assembly govern. This motion was adopted, and Seabury jumped to his feet again, racing down the aisle. "And now, Mr. Chairman," he declared, "under the rules of the convention, I ask permission to read my resolution without debate." Patrick ("Packey") McCabe, head of the Albany delegation, and a politician who sided with Hearst, got up.

"This is a Democratic convention," he said, "and I have no doubt that at the proper time it will be glad to hear Judge Seabury."

The helpless Chairman Kellogg, unable to cope with the situation, finally pounded his gavel and said, "Judge Seabury may proceed."

Dramatically, Seabury began to read in his resonant baritone voice:

> Resolved, that this conference of Democrats of the State of New York do renew to the President of the United States their wholehearted support and confidence in his magnificent struggle to make the world safe for democracy; and as an earnest of their loyalty, repudiate every truckler with our country's enemies who strives or has striven to extenuate or excuse such crimes against humanity as the rape of Belgium, the sinking of the *Lusitania* and the German policy of assassination by submarines; who seeks or has sought to sow dissension among our allies, or who now seeks to capitalize by election to public office, the latent treason whose total annihilation is the most pressing need of the hour.

As he emphasized the words "every truckler with our country's enemies," applause broke out, and by the end of the resolution, there were cheers. Everyone in the hall knew the resolution referred only to Hearst. It was carried unanimously by voice vote. Seabury had stirred the patriotic instincts of the delegates. That night all the Hearst headquarters were closed; all the delegates who had come to vote for him had checked out of their suites. The next morning, *The New York Times* said: "Although the resolution was blind as far as naming any person, there was not a delegate in the conference who did not grasp in an instant its thinly veiled meaning. Former Governor Glynn, who was supposed to sponsor Hearst on the floor of the conference, slipped out of town." With this resolution, Seabury effectively killed Hearst's bid for governor and forevermore ruined his personal political ambitions.

It was this convention that nominated Alfred E. Smith for Governor of New York. Speaking as a Suffolk County delegate, Seabury made his familiar attack on Tammany Hall's dominance of the state convention. His remarks were greeted with hisses. Of Smith, however, he said, "I believe he is a man of fine character, strong intellect, and unquestioned loyalty." When cheers greeted this statement, Seabury raised his hand in impatience. "You were hissing a while ago and you will have your chance to hiss again if

you let me go on. Mr. Smith is the best representative of the worst
element in the Democratic party in this state." Hisses, catcalls, and
groans followed his latest broadside. "Through it all," *The Times*
noted, "Judge Seabury stood majestically before the conference, gaz-
ing toward Boss Murphy, silent, smiling, serene, and even amused.
Murphy likewise smiled at him."

Thereafter Seabury supported Smith. He accepted a place on
Smith's campaign committee and endorsed him for re-election in
Albany and during his bid for the Presidency. Although Seabury and
Smith had their disagreements, these were honest spats about what
was good for the City of New York. The first time they locked horns
was over proportional representation, a system of voting by which
the city council members would be elected in proportion to the number of voters, thus insuring minority-party representation. Governor
Smith was in his apartment on Lower Fifth Avenue, nursing a bad
cold. When Robert Moses informed Smith that Seabury was on the
way up with his friend William Church Osborn, a man of great
dignity, Smith wisecracked, "You mean William *Cathedral* Osborn—
'Church' isn't stuffy enough." Seabury delivered a short lecture on
the need for nonpartisan government. "What's your alternative?"
Smith asked in a husky voice. "Proportional representation," Seabury
said, advocating one of his favorite governmental aims. Smith and
Moses, who had drafted legislation for the Governor, disagreed, and
that particular encounter was a standoff.

Nevertheless, Seabury strongly encouraged Governor Smith's presi-
dential hopes. In a letter to Franklin D. Roosevelt, chairman of the
New York committee for Smith's nomination, Seabury praised
Smith for not hounding the Socialist members of the state assembly.

Smith's, Roosevelt's, and Seabury's paths crossed at the 1920 Democratic national convention in San Francisco. All three, to greater or
lesser degree, were presidential possibilities. William Jennings Bryan,
still a sentimental force in politics, told the *Chicago Tribune* that
summer that among those best qualified were Justice Louis Brandeis and ex-Justice Samuel Seabury. Neither was ever seriously considered. Roosevelt and Seabury were both leaders in the independent
anti-Tammany or non-Tammany Democratic groups in the New
York delegation. Roosevelt seconded the nomination of Smith, and
later Smith made a seconding speech for Roosevelt as Vice President.

And Roosevelt and Seabury teamed up to break the "unit rule" at the convention, joining forces with a former Socialist, Mayor George R. Lunn of Schenectady, though later Roosevelt side-stepped the fight to help his personal position with the convention delegates.

The question was whether the New York delegation would vote as a unit or, more democratically, if minority opinions could stand apart from the Tammany-dominated conservative platform views. The Tammany leadership was anti-Wilson and anti–League of Nations; Seabury and, to a lesser extent, Roosevelt, were both demanding that the internationalist policies of the Federal Government be continued in peacetime. Tammany scornfully labeled these insurgent New Yorkers as "the Federal crowd." "Only Franklin Roosevelt, Judge Seabury and Mayor Lunn have the spirit to break loose from the body of dullness, stupidity and party disloyalty instead of surrendering their souls and voices to Tammany," declared a *New York Times* editorial. Seabury led the fight in person before the committee on rules, freeing the votes of the New York delegates, even though he was a challenged Suffolk County alternate and the word had gone out from Boss Murphy, according to a convention report, to "snap the whip and lick Seabury, Lunn and Roosevelt in one stroke." Because of his show of independence—which had been articulated by Seabury in the rules victory—Roosevelt received the vice presidential nomination, and the Smith and Tammany leadership formed a supporting alliance during the hopeless campaign against Republican "normalcy" that followed.

Judge Seabury's political activity during the rest of the 1920's was largely confined to anti-Tammany utterances during various state and city elections. His own political career was eclipsed as time dimmed the name he had made as a former gubernatorial candidate. His anti-Tammany stand was not merely a cause; it was a mania that prevented him from reaching any accommodation with the New York county leaders. His public service now was devoted more and more to the improvement of the courts and his profession.

These were his flourishing years, both in his practice and in his personal life. There was a select circle of corporation lawyers, estate lawyers, and appeals lawyers who practiced as much in the lawyers' and bankers' clubs—where matters could be settled by gentleman's agreement—as before the courts. Not for them the criminal and negligence and accident cases, which were left to young lawyers in the lower courts. Among this elite, the prestige of Samuel Seabury, Esq., formerly of the court of appeals, was great.

He carried off his part as if to the manner born. Most of the huge Gould estate fee had gone into acreage in East Hampton. In 1927 he paid the estate of Walter Lewisohn $160,000 for a magnificent town house, at 154–156 East 63rd Street. He and Maud filled it with $85,000 worth of fine European furnishings, rugs, books, draperies, silver, and works of art. The six-story mansion had twelve bedrooms; five, on the fourth floor, were set aside as rooms for the servants. A cook and two maids lived there; Nick Livingston, the Judge's chauffeur, stayed in town during the week to drive Seabury to and from the office. On week ends, part of the entourage moved to East Hampton to relax on the farm.

The house on 63rd Street, as the Seaburys referred to it, was decorated traditionally. Its elaborately carved dark wooden furniture, its brocaded draperies, its antiques and curios, gave an impression of substantial well-being. It was virtually a self-sustaining enclave on the correct East Side, with its own music room, billiard room, master's dining room, and servants' dining room, laundry, and storerooms. The glory of the house was its library; eight rows of walnut bookshelves circled the room above the mauve carpet and overstuffed reading chairs. At one end was a carved stone fireplace that might have come from a hillside castle in Tuscany; at another, an oil painting of Maud Seabury, by Alfred Hoen, for which the Judge had paid the artist $2,500. Among the other paintings in the library was one of Sir Walter Raleigh, whose chivalric manner fascinated the Judge. The books—a mere supplement to the thousands of volumes in the two-story library at the farm—ranged from *Trials of the Chartists* to Mark Sullivan's *Our Times,* with a whole row of books devoted to the origins of various English trade guilds, a subject which Seabury studied sympathetically most of his life.

In this library, not many years from then, Fiorello H. La Guardia would be sworn in as Mayor of New York to honor the man who had fought hardest for his candidacy.

East Hampton, 63rd Street, and Europe—a most agreeable yearly routine. Young attorneys, nephews and nieces, and friends filled the house and farm on week ends. Sam and Maud enjoyed the company of young people; "as long as they're not dumb breathing stones," he was fond of saying. He and Maud still went occasionally to the theater—they were especially fond of Gilbert and Sullivan—but ordinarily they stayed home in the evenings. After midnight, Seabury read in the library, alone, for an hour or two; sometimes, he awakened Bill Northrop to challenge him to a chess game.

The annual trip abroad always ended in England. Seabury roamed the countryside of Devon, searching county and church records for information about his family. He went to Edinburgh and, eventually, to Aberdeen, searching for clues to the past of that more notable Samuel Seabury, Bishop. In London, the Seaburys visited the bookstores and the art dealers together. Each trip they bought many volumes of social philosophy and political science. They acquired portraits of British lords and leaders at the bar in wigs and white, as well as such valuable paintings as an alleged Pieter Brueghel II, "Collecting the Tithes," and a William Hogarth, "A Midnight Conversation."

On the Continent the gourmet pleasures of Italy and France eluded him; he preferred the solid beef pies of England. Once he was taken on a cultural swing through nighttime Paris, winding up at the Opéra, and he found himself bored by it all. The next day, while Maud went shopping, he went off to indulge his real tastes. He and one of his nephews spent the day in the Paris *cour d'appel,* listening to arguments they did not understand but enjoying every moment of the proceedings. He was at home in the court.

The political paths of Samuel Seabury and Franklin Roosevelt ran parallel for a few exciting years. The Hudson River patrician-turning-radical and the Chelsea radical-turning-patrician could meet on common ground. Early in 1930, a group of distinguished Americans started an organization called the Anglo-American Records Foundation. The purpose was to establish a fund for research into the official British records from 1580 to 1600 in order to shed light on the birth of the American colonies. Samuel Seabury was named president; Franklin Roosevelt became one of the directors.

The past is important—for some to cling to, for others to abandon. Roosevelt and Seabury both had an acute historical sense. Their broad visionary goals could be the same. But Roosevelt was flexible enough to bend to the new age and Seabury could do so only on a municipal level. In the revolutionary 1930's, a genius for recognizing the public weal would lead one of these men to the Presidency; the other would meet political disappointment. Yet for a time the Judge would be like a Roman candle, brilliant and steady and then sputtering out—a great municipal servant to the greatest of American cities who might be forgotten by history but for an investigation that assumed the name Seabury.

BOOK II

The Great Investigator

1930-1933

The three things a Tammany leader most dreaded were, in the ascending order of repulsiveness, the penitentiary, honest industry, and biography.

Edwin L. Godkin, *The Nation*

Samuel Seabury is the most terrifying biographer that Tammany has had in modern times.

Walter Lippmann, the *New York Herald Tribune*

CHAPTER

Wanted: Man to Fight Tiger

AT eleven o'clock on the evening of August 26, 1930, the telephone rang in Judge Seabury's suite at the Carlton Hotel in London. A reporter for an American wire service was calling. Was it true that Seabury had been named to investigate the magistrates' courts in New York? Did he have any statement to make about his appointment, about corruption, about Mayor Walker? The Judge, puzzled, said he had no comment, not a word until he received official notification. He replaced the phone on the hook, pondered the cryptic information for a few moments, and then went back to reading *The Just Lawyer,* a rare first edition, printed in 1631, that he had tracked down after years of searching all over the British Isles.

The following morning a cable arrived from Edward R. Finch, the acting presiding justice of the First Department, Appellate Division of the New York State Supreme Court. It informed Seabury that he had been appointed referee to conduct an investigation of the magistrates' courts of New York City. Judge Finch's appointment order had come after consultation with Governor Franklin D. Roosevelt, who had requested a broad formal investigation.

He handed the cable to Maud, and when she had read it, he told her what he knew of the trouble brewing in Manhattan's criminal courts. He decided they would have to return to the United States at once. Maud, as usual, did not object. They got in touch with their nephew, Bill Northrop, who was in Paris, and asked him to meet them in Cherbourg. They arranged to take a fast boat, the *Aquitania,* home to New York.

It was not until the Seaburys arrived at quarantine, September 5, 1930, that they got the first inkling of the public reaction to the investigation. John Northrop, another lawyer nephew, came aboard with a packet of press clippings about Seabury's appointment. Reporters and photographers swarmed around them, demanding statements and asking them to pose. Did Judge Seabury have a plan? Would the investigation include just the magistrates under fire for buying their seats on the bench, or all the magistrates? Did he intend to investigate City Hall?

Seabury remained noncommittal. He said that any statement would have to come from the appellate division, which had appointed him. He said he would consult with the justices of that court, if possible, that very afternoon. He would not comment on the magistrates under investigation, but he promised to make a public statement in due time.

Before Seabury began work, he reviewed the circumstances that had led to his appointment. Many currents and crosscurrents of city, state, and national politics converged in the investigation. The grand sachems of Tammany and the illustrious personages of the Empire State—Franklin Roosevelt, governor and presidential office seeker; Al Smith, defeated presidential candidate and symbol of Tammany respectability; Jimmy Walker, mayor and beloved cloak of Tammany rottenness; Fiorello La Guardia, congressman and sidewalk reformer—would all be affected.

Tammany was riding high. The city was cut up into lucrative enclaves, each ruled by local club leaders, who were allowed to share the profits so long as they were co-operative. While Mayor Walker had his basic salary increased by subservient city legislators to $40,000 a year, eighty-five district leaders received salaries of more than $7,000 a year, for sinecures such as county clerk, register, deputy sheriff, and keepers of various records and seals. Those beneath the rank of leader had to content themselves with what they could get by extortion from fixing traffic tickets, on the lowest level, to arranging for judicial "contracts" and departmental licenses, on the highest.

If there was an indictment to be quashed—whether it was a charge of robbery committed by a juvenile or a charge of violation of fire laws by a businessman—the normal place to appeal for help was the Tammany clubhouse. There clever young attorneys with political ambitions loyally gave free legal aid, under the watchful eye of the district leader, in the hope of rich rewards. An adept lawyer might advance from assistant district attorney, secretary to a judge, city councilman, to state assemblyman or senator with a refereeship on the side, magistrate or municipal court judge, city, county, and supreme court judgeships. There was a sizable contribution "to the club" in return for each appointment or election. Sometimes it was legitimate: a contribution to help defray the cost of a political campaign; sometimes it was not: a contribution for which there was no accounting. Some officials and appointees paid outright, and Republicans as well as Democrats were involved. The usual payment for appointment as magistrate was said to be $10,000; for a general sessions or supreme court judge, $25,000 to $50,000. Payments were made in crisp, undeclared currency.

Under Mayor Walker, the Tammany district leaders flourished. When former Governor Smith opposed John F. Curry as head of Tammany Hall, hoping for someone with his own high integrity, he, in turn, was opposed by Mayor Walker. "The political history of our organization," Walker declared glibly, "shows that the successful leaders of Tammany Hall, such as Murphy, Kelly and Croker, were district leaders. There is nothing too big for a Tammany leader that democracy can give. They are the outstanding benefactors of this town." At the moment Mayor Walker failed to mention Boss Tweed.

After Charlie Murphy died in 1924, Tammany Hall loosened its reins temporarily. Boss Murphy had a certain dignity; his leaders addressed him as "Mr. Murphy." He had a businesslike reticence; it was said of him that even on the Fourth of July he refused to open his mouth to sing *The Star-Spangled Banner* for fear of committing himself. And he also had a certain way of operating that brought him the respect of his associates. For example, when John ("Red Mike") Hylan, the Brooklyn county judge, was being considered as the Democratic candidate for mayor in 1917, Murphy asked John H. McCooey, Tammany's Brooklyn chieftain, "Is Hylan a man we can trust and do business with?" McCooey said, "He certainly is—do you want to meet him?" Murphy answered, "No, but I want you to ram him down my throat." Thereafter, Democratic clubs in Brooklyn attested to Judge Hylan's independence, resolutions were passed, and Boss Murphy bowed to the public clamor and accepted him as candidate for the good of the party.

Sub rosa licensing in the 1920's was a lucrative source of income for the district leaders and Tammany Hall. The fees charged by the city's Department of Licenses for legal licenses were petty compared to the amounts that were charged unofficially for certain illegal licenses. Jimmy Hines, a West Side leader, "licensed" Arthur (Dutch Schultz) Flegenheimer's policy racket. Big Tim Sullivan "licensed" Arnold Rothstein's gambling places. The "license" frequently stipulated payment of a percentage of the income in return for immunity from police raids. Occasionally a token arrest was made for the record, but overeager policemen soon found themselves pounding night beats on Staten Island. "Recommendations" for transfers and promotions were made weekly by Tammany Hall to the police commissioner. The commissioner owed his appointment to the Mayor, who owed his nomination to Tammany Hall.

Murphy was a frugal man apparently; after his magnificent funeral at St. Patrick's Cathedral, it was discovered that he left an estate amounting to $2,170,761. His Tammany successor, between 1924 and 1929, was George W. Olvany, who came in, with a comparatively clean reputation, at the strong suggestion of former Governor Smith. After all, it was said of Olvany that he was the only member of the board of aldermen in the early 1900's who had remained seated when a youngster poked his head into a meeting and shouted, "Alderman, your saloon is on fire!" Olvany was to prove as culpable as his predecessors but, temporarily, he was hailed as the leader of the "New Tammany." Like the clubhouse attorneys in the districts, he, too, had a diploma; indeed, he was the Hall's first leader with a college degree. He was called "Judge" Olvany because he had served as a judge for six months in general sessions. He was a Greenwich Village boy, who somehow avoided membership in the Hudson Dusters, the local gang, and instead played with Jimmy Walker and went to church with Al Smith. He progressed through the clubs to become deputy fire commissioner and sheriff's counsel, a sachem of Tammany Hall, and a criminal court judge. No sooner did he step into the leadership of the Hall than he began to make the party professionals long for the taciturn Boss Murphy. Olvany had a big mouth into which he too often put both his feet.

He declared in the apostolic publication *World's Work:* "The Irish are natural leaders. The strain of Limerick keeps them at the top. They have the ability to handle men. Even the Jewish districts have Irish leaders. The Jews want to be ruled by them." This came as news to Jews, Italians, and other religious and ethnic political groups commingled in New York. And the party professionals did not savor such self-righteousness as: "If there is the slightest suspicion of grafting fastened upon anyone in our organization, his resignation is demanded at once. We will not tolerate it for a moment. I state with positive conviction that New York is the best-governed city in the world. There is less corruption in New York than in some cities one-tenth its size."

During the years before he was forced out by a revolt of disgruntled Tammany leaders and house lawyers, whose own firms were not getting their share of the spoils, "Judge" Olvany's law firm made more than a million dollars annually. Seabury showed during the investigation that Olvany, Eisner and Donnelly, Esq., made bank deposits of $5,283,000, without counting private deposits by the "Judge" and his law partners. In his dealings with city officials, Olvany played the role of, to use his own phrase, "a good Samaritan." Olvany, the college man whom Al Smith had hand-picked to raise the tone of Tammany, turned out to be greedier than most. Before he lost control of the Hall, however, he made a memorable admission. When an interviewer asked him if his political leadership of Tammany might possibly be of help to his private law practice, Olvany was reported to have grinned and declared, "Well, it won't hurt it any."

John F. Curry, Olvany's successor, was elected by Tammany's district leaders in 1929. More accurately, Walker picked Curry over, among others, Senator Robert F. Wagner. Within the party, Smith and Walker were drawing apart. Walker's personal life did not meet Smith's own standards for a public official. Smith's men were being pushed out by Walker's cronies. Olvany, a vigorous man, said that the condition of his health caused him to resign. Walker irked Smith by inquiring after Olvany's "health" at a dinner of the Inner Circle, the City Hall reporters' organization. Later Walker admitted that he had "brushed Al's silk hat the wrong way."

Curry was in the old mold of the Tammany regular, full of personal loyalties and hatreds, silent, noncommittal. He was formally elected by the district leaders by a bare margin of half a vote in June of 1929, but the re-election of Mayor Walker that November, by a majority of half a million votes over Representative Fiorello H. La Guardia, solidified his position. "In all appointments and other phases of official duties," Mayor Walker promised, he would "follow the judgment of that outstanding Democratic leader, John F. Curry."

Curry, the chief sachem of Tammany Hall all through the Seabury investigation, was a product of Manhattan's West 60's. He attained leadership of the new Hall on 17th Street through classic operations. Born in Ireland, he had been brought to New York before he was a year old, and he grew up along the Hudson River badlands. He became a Western Union messenger boy at thirteen, then a telegraph operator and accountant. Like Boss Murphy, he entered politics by way of athletics. The Palisades baseball club used him at shortstop; the West Side Athletic Club, in the hundred-yard dash. He caught the eye of "Two-Spot" Dan McMahon (also called "Sport"), his district leader. Sport taught him some of the rules of the vote-delivering game as played in the old Seventeenth District. Then he got him a job in the city's tax department. From there Curry became a sewer inspector. This led to a seat in the New York State Assembly.

McMahon was living a rich life in California and Florida by that time, and Curry saw his chance to assume the county leadership. He would have succeeded in his first try except for a small detail: McMahon came back and counted the votes himself. Curry was declared the loser. The following year, when Curry was prospering in the insurance business and also held the post of commissioner of records of the city's surrogate's court, he defeated the aging leader after another local dispute. Curry was regular; he was stubborn; he was a family man and a churchgoer. What if he lacked a high-school diploma? Olvany's college degree had contributed little to the party. As it happened, shortly after he came into the county leadership, an obscure institution of higher learning, Mount St. Mary's College, in Emmitsburg, Maryland, conferred on him a degree: "For philan-

thropy, knowledge of governmental affairs and executive ability."
He was now John Francis Curry, LL.D.

"I am the political leader of the dominant party in New York
City," he declared. As for reform, "The New Tammany is a fiction.
I will carry out the policies in which [sic] I grew up." He made no
attempt to conceal his dislike for former Governor Smith or present
Governor Roosevelt. He wanted no lectures about ethical behavior
or examples held up by Hyde Park aristocrats. He had work to do.

New York in the early 1930's was a big city to play with. Its population was 7,000,000. There were 20 billion dollars' worth of taxable
real estate. This property was taxed annually to the amount of $535,-
500,000; low assessments for knowing property owners were a key to
the Tammany spoils system. Six hundred million dollars a year went
to run the city government—$286,000,000 was paid to the 148,000
men and women holding city jobs. Many of these employees came
under the direct purview of Walker and Curry. Still the city was in
constant financial trouble trying to meet its bonded indebtedness.
At best, even for men of dedication and real ability, running New
York was a superhuman job. And New York had only Walker and
Curry.

What happened in the city affected the political lives of those who
ruled the state. "The Tammany policy as conducted by Mr. Curry
and Mayor Walker," wrote Walter Lippmann in his "Today and
Tomorrow" column in *The Herald Tribune,* "has been to get rid
of the Smith leadership in the local democracy. In the distribution
of state patronage in New York City, Governor Roosevelt has lent
his support to the Curry regime, and, therefore, to this policy.
Though he [Roosevelt] is unpopular with the rank and file of Tammany, he has had their organized support on election days. The political co-operation has been ruffled but not broken by the unhappy
necessity of investigating corruptions [sic] in New York, and a break
between Governor Roosevelt and Tammany has been avoided by a
kind of tolerant understanding on the part of the Tammany leaders
that what Governor Roosevelt had to do under pressure of public
opinion to let New York be investigated he had to do, and that what
he did not have to do he would not do."

Crime and corruption reached such proportions that the Citizens
Union, the City Club, and various other civic organizations de-

manded a cleanup. Governor Roosevelt had to act if the city wouldn't. The murder of Arnold Rothstein pointed up the general state of decay. Rothstein was the gambling czar of New York whose wires reached across the country. He was the banker for fixes in baseball and at the track, and he handled stolen and smuggled goods. "Rothstein is a man who dwells in doorways," his lawyer, William J. Fallon, said of him. "He's a gray rat, waiting for his cheese."

A trap was laid by other gamblers, to be sprung a week or so before Election Day, 1928. Rothstein sat at his table in the original Lindy's at 1626 Broadway, listening to the reports of his runners on gambling and drug peddling. He made this his headquarters, in spite of Mrs. Lindemann's efforts to discourage his patronage and that of the mobsters; in another corner of the boiled-chicken-and-cherry-cheese-cake emporium sat Damon Runyon, making mental notes on the prototypes of Harry the Horse, Milk Ear Willie, Big Nig and Sorrowful Jones. The rumor picked up by detectives was that Rothstein was supposed to be gunned down as he departed from Lindy's, picking his teeth, but this did not happen. It was not until two days before the election, while Rothstein sat in a big floating card game at the Park Central Hotel, that an "unknown man" upbraided him for welshing on his gambling debts, pulled out a pistol, and shot him in the groin. On Election Day, Rothstein died. The report was that Rothstein would have collected a million dollars in bets on Al Smith's loss in the presidential election.

The unsolved Rothstein murder dogged Walker's administration. The state Republican leader, W. Kingsland Macy, demanded an investigation of the police department. The Mayor replaced his ailing police commissioner, Charles B. Warren, who by a coincidence had been his law partner, with Grover Whalen, general manager of Wanamaker's department store and a former commissioner of plants and structures in Mayor Hylan's administration. Whalen ordered new uniforms for the policemen, carried on traffic campaigns and anti-Communist demonstrations, and greeted many dignitaries at City Hall; but he failed to find Rothstein's murderer.

Congressman La Guardia made the Rothstein case an issue in the fall of 1929, during his unsuccessful campaign for mayor. He charged that Magistrate Albert H. Vitale, who was lining up the Italian vote for Walker in the Bronx, was a friend of Rothstein's and had borrowed $19,600 from the gambler. This revelation could not defeat the idolized "night mayor of New York," as some called the night-clubbing Walker, but it did eventually bring an investigation by the Bar Association that led to Vitale's downfall. A month after the election, a seriocomic incident took place that proved Magistrate Vitale's underworld connections to be of the finest.

It happened at a testimonial dinner of the Tepecano Democratic Club at the Roman Gardens in the Bronx. The guest of honor, the Honorable Albert H. Vitale, stood up to acknowledge the plaudits of the crowd. Among the guests were various men with police records, including Ciro Terranova, the "Artichoke King." Suddenly six masked men, pistols drawn, entered the private dining room and lined the guests against the wall. A city detective handed his revolver to the robbers without attempting to use it. Vitale slipped off his diamond ring and hid it in his pants; a former magistrate, Michael Delagi, hid his diamond ring in his shoe. The six masked men took thousands of dollars from the guests, and disappeared. This unscheduled entertainment embarrassed Vitale, the honorary president-for-life of the Tepecano Democrats. He left the Roman Gardens at 2 A.M. and dashed to his Democratic clubhouse. Within two hours, he had rounded up all the money and jewelry that had been stolen at his party, restored the loot to the rightful owners, and seen to it that the detective's stolen gun was returned. The incident proved that Vitale knew how to reach "the boys."

In the same month that Seabury was appointed referee to investigate the magistrates' courts, and two years after the murder of Rothstein, a supreme court justice, Joseph Force Crater, stepped into a taxi in front of a restaurant on West 45th Street, waved good-bye with his Panama hat to two friends, and was never seen again. The case crisscrossed the investigation of the courts and, later, of the district attorney's office. Crater eventually became case No. 13595 on the records of the Bureau of Missing Persons as well as the object of a search that cost an estimated quarter of a million dollars.

The judge's disappearance was concealed for nearly a month, and then some extrajudicial matters about his off-bench activities were brought out. One of the friends he had waved good-bye to was Sally Lou Ritz, a striking Follies girl; Crater had a name as a skirt-chaser and big spender who played the Ziegfeld chorus line. At the same time he kept a divorcee for seven years in a midtown apartment, while downtown, on lower Fifth Avenue, he played the role of the devoted husband. Crater was close to the New York Democratic machine. He had served as president of a Tammany club on the Upper West Side of Manhattan and as Senator Wagner's law secretary. When Joseph Proskauer resigned from the bench, Governor Roosevelt, on the advice of Senator Wagner and Tammany, appointed Crater to the supreme court. The special grand jury investigating Crater's disappearance looked into his finances for clues. They discovered a shady real-estate deal, and they also found that when he had been appointed to the supreme court, there was a shift in his bank account of $22,500, a sum equivalent to one year's salary. In a time of bought judgeships, the natural conclusion was that Crater had paid Tammany for the opportunity to dispense justice.

The revelation that Crater might have bought his appointment suggested that an investigation of his affairs might overlap with the investigation of Magistrate George F. Ewald, who was charged with paying $10,000 for his judgeship to Martin J. Healy, deputy commissioner of plants and structures and a well-heeled Tammany leader. Ewald succeeded Vitale, who had been removed because of his link to Arnold Rothstein, and now Ewald was forced to resign not only because of the $10,000 payment, but because he was charged with using the mails to defraud in connection with the sale of mining stock.

"Till now nothing has come from the City Hall to indicate that Mr. Walker is aware of the discredit brought by his associates and subordinates upon his own record," *The New York Times* commented editorially. "When so many cracks show in the structure, there is lowered resistance to stress. The hour has come for the Mayor to summon both the demolition and reconstruction crews. It is not too late for Mr. Walker, who has in no personal way been even slightly connected with any of these scandals, to voice the indignation of the community which has twice elected him. A Republican investigation is both inevitable and desirable, however his own chances of re-election are shown to be affected by what is happening here."

But Mayor Walker had no time to pay heed to ivory-tower editorial writers. Hadn't the electorate reaffirmed its support of his administration and way of life? The ironies of the moment were pointed up by two news items that appeared the same day in the *East Hampton Star*. One announced with pride that a local resident, Judge Seabury, "who is very popular with both the summer colony and the permanent village," had received the investigative appointment and that "East Hampton will watch the proceedings with great interest." The other item was headlined: "Walker's Touch of Comedy Ends Montauk Raid Talk." The story disclosed that Mayor Walker had been caught in a gambling raid at the Montauk Island Club, but claimed to be a patron of only the restaurant part of the establishment. The Suffolk County district attorney, a gentleman called Wednesday Blue, was quoted as saying, "That satisfies me. I see the Mayor admits he was around when the raid occurred. I'm willing to let it go at that." What the local newspaper failed to mention was that the Mayor's girl friend, Betty Compton, was playing hazard for high stakes and His Honor was at her elbow. When the sheriff's raiders pounced, Walker hastily retreated to the restaurant and disguised himself in a waiter's apron. After the raid was over, the Mayor and Miss Compton sailed off on a getaway yacht moored in Montauk Harbor.

There were lots of laughs in the Walker nature; few mean bones in the slight body of the Broadway-tailored Mayor. Above all, he was loyal to incompetents and the political funhouse in City Hall. In addition to appointing the questionable magistrates, Walker appointed "Red Mike" Hylan to be judge of the children's court in Queens. When Alva Johnston asked him why he had appointed a man who had impugned his character, Walker told the reporter: "Alva, the appointment of Judge Hylan means the children now can be tried by their peer."

Unfortunately for Mayor Walker, however, what happened in Manhattan was watched closely by the Democratic governor in Albany. Indeed, as Al Smith pointed out to Walker before the 1928 presidential convention, a scandal involving the Mayor could harm a candidate from New York running for President. It could also embarrass a governor, and Governor Roosevelt was coming up for re-election in November, 1930, only a few months away. Roosevelt needed the co-operation of Tammany. He could afford to alienate neither Walker nor the independent voters who were watching him closely to see how he would handle Walker. In the state, he had to accomplish the familiar balancing act between Republican upstate and Democratic downstate—a feat that would be made even more difficult when, in the midst of the enlarged investigation by Seabury of the affairs of the City of New York, Roosevelt played the role of Walker's judge before the 1932 Democratic convention.

It is to Roosevelt's credit that his training as a lawyer prevailed. The leaders of the New York Bar encouraged him and so did the reform and religious groups in the city. He took an absolutely legalistic position about the investigation of the magistrates' courts. Roosevelt asked for the dangerous inquiry before the election and approved Seabury as referee, "by virtue of the Constitution and statutes of our state." Governor Roosevelt pointed out that the appellate division of the state supreme court (the First Judicial Department covered Manhattan and the Bronx) had supervision of all the inferior courts —and thus could remove any delinquent magistrates. Anticipating personal criticism, he stressed that "no other authority, not even the Governor," had the power of removal.

Mayor Walker's reaction to this intrusion was immediate and self-righteous. He, after all, had appointed the magistrates, usually upon the recommendation of Tammany district leaders. "No one welcomes such an investigation more than myself," he said. "If I didn't I would have been out long ago." However, he had a few more words on the subject. Referring to a letter written by Alderman Joseph C. Baldwin to Governor Roosevelt requesting that the investigation of Magistrate Ewald be extended to the office of the Mayor, Walker said, "Baldwin has done nothing but play politics. He is nothing but a politician, and a poor one. This letter seems to me to be a political hash of the last ten, perhaps twenty, years. If he can't cook up something better, then he ought to get out himself."

The city split into factions. Norman Thomas, Socialist leader and congressional candidate, said that Governor Roosevelt was "apathetic and subservient" to Tammany Hall. General James Harbord, chairman of the Republican advisory committee of New York County, said that Roosevelt had "chosen to stand for Tammany's crimes in the chief city of Tammany" in order to get the club's support at the polls. Heywood Broun, Socialist candidate for Congress in the Seventeenth District, took the broad view and threw the blame for local corruption on the Administration in Washington. The famous columnist wrote that President Hoover was adopting a politically partisan attitude "toward the tragic national crisis of unemployment." But all who commented approved Seabury's role in the investigation. C. C. Burlingham, ex-president of the Association of the Bar, and the most respected civic leader in the city, said that the appellate division "could not have selected a better man." From Hyde Park, Governor Roosevelt agreed.

As the investigation progressed, Mayor Walker appealed to the citizens to send him any information of petty graft. He pledged a cleanup of any little misdemeanors that might result from the day-to-day activities of 140,000 city employees.

Congressman La Guardia, whose accusations of graft and corruption in his unsuccessful campaign for mayor the previous fall now were emerging as facts, called Jimmy Walker's plea "a joke." La Guardia said: "How does he get away with it? Had I been elected, I would have cleaned out every city department myself. I would have removed every Tammany commissioner. The mere fact that the Mayor publicly states that there is petty graft is proof that the commissioners of the departments know there is. What chance has a poor pushcart peddler when a demand is made on him to pay his tribute? What chance has the plumber who cannot get a license unless he sees someone? And so it goes all down the line."

Seabury remained silent as the grand jury summoned various city officials. A pattern of reticence and hostility began to emerge. Seabury regarded the grand jury procedure as a warmup for his big show. An important matter was at issue: waiver of immunity from prosecution by city employees. Once again Roosevelt set down the law firmly in a letter to Walker which noted that a number of Walker's appointees had declined to waive immunity. "Whether they are within their legal rights in so doing is not the question," Roosevelt wrote from Hyde Park to City Hall. "Their action as government servants is contrary to sound public policy. I am asking therefore that you advise these gentlemen of this letter, and further, that you will suggest to them that they return before the special grand jury and voluntarily offer to waive immunity. They should freely answer any questions relating to their official acts. What I ask is that pleading of immunity by public officers in regard to public acts shall cease."

The Democratic state convention was about to begin and new complications developed. Walker replied publicly to Roosevelt by saying that his suggestion would be carried out promptly. Tammany chieftain Curry, who had refused to waive immunity himself, was packing his bags for the convention in Syracuse, and said merely that "a correspondence between the Governor and Mayor calls for no comment from me." His district leaders were spotted in key places in the city: sheriff, county clerk, commissioner of purchase, director of the budget, deputy commissioners of plants and structures, real-estate appraisers. They followed the leader. Even when Walker set a deadline for compliance with the Governor's "suggestion" that all public officers sign the waiver, the leaders refused to do so. Walker tried to save a little face by saying that they did not sign because of a Jewish holiday; in reply the newspapers ran a picture of Commissioner of Docks Michael Cosgrove as typical of those "observing" the holiday.

At the convention, however, the Democrats nominated Franklin Roosevelt again, and called for repeal of the Eighteenth Amendment and for a law forcing public officials to waive automatically their privilege against self-incrimination in respect to official acts. It was feared that Charles H. Tuttle, the Republican nominee, would make an issue of the refusal to testify; hence, the addition of the high-minded plank. Curry told his Tammany lieutenants that they would have to sign the waivers, but he placated them with promises that when the city put across the Democratic candidates, the Governor would ease up. Election Day came, the Democrats returned Roosevelt to Albany, and Walker, Curry, and the leaders felt that they were stronger than ever in spite of their unseated judges and magistrates. After all, they had delivered a huge plurality for F.D.R.

Meanwhile, Seabury quietly began to make his first moves. The revelations of the grand jury and his own talks with the appellate division justices impelled him to broaden the scope of the inquiry immediately. He insisted that not only the magistrates but the attorneys practicing in the lower criminal courts be investigated for "corrupt, fraudulent, unlawful or unprofessional" conduct. He was authorized to so enlarge his investigation, and appointed as his chief counsel Isidor Jacob Kresel, on advice of the city's Bar Association.

Kresel—who later became the target of Tammany's counterattack —was an important member of the New York Bar. At the age of

Samuel Seabury—A painting by Alfred Hoen that hangs in the library of the Association of the Bar of the City of New York.

The consecration of Samuel Seabury, the first Episcopal bishop in America and namesake of the Judge, took place in Aberdeen, Scotland, November 14, 1784. This mural, painted by John De Rosen, is in Grace Cathedral, San Francisco.

Samuel Seabury and Maud Richey were married on June 6, 1900, in the Chapel of the Good Shepherd at the General Theological Seminary, New York. Left to right: Lydia Seabury (Samuel's younger sister); Samuel and Maud; Emma Richey (Maud's sister), and two unknown bridesmaids.

Seabury, age twenty-seven, as a candidate
for the City Court of New York in 1901.
He took office January 1, 1902 — at
twenty-eight the youngest judge of that
court in the city's history.

Supreme Court Justice Seabury. As a
member of the New York State Supreme
Court before World War I, he wrote a number of important decisions upholding the rights of labor and the constitutionality of progressive social legislation.

This slide (originally in color) was used in Judge
Seabury's successful campaign for election to the court
of appeals, which he joined in 1914.

This campaign photograph showing Judge and Mrs. Seabury and their pet collie, Lassie, appeared in the *New York World* picture section, October 22, 1916, as part of a full page of pictures labeled "Samuel Seabury, Democratic Candidate for Governor of New York." The location is Wyandanch Farm, the Seabury's summer home in East Hampton, Long Island.

Campaigner Seabury. The Judge resigned from the court of appeals to run for governor on the Democratic ticket in 1916. He lost to Charles S. Whitman, who received Theodore Roosevelt's support, which the former President had promised Seabury. With the Judge is William F. McCombs, Democratic candidate for United States Senator.

Mrs. Samuel Seabury in the 1920's. This painting by Alfred Hoen hung in the Seabury town house on East 63rd Street, New York.

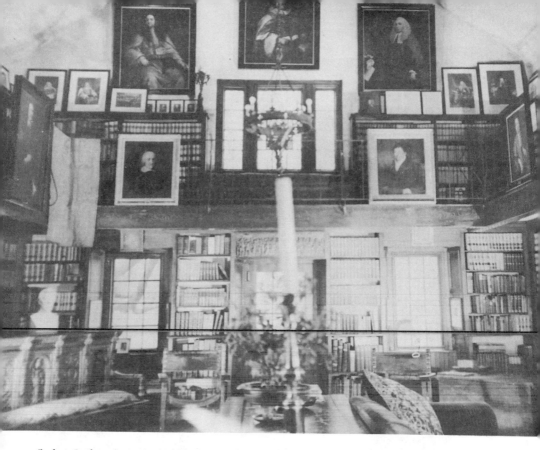

Judge Seabury's two-story library at the farm in East Hampton was filled with books on law, genealogy, social studies and literature—plus paintings of the Judge's ancestors and distinguished British jurists. (*Below*). Investigator Seabury (seated, sixth from left), with most of the members of his staff, at investigation headquarters, 80 Centre Street. To the left of Seabury is State Senator Samuel H. Hofstadter, chairman of the Joint Legislative Committee looking into the affairs of the City of New York.

Governor Roosevelt and investigator Seabury. On July 25, 1931, Governor
Roosevelt was the guest of Mr. and Mrs. Basil O'Connor at an informal
luncheon in Southampton. Several leaders of the Democratic party were
invited, including former Governor Alfred E. Smith. Judge Seabury, counsel
to the state committee investigating the City of New York, motored over from
his summer home at East Hampton to join Roosevelt.

Courtesy of the Franklin D. Roosevelt Library.

Sheriff Tom Farley was removed from office by Governor Roosevelt early in 1932 after Judge Seabury's revelations about the sheriff's "wonderful tin box." Drawing by Rollin Kirby in the *New York World-Telegram*.

Mayor Walker led paraders down Fifth Avenue during the "beer parade" of May 14, 1932. It was Walker's last moment of glory. On May 25 he was put on the witness stand by Judge Seabury and admitted receiving "beneficences."

Courtesy of Wide World Photos.

The Big Story. When Judge Seabury put Mayor Walker on the witness stand in the county courthouse, it was the major news of the day. This is the way *The New York Times* played the story—four columns on page 1, plus several pages more of text and reactions inside. The "minor" news reported on the front page included such items as a pitched battle between Nazis and Communists in the Prussian Diet Hall and President Hoover's campaign for renomination. (*Below.*) Confrontation. Judge Seabury had Mayor Walker on the stand for two days, May 25–26, 1932. Members of the state committee are on the bench as their counsel, Judge Seabury, reads evidence into the record. Thousands of citizens (many of whom were turned out by Tammany) cheered and booed the antagonists outside the jammed county courthouse.

Courtesy of Wide World Photos.

Judge Seabury's interrogation of Mayor Walker came as the culmination of more than a year's scrutiny of His Honor's private sources of income.

Courtesy of Wide World Photos.

Political interlude. Judge and Mrs. Seabury at the Democratic national convention in Chicago, June 30, 1932. The Judge was mentioned prominently as one of the dark-horse candidates if Governor Roosevelt's campaign faltered.

Courtesy of Wide World Photos.

"A Case for the S. P. C. A."—a drawing
by Rollin Kirby in the *New York World-Telegram*.

"Where It Hurts!"—a drawing by John
Cassel in the *Brooklyn Eagle*.

Judge Seabury and some of his associates arrive in Albany, August 10, 1932, for the hearings before Governor Roosevelt of the charges against Mayor Walker—the climax of the city-wide investigation. On the far right is George Trosk, Judge Seabury's chief assistant, and on the ground are some of their briefs and bundles of evidence.

Mayor Walker in Albany. Summoned to appear before Governor Roosevelt in the executive chamber, August 11, 1932, the Mayor arrived flanked by George Collins and John J. Curtin (his vociferous attorney, shown with his mouth open). The latter attempted—unsuccessfully—to lecture the Governor on the law.

Counsel Seabury in Albany in 1932. Here he poses on the steps of the Capitol: brief case in one hand, cigar and cane in the other, starched white shirt, chesterfield, derby, and characteristic enigmatic look behind the pince-nez.

Courtesy of the Associated Press.

(*Below*.) On December 1, 1932, Alfred E. Smith appeared at the invitation of Judge Seabury to suggest reforms in the New York City Charter. To the right of Smith are Assemblyman Hamilton F. Potter, vice chairman, and State Senator Samuel H. Hofstadter (wearing glasses), chairman of the Joint Legislative Committee.

Judge Seabury relaxed at Wyandanch Farm nearly every week end, with family, friends, and, during the investigation, members of his staff.

Campaigner at Cooper Union. On October 2, 1933, Judge Seabury addressed a Fusion mass meeting, formally launching the mayoralty campaign of Fiorello H. La Guardia. An overflow crowd heard him denounce Tammany's grip on the city.

Election night, November 7, 1933. The new Mayor of New York, "Major" La Guardia, and his chief supporter, Judge Seabury, celebrate the returns at Seabury's home. La Guardia was sworn into office on December 31, 1933, also at Judge Seabury's home, beginning the first of three terms of office as Mayor of New York.

Anti-Nazi stand. Judge Seabury sums up "The Case of Civilization Against Hitler" at a mass meeting of liberals, anti-Nazi activists, trade unionists and members of Jewish organizations at Madison Square Garden, March 7, 1934. As a result of his speech, Seabury became a target of the German-American Bundists.

Courtesy of the Associated Press.

To the father of good
city Government — now
three years old. The child
has grown into a sturdy
promising Youngster.
Marie & Fiorello La Guardia

"To the father"—an invitation from the La Guardias to the Seaburys to attend a ceremony before the start of the Mayor's second term. The hand-written note says: "To the father of good city government—now three years old. The child has grown into a sturdy promising youngster. Marie & Fiorello La Guardia."

Second term. Mayor La Guardia was sworn in for a second term on January 1, 1938, by Justice Philip J. McCook of the New York State Supreme Court. The Mayor had insisted that the ceremony be held where he first took the oath of office—in Judge Seabury's home.

Seabury and his "boys." On February 19, 1940, a group of associate and assistant counsel from the investigation staff of 1930–32 assembled at the Hotel Lafayette to celebrate the Judge's sixty-seventh birthday. The white-haired Seabury sits at the center of the table on the left.

La Guardia's funeral. Judge Seabury attended the services for former Mayor La Guardia in the Cathedral of St. John the Divine, September 22, 1947. At this time, the Judge was seventy-four.

Courtesy of The New York Times.

twenty-three, in 1901, he had been an assistant district attorney under William Travers Jerome. He was counsel to the New York State Assembly during the impeachment of Governor Sulzer. He served the Federal Government as a special Assistant Attorney General in antitrust and bankruptcy scandals. He frequently gave up his private practice as a trial lawyer and counselor to the major law firms in the city in order to help the Bar Association carry out a crusade. Only the year before he had prosecuted and caused to be disbarred dozens of lawyers involved in ambulance chasing. An immigrant from Galicia, who had gone through college from a crowded Stanton Street tenement by helping to tutor less gifted men at Columbia, he had lifted himself to the top of his profession.

The imperious Seabury and the diminutive Kresel (it was said that "he could run under a table wearing a high hat") made a formidable combination. It was Kresel who set the pattern for the investigation. From long experience as a prosecutor he knew where facts were buried. He knew that neither juries nor Tammany judges could dispute records. His technique, therefore, was to perform the unspectacular job of research: income-tax returns, bank-deposit slips, savings accounts belonging to members of a witness's family, brokerage statements, real-estate records, and other papers filed in the county clerks' offices.

The first public hearing was conducted by Seabury a little over a month after his appointment. On September 29, 1930, Seabury addressed a meeting of leaders of the bar and members of the press in the county courthouse. Anyone expecting spectacular revelations was disappointed. The newspapers played the story on the inside pages. Seabury simply defined the scope of the inquiry. "There are two paramount questions," he said, seeming to speak to his chief counsel more than to the crowd in the room. "What are the conditions in the magistrates' courts? Is justice being done?"

He promised that preliminary investigations would precede public hearings. "The essential facts can be ascertained only by laborious investigation," he said. "They do not lie patent upon the surface—they must be brought to light." And he then looked around the room and added something of significance to a score and more of young lawyers. "Especially to the junior members of the bar, from which the necessary legal staff must largely be recruited, I say: Give me your services in this work and you will have no cause to regret the sacrifices you may make, because your labors will be contributory to promoting justice in a judicial tribunal where the interests of the poor and helpless are primarily affected."

The response to his plea was not overwhelming; no large numbers of attorneys turned up at Seabury's law office or at the state building on Centre Street the next day. But, slowly the Judge began to assemble a group of young attorneys he was forevermore to call "my boys." Some seemed to come in almost by chance; others, after careful recruiting and recommendation. Most were under thirty-two years of age, and some were barely out of law school. Each was interviewed privately by Seabury, and, as they recall, enthusiasm for the cause was more of a qualification than experience. They proved to be inspired and often brilliant as legal bird dogs and general roustabouts in municipal affairs. Later they marveled at the quiet way in which Seabury brought out their best work and instincts. And loyalty.

Judge Seabury's staff included several of Kresel's own bright young men. Irving Ben Cooper had proved to be ingenious and tenacious during the ambulance-chasing investigation. Sidney Handler had also worked for Kresel on that inquiry. Philip W. Haberman, Jr., a friend of Kresel's, was offered an unpaid job for two months, which he gratefully took, and then was put on the staff and remained for two years. Herbert Levien asked the chief counsel for a job the moment he graduated from law school, because his brother had worked in Kresel's law office.

Others came for this, and, later, the bigger city-wide investigation, because of Seabury's appeal. When James H. Goodier, a former United States consul to Tahiti, returned to private practice, he found it lacked adventure. He read Seabury's plea, barged into the office unannounced, proved his enthusiasm, and was hired on the spot. Robert M. Davidson, a graduate of Harvard Law School, was the son of Maurice P. Davidson, a leader of the city's reform forces; the young Davidson was a member of the legislative committee of the Citizens Union and the City Club and therefore was aware of the need for the investigation. Oren Herwitz, George B. Levy, and Harold Melniker all joined the staff before they were admitted to the bar.

Seabury made a special effort to keep political considerations out of his selections. Yet he was aware that he had to strike a balance between Democrats and Republicans in order to bring full support behind his investigation from independents in the city. Jacob Gould Schurman, Jr., son of the former ambassador to Germany, and himself a former assistant district attorney, was a Republican, as was Harland B. Tibbetts, who had been a member of Kresel's law firm. Walter B. Walker, who had worked with Seabury on the Gould estate case, was also a Republican. It was through his friendship with Walter B. Walker, but at the prodding of Felix Frankfurter, that William G. Mulligan, a Democrat, joined the staff. Professor Frankfurter had advised Mulligan, who had been one of his best students at Harvard Law School, to get some experience in public service before going into private practice.

One of the assistant counsel, J. G. Louis Molloy, recalled later that religion as well as politics came up during his private interview with Seabury. Louis Molloy was a friend of a golfing friend of Bill Northrop's, who had suggested that he see the Judge. Their brief talk went:

"Why do you want to be part of this investigation?"

"I'm a Democrat and hope some day to be in politics."

"Have you ever been connected with Tammany Hall?"

"Yes, for one year. In 1927, I was an election district captain because I thought there might be a chance for younger Democrats in the party."

"Are you a Catholic?"

"Yes, a fallen-off, nonpracticing one, but if I have any religion at all, it's Catholic."

"I ask you that for only one reason. I am afraid that Tammany is going to counterattack by saying that we are going after Walker, Curry and the others on religious grounds."

A month later Seabury put Molloy on his staff. Carroll Hayes, a former municipal court justice and a vice president of the Catholic Lawyers Guild, also joined at the Judge's request. Seabury was prepared for any tricks. Personally and professionally he had repeatedly taken a stand against intolerance; now he enlisted a staff that covered a cross section of the city's legal talent.

The staff included some experienced men and some close associates of Seabury's. As usual, George Trosk prepared most of the papers and served as guide for the others. Henry J. A. Collins, who had been practicing in Seabury's office since 1924, served without pay during the magistrates investigation. So did Bill Northrop, acting as the Judge's confidential assistant. Another nephew, Andrew Oliver, had just finished Harvard Law School when "Uncle Sam" put him to work.

Judge Seabury turned to Raymond Moley, professor of public law at Columbia, for advice on matters of bail, probation, social welfare, and the administration of the criminal laws of New York state. "I came to know Seabury in the early days of the magistrates investigation," Moley later recalled, "because of my book *Our Criminal Courts*. It was in part a summary of my findings and conclusions after ten years of study in law administration in various states. The book was given to Seabury by my friend Basil O'Connor, Roosevelt's law partner. Seabury felt that I could be helpful and summoned me from California, where I was on vacation. I was a member of his staff for a year or more, formulating plans for reforming the courts and working on his final report to the appellate division." Conducting an investigation required a varied and dependable staff, and Seabury, like Roosevelt, knew how to engage the best talents of his brain trusters.

At the first full staff meeting, Seabury uttered a slogan to remember: "Old heads for counsel—young heads for war."

That was to be the line of attack in the next two years. He spoke frankly to his men: "The public will not be aroused to an awareness of conditions in the magistrates' courts through a series of graphs, charts and reports. We must divorce this investigation, as far as is possible, from legalistic machinery. There is more eloquence in the testimony of an illiterate witness telling of oppression suffered from legal processes than in the greatest sermon, editorial, or address ever written. Where preachers, editors, and lawyers have failed in arousing the public to a consciousness of unjust conditions these simple, unlearned witnesses will succeed."

If the people were being rooked, Seabury's group would go to the people and find out how and why.

At this point, Lincoln Steffens attempted to bring his great prestige to help calm the storm under way in New York. The crusades in *McClure's* and *The Shame of the Cities* were a quarter of a century behind him; his personal reputation was bonded strongly in publishing history. He had been a journalist *engagé,* associated with liberal and radical movements, helping to change governments by exposure in St. Louis, Minneapolis, Pittsburgh, and Philadelphia. Now, at age sixty-four, he met with Maurice P. Davidson, a leader of both the Citizens Union and City Club, which were marshaling support for Judge Seabury's investigation.

"The thing to do," said Steffens, "is to have a frank talk with Jimmy Walker, and say, 'This won't do. Of course we know that vice, lawlessness and civic corruption cannot be eliminated but at least it should be kept under control. After all, the people will be satisfied with nothing less than the outward appearance of decency, no matter how bad things are beneath the surface.' "

Steffens was a little old, a little cynical, by now, and Davidson said that the citizenry would not submit to anything less than full exposure of the conditions in New York City. The ties between crime and politics were too strong to be overlooked. It was now the time for new voices—voices such as those of the fighting journalist Heywood Broun, and of the anti-Tammany Democratic lawyer Samuel Seabury, both of whom knew what was going on in Manhattan and felt an obligation toward their city.

Few ever knew this man Seabury intimately. Few were ever aware that what he was undertaking would turn out to be not one investigation, but three: the magistrates' courts; the office of the district attorney; the affairs of the entire City of New York. These full-scale inquiries, culminating in the resignation of Mayor Walker and leading to the Fusion government of Mayor La Guardia, would last two years. Certainly only Seabury's intimates knew that his whole life's bearing was behind the fierce brief he was about to present against Tammany.

CHAPTER **10**

The Magistrates' Courts Investigation

EACH morning at 8:25, Nick Livingston, at the wheel of the dark green Lincoln with SS–19 on the license plates, pulled up in front of the six-story mansion on East 63rd Street. Seabury asked him to be there promptly at 8:30. But ever since the Judge had begun to drive to the state building at 80 Centre Street instead of to the private law office at 120 Broadway, his eagerness to get going made him step out the front door five minutes early. There seemed to be a new spring in his stride as he walked toward the limousine. Once inside, he settled back, lit his pipe, and read a newspaper (turning first to accounts of the investigation) during the brief ride downtown.

Seabury was the fulcrum about which his assistants turned. He devoted his energies equally to planning strategy with Kresel and to following the progress of the investigative attorneys. At the outset of the magistrates investigation, he had abandoned his own practice. Trosk remained at 120 Broadway for a while to finish up the private cases, but he, too, soon gave most of his time to preparing the reports at 80 Centre Street. Dorothy Benner found herself reporting directly to the Judge at the state building; he would not trust a strange secretary with the confidential information culled from the private hearings. Someone had to handle the affairs at the law office, however, and the thankless job was given to Bernie Richland, who spent most of his time redirecting people with complaints to the investigation office. No new business was accepted by Samuel Seabury, Esq., for the next two years, and his practice shrank to nothing, but he continued to pay the salaries of his personal staff out of his own pocket.

The investigation got down to business. The young lawyers began to gather the evidence. One day in that fall of 1930, Judge Seabury called out, "Let me know when you're ready, Mr. Cooper." Irving Ben Cooper shared an office with George Levy and Philip Lowry, and he was told to develop his own cases. Police corruption and the vice ring were the core of the troubles in the magistrates' courts, and Cooper plunged into the muck enthusiastically. He worked twelve and fourteen hours a day, lunching on sandwiches and milk shakes. "I was full of fight and inspired by the Judge," he later recalled. "I would ride with a police car when a witness was being brought in to make sure that nobody was tipped off ahead. It was not exactly a safe occupation, because you didn't know which cops were on the side of the law. This was brought home to me when I applied for life insurance during the investigation—and was turned down as a bad risk."

All day Cooper tracked down leads in the courts and around the city. Then witnesses were brought in for a private cross-examination. The usual procedure was to tender them a "request" subpoena: "You are hereby requested" (rather than "ordered"), the subpoena read, though few witnesses realized that they had a choice in the matter. Those who were tipped off in advance that they were about to be requested to come into 80 Centre Street avoided the process server. In some such cases, Seabury used the newspapers to determine their whereabouts; many a co-operative reporter helped to flush a recalcitrant witness. And, suddenly, there were many tipsters—mostly people with vivid imaginations, but some with real information—who saw in Seabury and his investigators an outlet for their long pent-up grievances.

Once Cooper presented Judge Seabury with a problem. One of his witnesses, who had worked with the higher-ups of the underworld, had been promised that, in return for his testimony, Cooper would not refer to a lesser phase of his activity. Later, it developed that the witness had lied about this part of his underworld life—and, independently, Cooper had discovered the true information. Cooper asked Seabury if it would be all right to pursue this untold aspect of his informer's life openly.

"There is an implied promise on our part not to," Judge Seabury said. "The witness spelled out a promise from us and we cannot renege."

"But he was not telling me the whole story," Cooper said, "and, therefore, we are no longer obliged to suppress this aspect of his life."

"It's a matter of fair dealing," Seabury replied. "If you bring this out, the witness will feel that he has been betrayed."

"But this witness is an underworld character!" Cooper argued. "He's a nobody!"

Judge Seabury looked above his glasses for an instant at his eager assistant. "Not a nobody," he said gently.

Hearings were held in private and in public. In the private hearings, which began October 9, 1930, and ended a little over a year later, 1,059 witnesses were examined. The minutes of their examinations covered 15,356 pages. "Some of this testimony seemed to me, in view of the public interests involved, to require presentation at public hearings," Judge Seabury told the appellate division. The public hearings began September 29, 1930, and continued for nearly eight months. At these open hearings, 299 witnesses were examined, the transcript of their testimony covering 4,596 pages.

Before a witness appeared in public, Seabury insisted that the facts be recorded in private testimony. By the time a witness went on the stand, the referee was no longer stalking but closing in for the kill. With the testimony of over a thousand witnesses recorded privately, Seabury's big task was to separate the small-time malefactors from the big-time operators. Before a public hearing, the assistant counsel who had interrogated a witness was called in to brief the referee, who would cross-examine the witness personally, or direct his chief counsel, Isidor Kresel, to do so.

Seabury had a favorite expression: "Educate me." It was the job of his staff to "educate" him on every detail of a particular case. They found him dogged in the pursuit of the significant facts behind a witness's testimony. Often briefing sessions took place at the house on 63rd Street, with the young staff attorney properly awed by his surroundings. After dinner he was offered a Scotch and a Havana cigar, and was then asked to present the background of a witness to be examined publicly the following morning. Seabury seldom displayed anger when the attorney described the activities of underworld characters. But listening to the tale of a rogue magistrate on the bench who had bribed his district leader and paid obeisance to Tammany, Seabury could not restrain himself from uttering the closest thing to a profanity that ever crossed his lips. "That's despicable!" he muttered, and he made it sound like a thunderbolt delivered to earthlings from a Higher Authority.

The magistrates' courts inquiry almost immediately uncovered a racket in which innocent women were framed as prostitutes by an alliance of police officers, bondsmen, lawyers, assorted court clerks and fixers, magistrates and, inevitably, the politicians in power who were responsible for political appointments around the lowest criminal courts in New York City. The most notorious tale was told by a stool pigeon, Chile Mapocha Acuna, thereafter the subject of a limerick in which he was called the "Human Spittoona." Acuna was only one of a handful of Runyonesque characters who hung around the police department vice squad, acting as *agents provocateurs* in false arrests. Others included such fine types as "Dove," "Pinto," Meyer Slutsky, "Chico," Harry Levey, and "Harry the Greek." All worked for the headquarters or Nineteenth Division roving squad as well as for the various vice squads in every borough of the city.

As Acuna, a thirty-one-year-old native of Santiago, Chile, began to tell his story on the witness stand before a packed courtroom, Judge Seabury ordered all women present to leave. The story, he decided, was too sordid for delicate ears. He had heard it in private after Cooper had persuaded Acuna that the investigation was on the level and that he would be protected. Seabury, Kresel, and Cooper first had to prove their good intentions before Acuna would talk. It took them three days to do so. Acuna, who had been double-crossed and jailed for a year by the vice-squad police, knew that his life was worth little once he testified. Police Commissioner Edward P. Mulrooney assigned six police lieutenants to guard him in shifts around the clock, letting them know that if Acuna died they would never reach captain.

Acuna lived. His testimony alone was sufficient to frighten and

shake up a large part of the police department—the first in a series
of revelations that reached higher and higher. "He was a witness
without parallel in the history of American jurisprudence," Judge
Seabury said.

Acuna testified that his job framing women in vice raids paid him
about $150 a week in 1929. He always received a share of the take
from raids on real houses of prostitution whose addresses he furnished. When business was slack, the vice squad swooped down upon
the Negro section of Harlem, crashed flats, and made arrests at random. But the vice squad's major activity was staging raids in which
Acuna or one of the other stool pigeons was "caught" passing money
to an innocent woman. After the stool pigeon named twenty-eight
vice-squad police who had employed his unique services, Seabury
asked him if any were present. Acuna stepped down from the witness stand and, walking through the audience, identified twenty-
eight policemen by name. Police Commissioner Mulrooney, sitting
in the court, took down their names. (Their activities dated from
Commissioner Whalen's term of office.) The men squirmed uncomfortably, but none protested.

"Tell us," suggested Kresel, "how you went about gathering evidence in these cases."

"Well," said Acuna, "we usually ate about one P.M. and nine P.M.,
while the roll was being called in the station houses. Then we'd stroll
around in front, where a detective friend would meet us. If we had
any addresses, we gave them to him. He would give us five or ten
dollars in marked bills. Then we would all set our watches together.
We would arrange it so I would just have time to give the marked
bills to a girl and watch where she put them, so the detectives could
get the evidence. Then when the policeman entered they would go
through their little comedy with me. They would insult me and
accuse me of everything they could imagine, and I would deny it all,
insisting that the woman was my wife and I had been there for days.

"Then they would take me into another room and pound on the
wall, to make it sound as though they were beating me, but it was
just more of the comedy. Finally I would give them a fictitious name
and address and hurry back to the station house. They would always
bring in the girls as prisoners. The next day when the case came up
in the magistrates' court the officer would testify that the man in the

case was unknown and could not be found. I was always the unknown man."

"Did you always succeed in getting the evidence you went after?" Kresel asked.

"Oh, no," Acuna said, smiling, "lots of times, thirty or forty times, there was no evidence."

"Now this is important," Kresel broke in. "Tell us whether you informed the arresting officer in those cases that there was no evidence."

"Yes, lots of times the police would come before I had time to get the evidence. Once I was standing in the doorway arguing with a woman when they came in. I told them I had not had time to get the evidence and gave them back the marked bills. They kicked me out and made the arrest, anyway."

A pattern began to emerge. The vice squad carried out direct and indirect types of arrests. In the direct type, the officer himself was a party. He approached a woman and arrested her after she had accepted money for prostitution and was prepared to carry out her bargain. In the indirect, the stool pigeon, the "unknown man" of police blotters, was the customer when the police broke in. The police developed a number of ingenious variations in making indirect arrests. In the "doctor's racket," the stool pigeon, posing as a patient, entered a doctor's office while the doctor was away and demanded treatment. He placed money in a conspicuous spot and, despite the protests of the nurse, began to undress, whereupon the police officers entered and placed the nurse under arrest for prostitution. The "landlady racket" was also popular. After renting a room in a boarding house and paying for it with marked money, the stool pigeon brought his alleged wife to the premises. Almost immediately, the police officers broke in, arrested the girl for offering to commit prostitution, and arrested the landlady for maintaining a house of prostitution. Thus the vice-squad officers obtained double graft.

In between Acuna's testimony incriminating the police, Referee Seabury subpoened the records of the magistrates' courts in the prostitution cases that had resulted from the stool-pigeon arrests. In some cases, innocent women languished in prison, merely on the word of arresting officers. Now Seabury had Kresel reveal the stories of these women in court. New Yorkers found it hard to believe that such things could happen in broad daylight in their city; Seabury, recalling for his colleagues Dr. Parkhurst's revelations in the 1890's, assured them that they had happened and could happen again.

One case was that of "Betty Smith"—a fictitious name assigned by Seabury for the record to a young married woman. Shortly before Christmas, 1929, "Betty Smith" was in her apartment with a Mr. Hazelton, a friend of her husband's who was their agent in a real-estate transaction, waiting for her husband to arrive for dinner. Two vice-squad officers broke into her home, and after abusing Mr. Hazelton, placed her under arrest and took her away. Seabury noted in his report of the "Betty Smith" case:

> I shall not mention the wholly disgusting indignities suffered by "Mrs. Smith" prior to her trial. Suffice it to say that when she went on trial charged with committing an act of prostitution with one "Joseph Clark," who was not produced at the trial and who, according to the police officer, gave an address which would locate him somewhere in the midst of the Hudson River, the vice officer took the stand before the magistrate and delivered himself of the case-hardened, stereotyped story customarily employed when a conviction was desired. Three witnesses testified to her good character. The vice officer changed his testimony and said that there were two men in the apartment when he made his unlawful entry. Incredible as it may appear, "Betty Smith" was convicted by Magistrate Stanley Renaud and locked up in a cell in Jefferson Market Prison. She was later taken to Harlem Prison, pending a medical examination and probationary investigation. By reason of the shock inflicted upon her sensibilities, and the brutal treatment she received in the prison, her nervous system suffered a reaction which kept her in confinement, surrounded by hardened and despicable characters, for over two weeks, before the necessary medical examination could be made. After this lapse of time, "Mrs. Smith" was returned to the women's court and placed on probation for six months. Near the end of the probationary period, her conviction was reversed by the court of special sessions.

Such stories had their effect on the city and state. Commissioner Mulrooney suspended every policeman—from patrolman to deputy inspector—identified by the stool pigeons. Departmental trials were held, as the district attorney's office went through the motions of presenting evidence against policemen accused of testifying falsely against innocent women. Speaking to a group of social workers at

City Hall, Mayor Walker took official notice for the first time of the sordid crimes going on under his nose. "I will confess," he declared, "I have been more or less shocked by the reports of the framing of innocent women."

Heywood Broun commented on the Mayor's belated discovery:

> In this duel between "less" and "more" the former has won the day, for the city's chief executive is about to take a vacation of three or four weeks at Palm Springs, since of late he has been more or less under the weather. I have no doubt that James Joseph Walker is ailing. In fact, I am surprised that he feels as well as he does. It seems to me unlikely that his health can be as precarious as that of the City of New York at the present moment. "Some of these reports have been exaggerated," says the Mayor. Suppose only one woman had been framed. And even suppose that lone case had concerned a notorious harlot. Even then I think we should expect from the Mayor something much stronger than "more" or "less."

If the Mayor decided he would rather be in Palm Springs than in New York that December of 1930, at least Governor Roosevelt was concerned. Now he addressed himself to Judge Seabury:

> In common with thousands of other citizens of our state I have been deeply disturbed and greatly incensed by the unearthing by the investigation being conducted by you showing framing up of women by some members of the so-called police vice squad. The investigation by you is, of course, continuing, but another question has been raised by the definite disclosures which have already been reported by the press. I refer to the cases of women who have already been convicted and sentenced under similar conditions of frame-up. Something should be done immediately to determine whether, if these charges are found in any way to be true, these women previously convicted should have their cases reopened or brought before the Governor with recommendations for executive clemency.

Seabury immediately recommended that six women, on parole after serving sentences for prostitution, be granted pardons—and Governor Roosevelt did so. At the same time, the Governor suggested that District Attorney Crain get busy and follow up with prosecutions of the offending police officers. As referee, Seabury had no power to initiate criminal actions; he could only make recommendations. His authority ended when he forwarded copies of the record of testimony to the district attorney and police commissioner.

But Seabury was aware of the power of publicity and of the press. He was learning how to make headlines for the afternoon papers and at the same time leave a promise for the morning papers. The frame-up cases had produced results quickly. The accounts appealed to readers of the *New York Daily News* as scandal and readers of *The New York Times* as sociology. When Polly Adler, billed as the city's most notorious vice "entrepreneuse," made her appearance before Seabury and his assistants at 80 Centre Street, even the stuffiest citizens of the metropolis were interested. Everyone wanted to know "who's who after the sun goes down," as the *New York World-Telegram* phrased it, "and what connection if any exists between the police and the profession of which she is the acknowledged chatelaine." If police officers could make a healthy profit from vice as a sideline, surely those who were running the "business" were making a fortune.

Miss Polly Adler herself later described what it was like to be a witness at the Seabury investigation—though she concealed many details. On the day she was subpoenaed, her friend "Irwin O'Brien," a vice-squad officer, was in her apartment. She claimed to have stalled the process server long enough for O'Brien to slip out the window and flee down the fire escape—a sixteen-flight walk—unnoticed by the raiders or reporters. "I learned that the Seabury staff had been instructed to knock themselves out to be courteous, and I was treated with unusual consideration so long as they thought there was a chance I might prove a co-operative witness," she recalled. "On that first day, the questioning was conducted by Harland B. Tibbetts, a mild-mannered, soft-spoken man. Also present were two assistant counsel—Philip W. Haberman, Jr., and the man who, I sensed, would be my real antagonist, Irving Ben Cooper. Although he never spoke during the questioning, his piercing eyes never left my face and his silence was like an attack."

The first session with Miss Adler was devoted to an examination of police docket books to confirm the dates of her arrests (she had used many aliases). On her next trip to Centre Street, she was turned over to Irving Ben Cooper:

He wasted no time on the amenities and began firing questions at me the moment I came into the room. Did I know a certain man? No. Had I been at a certain place at a certain time? I didn't remember. For what seemed hours he continued to throw names at me, and I continued to deny knowing all except those who could not possibly be hurt by our acquaintanceship. At the end of the long afternoon, Cooper glared at me out of sharp blue eyes that seemed to bite into me: "You are positive you don't know these men?" "Positive." "You understand, Miss Adler, that everything you say is being taken down by a court stenographer?" You're telling me, brother, I thought to myself. But aloud I said demurely, "Yes, I understand."

Cooper delved deeper and deeper into her financial affairs. Photostatic copies of her bank and brokerage accounts were turned over to him, and he questioned her about every deposit and transaction, looking for payoffs to public and police officials. At one point Cooper, exasperated by her unwillingness to admit to bribing the authorities, said, "Why don't you tell the truth?" "I am telling the truth," she said. Finally, he said, "I think we'd better let you have a talk with Mr. Samuel Seabury."

Miss Adler, a self-described student of the human condition, recalled Judge Seabury as "a gray-haired, fine-looking man who treated me with meticulous politeness." Seabury named a number of Tammany leaders, including the Mayor himself, and delicately asked her if it was not true that they had "celebrated" important events at her house. She responded with "No" or "I don't recall" to most of his questions. Then, still politely, he confronted her with one of "O'Brien's" checks. "It's a policeman's paycheck, is it not, Miss Adler? And you will notice that it is endorsed with a capital *P*," he said. He showed her the letter *P,* but held his finger over the signature above it. Feebly, she denied that it was her handwriting. Seabury did not press her but merely said, "Think it over, Miss Adler. Refresh your memory, and give me your answer tomorrow."

It was obvious that Seabury was not trying to persecute Miss Adler or to wipe out sin. And, indeed, so far as she was concerned, the Seabury investigation turned out to be beneficial. "The police no longer were a headache; there was no more kowtowing to double-crossing vice-squad men, no more hundred-dollar handshakes, no more phony raids to up the month's quota. In fact," she said, "thanks to Judge Seabury and his not-very-merry men, I was able to operate for three years without breaking a lease."

If the effects were unintentionally helpful to Miss Adler and her sisters, the police officers themselves were permanently exposed. After dismissal from the force, some were jailed for income-tax evasion. The swollen bank accounts of the vice-squad officers were explained in odd ways—giving birth to the famous "tin box" tales.

The thoroughness of the Seabury–Kresel technique was shown when more than a hundred patrolmen, officers, and members of their families were checked, through birth certificates, marriage licenses, and other public records. Two thousand banks and brokerage houses were served with blanket subpoenas to determine who held accounts under what names. One policeman banked $90,000 in five years; a lieutenant in the same period was able to deposit $184,000 in his own and his mother's name. How? The answers were nearly all the same: racetrack winnings and generous gifts from rich uncles. But why so many visits to the safe-deposit box? One police lieutenant claimed it was because he put in and took out his wife's earrings once a week.

Lieutenant Peter J. Pfeiffer had the historic honor of being the first person during the Seabury investigations to claim the existence of a magical tin box in a bank where he kept his cash and insurance papers. A check showed that he made five visits a month to the vault. The lieutenant explained that he did so not to put in cash but to inspect, over and over, his insurance papers. Officer James Quinlivan kept his money at home in a box and a trunk. He had won $9,000 on a horse named Flora Belle, on a tip given to him by a drunken jockey, but, when the officer was pressed for details, nothing more about either the unnamed jockey or the named horse could be discovered. Officer Robert E. Morris had a wonderful "Uncle George" who handed him forty $1,000 bills on a street in Coney Island and, thereafter, dropped dead somewhere in California.

"Where did you keep the forty thousand dollars?" Kresel asked.

"Right in the house," Morris replied.

"Where in the house?"

"I had it in a box."

Seabury interrupted to ask innocently, "In a tin box?"

"In a tin box," Morris said, in the reply that was becoming a standard joke.

But it was the magistrates who were the object of this inquiry. Magistrate Albert H. Vitale, shortly before Seabury's appointment, had been removed by the appellate division because of his friendship and business dealings with Arnold Rothstein. Magistrate George Ewald had been obliged to resign because he had bought his position for $10,000. The Seabury investigators now began to accumulate testimony showing that some of the people who worked in or around the lower criminal courts—bondsmen, clerks, court attendants, assistant district attorneys, certain favored lawyers—were receiving a share of the payoffs in the vice cases as well as in cases resulting from gambling arrests and convictions. Referee Seabury declared:

> The ring operating mainly in the women's court was a shocking example of the lengths to which distortion of law to illegal ends was carried in the magistrates' courts. It was made up of interlocking halves, the lawyers, the bondsmen and the fixers, on the one hand, and members of the so-called vice squad of the police department and their stool pigeons, on the other. Whatever the motives of the magistrates may have been in sitting back and permitting this outrageous spectacle to be enacted before them day in and day out, the effect of it is not in doubt: it permitted the lawyers, the fixers, and the bondsmen who operated in these courts to reap a rich harvest. What I am criticizing is the supineness of the magistrates in the face of palpably perjurious testimony by police officers.

Seabury and Kresel decided that their mandate required them to investigate every magistrate in New York City. They called in these judges one by one to see if they were fit to hold office. The first interrogations were held in private; then some judges were asked to repeat their testimony in public. Suddenly there was a wave of resignations.

Magistrate Francis X. McQuade, who had held office for nineteen years, resigned on the eve of his appearance, "obviating the necessity for a trial," the referee said. Through a dummy, Magistrate McQuade was a stockholder in the Polo Grounds Athletic Club, a corporation organized to sponsor fights in New York. He had also served as treasurer of the New York Giants before his services were dispensed with by Charles L. Stoneham and John J. McGraw, the team's owner and manager respectively. The sports-minded magistrate's interests included stock in highly speculative oil corporations and, most serious of all, in the Havana Casino, the Cuban gambling establishment. The magistrate was entitled to 5 per cent of the casino's income. His resignation was considered a triumph for Jacob Gould Schurman, Jr., who had been assigned by Seabury and Kresel to conduct the preliminary inquiry of McQuade. In spite of the resignation, Seabury refused to rub it in, saying, "There was much evidence submitted tending to show serious defects of temperament manifested in the discharge of his judicial duties. Notwithstanding what has been said about him, it is only fair to state that no evidence was received by the referee showing any act of corruption."

Magistrate Henry M. R. Goodman was the next to resign, giving "ill health" as the reason, and again Seabury refused to pursue his case further, saying: "I think it is fair not to comment in detail upon matters as to which no investigation was really completed." Then Magistrate George W. Simpson hurriedly resigned, also for the good of his health—he suffered from arthritis in one finger. Seabury's men found out that Simpson, who had sat for many years as presiding magistrate in the commercial frauds division of the magistrates' court, had disposed of cases in suspicious ways. "In one case," said the referee, "examination of witnesses concerned in the sale of obscene literature disclosed irregularities which, if known to Magistrate Simpson, would have necessitated the filing of charges against him [Simpson]."

Louis B. Brodsky was New York's "wealthiest magistrate," and Seabury wanted to know why. He got his answer when Brodsky decided to fight to retain his post. He was president and director of six real-estate corporations and an officer in several more; these corporations bought and sold numerous parcels of improved real estate in New York City. He was also a stock-market speculator with eleven brokerage accounts; his marginal operations while on the bench amounted to $7,000,000. Brodsky's real-estate and stock losses amounted to hundreds of thousands of dollars. During his hearings, he refused to produce any financial records, but again a tin box was discovered. Seabury reported that Brodsky had given Edward J. Byrne, son-in-law of James J. Hagan, the political leader responsible for this appointment, power of attorney in one brokerage account. Mr. Byrne held a political job as secretary to the tenement house department at a salary of $4,250 a year, yet admitted that he had some $40,000 in his tin box at home—not including $6,000 he received from Brodsky as "repayment of a loan."

The Seabury–Kresel technique was becoming well co-ordinated: one would ask the questions and the other would pin down evasive witnesses. In the Brodsky hearings, politeness and anger alternated. "I want to give you now an opportunity to make explanations about anything you choose," Kresel told Brodsky. "But I am unprepared to take advantage of your kindness," Brodsky replied. "I told you at the last hearing that you would have an opportunity," Seabury said sharply, "and you have had since last October to produce your checks and always you have asked for more time. You will have to make your statement now."

Brodsky did not reveal anything of an incriminating nature about himself and had explanations, though no records, for most of his huge business dealings. Referee Seabury turned over his evidence to the appellate division, and three trials followed, with Kresel and Seabury acting as prosecutors. These trials were memorable only for one incident—Magistrate Brodsky's peroration on his own behalf, in which he produced a copy of former Senator Vest's corny prose tribute to dogs: ("A man's reputation may be sacrificed in a moment of ill-considered action. . . . But a man's dog stands by him in prosperity and in poverty, in health and in sickness," etc.) and read it at length to the court. The majority of the appellate division judges found that Brodsky's outside business speculations were not sufficient cause to remove him from the bench. It was Seabury's first setback; Tammany considered the Brodsky acquittal a major victory.

But then came the trial of Magistrate Jean H. Norris, the first woman judge in New York City history. She had been George W. Olvany's coleader in the Tenth Assembly District of Manhattan, a fiery suffragette who had been held up as a shining example of woman emancipated. As a loyal Democrat, she had appealed to Boss Murphy in 1919 to give her a judgeship and Murphy had nodded and said, "Go home and say nothing more about it." In the fall of 1919, she was appointed a temporary magistrate by Mayor Hylan. From Harlem Court to women's court, she immediately gained a reputation for harshness, in spite of her pledge that the prostitutes and "poor unfortunate members of the weaker sex who appear before me will be dealt with in kindness; they will be handled with gloves of velvet rather than fingers of steel." Her record showed many severe jail sentences and few acquittals. She spoke in an affected manner with the acquired accent of a self-important person; nobody would ever have guessed that Judge Norris was a Brooklyn girl. "More than one humble streetwalker," noted Milton MacKaye of the *New York Evening Post,* "incarcerated in the workhouse for one hundred days, was warmed and comforted by the knowledge she had been sentenced by a lady."

Seabury's investigators learned that Magistrate Norris often convicted "prostitutes" on uncorroborated testimony of vice-squad police. They were tipped off about a case in which she had changed the court record in order to conceal her highhanded treatment of an unjustly convicted woman whose attorney was not allowed to present a full case in defense. Fortunately, the court stenographer had saved the true record of the minutes of the case before the prejudicial remarks by Magistrate Norris were stricken out. Whole pages of the stenographer's transcript had been cut by the lady magistrate.

When she was summoned to a public hearing by Seabury and confronted with her falsified records, she gave tedious explanations. Seabury scored several points when he questioned her about certain business dealings. She was a stockholder in the Equitable Casualty and Surety Company, which issued bail bonds she was frequently called upon to approve in her judicial capacity. And she picked up a little extra money by posing in her judicial robes for national-magazine advertisements that quoted her as saying, "Recently one of my friends suggested that I try eating Fleischmann's Yeast, which I did— skeptically enough in the beginning but thankfully enough at the expiration of only two weeks, as the improvement in my digestion resulted in more restful sleep than I had had for years."

Seabury brought Magistrate Norris before the appellate division. Martin Conboy, a prominent Catholic layman, served as her attorney, and all of Tammany's leaders were rooting for him. Seabury, aided by Harland B. Tibbetts, George Trosk, and Sydney Handler of his staff, personally presented the case against her before Presiding Justice Edward R. Finch and the four other justices of the appellate division. They found her conduct in the courtroom unworthy of a magistrate.

In the course of his presentation, Referee Seabury showed that he was much more broad-minded about human behavior than many of his accusers, then and later, who looked at his dignified mien and immediately pronounced him a stuffed shirt. Conboy tried to trip up Seabury in his defense of Magistrate Norris by pleading her high moral purpose in one particular case where she had convicted a twenty-year-old girl as a wayward minor on hearsay evidence. The young lady had been living with a gentleman not her husband while attending the Art Students' League.

"The girl was living as a mistress when she came into court, and Judge Seabury says that she should have been permitted to go back and live as a mistress," Conboy cleverly argued.

"Look at the record of that case," Seabury retorted. "There is not a scrap of legal proof there. The girl was living with a man, but that is not a crime in this state. It is not a question of Judge Seabury sending that girl back to a life of sin. That is not the issue. It is simply that there was no legal evidence that she was a wayward minor. It was none of Magistrate Norris' business what happened to the girl after she was out of court. It was the magistrate's business to see that the girl's rights were protected. She should have reprimanded the arresting officer for bringing that child into court on such evidence."

The appellate division unanimously ordered Magistrate Norris's removal from the bench. So ended the career of New York's first lady judge and the darling of Tammany Hall.

"Judge Seabury gathered up his papers and passed from the courtroom," Walter Chambers of the *New York World-Telegram* reported. "As he walked down the steps of the building a crowd of several hundred young girls, out at lunch-time from nearby office buildings, burst forth in a salvo of cheering. He stopped short in annoyed amazement, quickly assumed the impassive dignity of the judge and entered his car. The girls pushed and jammed about it as though he were a Lindbergh."

Now Seabury saw his opportunity to disclose how inept and unethical attorneys had obtained positions as magistrates. He uncovered the links between politics and the courts, revealing them in his official reports as referee. He had a mandate that he broadened on his own, and no one tried to stop him as he questioned the magistrates and discovered that one after another of them had received their appointments as rewards for service to their political party.

"In practically every such case, the evidence shows the applicant for judicial office standing abjectly and, figuratively, with his hat in his hand, before the political district leader, begging his recommendation to Tammany Hall, which was recognized to be the *sine qua non*. This evidence presents a situation which is a scandal and a disgrace, as well as a menace, to the City of New York. I propose," Seabury declared, "to reproduce the testimony of some of the magistrates on this subject, because, as far as I know, the common-law proof of the condition has never before been laid before the supreme court."

The testimony of one magistrate, Jesse Silbermann, showed what the procedure was for obtaining a bench appointment from the Mayor. First, a lawyer went to his district leader with an account of how hard he had worked for the club. Second, the district leader went to the county leader and pleaded the case. Third, the county leader went to the leader of Tammany Hall and made the recommendation. If Tammany found the applicant acceptable, the Mayor was then informed whom he should appoint for the next vacancy. In addition, the Silbermann testimony disclosed that religious- or nationality-group representation, rather than legal qualifications, was a primary consideration in appointing magistrates.

"After my appointment," Silbermann said, "I learned that the Mayor decided to appoint a Hebrew from the Bronx, and he communicated with Arthur H. Murphy [the Democratic county leader] and asked him to suggest a name of some Hebrew."

"Now, Judge Silbermann," the referee asked, "what I am anxious to have you state, if you will, and if you know, is just why you, Jesse Silbermann, were selected to be magistrate up there rather than some other Hebrew in the Bronx who was a member of the Bar in good standing."

"I was active in the party. I was chairman of the Law committee of the Democratic party up there prior to my appointment. I was active in politics."

"Now, what did you do toward getting your second appointment for a full ten-year term?" Seabury asked cordially.

"I saw my local leader, James W. Brown. I told him my term was expiring and I asked him to go up to see the county leader then, the present county leader, Edward J. Flynn, and ask him whether he was going to, or whether he would, recommend me for the appointment for the full term."

"What did Mr. Brown say?"

"He said he would go up to see Mr. Flynn. Then he said that Flynn was taking it under advisement, and that he didn't see any objection to my appointment and that he would let me know."

"Did he subsequently let you know?"

"He did. He said I was to be appointed. And I was."

Once on the bench, a magistrate had to pay off his obligations to the district leaders again and again. He was, after all, their boy. Seabury followed through in his cross-examination on the number of "visits" the magistrates received from district leaders. One admitted to forty such intercessions in cases before him; another confessed that he was "reached" by nearly every leader in New York and Bronx counties. Leaders would get in touch at the club, at home, or in chambers; bashfulness was not one of their characteristics. Occasionally the district court clerk would act as the intermediary between a magistrate and the leader.

Seabury called in the district leaders themselves. They were frank in their testimony. District Leader James W. Brown of the Bronx, for example, said that leaders regarded it as their "civic duty" to intercede with magistrates in cases pending before them. He admitted that his duty had taken him on many occasions into different courts. Nor could he see anything wrong with this practice. Rabbis, priests, and social workers intercede for people—why not district leaders?

"That," Leader Brown testified, "is the way we make Democrats."

When a grateful constituent for whom he had interceded with a magistrate asked how he could show his appreciation, Leader Brown said he told him: "The only thing you can do for me is to vote the Democratic ticket."

From such revelations of political fixing in the courts, Seabury concluded:

The demoralization of the magistrates' courts resulting from the political considerations finds expression not only in the subserviency of the magistrates but also in the very type and quality of the men appointed. Ability and fitness for office, where they exist, are, as a rule, purely accidental. The selection is made primarily to strengthen the power of the party. This explains the principle by which appointments are parceled out to meet the alleged claims of particular political districts; it also explains the even more vicious principle by which race, nationality and creed often dictate the selection of magistrates. The activities of the Steuben Society, in the selection of judges as a compliment to the German voters, are well known. In the case of Magistrate Vitale there seemed to be no doubt that he was selected as a representative of his Italian group in the Bronx. Magistrate Silbermann spoke with perfect naïveté of the reasons why he felt that his appointment was dictated— partly because of his activity in the party and partly because he happened to be of the Jewish race. As long as candidates are selected upon such considerations, we cannot hope to have the best.

Tammany Hall fumed. Exposure of a little rottenness and corruption was one thing; every starry-eyed reformer in the last half-century had been able to dig up some dirt. But this man Seabury was trying to uproot the system of favors and rewards itself; and he was digging in with a fanatical thoroughness. He had to be stopped.

The Tammany counterattack came sharp and low; they knew how to gouge and elbow in the municipal clinches. From Mayor Walker on down to the lowest clerk in the Hall of Records, suddenly the Seabury staff was blocked and kicked around.

At the outset of the investigation, Mayor Walker commended the action of the appellate division and the appointment of Seabury as referee. But when Seabury began to embarrass his administration by exposing the crooked magistrates whom he (or, rather, the county machines) had appointed, Walker changed his tune. Since Seabury's law staff was essential to the investigation, what better way to ruin the show than to cut down on his budget?

The city's corporation counsel, Arthur J. W. Hilly, refused to pay the salaries of the assistant counsel. When Seabury issued a statement that failure to do so was an obstructionist move, the corporation counsel replied that the whole inquiry was unconstitutional. "The statute authorizing the inferior courts investigation provides that the city shall pay the reasonable expenses of it, but makes no statement in regard to the employment of counsel," Hilly said. "A referee is defined by the rules of practice as an attorney in good standing, and certainly it was not contemplated that he should be assisted by seven other attorneys in carrying on the investigation."

Seabury decided to take his troubles to the Mayor. Walker gave him "positive assurance" that the lawyers' salaries (which were between $50 and $100 a week) would be paid immediately and that he had so instructed his corporation counsel. The next day the corporation counsel told Seabury that he would pay all the clerks and stenographers and process servers but would continue to refuse payment for the assistant counsel. Thereupon Seabury again got in touch with the Mayor, reminding him that he had given his assurances that the lawyers would be paid. To this letter, the Mayor never replied.

The next step Seabury took was to go to court. He had his process servers hand notices to the Mayor and comptroller informing them that a mandamus proceeding was being instituted in the supreme court to compel payment of the salaries. Walker replied innocently that he knew nothing about this case, adding it was merely one of thousands of cases that had been brought against the City of New York. Furthermore, the Mayor insisted that the act of the legislature under which the inquiry was ordered was unconstitutional and void. "This last argument," Seabury declared, "is frivolous on its face, since the city officers already had paid other disbursements by the referee for stenographers, clerks and others."

Governor Roosevelt declined to comment on Seabury's court action until he had had an opportunity to examine the record. Seabury said the suit would not be allowed to impede his investigation, and pressed the matter in the supreme court. To save his own time and the city expense, he made a test case for only one of his lawyers, Sydney Handler. To no one's surprise, the court determined that the objections to the payment of the expenses were without merit, that the act was constitutional, and that the referee was within his authority.* The comptroller promptly announced his refusal to participate in any appeal from the decision; the corporation counsel also announced that he would abide by the decision. The assistant counsel finally received their pay. Seabury later said that Walker's assurances of co-operation were "as insincere as they were loud."

* Matter of Handler, 138 Misc. 584.

In the midst of the investigation, a great opportunity came to Tammany. On February 10, 1931, Isidor J. Kresel, Seabury's counsel, resigned. He did so to spare the Seabury investigation from being marked with the same taint that had suddenly been put on his own name.

The resignation was the result of a combination of circumstances: the Depression, the failure of a big bank, and the desire for revenge on the part of one of Tammany's most cunning lawyers. At the end of 1930, the Bank of United States, with some half-million depositors, failed. It was one of 200 banking institutions in the state that were in a weakened condition after the stock-market crash. Governor Roosevelt and his state banking superintendent were criticized for not having taken stronger supervisory measures. Roosevelt approved amendments to strengthen the state's banking laws, but neither his banking department nor the Republican-dominated legislature acted quickly enough to prevent bank collapses. Examiners from the banking department and the Federal Reserve Bank studied the books of this private bank with the official-sounding name and condemned Bernard K. Marcus, president, and Saul Singer, vice president, as unfit to conduct the affairs of such a large bank.

Kresel was the bank's general counsel. His acts, together with those of the bank's chief officers, became subject to District Attorney Crain's investigation, conducted at the request of Governor Roosevelt, into the reasons behind the failure. Crain welcomed Max D. Steuer, who volunteered eagerly, as his special assistant to handle the Bank of United States inquest. There was more than one reason for Steuer's—and Tammany's—glee at the chance to put Kresel on the spot. Steuer had been Marcus's lawyer before Kresel acquired the wealthy client. Steuer was once almost disbarred for allegedly coaching a client, Edith St. Clair, a musical-comedy actress, in a suit she had brought against Abe Erlanger, the producer, for life support as a result of extramarital favors and services rendered; former District Attorney Jerome and Kresel represented Erlanger, who had to pay Miss St. Clair, and Steuer always considered Kresel responsible for the subsequent disbarment proceeding, in which he was cleared. Furthermore, Steuer was a trusted adviser of Boss Curry's and the most influential Tammany lawyer in New York.

Steuer later touched off one of Al Smith's famous retorts. At the

Democratic state convention in 1932, Smith and Roosevelt advanced
the case for Herbert H. Lehman for governor. Steuer fancied himself
a political sage. "The nomination of Lehman would not be good
politics," Steuer said. Smith turned to Steuer and Curry in the latter's hotel room and replied, "Steuer, you may know a lot of law. I
don't know law. But you don't know a damn thing about politics.
I do. If Lehman isn't nominated I'll come down to New York and
run for mayor and take the town away from you." Curry said, "On
what ticket?" Smith turned on his heel and declared, "Hell, on the
Chinese laundry ticket."

Kresel was a witness at the trial of Marcus and Singer, who were
found guilty of violating the state's banking laws and given jail sentences; later, he was tried himself on the charge that he had committed perjury during the case against the bank's officers. He was
also indicted for misappropriation on the grounds that as the bank's
attorney, he had advised Marcus and Singer.

Seabury recognized the selflessness of Kresel's resignation and
refused to turn his back on his first assistant. "Kresel served with an
unflagging industry and devotion and he performed with outstanding skill and ability," he reported to the appellate division. "His contribution to the results of the investigation cannot be overestimated."

Tammany Hall hoped that the removal of Kresel would be sufficiently embarrassing to kill the investigation. They were mistaken.
Harland B. Tibbetts was advanced to Kresel's job, and Seabury himself stepped into the breach. He became not just a referee sitting in
judgment, but assumed new burdens as investigator and cross-ex-
aminer. The investigation continued in private and public hearings
under his command until October 26, 1931, and he filed his final report, with recommendations for reform, on March 28, 1932. Although his original mandate called upon him to investigate only the
magistrates' courts in New York and Bronx counties, his recommendations affected all the lower criminal courts in the city.

Seabury called for consolidation of the magistrates' courts, children's court, and court of special sessions into a single new court of
special sessions. "The true reason for consolidation is found not in
the mere financial benefits; an even more important reason is that
upon such consolidation the present haphazard and illogical distribution of the work could be eliminated, a new and better distribu-

tion could be substituted, considerable duplication of work avoided and a much smoother and better co-ordinated system put into operation. This would not only be of benefit to the courts, but of great advantage to the members of the public having to do with them."

The most radical revision he proposed was to take the power of appointment of judges out of the hands of the Mayor. "Those justices of the present court of special sessions and of the children's court, and those of the present city magistrates who have shown their fitness to hold their respective offices, would, presumably, be appointed by the appellate division to the proposed new court of special sessions upon its creation; the places of the others, to the extent that successors were needed, would be filled by the appellate division with new and properly qualified judges." A "president justice" was suggested, similar to the presiding justice of the appellate division, with power to assign the judges and administer the consolidated court.

To break the political hold of the district leaders on various lesser jobs around the courts, Seabury recommended that all the clerks be placed under civil service. He also advised that fines be taken out of the hands of lesser officials in the courts and that a central office be set up where traffic fines could be paid directly. This proposal had been made by Mayor Walker, and Seabury commended it as a step in the right direction. To protect the rights of arrested citizens, he called for immediate arraignment before a magistrate instead of at police stations. This, he said, would help to destroy the "dirty work of bribery and fixing" as well as "third degree" police methods.

"The abuses that have been disclosed do not strike at people of wealth and power," he declared, sounding like the young Seabury.

They oppress those who are poor and helpless, under circumstances where the oppressor enjoys practical immunity. A court in which these practices could have obtained, or in which they may obtain again, is not a court of justice. True, we are assured that the vice squad has been abolished, that the employment of stool pigeons has been discontinued, and that other changes of like character have been made; but what assurance is there that these evils will not be revived?

There can be no remedy for these conditions unless the court can be entirely free of political control. That will not be a task easy of accomplishment, necessary and vital though it is to the proper administration of justice. There is too much patronage and rich opportunity for spoils to allow the necessary changes to be made, if the political forces that now dominate can prevent it; but change there must be if these evils are to be severed from the administration of justice.

The recommendations for consolidation and streamlining the courts were eventually adopted in part in New York City and other municipalities, but the idea of removing judgeships from politics remained a reformer's dream.

In January, 1933, a grateful appellate division thanked Judge Seabury for his accomplishments in the magistrates' courts investigation. Their public letter to him noted that, as a direct result of his work, two magistrates had been removed by unanimous vote of the court, three had resigned and one had decided to leave the state hurriedly. They said that the resulting improvement of the conditions in these criminal courts would be lasting. They agreed with his recommendations and called for legislative action to put them in force. They regretted but one thing: Judge Seabury refused to accept payment for his work, which had begun over two years before, back in the fall of 1930.

Seabury had kept secret that he had never accepted a penny for himself; that he had paid out of his own pocket two lawyers from his business office who worked exclusively on the investigation staff; that he had personally defrayed some of the printing and other costs and had refused to submit a bill to his city or state.

Presiding Justice Edward R. Finch and his colleagues in the appellate division then made public Seabury's brief letter, insisting that the citizens of New York had a right to share it:

I have considered the willingness of the court expressed to me by you to allow me $75,000 as compensation for my services while acting as referee of the appellate division in the conduct of the investigation into the magistrates' courts, which continued from September, 1930, to March, 1932. I prefer, however, to give my services without any charge to the City of New York as a contribution which the profession of which I have the honor to be a member rendered in the effort to remedy the gross injustices which prevailed in that court.

Around the courts and lawyers' associations, the consensus was that he should have accepted the $75,000 fee instead of giving the city treasury a gift. It was, after all, for services rendered. Some said he was a civic fool; others tried to explain it by calling him a man with a vision of himself: a modern St. George slaying tigers. Seabury said nothing.

CHAPTER **11**

The District Attorney Investigation

ON March 10, 1931, in the middle of the investigation of the magistrates' courts, Governor Roosevelt appointed Judge Seabury commissioner to inquire into the conduct and competency in office of
Thomas C. T. Crain, district attorney of New York County. Because
of the delicate relationship existing between the Democratic governor in Albany and the Democratic mayor in New York City, Roosevelt had to move cautiously, often behind the scenes, to prepare
what amounted to an investigation of Tammany Hall.

Few persons, then or later, were aware that Roosevelt had suggested Seabury for the magistrates' courts investigation. But early in
the summer of 1930, Victor J. Dowling, the presiding justice of the
appellate division, had an unpublicized meeting with Governor
Roosevelt to discuss the choice of a referee. They agreed on three or
four candidates who could do the job, but came to no decision. Dowling was in Europe when the scandal broke about Magistrate Ewald's
purchase of office, and in his absence, Acting Presiding Justice Finch
named Seabury referee at the suggestion of Governor Roosevelt.

As more and more examples of malfeasance were revealed during
the hearings, it was only natural for the public to wonder how deep
the corruption went. If the Seabury investigation implicated so many
officials, how many more rackets were undiscovered, and who was
covering up? Why, for that matter, did a special referee have to be

called in to conduct such an investigation to deliver the culprits? Where had the district attorney been all this time?

From civic organizations, the bar, press, and pulpit, howls of indignation arose. They had heard, for example, the story of Mme. St. Clair, a Marseillaise Negress, who was banker for one of the big policy games in Harlem. She had an income of a quarter of a million dollars a year and traveled with her own bodyguard. The lottery tickets, selling for as little as a penny and paying off at 540 to 1, amounted to a multimillion-dollar business. Mme. St. Clair's bribes to the police were delivered to the West 123rd Street station house by an underling named "Mustache" Jones. Forty murders and half a dozen kidnappings were laid at the door of policy gambling in the city.

The corruption came a little closer to the district attorney's office with the disclosure that John C. Weston, a former process server who had acted as an assistant district attorney from 1921 to 1929, had enriched himself by receiving bribes from lawyers, bondsmen, and policemen. He was responsible for the discharge of 600 vice and immorality cases involving nearly a thousand defendants. Never, in all the time he was assigned to the Jefferson Market Court, was he asked to report on his activities. "The only time I went to the district attorney's office," he said, "was to get my salary check."

At this time a shocking murder further aroused the people of the city against the police and the district attorney. In February, 1931, Vivian Gordon was questioned privately by Irving Ben Cooper; she told him that she had been framed in the past on a prostitution conviction. She arranged to come to his office again with evidence, but before she could do so she was found in Van Cortlandt Park in the Bronx, strangled. A week later her shamed teen-age daughter committed suicide. Miss Gordon was said to have had "five hundred sugar daddies," in the words of the tabloids, while the more long-winded full-sized papers described her as "a misled woman who followed the tinsel path." Polly Adler, whose phone number was found in the murdered woman's address book, said that Miss Gordon was just another attractive woman "out to feather her nest quickly." Police Commissioner Edward P. Mulrooney said there would be "a stain on the shield of every policeman in New York" until the murder was solved. Governor Roosevelt sent word from Albany that the police were "on trial."

The fact remained that (as the gangland phrase went in the 1930's) Miss Gordon's lips were forever sealed. No longer could she implicate others before Seabury's investigators. That her murder had been flagrantly committed in a city park was a horrifying indication of the defiant attitude of the racketeers toward the Walker administration's law-enforcement machinery.

A specific demand for action came to the Governor from the City Club of New York, whose president, Richard S. Childs, and board chairman, Joseph M. Price, petitioned for the removal of District Attorney Crain. They charged that his conduct in office was "incompetent, inefficient and futile"; that he "failed properly to conduct prosecutions for crimes and offenses cognizable by the courts"; that he initiated many investigations, "but conducted them inadequately and ineffectively"; that he made misleading statements about indictments and prosecutions, including "frauds in relation to freight and delivery business and dock racketeers"; that he failed to expose "grafting in the Department of Purchase and crimes connected with the Board of Standards and Appeals"; that he did not investigate or prosecute various stock frauds and other specific cases; and that he "assumed a semblance of activity only after other agencies aroused public opinion which he could not wholly ignore."

The City Club was not the only civic group registering alarm. The City Affairs Committee of New York, whose members included John Dewey of Columbia, Bishop Francis J. McConnell, and Rabbi Stephen S. Wise, blasted the "inertia and timidity" of Crain. "It is obvious that popular cynicism and mistrust of the processes of government have been greatly increased by District Attorney Crain's statements on racketeering," said Norman Thomas, who added that "racketeering could not flourish without political alliance." Heywood Broun put it: "The crane is mightier than the Crain and much more stalwart. The crane stands on at least one leg."

Governor Roosevelt called in Crain and Curry, his Tammany sponsor, and confronted them with the City Club charges. It was disclosed that in the meeting at Roosevelt's home in New York Crain had requested an immediate investigation, but there were rumors that Roosevelt had offered the district attorney a chance to resign.

Tammany Hall now vented its anger on Roosevelt, spreading the story that he had encouraged the private citizens' group to petition him to remove Crain. Roosevelt retaliated against Tammany's outcry by appointing its archenemy, Samuel Seabury, to be his commissioner. At first Seabury declined to accept the post because he was making progress in the magistrates' courts investigation and did not want to divert himself and his staff from it. But Governor Roosevelt prevailed upon him, as the logical candidate, to accept the assignment for the good of the city. The Governor formally wrote him:

> I have decided to appoint you commissioner under Section 34 of the public officers' law to hear and investigate formal charges which have been filed with me against the district attorney of the County of New York, and to take evidence relative thereto. I sincerely hope that you will be willing to accept this appointment in addition to the other public service which you are rendering.
>
> I shall be glad to have you start your duties as commissioner at the earliest possible moment; and, as you are in the very strict sense, acting as the commissioner of the Governor in this matter, I shall be glad to confer with you at any time. I am very confident that your fine reputation for fairness and justice peculiarly qualifies you.
>
> You will, of course, note that the charges made do not in any way involve the personal integrity of Justice Crain, but relate solely to his competency to fulfill the office which he holds.

Crain himself seemed worth no more than a municipal skirmish. An old Tammany sachem, he had served quietly on the bench of the court of general sessions and on the supreme court. He lived genteelly on his inherited millions in an old Manhattan mansion and attended the Episcopal Church regularly. His appointment to the post of district attorney seemed, because of his advanced years, ludicrous—unless, of course, Curry preferred a tame prosecutor. Crain had lost no time proving how foolish he could be by promising to solve the year-old Rothstein murder within two weeks after taking office.

However ineffectual he might be personally, he was the center of a pitched battle. On one side was Governor Roosevelt, trying to do his duty, looking ahead to 1932, yet aware that much of his political strength depended upon Tammany, aided by a reform-minded, hell-bent-for-glory commissioner, who was hardly an ally or confidant. In opposition were Mayor Walker, the beau of the city ball; Boss Curry; the wily Tammany legal talents, including Max D. Steuer and Samuel Untermyer; a gaggle of judges, and assorted foot soldiers who marched in tune to the Machine.

Mayor Walker decided that this would be a propitious moment for him to take a winter vacation. He took a train to Palm Springs, California, where he stayed at the desert estate of Samuel Untermyer. An Indian chief from a nearby reservation offered the Mayor a free thermal mud bath, to which he replied, "Thank you, no. I've been in one constantly during the past eighteen months." More to the point was Heywood Broun's response to the Mayor's Palm Beach trip: "Though I grant that James Joseph Walker is sick, it seems to me unlikely that his health can be as precarious as that of the City of New York at the present moment. It is a pity that the Mayor cannot take the metropolis with him on the trip. The city stands in need of scathing sunlight, fresh air and a fine rousing wind to cleanse its lungs and vitals. In Palm Springs, I trust, the palms will be straighter and itch less than those of Tammany."

At 80 Centre Street, meanwhile, Seabury was juggling his two investigations. He assigned John Kirkland Clark to head the staff looking into Crain's conduct, and asked Raymond Moley to assemble statistical and graphic evidence on Crain's record. Samuel Untermyer, Mayor Walker's Palm Springs host, who was seventy-four years old, became seventy-year-old Crain's defense counsel.

Mr. Untermyer immediately began to try his case in the newspapers. He released copies of a letter he had mailed to the Governor to the effect that the City Club's charges were preposterous, that the Governor had no right to name Seabury his commissioner, and that Seabury could not possibly be free of bias and prejudice. Thereafter, Untermyer and Crain paid Judge Seabury a visit and offered to cooperate with him if he would agree not to examine any witnesses in private hearings. Seabury refused to make any agreements, maintaining that he had a statutory right to examine witnesses in private. Untermyer said he would test the matter in the courts. Seabury responded by calling in Crain's chief assistant the next day for a private session, denying Untermyer representation. Seabury continued to

collect evidence in private hearings, as he had done in the magistrates investigation.

In order to examine Crain's conduct in office, Seabury asked to
see the minutes of the grand jury which was investigating the "business" activities of racketeers in the city. Crain and Untermyer, of
course, attempted to block him. Crain argued that the grand jury
minutes could not be disclosed "for use solely in a private investigation"; that the commissioner was "legally disqualified" from asking
for the minutes; and that "by reason of the bias and prejudice of the
commissioner and the unfairness with which the proceedings have
been conducted," these minutes could not be divulged. Fortunately,
when Seabury asked for a court order granting him a copy of the
minutes, Judge Charles Nott said that the public interest as well as
sound legal procedure required him to grant Seabury's request.

The grand jury minutes and the private hearings revealed another
shameful situation. There were few businesses in the city untouched
by the racketeers, who received bribes, payoffs, and shakedown
money—sometimes merely for promising to leave a company alone.
Seabury and his staff were not immediately concerned with the existence of these rackets, but they were concerned with Crain's failure to prosecute the racketeers.

One sordid story, especially shocking to housewives and restaurant
owners, was the account about racketeering in the Fulton Street fish
market, which supplied sea food to most New Yorkers and many
people along the Atlantic seaboard. The man in charge of labor
"negotiations" was Joseph "Socks" Lanza, who was the delegate representing Local 16975 of the United Sea Food Workers. On behalf of
hotel-supply dealers, a management representative telephoned Lanza
and stated flatly that the employers could not afford to pay steeper
wages. "I guess we can fix it up," said Lanza, suggesting that he
receive $7,500 for a sweetheart contract, undercutting the union, at
the same rate as the year before. The management representative
said he couldn't afford to pay that much, and Lanza settled for
$5,000. Similar payments had been made before to Lanza at contract
renewal time.

"The gangsters shake down the dealers every two years at the time
of the renewal of labor contracts," a complainant said. "During October this year's shakedown must have amounted in all to somewhere

around $25,000. A specified amount was set for each union man employed and I know for a fact that the eighteen stands in Fulton market proper paid them around $8,700 and the hotel-supply dealers $5,000." In addition, Seabury revealed that certain fish firms made annual payments of $2,500 to Lanza to keep their plants nonunion and that Lanza himself was on the payroll of one of the companies. The 600 retailers trading in the Fulton market were each paying forty to fifty dollars a year to Charles Skillen, another delegate from Local 16975, in order to get delivery of the fish they bought.

"I am forced to the conclusion that the district attorney did not do all that the situation required or all that he could and should have done to bring these racketeers to justice and to break up the hold which they had and still have upon these dealers who serve approximately one-fifth the population of the United States," Commissioner Seabury reported. "The official inaction engenders the belief in the employers who submit to extortion that there are no law-enforcing agencies within the County of New York willing and powerful enough to bring to justice those practicing extortion upon them."

Next, Seabury and Clark turned to racketeering in the millinery trade. Here, the cast of culprits included "Little Augie" and "Tough Jake" Kurzman, who received their payoff from the manufacturers of ladies' hats. These union organizers were in the business of selling protection against organization. "Little Augie" was about to receive $2,000 from one hat company when he was gunned down; Kurzman made a deal with the same company to continue the service for $100 a month, and honored his obligation. He received $10,000 a year from various hatmakers, who carried the payoffs on their books as "protection."

Seabury chided Crain for not prosecuting Kurzman until after his activities were exposed at public hearings. But, with typical fairness, Seabury said that credit had to be given to Crain for making an effort to secure testimony from the employers about their extortion payments. Kurzman himself managed to slip in and out of the magistrates' court during the public hearings, but he was never jailed, and he finally fled the state when a bench warrant was issued for his arrest.

The cloth-shrinking business, a major activity allied with the garment industry in New York, proved to be a successful racket for Joseph Mezzacapo, who dissolved the Cloth Shrinkers Union and set up his own union to replace it. Mezzacapo ruled upon who could work where, and no one could work who was not a member of his personal union. Seabury's staff followed the procedure that had worked so well with the investigation of the vice squad and district leaders: checking bank accounts and other records. During the five years prior to the investigation, Mezzacapo had made deposits in excess of $332,000 in a single account with the Federation Bank and Trust Company. Seabury again was forced to conclude: "Judge Crain did not examine the activities of Mezzacapo to ascertain the extent of his activities and their unlawful character. A survey of the investigation of racketeering in the cloth-shrinking trade points to the same ineffectiveness on the part of the district attorney which he demonstrated in his attempts to cope with this evil in other industries."

Every day Mr. Untermyer, wearing a buttonhole orchid to match his tie, arrived in court with his client, District Attorney Crain. Untermyer sat at the counsel table, mumbling, "Louder, please!" at witnesses, and objecting to Commissioner Seabury's questions on the grounds of "bias." At one point Untermyer began a harangue in which he questioned Seabury's motives in the investigation, but Seabury interrupted him with a sharp rap of the gavel. "That remark I regard as gross impertinence, and it must not be repeated," Seabury declared.

Untermyer tried to prove that the district attorney's office was indeed striking back at the racketeers. The record showed that the district attorney had tried to collect evidence of criminal interference in areas of employment that concerned the livelihoods of millions of people in New York: master barbers, kosher butchers, operating engineers, night watchmen, bead makers, cinder removers, clothing, laundry, and leather workers, flower and fruit sellers, fur dressers, hod carriers, paper hangers, window cleaners, and many more. This sounded impressive, on the surface, but Clark put Charles C. Pilatsky, Crain's deputy assistant district attorney, on the witness stand, and asked him to describe what was being done about the rackets in these "protected" areas.

"Well, we had an office on the same floor and almost as big as

Judge Crain's and we had a sign painted on the door," said Crain's "racket buster." The sign read, "Racketeering Complaints Here." At the office he investigated 150 complaints.

"How many indictments came out of your investigation?"

"Two," Pilatsky replied.

"And how many of those were dismissed without trial."

"I understand, both of them."

As a result of these admissions, Seabury concluded: "The actions which [Crain] took in this field—preceded by his promises of successful warfare upon them—manifest not only ineffectiveness but, in my judgment, incompetency on the part of the district attorney. Indeed, I think it is a fair conclusion to say that the district attorney of the county, confronted by the problem presented by the aggressive tactics of the racketeer, has thrown up his hands and recognizes that, even with the co-operation of the police department, he has not been able to do anything of substantial value toward stopping the practice or bringing these criminals to justice."

But in reporting on his discoveries of the extent of the racketeers' activities, Seabury was careful to point out to Governor Roosevelt that labor could not be judged, as a whole, by "Socks" Lanza and "Tough Jake" Kurzman. He was consistent here with his youthful stand about the rights of labor:

> The trade union accomplishes a useful and necessary purpose when it is honestly administered. The system by which a blackleg labor leader is permitted to extort money as the price of nonenforcement of union requirements not only strikes a direct blow at the whole trade union movement, but is clearly illegal. Furthermore, it permits employers to buy immunity and subjects them to the necessity of entering into contracts the terms of which are not prescribed by market conditions but are fixed and determined by the amount which may be extorted from them by an unscrupulous labor union delegate. The public has a real and substantial interest in the abolition of these abuses. The extortions of the racketeer are, like taxes or charges enhancing cost, shifted to the consumer, who, in the last analysis, must pay the tribute.

The City Club also assailed Crain for his puerile investigation of the magistrates' courts—and here, in the light of Seabury's own investigation, the obvious shortcomings of the district attorney were apparent. Indeed, Untermyer had frankly admitted that Seabury's own inquiry was so vigorous that his client's would look slight by comparison. Nevertheless, Seabury was forced to conclude that here, too, Crain failed to follow through on the scandalous conditions in the courts. "Unscrupulous bondsmen, corrupt policemen and dishonest attorneys at law operated for many years, especially in the women's court, where their activities were facilitated through the connivance of a bribe-taking representative of the district attorney's office who resigned prior to the beginning of Judge Crain's term." Seabury listed several instances where criminal proceedings had been started against bondsmen who connived in the fraudulent vice cases, but were dropped. Again, however, he was impartial, noting that the district attorney had acted "with a reasonable degree of efficiency" in the prosecution of vice-squad officers.

The City Club's indictment cited a number of particular cases where the district attorney had been "guilty of misfeasance in office." Individuals in the Department of Purchase and the Board of Standards and Appeals were charged with graft and other crimes. The grand jury provided information about William E. Walsh, chairman of the Board of Standards and Appeals, and Dr. William F. ("Horse Doctor") Doyle, who practiced before the board. The board had discretionary power to permit variations in the Building Zone Regulations, and therefore was the prey of the real-estate interests—and, of course, a rich source of graft.

Some suspicious payments and bank accounts were revealed by the grand jury. Doyle's accounts disclosed that he had received retainers by check and cash payments; there was a strong indication that fee splitting was taking place. Seabury put Crain on the witness stand and asked him why he had never called Doyle in for an accounting. Crain explained meekly that he feared doing so would grant Doyle immunity from prosecution. As for the Walsh case, which involved a loan from a property owner to the board chairman, the grand jury refused to indict Walsh, and therefore Seabury could not find the district attorney at fault.

On the question of immunity from prosecution, however, which arose many times during the city-wide investigation, Seabury took a practical stand:

The district attorney was quite correct in his statement that he could have given Doyle immunity. I think he was in error in his conclusion that it was not in the public interest that he should do so. As the case stood, by reason of Doyle's silence nobody was being prosecuted, neither Doyle nor those with whom he may have entered into conspiracy. Nothing was being done; no progress was being made toward bringing anybody to justice in relation to this transaction. Doyle was secure because the district attorney was unwilling to accord him immunity and those with whom he may have conspired were secure because Doyle refused to speak.

Seabury indicated that his own course would have been to accord Doyle immunity and compel him to speak. He found the district attorney merely guilty of an error of judgment here. The case of Doyle, however, was carefully filed away in Seabury's mind. It was obvious, he confided to his assistant counsel, that the Tammany-dominated Board of Standards and Appeals was worth close investigation. He knew that he did not have the authority to investigate this or any other city unit under his delimited refereeship or commissionership. But the Doyle case was one for the future.

Raymond Moley's charts and statistical analyses showed that the tendency during Crain's term of office was to indict defendants for major crimes and allow them to plead guilty of misdemeanors. For example, there were 1,279 indictments for grand larceny filed in 1930. Of these, 623 resulted in convictions, but of this number only 72 resulted in a conviction of the crime charged; 128 resulted in convictions on charges of lesser felonies, and 423 in convictions on charges of misdemeanors.

Recalling his presentation of this damning graphic evidence of the district attorney's incompetency, Moley said later, "I did this with considerable zest and, I believe, proved a case of gross inefficiency, despite the artful cross-examination of Samuel Untermyer."

After all the evidence was presented, and after all the charges against Crain were sustained or dismissed, Seabury summed up: "Truth compels the conclusion that in many instances he busied himself ineffectively, and that he did not grasp or act upon opportunities for high public service which some of the matters referred to presented to him. I am satisfied that wherever he failed, and I think he did fail in many cases to do all that he should have done, his failure was not due to any lack of personal effort or any ignoble motive." Here, Roosevelt and Seabury were in agreement about Crain's integrity. In victory, Seabury now turned magnanimous, despite the fact that his investigation had clearly proved Crain to be unworthy of the office of district attorney of New York County.

"The question whether an elected public official should be removed is not to be determined by individual opinion as to what may promote public interest. Proof, not opinion, is the standard which must be applied in solving such a question. Public interests are to be served, but such interests cannot be truly served at the expense of injustice to an individual." He therefore recommended to the Governor that the petition to remove Crain from office be denied. That he was being a gentleman and looking at the equities here was indicated by his statement that, in reaching his conclusion, he was much influenced by Crain's honorable public career as a judge before he became district attorney.

Commissioner Seabury submitted his report to Governor Roosevelt on August 31, 1931, and immediately afterward Crain's counsel announced that he would ask for a new hearing.

"At the risk of appearing ungracious," Untermyer said, "I will say that, in my opinion, if any other result than a dismissal of the charges had been possible it would have been achieved. The proceedings were conducted with a degree of bias rarely known by a distinguished judge who appeared to be acting throughout as a prosecutor."

Untermyer was seeking publicity, as he had done throughout the investigation, and his announcement that he would seek another hearing came to nought. Governor Roosevelt, however, made it clear that he did not appreciate Untermyer's pronunciamentos. He authorized the statement that "the Governor resents, and long has resented, the tactics employed by Mr. Untermyer and his unfair criticisms of Judge Seabury." And, personally, he wrote to his commissioner: "I desire to compliment you and thank you for your painstaking, considerate and tireless efforts in this case. The reading of your report impresses me with the soundness of your reasoning and the complete fairness of your conclusions."

As in the magistrates investigation, Seabury did not ask for any fee. But he did accept $10,000 for his services in the district attorney investigation.

Some people wondered why Seabury was lenient with Crain. His report of Crain's inept conduct seemed to be heading in one direction—toward a recommendation for removal—and suddenly the course changed. The suspicious would not accept Seabury's legal reasoning that the incompetency was not gross nor was the failure to act in specific cases induced by improper influences; in other words, that Crain was incompetent but honest. The distrustful said that one reason Crain was not removed was that he was an important layman in the Episcopal Church.

There was, indeed, a behind-the-scenes reasoning for Seabury's decision. Long afterward, George Trosk remembered: "There was no question that we could have, if we wanted to. But we had advance information that, regardless of what the report said, Tammany's leadership was going to nominate Crain anyway. And that meant he would win in controlled Manhattan. We knew we would be left looking silly—that it would look like a repudiation of our efforts. So we decided to do the practical thing, set out all the damaging evidence that we uncovered but not recommend removal. We knew that there was much more to be gained by continuing the investigation into the whole city's affairs."

Seabury did not set out to malign the aging district attorney. His concern was greater than that. There were elections ahead in the city, state, and nation, and the result of the investigations in New York would have a powerful effect on all three. Who could predict what might come of them? There were new challenges ahead—and old scores to settle.

CHAPTER **12**

The City-Wide Investigation

IN the early fall of 1931, the Joint Legislative Committee to Investigate the Affairs of the City of New York met in the county courthouse. Among the most important witnesses—and a gentleman who brought laughter to the otherwise somber city—was the Hon. Thomas M. Farley, sheriff of New York County, president of the Thomas M. Farley Association, leader of the Fourteenth Assembly District, and Tammany Hall sachem. Samuel Seabury, counsel, with consummate politeness, asked him to explain how he had accumulated nearly $400,000 within six years on an annual salary of $8,500. Their dialogue was a source of new phraseology for the American political vocabulary:

SEABURY: Where did you keep these moneys that you had saved?
FARLEY: In a safe-deposit box at home in the house.
SEABURY: Whereabouts at home in the house did you keep this money that you had saved?
FARLEY: In the safe.
SEABURY: In a safe?
FARLEY: Yes.
SEABURY: In a little box in a safe?
FARLEY: A big safe.
SEABURY: But a little box in a big safe?
FARLEY: In a big box in a big safe.

SEABURY: Was the big box in the big safe fairly full or crowded when you withdrew this money?

FARLEY: I didn't withdraw it all at once. That is money that was in the safe-deposit box——

SEABURY: When you first drew it, Sheriff, was the box then crowded or very full?

FARLEY: Well, it was full and plenty in it.

SEABURY: More and plenty?

FARLEY: Yes.

SEABURY: And, Sheriff, was this big box that was safely kept in the big safe a tin box or a wooden box?

FARLEY: A tin box.

SEABURY: Is it the type of tin boxes that are specially manufactured and designed to serve as a receptacle for cash?

FARLEY: It is.

SEABURY: Giving you the benefit of every doubt on sums from your official vocation and other gainful pursuits, the eighty-three thousand dollars extra you deposited in 1929 came from the same source that the other money came from?

FARLEY: It did.

SEABURY: Same safe-deposit vault?

FARLEY: Yes.

SEABURY: Same tin box, is that right?

FARLEY: That is right.

SEABURY: Now, in 1930, where did the extra cash come from, Sheriff?

FARLEY: Well, that is——. My salary check is in there.

SEABURY: No, Sheriff, your salary checks are exclusive of the cash deposits which during the year you deposited in those three banks.

FARLEY: Well, that came from the good box I had. [*Laughter.*]

SEABURY: Kind of a magic box?

FARLEY: It was a wonderful box.

SEABURY: A wonderful box. [*Laughter.*] What did you have to do— rub the lock with a little gold, and open it in order to find more money?

FARLEY: I wish I could.

Farley, one of the more delightful members of the tin-box battalion that marched before Judge Seabury, eventually was removed from his shrievalty, by order of Governor Roosevelt, because of his unfitness to hold public office and his failure to explain the sources of his wealth. The fact that, as an upstanding Democrat, he had once contributed $20,000 to Roosevelt's campaign fund did not save him. In subsequent years his "tin box" phrase has been misquoted in song and story as a symbol of municipal mishandling of money. This is an injustice to Sheriff Farley and to history. He did not claim to have a measly "little tin box" but "a big box in a big safe."

The Seabury investigations touched peripherally the incumbents in lesser city offices. Fouled lines of municipal government criss-crossed and inevitably led to Mayor Walker's office. The Tammany leaders were indignant, calling Seabury merely another politician; worse, he was the insulter of the people of New York, because he maligned the officials they had chosen. But there were growing numbers of New Yorkers who refused to let the soft soap of chauvinism blind them to the scandals before their eyes. They set up a renewed clamor for a housecleaning, for a full-scale investigation of all the departments in all the boroughs of the City of New York.

However, there were complications for Republicans and Democrats. Early in 1930 an attempt was made in the Republican-dominated state legislature to push through an investigation of the Democrat-dominated city. Governor Roosevelt let it be known that an investigation of Republican Westchester, Nassau, Suffolk counties—and other Republican counties upstate—might be in order, too. In spite of this threat of retaliation, the legislature passed a resolution authorizing an investigation—which Governor Roosevelt immediately vetoed, declaring that the Republican legislators were not acting in good faith and that the proposed investigation was wholly political in motivation. He had, however, a more serious objection to the measure. "If logically pursued," Governor Roosevelt said, "it would compel future governors at one time or another to meddle in the affairs of every county and city in the state. It would foist upon the Governor the new and unheard-of function of assuming the responsibility for the selection and general supervision of a commission to investigate any or all of the vast governmental machinery of one particular city."

The veto did not endear Roosevelt to Seabury. As Roosevelt's referee and commissioner in two other investigations, he maintained a judicious silence. But among his intimates he deplored the Governor's stand. He found some little comfort in Senate President John Knight's statement that the reason given for the veto was the "feeblest" he had ever heard, that the corruption being exposed by Seabury "paralleled [that of] the Tweed regime."

A year later, on March 23, 1931, the senate and assembly adopted a joint resolution for the appointment of a committee for "the investigation of the departments of the government of the City of New York." This time the Governor did not interfere. Fresh evidence of corruption was emerging nearly every day. Rabbi Stephen S. Wise of the Free Synagogue and John Haynes Holmes of the Community Church, on behalf of the City Affairs Committee, had brought charges against Mayor Walker to Governor Roosevelt. The clergymen who had dared to question the Mayor's ethics were branded Socialists by Tammany Hall. But the city could no longer avoid a full inspection. Governor Roosevelt approved a $250,000 appropriation and backed the committee's designation of Judge Seabury as counsel. The most far-reaching investigation in New York City history was under way.

When Seabury received word that he was to be named counsel, he was having lunch at the Bankers Club at 120 Broadway with George Trosk. After finishing his roast beef and lighting a cigar, he looked thoughtful for a moment and then said: "This presents a certain small problem for me, because I own some stock in one of the transit companies in New York."

Trosk said that surely no one would question his integrity.

"Nevertheless," Seabury continued, "my position must be absolutely correct. Under the circumstances, there are several alternatives. One, if something came out about this transit company and I should fail to investigate, people would say I did so for private gain. Two, if I do investigate the company, there are those people who are bound to say I did so simply to whitewash it. Three, if I give the stock to a member of my family, it will be regarded as a subterfuge. There is only one feasible way for me to handle this if I am to serve as counsel."

Puzzled, Trosk asked him what that alternative was.

"The only thing to do is give my stock away to charity," Seabury declared.

They returned to the office, and Seabury gathered up his stock certificates. He handed them all to Trosk.

"George, I would appreciate it if you would take these certificates

and have them sold anonymously. Give the proceeds—without anyone knowing where the money came from—to the treasurer of the
charitable hospital-fund drive that is now on."

Trosk did so that afternoon. Seabury's stock sale amounted to
$19,000. When he returned to the office, Seabury thanked him, and
the matter was never mentioned again. At times in the next year and
a half when the Tammany tiger was stalking Seabury, Trosk wanted
to reveal this amazing act of integrity. But he knew Seabury too well
to do so. To this day the story was known only to Trosk and Judge
Seabury's nephews.

On April 8, 1931, Judge Seabury officially accepted the appointment as counsel to the legislative committee. He informed State
Senator Samuel H. Hofstadter, the chairman of the committee, that
he considered the job a legal one in which he would act in the same
manner as if for a private client. He underscored the idea that he do
his duty without regard to any political consideration. And then, in
a rather unusual statement, he insisted that he take "the fine old oath
which grand jurors were required to take." He quoted his own oath
before the committee chairman: "You will diligently inquire and
true presentment make. . . . You shall present no one for envy, hatred
or malice; neither shall you leave any one unpresented for fear, favor,
affection, hope of reward or gain, but shall present all things truly as
they come to your knowledge, according to the best of your judgment." He added that he pledged to adhere to the letter and spirit of
this oath.

With these ringing words, he began the private and public hearings that went on until December 8, 1932. More than 2,260 persons
were examined privately; their testimony covered 47,000 pages. Another 175 witnesses appeared in thirty-seven public hearings; their
testimony added another 5,000 pages to the mimeographed record
compiled by Marshall & Munson, the official stenographers of the
senate and assembly. In addition to the testimony, hundreds of thousands of pages in books of account and other documents were
combed by the counsel's staff of lawyers and accountants. Assaying
the task, Seabury asked for additional funds to do the job; Roosevelt
and the legislature went along. Eventually, this became a half-
million-dollar state investigation of the City of New York.

The Joint Legislative Committee that appointed Seabury as its counsel soon divided along party lines. Chairman Hofstadter was a Republican who had defeated a Tammany candidate in the Fifteenth (Silk Stocking) District of Manhattan. The vice chairman, Hamilton F. Potter, a Suffolk County Republican, was a descendant of the famous American statesman Hamilton Fish. The Republicans outnumbered the Democrats in the executive sessions of the group, and in order to hamper the investigation, the Democrats almost immediately began to harass Seabury.

This group of Democrats was made up of petty statesmen of the caliber frequently found in the Albany legislature. They included Senator John J. Dunnigan, Senate Minority Leader John J. McNaboe, and Assemblyman Louis A. Cuvillier, each of whom took turns in directing obstructive tactics. McNaboe was Boss Curry's man on the committee, and he later admitted that he had actually "received instructions" to attack the investigator. Cuvillier was also under the sway of Tammany Hall. Dunnigan was an architect in the Bronx, and he was linked to the influential Democratic political machine there. All three made no bones about it: they were out to embarrass and break the investigation. They were abetted by Irwin Steingut, assembly minority leader, who relayed orders from his Brooklyn stronghold.

Assemblyman Cuvillier was known for his long speeches, his ability to recite long passages from the Constitution, and his naïveté. His colleagues in Albany made him the butt of their jokes. They would draw fake bills and place them in his box. As a good Democrat, he was asked to approve a bill to put up a tollgate on 42nd Street and tax every blonde that walked by. He was also asked to introduce a bill that would take the last car off every train going from New York to Albany.

Early in the hearings, Senator Dunnigan turned to Seabury and remarked, out of the blue, that he understood that the Judge had received a million-dollar fee from the Gould estate accounting. "Yes," Seabury replied, "over a ten-year period."

"But I never heard of anyone receiving such an amount," Dunnigan said. "*I* never got such a fee."

Seabury replied, "Senator, the reason is obvious—you were never worth that much to anybody."

Senator McNaboe, the most vociferous of the three, threatened

Seabury and his assistants, telling the young lawyers that they would never get anywhere in law practice or politics if they stuck by their chief. At one point, he was responsible for the rumor that Judge Seabury was "keeping a woman on Park Avenue." He told one of Seabury's assistants that unless the investigation cooled off, he would produce her. Somewhat embarrassed, the assistant counsel reported the story to Seabury, who found it amusing. "Tell McNaboe that if he can produce such a lady, I will put her on the witness stand," Seabury said dryly.

A key case in the city-wide investigation concerned Dr. William F. ("Horse Doctor") Doyle, one of the biggest grafters in municipal history. Doyle's case was an illustration of the way one city department could be controlled by a political machine; the ease with which profits of millions of dollars could be diverted for a favored few, including those outside the city government, such as law firms; how bribery could become the accepted method of setting appeals for arbitrary changes in building laws.

Doyle, a veterinarian, practiced before the Board of Standards and Appeals, which treated real-estate problems, not animals. This tribunal in its discretion could permit variances in the regulations concerning the heights of buildings, setbacks, the location of garages, gasoline stations, the nature of the occupancy in factory and home areas. They could make changes that would permit factories to be built in residential neighborhoods; make allowances so that skyscrapers would cut off light and air; affect the lives of many people by turning residential streets into dark and unwholesome canyons. On this city board sat five men, four appointed by Mayor Walker and one by the fire commissioner, himself the Mayor's man.

Doyle had entered politics in the early 1900's, getting an appointment as chief veterinarian of the fire department. The record failed to disclose any complaints from his patients, the city's fire horses. Mayor Hylan named him chief of the Bureau of Fire Prevention. Away from the stables, he performed with some difficulty, retiring after several years when he was indicted for malfeasance because a building he failed to check went up in flames. This circumstance turned out to be a happy one, for it sent him on the road to riches. He started to practice before the Board of Standards and Appeals, pleading cases for builders, contractors, and landlords. (No law degree—or any degree—was necessary.) His skill as an advocate must have been great, for between 1922 and 1930 he put over a million dollars into his bank accounts. In one remarkable year, 1927, his fees amounted to $243,692.60.

The Federal Government began to question his income-tax returns; subsequently he was acquitted of tax evasion, but pertinent records were turned over to the district attorney of New York County. Here they fell under the scrutiny of Judge Seabury and his staff, who found that he had won 244 permits for garages where they were forbidden; 52 applications for gasoline stations where applications had previously been turned down by the Bureau of Fire Prevention; 187 modifications of departmental orders issued under the state labor and tenement-house laws; numerous permits to raise building heights, install wet-wash laundries, and other businesses in residential areas. He was also successful in making the board reverse itself in many cases. His bookkeeping system, incredible for a former city official, included payments partly by check and partly in cash, balances unaccounted for, and blank stubs under the general heading of "disbursements." He obviously was splitting his huge fees.

Seabury decided to put Doyle on the witness stand at the first public hearing of the Joint Legislative Committee. Doyle had fled the city, and the jurisdiction of the committee, but a charge of Federal-income-tax evasion brought him into Manhattan briefly. As Doyle left the Federal building, Seabury's men subpoenaed him and took him to the state building. He was interviewed privately for fifty minutes by Chairman Hofstadter and Counsel Seabury.

"Are you willing to tell us with whom you split fees when you were practicing before the Board of Standards and Appeals?" Seabury asked him.

"On advice of my counsel, I must say that I am in no position to answer such a question," Doyle responded. His counsel was Samuel Falk, son-in-law of Republican County Leader Samuel Koenig, a relationship that did not go unmentioned in the press. Some observers felt that the Republicans had a vested interest in the "system." Doyle was then scheduled to appear at the end of July, 1931.

Judge Seabury, elegantly attired in dark business suit, starched collar and fine silk tie, entered the county courthouse on the appointed day, handed his straw boater to an assistant, and sat down at the counsels' table. State Senator Hofstadter first read into the record Judge Seabury's letter of acceptance to him as chairman, which stipulated that the counsel would have "an absolutely free hand" in presenting the evidence. Seabury then began quietly by calling a clerk of the Board of Standards and Appeals and a Corn Exchange Bank official. These witnesses presented facts about Doyle's practice—and his bank accounts.

Seabury next put Doyle on the stand. He gave some obvious facts about his practice. But when Seabury asked, "In practice before the board, wasn't it your practice to take part of the fee by cash and part by check?" Doyle replied, "I refuse to answer that question because it might tend to incriminate me." Seabury asked him if he had ever split a fee with board members, and Doyle indignantly replied, "Not a nickel." Thereafter, Doyle refused to answer a series of questions about whether he had ever split fees with anybody else. To Seabury's question, "Did you ever bribe any political leader in the County of New York?" again Doyle refused to answer on grounds of possible self-incrimination.

Now Seabury turned to the nine members of the Joint Legislative Committee and demanded: "I want to ask the committee whether this witness should not be required to answer this question or whether it is in the public interest that he be excused from answering."

Chairman Hofstadter called his committee into executive session, after which he announced that the committee had decided, 5 votes to 4, to empower the inquiry to force Doyle to testify. At this point, Assemblyman Cuvillier, speaking for the Democratic minority, turned on Seabury: "What I want to know is this—isn't W. Kingsland Macy, the Republican state chairman, behind this whole machinery to bring Doyle to testify in order to assist the Republican party at the polls?"

Judge Seabury's face reddened. He stood up before the legislators and stated, "If that were a fair question—and I don't admit that it is—it would be perfectly in line for me to ask you whether or not these activities and attempts to obstruct the work of this committee are not actuated by the leader of Tammany Hall."

There was a roar and outburst of applause in the courtroom, according to the *New York Evening Post,* and Senator Hofstadter pounded his gavel and threatened to clear out the spectators.

Thereafter, Judge Seabury continued to ask questions about fee splitting and bribes and bank accounts, and Doyle continued to refuse to answer. Each time, Chairman Hofstadter directed him to do so for the record. Finally, Doyle was cited for contempt, and Justice William Harman Black sentenced him to thirty days in jail. If there was any doubt that Tammany Hall had an interest in the welfare of Doyle, it was dispelled by a startling legal maneuver in the next few days.

Boss Curry himself put through a phone call to a more sympathetic judge, Henry L. Sherman of the appellate division, who was vacationing in Lake Placid, New York, 300 miles north of Manhattan. Justice Sherman granted a stay of the order jailing Doyle. Doyle was liable to become talkative unless Tammany kept him out of jail, and Tammany's chief sachem had taken the matter into his own hands with an injudicious call. The press reported that Max D. Steuer instigated the maneuver; he had actually been in Curry's suite at the Park Lane Hotel when the call went through. This so infuriated Seabury that he called upon Curry to explain his actions before the committee.

The Tammany leader admitted that he had "reached" the judge at Lake Placid but quickly added, "Wait a minute, I don't like that word *reach*." Seabury smiled and said, "Very well, Mr. Curry, I don't want to injure your sensibilities." Seabury asked him why he had interfered in a judicial proceeding, and Curry replied, "I wanted to have the powers of the committee tested with regard to the immunity clause. I want to tell you, Judge Seabury, I didn't try to influence justice. I tried to get a judge to hear a case." Seabury asked, "You thought it part of your political duty as leader of the Democratic organization of this city to interfere in a case when the courts of justice were concerned. Did you do it as a personal favor?" Curry answered, "Yes, but that was only secondary."

Under constant pressure, Curry finally gave his real reason for defying the committee so flagrantly. All along, the Democratic legislators had maintained that they were for the investigation and resented Seabury's statements about obstruction. Now Curry said, "I as representative of the Democratic organization of the City of New York was expecting someone to test the constitutionality of the committee's powers to grant immunity, and therefore when the request came for my aid, I was glad to be of service." In reply to Seabury's question as to why he had telephoned a justice of the appellate division, Curry finally declared, "This is a crucification, if it can be had, of the Democratic party of the City of New York."

It was obvious that two codes of morality were in conflict, that Curry and his cohorts had somehow convinced themselves that their party had extralegal authority. This above all shocked Seabury. That the leader of Tammany Hall could actually say so before a state legislative committee indicated a certain malign sincerity. Years of holding power by controlling courts and city departments had turned illegal actions into acceptable behavior. This was the system; the politicians who followed the rules wanted to preserve the system; they were, in this sense, archconservatives.

"The truth of the matter was that the political organization with which Doyle had had his relations was taking up the cudgels when an exposure of those relations was threatened and particularly when there was danger that continued incarceration might weaken Doyle's resistance to disclosure." Thus Seabury interpreted the matter to the legislators.

Meanwhile, the wags summed up the situation in a song:

> *Tammany Hall's a patriotic outfit,*
> *Tammany Hall's a great society,*
> *Fourth of July they always wave the flag, boys,*
> *But they never, never waive immunity!*

Now a legal question emerged that could destroy the whole investigation: Did Seabury and this legislative committee have the power to grant witnesses immunity from prosecution? An appeal was taken to the state's highest court in the Doyle case. Judge Cardozo heard the arguments and postponed a decision for ten days. "What happens to Dr. Doyle in the meantime?" his attorney asked the court on behalf of his jailed client. "He stays where he is, of course," Judge Cardozo answered. Then Cardozo reversed the judgment of the lower courts and held that the legislative committee did not have the power to grant immunity. Even though the ruling was against his authority, Seabury called it "a learned decision."

For Cardozo was thinking of the rights of law-abiding men as well as rogues. And in his opinion, he suggested that there was a proper way for immunity to be granted: "The way to compel disclosure as to conspiracies and attempts is not obscure or devious. A grant of immunity similar to the one contained in the resolution may be embodied in a statute. The legislature, when it convenes, may pass an act of amnesty with the approval of the Governor, an act of amnesty coextensive with the privilege destroyed. The appellant as well as other witnesses will then be under a duty to declare the whole truth, irrespective of the number or nature of crimes exposed to view."

It was now up to Governor Roosevelt to call an extraordinary session of the legislature. Judge Seabury drafted a bill giving the committee power to force witnesses to testify by granting them immunity. It was forwarded to Roosevelt with a personal letter from Seabury in which he spoke as one Democrat to another. "I deeply regret to say, but truth compels the statement, that a fraction of our party now in control of the City of New York has expressed its opposition to such a statute." He said that by granting immunity the last excuse for permitting malefactors to refuse to testify would be removed. "Fortunately, it lies within your power as governor to convene a special session of the legislature to unite with you, regardless of party, in enacting a statute that will empower the Joint Legislative Committee in proper cases to grant immunity to witnesses to the end that the facts about graft and corruption in the City of New York may be disclosed. With great respect, I ask that you exercise this power."

Governor Roosevelt, under political pressure because of his presidential aspirations, conferred with close associates, including Lieutenant-Governor Herbert H. Lehman and Samuel I. Rosenman, his legal adviser. New York City's Democrats were trying to force him to agree to a diversionary investigation of upstate Republican counties. Democrats outside New York State watched to see if the Governor would knuckle under to Tammany. He did not. He called an extraordinary session to enact Seabury's immunity proposal. "The purpose of the legislation," Roosevelt said, "meets with my entire approval." The legislature enacted the bills, and Roosevelt signed them into law. Although the Governor did not "flame out in wrath against plunder"—as an editorial in *The New York Times* wished he would—he did act to strengthen the Seabury investigation.

Now Seabury's staff began to roam the five boroughs of New York, to check on the distribution of funds for unemployment relief. Nearly $10,000,000 had been appropriated by the city for this purpose in 1931. The money, distributed through the borough president's office, was not allotted to the boroughs in proportion to the number of unemployed but rather on the basis of "work opportunities" for roads and other public projects. Judge Seabury dispatched the Herwitz brothers, Oren and Victor, fresh out of law school, to Staten Island. They examined the relief rolls, compared them with party registration, and discovered that nine out of ten people on relief were Democrats. They visited these recipients personally. A few of the Democrats on relief had two cars in the garage; others worked for the borough of Richmond. The relief applications were "handled" by the political clubs; Republican poor need not apply.

Judge Seabury called many witnesses (including one receiving relief but owning four cars, working women with maids at home, and one man paying taxes on $60,000 in real estate); all were Democrats and linked through their clubs to the office of Borough President John A. Lynch. The disclosure of the goings on in Richmond, and the revelation of a similar situation in the office of Manhattan Borough President Samuel Levy, aroused the populace. Manhattan's relief cards, distributed through the borough president's secretary, were approved with the blanks not filled in; that task was taken care of by the district clubs.

Shortly after these abuses were exposed, the City of New York appropriated another $15,000,000 for unemployment relief. By this time public indignation could not be ignored, and Mayor Walker appointed a nonpolitical board of distinguished citizens to insure an honest distribution of relief money. "It is highly gratifying," Judge Seabury commented, "to know that our efforts have been responsible for the selection of this type of board free from political control. It would seem conservative to say that the amount saved will be a very substantial sum."

The borough of Richmond had another scandal involving its bus transportation, and once again Borough President Lynch was the culprit. There were two bus lines competing for a franchise. One, the Staten Island Coach Company, had a decent record, offered lower fares and a better share of its income to the city; the other, the Tompkins Bus Corporation, was financially irresponsible. The Board of Transportation had recommended that the Staten Island Coach Company get the franchise. Why, Judge Seabury wanted to know, did the franchise go to Tompkins Bus?

He put Lynch on the witness stand, where it came out that the borough president had a substantial interest in the newspaper the *Staten Islander*. The periodical supported Lynch politically, and he helped to support it financially when it was losing money. A promoter, Minthorne T. Gordon, arrived on the scene and took over the paper, giving Lynch a note for $30,000. Less than a week later, Gordon was granted the bus franchise in the name of the Tompkins Bus Corporation. All such franchises went through the Board of Estimate, over which Mayor Walker presided. Judge Seabury revealed that, in spite of the evidence about the two bus companies, Mayor Walker had turned to Borough President Lynch and said, "Name the company." Lynch replied, "Tompkins," and the board approved the franchise unanimously. Shortly thereafter, residents of Staten Island had their bus fare increased.

Watching Seabury in action before the Joint Legislative Committee, his young assistants learned how a master prepared a case. "He did it by writing in one-line sentences a list of the facts he wished to elicit from a witness," Oren Herwitz later recalled. "Then he framed his questions to bring out the facts. The sentences were written out in longhand on white ruled legal paper. Opposite each fact was a page number from the transcript of private testimony. If witnesses balked, he would remind them of what they had said—they were under oath, of course. But he wouldn't indulge in fishing for evidence aimlessly, and he refused to browbeat a witness."

The borough of Queens was ruled by John Theofel, Democratic county leader whose sinecure was chief clerk of the Queens Surrogate's Court. There were some suspicious goings on there, and Judge Seabury assigned Louis Molloy and Harold Melniker to check. The borough had a noble tradition of graft, and Theofel could hardly be expected to measure up to Maurice Connolly, the borough president until 1927, who was involved in the $16,000,000 sewer-pipe swindle. Queens was one borough where the sewers could be said to be the finest, so thoroughly were they worked over.

Theofel was put on the stand by Judge Seabury and had some difficulty explaining his duties as chief clerk. When asked which departments he supervised in the surrogate's court, he replied, "I am not a lawyer, Judge." When Seabury asked him, "What do you do, Mr. Clerk?" Theofel replied, "Walk through, keep around on the job." The only item of service he recalled having performed was moving the clerk's office from the sixth floor to the fifth floor. However, these were preliminary skirmishes. He admitted that he, the clerk, had put the surrogate into office! Two weeks later, the grateful surrogate raised Theofel's salary by $2,000. Theofel also admitted humbly that he named other officials to high office—from district attorney to supreme court judge.

Theofel was very firm on one subject: Queens public officials had to uphold the dignity of their borough by riding around in Pierce-Arrows. All the "official" cars purchased by the city were Pierce-Arrows; it was also expected that officials would buy them for private use. When an assistant district attorney who could not afford one expressed a desire to purchase a less expensive Packard, he was told that he had better buy a Pierce-Arrow from Wilson Bros., Inc., where all the other cars came from. By a coincidence, Dudley Wilson was Theofel's son-in-law, and Theofel owned most of the stock of Wilson Bros., Inc. It could honestly be said that when the Pierce-Arrow was no longer on the market for the American motorist, it was through no fault of John Theofel.

He, too, had a tin box. Judge Seabury established that during his six years as Queens county leader, Theofel's net worth increased from $28,650 to $201,300. He controlled campaign contributions. When reporting these contributions to the Secretary of State, he would make an omnibus statement that "$40,000 was paid to watchers, workers, tabulators, messengers and so forth." He claimed to have destroyed all receipts. But he did disclose the code of Queens political morality established by his predecessor. The Democratic county boss had taken $6,000 in cash from a campaign fund and given it to his secretary. "I protested," Theofel said. The county boss then told him, "Take a thousand for yourself, John." Seabury asked, "Well, did you?" Theofel replied, "Sure."

When Judge Seabury asked Theofel where he kept his tin box, Senator McNaboe interrupted, "I don't think the State of New York is warranted in spending five hundred thousand to find out whether anyone has any money in a tin box or not." "Or a diamond box or a gold box," added Assemblyman Cuvillier. "It could be done more economically if the Senator did not interrupt," said Judge Seabury. The questioning continued, and Judge Seabury established that safe-deposit-box records and bank-deposit slips showed parallel transactions of large sums of cash. He continued to produce documentary evidence ferreted by his assistants every time that Theofel was unable to say whether he had kept his money "in a closet, in a shoe, in a sock or in a box."

In the Bronx, two men dominated Democratic politics. The county leader was Edward J. Flynn, an attorney who served as Governor Roosevelt's Secretary of State and remained loyal to him despite Tammany's antipathy to the investigation. His patronage came through state rather than city channels, and he was not tainted with personal scandals or impropriety. Boss Curry of Manhattan did not appeal to Ed Flynn. There was another Flynn, however, who remained in the Bronx. William J. Flynn, the former county coroner, served as commissioner of borough works, a traditional position for grafters. Irving Ben Cooper went up to the Bronx for Judge Seabury and discovered that the ex-coroner was trying to bury some of his nefarious deals.

William J. Flynn was no relation to Ed Flynn, as the latter pointed out again and again, but they were often confused by the public. William J. Flynn was a plunderer of Bronx real estate. When a private individual, Louis H. Willard, attempted to buy a vacant lot for the purpose of erecting a garage, he suddenly found his plans blocked by the commissioner of public works. Flynn, signing his letter of protest "Acting President, Borough of The Bronx," claimed that he did so as an individual, not as a public official. Having succeeded in stopping Willard, because such a garage "would be a detriment to our people," Flynn acquired a property across the street and built his own garage. Whenever Willard tried to obtain approval for curb cuts (necessary for vehicles to go over the sidewalk) so that he could rent to business concerns, Flynn, to avoid any possible competition saw to it that approval was not given. Willard lost his property and his home through foreclosures, his wife committed suicide, and he attempted to poison himself.

The crooked Flynn concealed his garage and other holdings behind dummy corporations. On one of his properties he managed to avoid paying taxes of $13,000 by getting the Board of Estimate to declare it to be part of a public park (though it was not). Flynn also authorized a bus line to operate on condition that the buses park in his garage. All these facts were dug out by Irving Ben Cooper.

Seabury's examination of Flynn before the Joint Legislative Committee revealed that his job as commissioner of public works had been fruitful. He had started as the owner of a two-family house and no other real estate. At the end of 1931, his bank deposits showed a total close to $650,000. His real-estate equities had grown to about $400,000. Before the motion was made to adjudge him in contempt for refusing to answer questions about his deals, Flynn blamed the terrible depression that had caused his property to go down in value: "I am sorry to say, and yet I don't need to be ashamed of it, because I am in the same position as the great City of New York, who have wonderful assets in their bonds, yet have no sale for bonds that are down to seventy-nine and eighty. I am in the same position as the U. S. Government today."

The investigation moved on to Brooklyn, home base for three men named McCooey, McQuade, and McGuinness. "Uncle John" H. McCooey, the Democratic boss of Kings County for more than two decades, was clerk of the surrogate's court. He had the Brooklyn Bar Association in his back pocket. Even when Judge W. Bernard Vause, one of McCooey's pals, was caught in a swindle, the local Bar Association blinked and turned away. Vause was convicted of using the mails to defraud, and despite the efforts of Tammany's favorite lawyer, Max D. Steuer, was sentenced to a six-year prison term. McCooey declared, "They have never proved that he was dishonest as a judge." In spite of this ringing endorsement, Judge Vause went to jail.

In the midst of the city-wide investigation, McCooey decided that five more supreme court judges were needed to keep justice flowing through Brooklyn's courts. These became part of a larger bipartisan judiciary deal in the Second Judicial District, in which supreme court judgeships went to Democrats and Republicans in four other counties as well. As a trader who knew how to make a deal —he proceeded to the fore, said newspaperman Paul A. Tierney, "with the triumphal progress of a jellyfish"—McCooey demonstrated how to "divide" five places in half. After fixing matters with the Republicans in the Albany legislature and the Republican leaders in metropolitan New York, McCooey said magnanimously, "We ought not to be the dog in the manger any longer. Let us give the Republicans recognition." In a great display of judicial love and cleanliness, the Democrats obtained three and the Republicans two judgeships in Brooklyn, each party endorsing the other's candidates.

The three new Democratic supreme court judges for Brooklyn included one whose name sounded familiar: John H. McCooey, Jr., the thirty-year-old son of "Uncle John." He was far from a brilliant lawyer, and received his principal income from refereeships given to his firm by his father. He also did well practicing before the Board of Standards and Appeals, where, as "Horse Doctor" Doyle had shown, a politician could make a handsome living. Judge Seabury, fuming at the bipartisan deal, put McCooey, Senior, in the witness chair and made him admit that all the Brooklyn judgeships had been agreed upon beforehand by Meier Steinbrink, McCooey's Republican opposite number, and himself. Steinbrink, to show his impartiality, stepped down as leader and took over one of the supreme court judgeships—with McCooey's endorsement.

Seabury asked McCooey to tell the legislative committee how his inexperienced son had received the $25,000-a-year supreme court nomination. "Oh," said McCooey, "nearly every leader in the party urged me very strongly to nominate Jack. I had no idea there was such a unanimity of opinion." McCooey added that he had allowed his leaders to twist his arm, and the Brooklyn Bar Association to approve Jack, because his son had "the poise and the character and the industry," and was, besides, "in a receptive mood."

Seabury took the matter up before both lawyers' associations in Manhattan. They strongly disapproved the deal and the rubber-stamp endorsements by the political bosses. "No-Deal" candidates were put up for office in opposition, but they could not defeat the combined machine vote. Judge Seabury reported these sordid facts to the legislative committee, pointing out that there was a price tag attached to this judicial palship. He quoted one Republican leader as telling a future supreme court judge: "Remember the address of the treasury of the county committee." Seabury exposed such deals

($5,000 in cash for one particular judgeship, plus the right of the county leader to appoint the judge's legal staff) for all the citizens of the city and state to see.

Brooklyn also had a county register, the Hon. James A. McQuade, who turned out to be one of the finest family men in the borough. He gave hilarious testimony when he took the stand as the "breadwinner" of what the tabloid press in New York called "the thirty-four starving McQuades." Seabury pursued McQuade, as well as other leaders of Democratic and Republican district clubs, because poker as well as politics was played in the clubhouses. The charitable McQuade came from the Greenpoint section of Brooklyn, and, appropriately, gave his address as "Noble Street."

Judge Seabury had a few questions to ask him: How had he managed to accumulate $510,000 in six years when his salary was $12,000 a year? And what about the fine "library" he maintained for "the boys" in the clubhouse where, strangely, the police raiding the club found bookies but no books?

"As I understand it," Seabury said innocently, "at the time of the raid the members were up in the library reading books?"

"We have a good library there," said McQuade, "and they could sit there and study or do whatever they wanted to do. There were eight or nine men, four in the library and four were at a table, playing cards, penny-ante or something—I don't know what they were playing."

Seabury said that it was a shame that men should be taken out of a library and arraigned in a police station, and McQuade heartily agreed. Then Seabury interposed with some of the literature that was discovered in the library by the policemen. The main periodical, he said, seemed to be *Armstrong's Scratch Sheet*. And among the literary efforts found in the club were small slips of paper with notations such as "Phillips, first entry and contract 0-2-0, parlay, Faithful Friend and Sir Murice." McQuade finally admitted that he regularly bailed out the gamblers in his club, but only as "a general act of good fellowship for friends and neighbors."

Seabury then asked McQuade how he happened to have more than half a million dollars deposited in his account.

"Money that I borrowed. If you want me to get to the start of it, I will have to take and go over the family in its entirety, without feeling that I am humiliated in the least or am not humiliating the other thirty-three McQuades. If this committee can take the time, I will go over it from the start." McQuade paused for a moment and then said, as if delivering himself of a state secret, "I unfortunately went into politics. I say that cautiously."

"You don't base that on that deposit, do you?" Seabury asked.

"I am going to get to that deposit, if you will let me." He explained that a family business had failed after an unnamed man had stolen money from the firm. When McQuade Brothers was liquidated, he said, "the thirty-four McQuades were placed on my back, I being the only breadwinner, and after that it was necessary to keep life in their body, sustenance, to go out and borrow money. I felt it my duty, being that they were my flesh and blood, part and parcel of me, to help them. I am getting along in fairly good shape when my mother, Lord have mercy on her, dropped dead. I am going along nicely when my brother, Lord have mercy on him, dropped dead. But doing nicely, when I have two other brothers, and when my brother died, he willed me his family, which I am still taking care of, thank God. The extra money that you see in this year or any year from that year on has been money that I borrowed, and not ashamed of it."

"Well, now, Mr. Register," said Seabury politely, "will you be good enough to indicate from whom you borrowed this money?"

"Oh, Judge, offhand I could not," McQuade said.

Seabury reworded the question and continued to cite figures from McQuade's bank deposits, getting the evidence into the record.

"I would, for instance," McQuade said, "borrow a thousand dollars off John Brown. In two weeks time John wanted that thousand dollars, and I would borrow a thousand dollars off John Jones. Another, maybe two weeks he would want that. I would get it off John Smith, where in reality there would be possibly ten thousand dollars deposited for the thousand dollars that was actually working."

Seabury asked him if he had any records of the sums borrowed or paid off.

"As the money was paid, it was off my mind," said McQuade, "and I thanked God for it and destroyed anything that I might have."

"Why do you give thanks to Divine Providence?" Seabury inquired.

"I give thanks to Divine Providence for permitting me to pay those people who were kind enough to loan me the money."

Exasperated at McQuade's evasions and losses of memory, Seabury asked him to please omit the pathetic tale of the other McQuades and simply explain the deposits.

"I am under oath here," McQuade protested. "And an oath is calling upon God as witness to the truth of what I say. That's my truth, so help me God."

Seabury reminded McQuade that he had asked for a public hearing so that he could clear his good and generous name. "That's right," McQuade said. "It was my misfortune." Seabury then told him not to cry, because he was getting the hearing he wanted. "You never heard me cry," McQuade said indignantly. "With all my trouble, and I had plenty of that, I never cried. My name was McQuade." Seabury said, "That is what I understood it was"; and McQuade declared, "There are very few McQuades that do any crying."

Assemblyman Cuvillier interrupted to ask, "Mr. McQuade, what are you worth?"

"I got enough to do me the rest of my life if I die today."

"What's that?" asked the confused Cuvillier.

"Nothing. You can't be worth much when you have thirty-four in the family."

Thus, when McQuade left the stand, his half a million dollars was still a mystery. Outside, he grinned and asked a group of reporters, "How did my story go over?" It went over well, apparently, with McCooey, who decided McQuade deserved a higher office in Brooklyn at an increase in salary, and thereupon entered McQuade as the Democratic candidate for sheriff in the fall election of 1931. The good Democrats of Kings County dutifully elected him.

The investigation of Brooklyn gambling starred another unusual citizen from Greenpoint, the Hon. Peter J. McGuinness. He held the post of assistant commissioner of public works and was, he declared proudly, "executive member of the Greenpoint Peoples' Regular Democratic Organization of the Fifteenth Assembly District." McGuinness had the charm that McQuade lacked. As political rivals in the same neighborhood, McGuinness had labeled McQuade "Payroll Jim, the Jesse James of Greenpoint," thereby taking notice of all the starving McQuades on the city payroll. McGuinness called Greenpoint, with its Newtown Creek serving as a small harbor on the East River, the "garden spot of America."

When he left the board of aldermen to take over Brooklyn's public works, he informed the board: "I drove nine gypsy bands out of Greenpoint, as well as three hundred Chinese coolies and all the cats and dogs that used to run down the streets. One of the best things I done was to establish a farm garden so children could learn the real value of vegetables. I got Greenpoint three playgrounds, the subway, the one-and-a-half-million-dollar bridge on Greenpoint Avenue, and two million dollars' worth of paving." With that, the retiring alderman concluded, "I done good. I thank you." He was disarming. Even Seabury could not suppress a twinkle when, upon being asked who had suggested him for his assistant commissionership, McGuinness replied, "Well, I couldn't pick a more better person to suggest for this job than myself."

Seabury wondered how McGuinness had managed to take the leadership of the assembly district from McQuade in view of "his large family connections," and McGuinness said, "Judge, I don't think Mr. McQuade has got anything on my family." Seabury continued lightly, "You think you could have outvoted him in that respect?" and McGuinness answered, "You can tell the world on that, Judge. There is fourteen McGuinnesses."

The byplay momentarily over, Judge Seabury asked McGuinness if he knew what went on in his clubhouse. "Sometimes, Judge," he replied. "But I can't be held responsible for everything that goes on. If a man murders another man, I hope they don't lock up McGuinness for the murder." Seabury said he referred to gambling, and McGuinness admitted that Inspector Lewis J. Valentine's detectives had shown an unusual interest in his political clubrooms. Indeed, McGuinness said that he was just heading for his club to tell his good members to please cease and desist any gambling henceforth when a funny thing happened.

"I went upstairs to the clubroom. It was just about five minutes after four. I got myself in the side of the clubroom—one light was lit and the other side it was dark. I put myself behind a pillar. They didn't know I was in the clubroom until a gentleman appeared at the door and he said, 'I would like to see Mr. McGuinness.' I said, 'Here I am,' and I jumped up and walked to the door. He said, 'Mr. McGuinness, would you be kind enough to give me a letter out to the new Maspeth Union Gas tanks, so I can get the job Monday?' I said, 'Come back tonight, I will only be too pleased to do it for you.' I turned quick on my heels and I said, 'Cheese it, here comes the cops.' "

At this Seabury found himself somewhat confused by the narrative. Was McGuinness warning the gentlemen in his club to avoid arrest or to close down the gambling? McGuinness said that he wanted to make sure that his club members were behaving. "You weren't spying on your own club members, were you, hiding behind this pillar?" Seabury asked. McGuinness replied, "Yes, I will spy on them, too. They were doing things there they shouldn't do." Seabury asked him if there was any agreement with the raiding police, and McGuinness said, "Judge, in my public life, me and the police never agreed." The courtroom roared.

"But you said, 'Here comes the police' or 'Cheese it, the police'?" Seabury inquired.

"No," said McGuinness. "Cheese it, here comes the cops."

Judge Seabury bowed and said, "I stand corrected."

But a moment later McGuinness admitted that he was not skilled in all languages. In his club "library," a rival to the neighboring club run by McQuade, certain literary notations were found, such as "Even money on Oh Susanna; Great Sport and La Camita, 0-20." Seabury asked him if he understood what those slips of paper meant, and McGuinness replied, "Judge, all that stuff you just read off is Greek to me." At this point, McGuinness pulled out two season passes to Belmont Park and declared that, despite these courtesies from the New York Racing Association, "I never went to a racetrack in my life."

Judge Seabury produced the police record to refresh McGuinness's memory about some papers found, during a raid, in a safe in his club. The safe bore the name "Peter J. McGuinness." At this McGuinness said, "I never seen anything in that safe—I never seen the safe opened." Judge Seabury lifted an eyebrow, and McGuinness looked hurt. "Now, I would like you to tell, with your characteristic frankness," Seabury said, "what these notations found in your safe

mean: 'January Play, $54,057; Pay Off, $46,015.23; Profit, $8,041.77.'"
McGuinness said, "Judge, that was not my safe. I never put a tooth-pick in that safe."

After elaborate thanks to Judge Seabury for mentioning his club's Christmas-basket fund and carnival receipts (all of which, he admitted, were commingled in his personal bank account), Assistant Commissioner McGuinness turned on his charm and said, "A pleasure, I assure you gentlemen, having this great pleasure of coming before you. I want to thank Mr. Seabury, too, for being so kind and courteous to ·me." In turn, Seabury told McGuinness it gave him great pleasure to return his savings-bank book. McGuinness swept off the stand, his savings intact, and his honor only slightly askew.

Seabury's investigation of Manhattan, where Boss Curry ruled and where His Honor the Mayor occasionally resided between junkets to California and the Continent, had no such amusing side lights.

Here, especially, Seabury's staff was attacked. Tammany lawyers in official positions told George Levy, "You're hurting yourself for life—after this investigation is over, Tammany is still going to control the city." One Tammany district leader turned on Louis Molloy and said, "How can you, with the name of Molloy, do such a thing? Seabury will never do anything for your career." But Molloy remembered a witness who complained to the press that he had been forced to give improper testimony during a private interview with Molloy. When his accusation appeared in the papers, reporters brought the news to Judge Seabury, whose immediate reply was, "I have not read the testimony in question, but I'm sure that any questions Mr. Molloy asked were pertinent to the inquiry." The reporters walked into Molloy's office, saying, "The Judge sure backed you up."

The records of private testimony were carefully guarded by Bill Northrop and a few others close to Judge Seabury. They were locked in large steel safes at night, and not even members of the legislative committee were permitted to examine them. Seabury was determined that no innocent witnesses would be slandered merely by reason of his appearance before the investigative staff. Tammany used various devices to try to find out where Seabury's blows would be struck next. One minor politician, who managed to work his way onto the Seabury staff as a process server, invited Bill Mulligan to a sinister night club in the Bronx. He tried to pump him for information, and a couple of thugs joined them, on signal. The cheap booze flowed, but Mulligan fortunately recognized the game. The next morning he warned his colleagues that one of their process servers could not be trusted, and thereafter the man was avoided.

A major blow to Tammany Hall in Manhattan was the testimony, and subsequent dismissal, of Thomas M. Farley, sheriff of New York County. When the police raided the clubhouse of the Thomas M. Farley Association, they found former associates of Arnold Rothstein and well-known gangsters with long felony records among the crapshooters. Judge Seabury asked Sheriff Farley if he knew what these habitués of his club were doing at two o'clock in the morning.

"The members that was there was busy packing baseball bats, skipping ropes, and rubber balls, because our May Day party took place the next day," explained the sheriff, with a straight face.

Judge Seabury marveled at the fact that these men were so dedicated that they were packing toys for children long past midnight. "By any chance," he inquired, "did any gambling paraphernalia get mixed up with those rubber balls and other children's playthings?" The sheriff assured him that none had, and Seabury asked what else was found there that night. "There were canopies," said Farley, "and Maypoles."

These fanciful tales, plus the earlier failure of Farley to explain how he had amassed $400,000 in his wonderful big tin box, resulted in charges brought by Judge Seabury to Governor Roosevelt to throw the sheriff out of office. The latent hostility between the administration in Albany and the investigators became apparent when the Governor's counsel, Samuel Rosenman, asked Seabury if he filed these charges as an individual or as counsel to the Joint Legislative Committee. Rosenman wanted to clarify the record, adding that "the Governor has stated that the same consideration will be given to charges" in either case. Judge Seabury—whose righteous indignation did not always serve his cause best—rather formally admitted that "my letter was an individual communication by me to the Governor of the state."

Judge Seabury did not trust Governor Roosevelt; worse, he felt a need to lecture him. While waiting for the Governor to act against Sheriff Farley, he wrote him a letter on February 1, 1932, saying:

I read recently with interest your stirring address pointing out the need that exists in our country for leadership. Will you not furnish the sort of leadership to which you referred in the present situation? The People of New York County have no agency to which they can appeal other than yourself. Every prosecuting agency within the five counties which compose the greater city is in the control of Tammany Hall. Surely upon the facts, you will not fail to respond. I have tried to put the issues before you respectfully, but plainly. I feel that the people of this county are entitled to prompt executive action.

Governor Roosevelt asked Sheriff Farley to come to the executive chamber in Albany. In morning coat and stand-up collar, the Tammany sachem again attempted to explain away Seabury's charges of personal and public corruption. But his greed had exceeded his grasp. At the end of February, 1932, Sheriff Farley was removed from office by Governor Roosevelt.

One sentence in Governor Roosevelt's decision against the sheriff became a standard citation for all such cases in the future, not only in New York but in other states of the union. It evolved into an unofficial code of conduct:

As a matter of general sound public policy, I am very certain that there is a requirement that where a public official is under inquiry or investigation, especially an elected official, and it appears that his scale of living or the total of his bank deposits far exceeds the public salary which he is known to receive, he, the elected public official, owes a positive public duty to the community to give a reasonable or credible explanation óf the sources of the deposits, or the source which enables him to maintain a scale of living beyond the amount of his salary.

Sam Rosenman watched the Governor write out this principle in his own hand.

Manhattan's Tammany leaders received a cut from every possible function, small and large: from getting married to renting a pier. For example, the man in charge of issuing marriage licenses was James J. McCormick, a deputy city clerk. McCormick, also a Democratic district leader, strongly believed in the sanctity of marriage and money. When a couple came to his municipal chapel, two dollars went to the city—and "tips" of ten or twenty dollars went into his own pocket. These were not exactly voluntary contributions from eager bridegrooms. All through the ceremonies, his top desk drawer was left open conspicuously—and he indicated that bridegrooms could put their tips there. An anxious couple could also get to the head of the marriage line by crossing the clerk's palm. Judge Seabury followed his normal routine; he confronted the official with transcripts of his thirty bank accounts and asked him for an explanation of deposits of $384,788. McCormick admitted taking tips (which the city treasurer then tried to recover by attaching his accounts), but said he had only one regret: "I'll get it at home for holding out." McCormick's wife had not known how much other people's marriages had enriched theirs.

When the North German Lloyd Steamship Company decided to dock its liners on the Hudson River instead of in Brooklyn or in New Jersey, they found their plans thwarted by red tape in the offices of the corporation counsel and dock commissioner. There was but one printed form in which a few blanks had to be filled in, yet it took years to "process." Finally, after waiting from 1922 until 1931 for a pier, the steamship company got the point. They hired William H. Hickin, president of the National Democratic Club and a lawyer well connected in Tammany Hall. He received a $50,000 "fee" for handling the arrangements. Judge Seabury called Hickin to the stand to explain, but he refused to waive immunity. "The foregoing review of the North German Lloyd pier lease transaction," Seabury reported to the Joint Legislative Committee, "shows too eloquently to require further discussion how arrangements for the granting of pier leases in the City of New York are made directly with Tammany Hall. It is also evidence of the subtle system by which graft is now extorted—to wit, the interposition of a lawyer to whom the money is passed under the guise of a legal fee."

The law firm to retain for any successful dealing with the City of New York, Judge Seabury revealed, was Olvany, Eisner & Donnelly. The senior partner was onetime leader of Tammany Hall the Hon. George W. Olvany, who maintained his practice while he was head of New York County's Democrats and even after he was replaced by John F. Curry. Magically, land was condemned, easements found, licenses granted, and laws circumvented when George W. Olvany, Esq., received his huge retainers.

All these exposures of corruption were made in the face of a steady attack by New York City's Democratic officeholders, as well as by Democratic members of the legislative committee. For several months Seabury's staff remained unpaid. When it came time for an extension of the life of the investigative committee in 1932, Assembly Minority Leader Irwin Steingut, who had witnessed the demise of the reputations of his Brooklyn colleagues, waxed eloquent. "Are you going to continue to play into the hands of a grand inquisitor who has not only failed to do what he was told but who is brazenly using you to help grind his own personal political axes? Are you going to continue to pour out the public's money when the state is facing a great deficit and when thousands of hungry mouths are yearning for a crust of bread? If so, then you can only be compared to Nero, who fiddled while Rome burned, or to Marie Antoinette, who, when she was told that the people had no bread, cried petulantly: 'Let them eat cake!'"

Despite the allusions to the Grand Inquisitor, Nero, and Marie Antoinette, the state legislature voted to continue the investigation in 1932. Assemblyman Steingut's comment after his oratory had failed was: "Seabury doesn't dare call Mayor Walker, because he knows he has no case against the greatest city in the world." Steingut was soon to be proved wrong.

Many New Yorkers wondered if anything concrete would come from the investigation. There had always been corruption, though few were aware of its scale. Exposure was only half the story; what preventative did Seabury suggest for the future? The legislature had specifically voted that its committee could review any matter "relevant to the general question of ascertaining and improving the administration, conditions, and conduct" of the courts and city government. In an editorial "Open Letter to Samuel Seabury," *The Nation* expressed the hopes of the enlightened citizenry:

Are you, Mr. Seabury, thinking of these further and permanent aims in the midst of your extremely tedious and difficult task of unearthing official misconduct? If not, you are merely wasting time. If, on the other hand, you, with the aid of the innumerable volunteers who will come to your assistance the moment you express the wish, will plan for the future, you will have served not only your city and your state but the whole country. As long as Tammany remains in charge of New York the entire system of city government in America is disgraced.

Seabury accepted the challenge. While his staff continued to collect information about corruption, he began to think about a new charter for the City of New York. At the end of 1932, when he made his final report to the Joint Legislative Committee to Investigate the Administration of the Various Departments of the Government of the City of New York, he included his suggestions for a completely revised charter.

The biggest investigation in the history of an American municipality thus came to an end. Judge Seabury could not restrain himself from taking a final swipe at the "city authorities and the leaders of the dominant political organization" who had obstructed the investigation "with intensity and bitterness at every stage." And then he declared his faith that the People of New York, with the facts before them, would exercise their sense of public decency. "Unless all the teachings of history are false," he wrote in his conclusion, "the people will not content themselves merely with remedying these evils, but they will relegate to the oblivion which they have so richly earned their apologists and defenders, as well as those who have fattened upon these evils at the expense of the poor and lowly of our city, who have been humbugged, swindled and betrayed."

CHAPTER **13**

"*The Boy Friend*"–*Jimmy Walker*

IN the summer of 1908, when Building Commissioner Walker's son, James, was a pointy-shoed character around Tin Pan Alley, resisting his father's efforts to send him to law school, he wrote a hit song, *Will You Love Me in December as You Do in May?* That same year, Dr. Seabury's son, Samuel, already sat as a justice of the New York State Supreme Court. Now another May was here, May of 1932, and the songwriter was His Honor the Mayor, a beloved man of fifty, with a subpoena in his hand. The subpoena had been served at the behest of Seabury, a respected but not universally beloved fifty-nine-year-old private citizen of New York, counsel for the state's investigation of the city. Up the Hudson, watching the investigation of Tammany's mayor, Governor Franklin Roosevelt maintained a judicious aloofness; what happened in the county courthouse could affect his chances for the presidential nomination. From the Bowery to Park Avenue, and across the cities of the nation, people wondered: Will Jimmy Walker still be mayor by December?

Judge Seabury and his staff began thorough preparations; even the prodigious power of Walker to charm was taken into account. "Don't look him straight in the eye when he's on the stand," an associate advised Seabury. "He has an uncanny ability to stare you down. Once he's caught you, you're liable to be stunned and confused." Seabury smiled and said that he had interrogated thousands of witnesses as attorney and judge; nevertheless, he said he would bear the warning in mind. Later, his staff noticed that he stood sideways toward Walker and did not face him unnecessarily.

Four members of Seabury's staff met in his private office before Walker's scheduled appearance. They could be heard arguing loudly by anyone walking in the corridor. Inside they were engaged in a mock trial. The actors were Jack Schurman, Harold Melniker, Louis Molloy, and Bill Mulligan, and each took a turn playing Mayor Walker. The others fired questions about his accounts, trying to contradict the expected answers with damaging records. Accountants working for Seabury on the Walker evidence also got into the act. None could possibly anticipate the fury of the obstructive counterattack by the Democratic legislators on the committee, the remarkable ability of Walker to fence on the witness stand, the roar of his claque. The rehearsals were amusing, but they were a waste of time.

However, the case built up against Walker by Seabury and his associates and assistants was worth the year of careful preparation. "By the time we were ready to present the evidence, we knew all about his finances and financial dealings," George Trosk later recalled. "Perhaps more than Walker knew about himself."

A year before a premature attempt to remove Walker had been made by the City Affairs Committee. The Reverend John Haynes Holmes and Rabbi Stephen S. Wise had moved courageously but precipitately, charging the Mayor with failure to administer the city government, appointing unworthy officials, and ignoring widespread corruption. They did not back up their charges, and Walker had merely replied that the civic organization was nothing more than "an annex of the Socialist party" and that the Reverend Dr. Holmes was "a leader in a group of agitators and Soviet sympathizers." Governor Roosevelt told the City Affairs Committee spokesmen that there was insufficient evidence to remove the Mayor. Walker, naturally, was gleeful.

"I seem to see," said Heywood Broun in his column, "It Seems to Me," "a willingness on Mayor Walker's part to shift responsibility. He expressed grave concern over the failure of civic organizations and great newspapers." The Mayor in a speech said that any reports of corruption should have been disclosed long ago by the press if they were doing *their* job. Cracked Broun, "In other words, the press has held out on James Joseph Walker. Apparently no reporter took the trouble to tell the Mayor the facts of life in a great city. Somebody should blurt out to him the news that there is no Santa Claus within the ranks of Tammany. At least, only for a very restricted set of good little boys and girls."

Seabury was determined not to file general accusations if evidence of personal corruption in the Walker system could be uncovered. Was it not possible that the Mayor, too, had a tin box? To find out, Seabury's group examined the subpoenaed accounts of Walker and many other public officials. For months they sifted records, trying to establish some clue as to Walker's real wealth. But they were unsuccessful until one of the tellers at the Chase National Bank said to James T. Ellis, an accountant diligently going through the bank's records for Seabury, "This will probably cost me my job—but you fellows left out one thing on your subpoena." "What's that?" asked Ellis. "Letters of credit," said the bank employee. Ellis had subpoenaed all forms of records, found nothing to implicate Walker, and had just about decided to give up.

Now he put on his hat and ran as fast as he could to 80 Centre Street. "I may be on to something," he told Louis Molloy and Phil Haberman. "Quick, make out a subpoena for letters of credit." They did so, and the trio went back to the Chase Bank. For the first time in their dealings with the bank, they got a runaround from one of the executive officers. At about three in the afternoon, after the bank had officially closed for business, they went back to their headquarters and burst into Seabury's office. They told him of the officer's evasive tactics. For a moment he became very agitated. Then he sat thoughtfully.

"I will make a suggestion," Seabury finally said, his composure regained. "If you think well of it, why don't you go over to the Chase right now, present my compliments to Mr. Winthrop Aldrich, and say that if there is such a needed document in his bank and it is not in my possession by tonight, his bank will not be open tomorrow."

His assistants questioned his means of carrying out his threat, and Seabury told them that he would subpoena every teller and officer so that it really would be impossible for the bank to conduct any business.

Molloy, Haberman, and Ellis went back to the bank and asked to see Mr. Aldrich. He was not available. They asked for the first vice president. He was not available. They asked to see *any* vice president. Unfortunately, they were all with Mr. Aldrich. . . .

"It was obvious," one of Seabury's assistants recalled, "that the impregnable Chase Bank was scared to death."

At this point, the young men turned to the secretary who had been giving them the runaround and delivered Judge Seabury's message for Aldrich. She disappeared, and a few moments later a vice president emerged and handed them a letter-of-credit record. Mayor Walker's flamboyant signature appeared on all the drafts drawn upon the document.

They dashed back to their office in the state building, and handed the evidence to Judge Seabury.

"This is a fatal blow to Tammany Hall," he said, excitedly. "It is the first time in the history of New York that a mayor is caught taking money with his actual receipts for the bribe."

The letter-of-credit evidence was too important to trust to the office safe. At Seabury's suggestion, Molloy and Haberman rented a safe-deposit box for it. They later had it photostated, but again they put the original in the private box, and did not remove it until Walker himself was confronted on the witness stand.

That letter of credit had been given to Mayor Walker out of a "slush fund" maintained by a group of politicians in New York and businessmen in other states who banded together as the Equitable Coach Company in a fantastic scheme to take over all the bus lines of New York City. Hidden beneath layers of concealed transactions was the fact that Walker had signed a purchaser's agreement for the letter of credit and then taken off for one of his many "much-needed rests" in Germany, Italy, and France during August and September of 1927. In one week in Paris with his cronies, for example, he drew $7,150 against the bank credit, found he was running a bit short, and began another week in Paris by negotiating an additional loan of $3,000 drawn on his New York accounts. The "slush fund" took care of the Mayor's payment here, too.

In one respect, at least, Mayor Walker was honorable: he gave services rendered for these "beneficences," as he liked to call them. The Equitable Coach Company aimed to control all surface transportation in New York, and received a franchise from the New York

City Board of Estimate. Walker himself pushed through the necessary votes in the city's highest executive council. There was one minor stumbling block—the Equitable Coach Company did not own a single bus. Furthermore, its financial setup was, to quote the State Transit Commission later, "paralytic." Nevertheless, Mayor Walker kept giving this fraudulent company extension after extension of its franchise in order to allow it time to begin operations. He did not even bother to use underlings; the franchise was kept alive in the Board of Estimate on the Mayor's own motions.

A combination of detective work and cryptanalysis broke the secret "code" used by the Mayor's business affiliates without his knowledge. It was clear that Walker was held in contempt by the financiers who were using him to try to gain control of the city's transportation system.

The grand scheme involved a go-between, a sly and vulgar state senator, John A. Hastings, from the Brownsville section of Brooklyn. He was one of the opportunists to whom the Mayor was attracted; Hastings and Walker had become close friends in the state legislature. Hastings was on the payroll of several companies, including those operating Manhattan taxicabs, because he was considered a close friend of the Mayor's. One advertising company paid him $10,000 a year to act as, he phrased it, "a glad-hander." His state senator's salary of $2,500 annually hardly paid for his cars, expensively tailored suits, and fat cigars (which were labeled, "These cigars made especially for Senator John A. Hastings").

Senator Hastings organized a small group of Ohio manufacturers in a master company to obtain the bus franchises. He introduced his associates to the Mayor at parties and shipboard sailings. This was the end of the trolley era in New York, and the franchise was supposed to capture control of the routes being converted from trolley lines to bus lines. When Seabury's men discovered that the Equitable Coach Company had paid for the Mayor's tour of Europe, they began to track down the financial backers. One was Frank R. Fageol, president of an Ohio bus company, who, while a witness, had said that he did not have his records with him but would be glad to produce them in Ohio.

No sooner had he said this than Messrs. Molloy and Haberman were at his office in Kent, Ohio, even though they had no authority to operate outside New York state. "We would have crawled to Ohio for Judge Seabury," they later said. The bus company president asked, surprised, "What are you fellows doing here?" "We didn't want to inconvenience you again in New York," they said innocently. Fageol called his secretary. "Those Equitable Bus files in your room—let these gentlemen see them," he said. Fageol knew that the current files revealed nothing about his secret negotiations involving Mayor Walker. But the moment Fageol left the room, Molloy took a chance and asked the secretary to show him the "dead files." The secretary led Seabury's investigators to the basement. Here, they discovered telegrams and memoranda that were invaluable evidence. When Fageol entered the room again he asked, "You gentlemen find what you were looking for?" They said, "Yes." Fageol asked, "Where?" They replied, "Down in the basement." He was thrown off balance, but, having given them permission to look at the records, he could not now protest.

In New York, Molloy, Haberman, and the staff working on the Walker records began to put the pieces together. The memoranda showed that the Equitable plan called for a $20,000,000 financial deal in which Mayor Walker's cat's-paw, Senator Hastings, had a substantial equity. But still Walker was not conclusively implicated. Everyone knew Hastings was a manipulator. The point of the search was to turn up evidence against Walker. That night, Haberman put all the papers in the Equitable case in front of him and began to piece them together. There were dozens of names and corporations from various places that made the puzzle all the more difficult. He drew up a dramatis personae, and suddenly realized that the key to the "code" was contained in two words: BOY FRIEND.

These appeared in a telegram he had picked out of the dead file in Ohio which went:

JOHN MADE MISTAKE AS HIS BOY FRIEND DID NOT WANT FURTHER NEGOTIATIONS WITH PHILADELPHIA BANKER BUT SAYS GO AHEAD WITH BROOKLYN PARTY. CHAIRMAN BOARD AGREEABLE AND LIKES YOU.

The "John" stood for Senator Hastings. The "boy friend" was Mayor Walker. The "Philadelphia banker" was Albert M. Greenfield. The "Brooklyn party" was the Brooklyn Manhattan Transit Corporation, whose "chairman board" was Gerhard M. Dahl. The wire had been sent to Fageol from J. A. Smith, who ran the New York office of the Equitable Bus group. Smith, who dealt with Hastings, was the man who had put up the $10,000 for Jimmy Walker's letter of credit. That connected Walker's "beneficence" with the bus franchise scheme in New York. The telegram had been sent while members of the Equitable group scurried about Ohio, Pennsylvania, and New York for financing. The Brooklyn Manhattan Transit was ultimately approached with a suggestion to support the deal. But the grandiose scheme began to fall apart; it was too big to swing and too politically vulnerable.

This telegram and another which Haberman decoded disclosed that the out-of-state interests considered the "war board" (the code name for Tammany Hall) and the "boy friend" their allies; that the "beneficence" of the letter of credit received by Walker was on account of services rendered. This was the real meaning to Seabury's investigators.

Haberman presented his discovery of the link between Walker and Equitable Bus to Judge Seabury, who pressed the staff to look for substantiating evidence on this deal and for other sources of Walker's income. Clearly, Walker's high mode of living as "night mayor of New York," plus his having to support both wife and mistress, required more than his official salary.

Now more accounts were traced. J. A. Sisto, the senior partner in a Wall Street brokerage firm, met Mayor Walker in Atlantic City, decided to "take the Mayor in" on some Cosden Oil stock, and, without Walker's putting up any money, soon had a mutual friend deliver to the Mayor at City Hall an envelope containing a "profit" of $26,000 in bonds. Supposedly this was money "made for" the Mayor on an investment. Sisto felt he was not obliged to give the Mayor anything but did so because he "felt an admiration for Mayor Walker." The real source of Sisto's admiration can be traced back to his firm's ownership of a large interest in the Checker Cab Corporation, which was then seeking to maintain its advantageous position on the streets of New York. Among the bonds the Mayor received from Sisto was $10,000 of Parmelee Transportation, a holding company controlling various taxicab subsidiaries.

Still another "beneficence" came from Paul Block, owner of the *Brooklyn Standard-Union* and other newspapers, and a speculator who sometimes acted for Hearst in buying up daily papers. His reason for deciding to subsidize the Mayor of the City of New York deserves mention. According to Block, he was walking along Fifth Avenue with his ten-year-old son when the bright young fellow questioned his father about the Mayor's personal finances. "Well," the boy said, "can he live on what he gets?" The boy's concern inspired the father to a most original action. "I was going to try and make a little money for him," Block explained innocently to Seabury later. A joint brokerage account was opened, "P.B. and J.J.W.," but "J.J.W." never invested a penny. Walker received $246,693 over a two-year period, in return for his friendship. The money came to him in cash or checks, and he put it either in his safe at home, gave it to Mrs. Walker, or to "an unnamed individual," who was, of course, Betty Compton, coyly shielded from indelicate mention on page 3 of the tabloids. And why was Block so generous? At the time he had an interest in a company that hoped to sell tiles to the contractors building the city's subways.

Finally a "tin box" was discovered—a joint safe-deposit box held by the Mayor and Russell T. Sherwood, his financial agent. Routinely, the Seabury staff had asked every bank and brokerage office in New York to disclose any accounts in Walker's name. After the brokerage firm of Hornblower & Weeks had denied any knowledge of any Walker account, the senior member of the New York office, John Wing Prentiss (whose name Seabury did not divulge), came in to see the Judge. He said that he was the only one in the firm who knew the true ownership of a huge account, opened in March, 1927, by "Sherwood," simply called, "Investment Trustee Account." The initial deposit was $100,000 in cash. There was no signature card or other evidence of ownership. Another $161,000 in cash was added in the next few months. Not a cent was withdrawn or a stock traded.

Sherwood was a bookkeeper in Walker's old law office, and, between 1924 and 1931, when he fled to Mexico rather than testify before Judge Seabury, he handled the Mayor's checkbook and accounts. The anonymous account was closed by Sherwood in August, 1927, and, at his request, he was handed $263,000 in cash by the brokers. "The following day Mayor Walker sailed for Europe," Judge Seabury noted. Sherwood maintained this and other accounts for Walker, using some of the funds to pay for Walker's obligations. For example, 500 shares of stock of the Brooklyn Manhattan Transit Company were taken out of Sherwood brokerage accounts and given to Betty Compton.

Judge Seabury and his assistants accumulated evidence that, from January 1, 1926, when Walker took office, to August 5, 1931, Sherwood deposited nearly a million dollars for Mayor Walker, of which $750,000 was in cash. Judge Seabury explained why the secret account had been kept in a brokerage house. "If it had been put in a bank, the name of the depositor and the existence of the fund would have become known," he said.

Obviously, Sherwood was a key witness. Suddenly, he disappeared. It was a tremendous blow to the Seabury investigative staff. The Joint Legislative Committee issued a subpoena requiring his attendance. Process servers chased him to Atlantic City and Chicago, unsuccessfully. Then it was discovered that the elusive Sherwood had at age forty-six succumbed to marriage for the first time, and was honeymooning in Mexico. At a staff meeting, Seabury said, "The wicked flee when no man pursueth, let us help them on their way." Thereupon, Haberman and Handler took a train to Texas, then a Ford trimotor plane to Mexico City, pursuing their witness. The bridegroom received them, but spurned their subpoena. The extradition pact with Mexico did not cover recalcitrant witnesses. After holding several press conferences in Mexico City announcing that Sherwood had been served and emphasizing that he was Mayor Walker's man, the two investigators returned to New York. "We felt that we had used the engine of publicity as Judge Seabury had wanted us to," Haberman recalled. The point was underscored for New Yorkers and the nation at large.

In 1932 Walter Lippmann made much of the story in a "Today and Tomorrow" column entitled "The Seabury Investigation." He wrote:

> Mr. Seabury has been investigating the office of Mayor Walker. In the course of it he discovered that a certain Russell T. Sherwood was so closely associated with Mr. Walker that since 1924 they have been the joint proprietors of a safe-deposit box. Sherwood fled the jurisdiction

of the committee and has ever since been a fugitive. The Mayor, who knows what Sherwood knows, has made no effort to have Sherwood return and testify. Tammany complains that Mr. Seabury has discredited the city government "from the top down." That is true. The city government is discredited from the top down. But until Sherwood is produced by Mayor Walker nothing else is possible but to regard the Mayor as discredited. Would any man of honor allow his agent to be a fugitive?

At last the confrontation between Seabury and Walker approached. On May 23, 1932, a *subpoena duces tecum* of the Joint Legislative Committee was served upon the Mayor, calling for the production, on May 25, 1932, of all records of his personal financial transactions from January 1, 1926, to date. The scene was to be the county courthouse off Foley Square. The audience, the city and country.

That morning, Walker's valet laid out a spiffy court costume for the show: a one-button double-breasted blue suit, blue shirt, blue tie, and matching blue handkerchief. "Little boy blue is about to blow his horn—or his top," the Mayor kidded. Then he stepped outside from the Mayfair and into his limousine. "Drive carefully," he told his chauffeur. "We don't want to get a ticket."

Judge Seabury, that morning, dressed early, had breakfast with Maud, and stepped into his limousine. He wore a gray suit, white starched shirt, and conservative dark tie. During the ride downtown to 80 Centre Street, Nick Livingston hinted that he would like to spend the day in the courtroom, and Judge Seabury provided him with a ticket. He was one of the few in the packed audience not cheering raucously for the Mayor. Five thousand persons were outside and a thousand inside when Judge Seabury arrived at the courthouse, flanked by his assistants carrying brief cases and exhibits. There was a little applause and a sibilant undertone of hisses as he mounted the steps. Judge Seabury raised his hat with a courtly gesture to the one and ignored the other.

At a quarter to eleven, the Mayor's blue limousine pulled up before the building. As the huge crowd cheered and whistled, a grin broke out on the face of the Mayor. The man beneath the light gray fedora, with its brim rolled down on one side, refused to move quickly within the pressing crowd. Unlike Seabury, he was one with these people. The police inspector in charge suggested that he enter a side door, but he snapped back, for the benefit of reporters, "I'm used to traveling in crowds." A number of persons wore neckties that advocated "Beer for Prosperity," which some had already had that morning. "Good luck, Jimmy," "Atta boy, Jimmy," "You tell 'im, Jimmy," they shouted, and the Mayor acknowledged their encouragement by clasping his hands overhead. Someone looking closely could have noticed he wore a ring with a blue stone.

Inside, the committeemen, led by Chairman Hofstadter, moved to their judicial chairs behind the rail of varnished oak. Judge Seabury and his assistants already were at the counsel table. As Mayor Walker entered, cheers and applause broke out. Senator Hofstadter cautioned the audience that he would clear the room if they interrupted the proceedings. "You all have to excuse me for wielding the gavel," he said, banging for silence. At eleven o'clock, he turned to the counsel. "Judge Seabury, the committee is ready, if you are," Senator Hofstadter said.

Among the members of the state committee, as its fifty-ninth hearing began, were majority Republicans, including Assemblyman Hamilton F. Potter, who served as vice chairman, and minority Democrats, including Senator John J. McNaboe and Assemblyman Irwin Steingut and Louis A. Cuvillier. Surrounding Seabury were George Trosk, Jacob Gould Schurman, Jr., and William B. Northrop, his associate counsel, and Philip W. Haberman, Jr., William G. Mulligan, Harold Melniker, and J. G. Louis Molloy, his assistant counsel. These were men who had worked together since the magistrates' courts investigation and now, at last, the target of their anticorruption campaign was in their sights.

"Mr. Mayor, would you be good enough to take the stand," Seabury said, and Walker sat down in the armchair to the right of the committee. Seabury leaned against the oak railing and said, "Since the immunity laws were passed, it has been our habit here to tender to witnesses that are called a waiver of immunity. In making the tender it has been my practice to say, in accordance with the fact and the law, that the mere fact of tendering a waiver to any witness carries with it no implication. May I, in the light of that statement, tender a waiver of immunity to you." The Mayor put on his horn-rimmed spectacles, looked at the document, and signed.

Judge Seabury asked the Mayor if he had produced any papers in response to his *subpoena duces tecum,* the Mayor said, "I have," and handed Seabury a box. It included canceled check vouchers from his account with the Chatham & Phoenix Bank & Trust Company for one month in 1930 and three and a half months in 1931, and check stubs for the same account for one month in 1930 and eleven months in 1931–32. When Seabury asked him why he had not produced check stubs or vouchers for the years 1926–29, he stated that if any records were in existence they were in his old law office, but he had not personally made inquiry about them. (Ten days later, Walker did produce some more vouchers.) No records were brought from any of Walker's brokerage accounts, savings accounts or, safe-deposit boxes.

Now Seabury got down to business, questioning Walker about the Equitable Bus deal which had led to the $10,000 letter of credit. Seabury pressed him to recount the details and asked him why he had used his influence on the Board of Estimate to renew the franchise of the bus company when the company owned no buses. The Mayor reminded Seabury that he had only three votes on the board and twelve votes were required for a franchise. Seabury asked Walker if it was not true that he had strongly "urged" his colleagues to vote with him, and Walker innocently replied, "The Mayor never has in six years asked a member of the Board of Estimate to vote for or against anything." Seabury asked Walker if he had not argued for Equitable Bus, and the Mayor admitted he did so, but only for the city's good. Seabury said the Board of Estimate record challenged the Mayor's contention that the Equitable franchise was sound.

"Mr. Chairman," Walker said, turning away from Seabury, "I don't believe that your counsel or you have any legal right to inquire into the operations of an executive's mind or to cross-examine him about why he reaches his conclusions, any more than I have a right or you have a right to examine the Governor as to why he makes an appointment or why the President of the United States vetoes a bill. But, notwithstanding that, let me tell you why I did it."

This was followed by laughter and applause. Walker was aware of his audience, which responded to his remarks, his diversions, and his indignation. Walker resorted to a series of tricks—breaking into Seabury's questions, jabbing lightly, asking for more and more details before answering a question, and then declaring that the question was so complicated that he dared not trust to his memory, since it was all in the record, anyway. When Seabury patiently went along with these tactics, and constructed another question from the facts, Walker would then ask him to repeat the question. But Seabury, having encountered this obvious ruse many times in court, refused to repeat any questions himself, turned his back, and had court stenographers read his words.

When the Mayor was finally backed to the wall with contradictory facts from the Board of Estimate records, establishing that he had worked on behalf of the Equitable Bus group, he merely stated that he could not be expected to remember what he had said specifically at meetings. Seabury asked him if he considered that an "answer," and Walker replied, "No, it is not, and you are not going to make it an answer." But then he refused to "answer," adding sharply, "Remember, I am still the Mayor of the City of New York." And again the spectators applauded, and Chairman Hofstadter banged the gavel and threatened to clear them out.

Mayor Walker was nothing less than brilliant in his repartee. He hid his anger better than did Seabury. His replies ranged from wisecracks to acidly phrased retorts. Since the complex transaction involving the Equitable Bus franchise was camouflaged by lesser financial arrangements, the audience found the details hard to follow, but they responded instantly to the Mayor's punch lines. He left them laughing.

Questioned about promises made by applicants for bus franchises, the Mayor replied: "Why, the best offer, according to that theory, that the city ever had for bus operations came from a company located upon Long Island, and upon investigation it turned out that they were in the hay-and-feed business."

During a committee dispute, when Seabury remarked that he was perfectly willing to answer the Democratic members one at a time, "but I would rather not have more than four or five at once," the Mayor interjected: "Give me the [same] preference, will you?"

One question about the details of the Equitable Bus scheme was a lengthy one, and Walker sharply remarked at various points: "You know that I won't answer a question that amounts to a speech." "Is this an inquiry or is this a prosecution of me?" "If it is an inquiry, give me another forum where I will be even with counsel, and then I will make it a personal competition."

When Seabury rebuked Walker for "making a speech," the witness retorted: "Well, they're not so bad. Did you ever listen to any of them?"

Asked about a detail in his disbursements, a question to which one of the Democratic assemblymen protested because it inquired into "a man's private life," Walker broke in, "Oh, run for mayor and you will read it all in the papers."

In between questions, Walker whispered under his breath, "You and Frank Roosevelt are not going to hoist yourself to the Presidency over my dead body." This, of course, did not show up in the printed record or in the newspapers. But Louis Molloy heard Walker say it several times. During a recess, Seabury inquired, "Louis, the Mayor keeps muttering something. I don't seem to be able to hear him—do you?" Molloy replied evasively, "I'm not sure, Judge." Then he asked George Trosk if it would be right to tell the Judge about the insulting remark, and Trosk said, "No, it will only serve Walker's purpose of distracting Seabury."

Walker and his cronies on the legislative committee stated that the whole investigation was a Red plot. This line did not surprise Seabury, who as a reform campaigner had been accused of radicalism many times in the past. When laughter and applause followed one of Walker's wisecracks, Seabury said, "You have an appreciative audience, Mr. Mayor." Senator McNaboe broke in, shouting, "You have had Communists and Reds in here!" The Mayor followed this with a comment that he was being confronted here with the same sort of "agitation" used by "our communistic friends." McNaboe later continued, "I want you people to go on record as approving prying into a person's private affairs, particularly his wife. I want a ruling, to find out whether this is the United States or Russia." When the minority members continued to drag in the red herring, Seabury uttered one word for the record. "Bosh," he said, contemptuously.

In the courtroom at Seabury's invitation sat Henry George's daughter, Anna de Mille, with her young daughter, Agnes, later to be a noted choreographer. Anna was despondent, watching the Walker claque. Seabury came over to her and said, "Cheer up! These yells are not in the record—what's in the record are those lies!"

As McNaboe, Cuvillier, and Steingut tried to trip up Seabury with interruptions, and Walker avoided direct answers to any questions the moment they came close to home, it soon became apparent that the game was to exasperate counsel, turn the investigation into a duel of personalities, a popularity contest. Nevertheless, Seabury managed to set out his main evidence about Mayor Walker's "beneficences." Late in the afternoon, the Mayor left the stand. "The cheering from the Tammany adherents," Raymond Daniell reported in *The New York Times,* "was just as strong as it had been when he came to court." The long day was neatly summed up by Doris Fleeson in one lead sentence in the *New York Daily News:* "Mayor James J. Walker fought with rapier-like wit against the ponderous legal attack leveled at him by Samuel Seabury."

The following morning and afternoon, Walker was on the witness stand again. This time he tried tears as well as laughter. He wore an air of hurt pride, humility, and civic indignation to begin with, acknowledging that his "day in court" had not been all pleasant and excusing himself for any discourtesy. He reminded the committee that he was "still a bit human" and "subject to human emotions." The crowd on this second and final day of his testimony lapped it up, cheering and applauding his histrionics. He elaborated on the Tammany line that the investigation was not authorized and that his beloved city was being hurt. "This investigation," the Mayor said, "has done much to undermine the value of New York City securities and has done much to make it difficult to market them."

But these tactics did not stop Seabury from continuing to examine Walker's financial records. Seabury asked Walker to explain how he had received nearly a quarter of a million dollars over a two-year period from a joint brokerage account with Paul Block. The Mayor replied weakly, "Mr. Block for several years had manifested a very genuine friendship for me. Mr. Block's life has been characterized by generosity and a very unusual friendship for a great many people. He has always kept his charities as far from publicity as he could. The regret is that any publicity was given to any beneficence."

Seabury also questioned him about his joint safe-deposit account with the missing Sherwood. "Didn't you have a safe-deposit box jointly with him?" Seabury asked, and Walker said, "I did not." Seabury rephrased it, "Didn't you sign an application for such a safe-deposit box?" Walker said, "I apparently did." He explained that the box was maintained to hold some papers from an old law case but that he never went to the box. As Seabury unfolded the facts about Sherwood's secret accounts, the Mayor cracked, "I hope he proves it is mine. I will try to collect it." The Mayor unqualifiedly repudiated Sherwood, declaring that Seabury was trying to make "a real scenario."

Again Walker was in good retort form. Following Seabury's denial of antagonism, Walker said: "I am here on an inquiry, but it looks as if somebody wants my life." When Seabury asked whether he remembered shaking hands with J. A. Sisto, the taxicab financier, Walker replied, "Due to the activity that I have been in since 1910, I do shake hands with a great many people I don't know, and try to make them believe I do, but please don't tell them about it." Long wrangling between Chairman Hofstadter—who displayed great patience and impartiality during the hearings—and the minority members of the committee led the Mayor to show a proper degree of indignation even toward his fellow Democrats: "The Mayor of the City of New York has a great many things to do. Will you please not keep me in this room any longer than you have to, away from the duties I have to perform?" This was the first time anyone had ever heard Mayor Walker complain that he had to leave the center of any stage to go to work.

On another occasion, he stood on his dignity. When Seabury scored a point, Bill Mulligan could not help grinning. Walker suddenly turned toward the table where the assistant counsel sat, pointed his finger at Mulligan, and said, "That man, who is an employee of the State of New York, is ridiculing me." All eyes were on the young lawyer. "I will take the trouble to find out his name and do something about him," Walker continued. Mulligan stood up, faced the Mayor, and declared loudly, "My name is William Mulligan." All in the court laughed; the manner in which he said his name, and the name itself, boomeranged on Walker, playing to the crowd.

Again the cries of "Red" were raised. One of the rumors in the court was that the Communists were coming to demonstrate. Word reached the police department, and five members of the "Radical Squad" arrived, but they found not one "Communist" to arrest. The only demonstrators turned out to be the Democratic committee members. Assembly Minority Leader Steingut shouted, "Why, in the darkest days of Russia nothing like this would ever take place." Senator McNaboe followed by calling it all "a trial balloon" for headlines. Finally, Seabury said, "If they may return from Russia and the balloon to New York, I would like to put a question." But Assemblyman Steingut persisted, "I would rather be in Russia than have this kind of persecution."

At the end of his second appearance on the Seabury stand, Walker concluded, "I hope with the close of the two national conventions in Chicago we will be through with some of the politics." This was an allusion to mention of Seabury's name as a candidate for high office. And he got a last word in against Seabury by hinting that he was one of the "men who don't know the difference between uptown and downtown." Applause and cheers followed his departure from the stand. He left the courthouse, literally, in a shower of roses. A dozen women had stationed themselves on either side of the main doorway and threw the flowers as he emerged. He smiled at each of the women before passing down into the cheering throng. No roses greeted Seabury as he emerged later in the afternoon, but, one of his associate counsel noted, at least there were fewer hisses and boos now.

The next day was a Friday, May 27, 1932, and Seabury and his lawyers read the newspapers carefully to see which way the public wind was blowing. They were disheartened by the fact that Walker still seemed to be able to manipulate the crowds in spite of all the evidence so carefully presented of his financial indiscretions. A headline in *The New York Times* was no help to their sagging spirits: "TAMMANY PLEASED BY WALKER SHOWING. Friends Hold He Came Off Better Than Even Against Seabury in His Two Days on Stand."

The young lawyers drifted into Judge Seabury's room in the state building. He looked at them with mock annoyance. Suddenly his eyes brightened. "This is the most discouraged group of lawyers I have ever seen," he said. "I am going to issue orders to all of you. I want everybody here to obey them instantly without question." They had never heard him issue "orders" before; he had only "suggested." With a half-smile, he said, "All of you are to go to your homes immediately, pack a bag, and meet in front of my house on Sixty-third Street two hours from now." To Haberman he said, "Phil, bring your

car, because everybody won't fit into mine. And remember—no
papers from the hearings are to be brought along. You're all coming
to the farm at East Hampton for the week end."

Two hours later, the automobiles carrying the Seabury staff were
on the road, with the Judge's limousine leading the way. On Northern State Parkway, a motorcycle cop stopped license plate "SS–19"
for speeding. Judge Seabury leaned out the window and asked innocently, "Officer, have you any children?" The cop said yes. "Then
you ought not to go that fast," Seabury said with a straight face. The
cop recognized him, saluted, and signaled him on. "The Mayor has
put our pictures in the papers," Seabury commented.

They arrived at the farm in time for a late supper. As they sat
down to eat, Seabury said, "Now, gentlemen, everybody is forbidden
to talk about the city investigation for two days." In the library later,
they discussed every subject but the forbidden one. Seabury, mixing
drinks, asked his assistants, "How much coloring matter do you want
in it?" The young lawyers relaxed for the first time in many months.
The next morning they walked over the fields and lanes of East
Hampton, and Seabury led them along the dunes to look out over
the Atlantic.

On Sunday evening, one of the men mentioned the forbidden
name: James J. Walker. They were sitting on the stone patio. "I
think that Walker talked himself out," the assistant declared. "I don't
think that he really made a good showing, and I think that the facts
we brought out are going to sink into the public's mind after the
wisecracks are forgotten."

Seabury's eyes sparkled behind his glasses. "Well," he said, "I dare-
say your spirits are revived now." He announced that the house rules
were now suspended. "Let's get down to cases again," he said.

With fresh vigor they discussed the two days of testimony, weighing admissions and openings for new attacks. By the time they returned to New York early the following morning, they felt that the
time had come to bring charges before Governor Roosevelt for the
removal of Walker as Mayor of New York.

But the Democratic presidential nominating convention was now
only weeks away. For reasons of his own, Seabury sat back and let
the case simmer for several days after the Walker hearings ended.
Seabury thought Roosevelt should move; Roosevelt thought Seabury

should. Both the Governor and the committee counsel allowed their favorite newspapermen to get stories, but neither took any step that might appear politically motivated. According to *The New York Times* of June 3, 1932: "To act on his own initiative now, the Governor's advisers have told him, would be to run the risk of being accused of political opportunism. The political effect of Mayor Walker's case on Governor Roosevelt's chances of winning his party's nomination for President cannot be minimized. Failure to act decisively if charges are filed with him might be interpreted as bowing to Tammany Hall, while precipitate action would alienate the local organization and cast doubt on Mr. Roosevelt's ability to carry his own state."

Judge Seabury, during the first week in June, gave no hint of his intention in the matter. He motored leisurely to Washington and Jefferson College in Pennsylvania, where he received an honorary Doctor of Laws degree. Letters and telegrams poured into Albany and New York, asking for Walker's removal, and praising the hard-hitting counsel. He was riding high.

Roosevelt felt frustrated by the requests that he take the initiative and "do something." Finally, through his secretary, Guernsey T. Cross, he issued a blunt statement:

> The only information before the Governor is in the form of very incomplete newspaper stories. It is not even clear from Judge Seabury's statement to Chairman Hofstadter whether he has fully completed his investigation. I act in each case definitely, positively and with due promptness. Get the law straight. It is the duty of the legislative committee and its counsel, if they believe they have sufficient cause, to present evidence to the proper authorities without waiting to make formal report to next year's legislature. You cannot get away from that obvious public duty. In the case of Sheriff Farley, Judge Seabury asked the legislative committee to present the evidence to the Governor. The committee refused. Judge Seabury sent it himself. I acted. If the evidence in any case now before the legislative committee, in their judgment or that of their counsel, warrants, it is time for the legislative committee and their counsel to stop talking and do something. It is not the time for political sniping or buck passing.

Having no other choice, Seabury took up the challenge. On June 8, 1932, he sent Governor Roosevelt the transcript of Walker's testimony and his analysis of the evidence. A majority of the members of the Joint Legislative Committee refused to back him up, so he filed the report alone. "This record is presented to you by me in my individual capacity as a citizen of the State of New York," he wrote Roosevelt, "not as the counsel to the Joint Legislative Committee. I submit the record to you not as formal charges but for your information so that you may determine what shall be done."

The analysis of the evidence he gave to the Governor summarized the series of "beneficences" received by Mayor Walker from various persons doing business with the city, or hoping to. Seabury referred to Russell T. Sherwood's deposits of close to a million dollars in banking and brokerage accounts, and to the Mayor's refusal to explain the sources of this fortune. The counsel averred that because of these and other unexplained funds, and his conduct in general, the Mayor was guilty of malfeasance and nonfeasance, rendering him unfit to continue in office. Seabury concluded: "I have no request or petition to make in reference to this matter, and my only desire is that it may be dealt with solely upon its merits and regardless of any other circumstance. In my judgment, the evidence presents matters of the gravest moment to the people of the City of New York. I therefore present it to Your Excellency, who alone, under the Constitution and the laws, is empowered to act."

In turn, Governor Roosevelt acted judiciously. He undertook a study of the transcript and analysis of evidence. On June 21, 1932, he forwarded to Mayor Walker the charges that had been filed by Seabury. Two days later Walker informed Roosevelt that he was leaving for the Chicago convention and would reply to the communications upon his return to New York—after the Democrats had nominated a presidential candidate. Thus the most controversial case in Tammany's long history of involvement with city-state politics and presidential candidates was left hanging. No one dared to take a false step before the convention. Not Walker, fighting for his good life as mayor; not Smith, playing a waiting game; not Roosevelt, counting his strength with the delegates; not Seabury, hoping that Tammany's mayor would not escape in a show of political unity.

In *The Nation* of June, 1932, George S. Kaufman wrote a parody of his own Pulitzer Prize play, *Of Thee I Sing,* calling it *Jimmy the Well-Dressed Man.* It was a witty summary of Seabury's cross-examination and Walker's protestations of innocence. In it Seabury said: "Now, to you it's old and hoary,/ But it's very new to us,/ So we'd like to hear the story/ Of the Equitable Bus." And Walker: "Fee, fi, fo, fum!/ Whoops-a-daisy, and ho hum!/ The whole committee is on the bum—/ Where do you get your questions from?" In Kaufman's final stage direction, Jimmy dances, the committee joins him, and "at this point the piper comes on to the scene—and the public pays him." It was a perfect curtain line, but, for the moment, the laughs were suspended as everyone but Roosevelt entrained for the Democratic convention.

Walter Lippmann in mid-June of 1932 took matters more seriously. He could not understand Roosevelt's indecision, and was surprised that the Governor had turned against Seabury.

> There has been something distinctly queer in Franklin D. Roosevelt's mental processes throughout this affair. He seems to be mostly deeply irritated at the fact that the Seabury investigation has been producing testimony which compels him to choose between condoning corruption and striking it. He has displayed a singular petulance towards everybody who has had any part in putting him in a position where he might have to make a decisive choice between breaking with Tammany and surrendering to it. It is, of course, an unpleasant thing to have to consider the removal of Mayor Walker just before the convention meets. If he removes the Mayor, Mr. Roosevelt will be accused of playing politics. If he does not remove him, he will also be accused of playing politics. It is a perplexing problem. But the problem is entirely the consequence of Governor Roosevelt's indecision during the last year.

James J. Walker, in top hat and swallow-tailed coat, had become the symbol of Tammany's arrogance. Corruption in municipal government wore fancier dress than when Seabury first began to combat it before the turn of the century. Seabury could not understand how New Yorkers could cheer Walker after he had exposed him for two days in court, but he was patient and he knew his city's history. When he was told about the Mayor's tumultuous reception by the crowd, he declared: "They gave one to Tweed, too."

CHAPTER **14**

Futile Dreamer, II: A Presidential Nomination

SEVERAL months before the 1932 Democratic convention, Governor Franklin D. Roosevelt was handed an undated, unsigned note in private by Louis Howe, his longtime adviser. An air of mystery surrounded its origin, but its message was clear: Look out for Judge Seabury—your investigator is after the nomination for himself.

The brief note said: "Walter Chambers, the man who wrote the book on Seabury, on a leave of absence from the *World-Telegram,* has been in Washington and talked to some newspaper people, whose names I cannot mention, because they are my sources of information. He approached some people on Capitol Hill, especially Wheeler of Montana, to get his viewpoint on Seabury as a presidential candidate."

This alerted the Roosevelt forces and caused the Governor and his staff to regard the investigation as more than an attempt to expose Tammany corruption. Rightly or wrongly, they felt that Seabury was out to capture the nomination. Every day Seabury's name made the headlines in the New York and national press; to the professionals weighing the political implications, the fact that Seabury was really uncovering graft and official misconduct was secondary. These professionals in the Roosevelt camp, who had been rounding up delegates all over the country for more than a year, knew that Seabury had no organization and therefore stood hardly a chance of obtaining the nomination. Yet while the investigation continued Seabury could be an embarrassment and a nuisance at the convention.

Did Seabury really want the nomination? "He definitely did," says William B. Northrop, "although he wouldn't do anything to jeopardize the success of the investigation or his own sense of dignity. As far as the nomination was concerned, he could be described as a quiet volcano, ready to erupt."

Chambers served as an advance scout with Seabury's knowledge but without his open approval. When Chambers spoke to Senator Burton K. Wheeler of Montana, he did so knowing that Wheeler was one of the Western progressives whom Seabury admired. Chambers was a reporter for the *New York World-Telegram* who had become so enamored of Judge Seabury that he had taken a leave to write a "campaign" biography. It was not labeled as such, but Seabury and his intimates considered the resulting work, *Samuel Seabury: A Challenge,* the opening gun in his presidential boom. Walter B. Walker, who had worked with Seabury on the Gould case in the 1920's, contributed toward the publication of the book. At his farm in East Hampton, Seabury put up Chambers for many week ends of interviews. So keen was Seabury about the book's value to the "campaign" that he asked Raymond Moley to write its introduction. Moley had worked on Seabury's staff up to the middle of 1931, but then he had been recruited for Governor Roosevelt's brain trust. He declined Seabury's invitation, and the book was launched without him. It was more factual than most campaign biographies, but its aim exceeded its achievements. Seabury came out too good to be true. The concluding paragraph illustrates the tone of the entire book:

Judge Seabury's accomplishments in New York cannot be regarded merely for their local significance. They are applicable to every community where apathy and lethargy of the people permit the machine politician to grasp the power of government. His philosophy on human rights has long influenced the administration of justice in the state in which he was born and in the development of which his ancestors contributed so much. Within the coming weeks, and months, he will certainly make clear, to honest citizens in every community, methods by which they can do much to reclaim their local governments from the selfish control of those who use public power for their private enrichment. Samuel Seabury comes then as a radiant challenge to youth to arm itself with convictions; to remain steadfast in its ideals; to hold its faith that there can be here in truth a government of the people, by the people, for the people.

Speculation about Seabury as a presidential candidate began in November of 1931. As a result of the interest aroused by the investigation of the City of New York in the big cities of the United States, Seabury became the subject for features in magazines and newspapers. There were references to the Tweed Ring, to Tammany's colorful sachems, to this descendant of the first American Episcopal bishop who was taking on singlehanded the forces of evil in Manhattan. Inevitably, the other principals in the New York "story" were mentioned as presidential possibilities—Smith and Roosevelt—and to their names was now added Seabury's.

Nearly every day Dorothy Benner, the Judge's secretary, showed him clippings from newspapers around the country mentioning the presidential nomination. "Seabury's Probe of Tammany Makes National Sensation," said a Connecticut newspaper. "Tammany Foe to Be Candidate for Presidency," said one in Michigan. "Judge Seabury, Controlling Genius Behind New York Investigations, Does Not Deny Aspirations," read an Indiana paper. Some papers reported that he was seeking the nomination; some reported that he was not interested; some assumed that he would be the Democratic nominee. With the great ability of newspapers to pick up and embellish one another's speculations, the rumor of Seabury's candidacy leapfrogged across the counties and states. Miss Benner clipped all the "President" articles and pasted them in a scrapbook. It became another book of illusions.

Chambers published an article in *The Forum,* as part of a series called "Presidential Possibilities." It was workmanlike and enthusiastic and filled with hints that there was fire beneath the Seabury smoke signals. He spoke of "independent Democrats now planning to sponsor the candidacy" who were convinced that "he will add immeasurably" to the party's chances. From "leaders in the party throughout the nation"—none of whom he named—came "assurances of support." He said there was a group of independents "well known in the country who have privately made plans to start the boom for Judge Seabury." If any independents were worried about the cost of a national campaign, Chambers reassured them that "ample financial assistance by millionaires reputed to be genuinely interested in the honest administration of government" had been promised. Again, neither the influential independents nor the millionaires were named. The "presidential possibility" had everything: "He combines the virtues of Franklin Roosevelt, Newton D. Baker, Owen Young, Albert Ritchie, and Alfred E. Smith."

When asked point-blank about his presidential aspirations, Seabury continually denied interest in anything but carrying forward his city-wide investigation. Nevertheless, at the end of February, 1932, he made a speech, at a City Charter Committee dinner at the Hotel Sinton in Cincinnati, that encouraged new speculation about his own ambitions. At the dinner Mayor Russell Wilson sat at Seabury's right, and most of the dignitaries in Ohio were present. The Judge began his speech calmly by complimenting the city on its achievements in cleaning up racketeering and decreasing bonded indebtedness. Then he summarized the situation in New York that his investigation was bringing to light. He warmed to his favorite subject, Tammany Hall. And then he dropped his bombshells on the Roosevelt candidacy.

Pairing Tammany with the Governor, he said: "Intoxicated with the absolute power which it possesses in the City of New York, and the great influence which it exerts in the state, it now reaches out to extend its power and use its influence in support of some candidate who will be friendly to it, if, indeed, he does not openly wear the stripes of the Tammany tiger."

In case those present and the radio audience did not know about whom he was talking, he went on: "The power of Tammany Hall drives public men, whose instincts would lead them to speak out in protest against the corruption that has been revealed, to a sullen silence. They know the conditions are evil, but they fear to antagonize the power of Tammany Hall, and politicians seeking its favors cater to it even where they feel they would be discredited if they openly lined up with it. Where they hold public office and are forced on given occasions to rule adversely to Tammany Hall, they soften their opposition so that while the public will not regard them as pro-Tammany, Tammany Hall will not regard them as opposed to it."

The Roosevelt forces kept their silence, but fumed at the insulting comments. Seabury's saying these things before a national audience in the Midwest could hurt them. For many months the Governor's political "cabinet" had been going around the country, lining up delegates, reassuring them that Roosevelt's investigation of New York City proved that he was not linked to Tammany Hall, that he was his own man and a winner. What mischief was Seabury doing to the plans?

The retort came not from Jim Farley, Ed Flynn, or Sam Rosenman but from Irwin Steingut, the Democratic leader of the New York State Assembly, who, from his Brooklyn stronghold, was one of the most important Tammany advisers in the period of the investigation. Steingut, a member of the Joint Legislative Committee investigating the city, immediately issued a statement that Seabury's Cincinnati speech clearly showed that "he hopes the Democratic convention next June will nominate him for President or Vice President." Since Seabury was playing politics, Steingut said, the "decent and honorable thing for him to do at this time would be to resign as counsel to the Hofstadter committee, for he has destroyed his future usefulness."

To which *The New York Times* commented editorially: "The indicated and honorable course is to pursue relentlessly his work of letting light into the dark rooms of Tammany Hall, and so to give the lie to the insinuation that he is looking for some other reward than the satisfaction of doing an honest and skilful piece of work for the public benefit."

The Democrats on the legislative committee did what they could, in statements made in the midst of the investigation, to encourage the idea that Seabury was after the nomination. He, and the reform forces in New York, now recognized the danger signals. If Tammany could prove that Seabury had political motives, then he was playing on their home grounds with their bats, balls, and tin boxes. And they always won on their own field.

Seabury began to make denials, mild at first and then vehement. As for the "honor," he said he intended to devote his efforts to the investigation, which he expected to continue for some time. Reporters asked him about various speculative writings, such as the one in the *Terre Haute Star* that said, "Suppose the man were meditating on the White House, what of it? The race is still open and there are worse recommendations for the job." Seabury replied that he had indeed seen the editorial but regretted its publication "because of its possible effect upon the progress of the investigation to which my whole energies are directed"—and he added, significantly—"at this time." Finally, he was forced to say that the supposed "presidential boom" was begun by "enemies to discredit the investigation." Thereafter he refused to answer any political questions.

Still there were encouraging signs. Arthur Brisbane, Hearst's chief editorial columnist and confidant, asked Seabury for a private conference to discuss the presidential nomination. Considering Seabury's antipathy toward Hearst, this was considered to be an important conciliatory move. There was another aspect to their quiet meeting, however. Brisbane's visit with Seabury followed a suggestion from a Tammany bigwig that the peerless investigator might emerge as a presidential possibility. Former Judge Daniel Cohalan had praised Seabury and his enhanced stature—a move some political analysts interpreted as a subtle thrust at his political ambitions. Nevertheless, Brisbane took up the suggestion, visited Seabury, and discussed the forthcoming convention. Both men felt each other out but made no commitments. When word got back to Tammany Hall that Hearst's man had met with Seabury, the rank and file felt that Cohalan had betrayed the sachems by giving the right people wrong ideas. The meeting was considered a boomerang because it opened doors for Seabury.

A wild hope was being nurtured in the minds of Seabury and his friends. They were beginning to believe that what they read in the newspapers—the universal praise for Counsel Seabury's force and style—would be reflected at the convention, and they envisioned a parade of banners labeled *Seabury* marching forward on the flagstaffs of righteousness.

All this without beating the bushes for delegates, without a central organization devoting its energies to lining up the neutral states, without the necessary half-promises to favorite sons in case of deadlocks, without, in fact, an avowed candidacy. The campaign, if it could be called that, was based on negative factors. The main strength in New York was divided between the old governor and the new. Smith and Roosevelt had their own delegates as well as numerous supporters outside the state. The Seabury camp's hope was to have the two men of power collide and knock each other off, so that their leader emerged as the strong man in New York. It had never happened before in the national ring, but, then again, there had never been such an investigation in the history of municipal reform. Smith's name was tied to Tammany's; Roosevelt's would be, too, if he continued to be cautious in condemning the wardheelers being exposed.

As the convention neared, Seabury did make a move toward a practical plan. A key figure at the convention would be William Gibbs McAdoo, whom Seabury had known as a practicing attorney in Manhattan. McAdoo, who had married President Wilson's daughter, was a contender for the Democratic nomination in 1920 and 1924; the Smith–McAdoo feud during the 1924 convention was still remembered in 1932. McAdoo had emerged as a power in the Western states. He was a California resident, a delegate to the convention —and Hearst's bargaining agent. Now Seabury attempted to enlist McAdoo in the ranks of those trying to stop Roosevelt.

They met privately for lunch at the Waldorf in New York. Their discussion was political and social. They talked about President Wilson and how Seabury had supported him for re-election in 1916 at no small sacrifice to his own candidacy for governor. Then the name of the leading dark-horse candidate came up: Newton D. Baker, Wilson's Secretary of War, a West Virginian, a former Mayor of Cleveland, a lawyer with service on the Permanent Court of Arbitration at The Hague. Baker had coined the word "civitism" as an expression of the municipal spirit he sought to arouse in America's cities. When he was in Cleveland before the world war, he became known as the "3-cent Mayor" because he fought for three-cent trolley fares, three-cent lighting charges, even three-cents-a-dance dance halls. Of such bounties to the citizenry, Seabury heartily approved.

From the secret meeting with McAdoo, Seabury came away with the impression that they had agreed to throw their full support to Baker for President. The ticket would include Seabury for Vice President—a real Wilson team to cope with the challenges of the Depression. Or, if the convention delegates willed it, Seabury could look higher—even to the top spot. In any event, McAdoo assured Seabury that he would never cast his vote for Franklin Roosevelt for President. So Seabury related the plan to his family and a small group of legal assistants on his staff.

Everything seemed to depend on stopping Roosevelt on the first ballot. Seabury's intimates spread the word that the history of contemporary Democratic conventions was in his favor. Champ Clark had been the leading contender at Baltimore in 1912 when Wilson was nominated; A. Mitchell Palmer had blocked the nomination of James M. Cox in 1920 until Cox had made a deal with the Southern delegates; McAdoo would have obtained the nomination in 1924 but for the opposition of Smith, which had caused it to go to John W. Davis. As a national figure now, Seabury was in the class of any of his Democratic predecessors before convention time. Once Roosevelt was stopped, the reasoning went, Seabury would become the leading candidate.

A month before the convention, Seabury's hammerblows fell on Mayor Walker. The two days at the end of May, 1932, when the investigator put the Mayor on the stand before the Joint Legislative Committee at the county courthouse in New York, captured the nation's attention. They were the climax of a year or more of intensive searching of the Mayor's private sources of income, and pay dirt had been struck. The Mayor was charming and his cheering section in excellent voice, but it was obvious that he had left the embarrassing questions unanswered. He had to. To do otherwise would have been to admit bribe taking and corruption; instead the Mayor preferred to hide behind the cloak of financial naïveté.

Now Walker's problem became Roosevelt's dilemma. Walker could only lose the mayoralty, but Roosevelt stood the chance of losing the Presidency. What would he do about the Walker scandal that Seabury had uncovered? The question was on the mind of everyone thinking ahead to the struggle for the nomination in Chicago.

"This fellow Seabury is merely trying to perpetrate another political play to embarrass me," Roosevelt wrote privately on June 4, 1932, to Colonel Edward M. House. "His conduct has been a deep disappointment to people who honestly seek better government in New York City by stressing the fundamentals and eliminating political innuendoes."

When Seabury sent the transcript and analysis of Walker's testimony to Governor Roosevelt—with the convention a scant week away—Roosevelt tossed this hot potato to Walker, requesting that he answer the charges. Walker stalled, and said that he would reply

after the convention. So the investigation stood as all three principals
—Walker, Seabury, and Roosevelt—prepared to go to Chicago.

From all over the country, Roosevelt was hearing from people who
had been following the Seabury investigation. A man in Easthamp-
ton, Massachusetts, wired: "I am a Republican but will vote for you
provided you avail yourself of the opportunity to dismiss Mayor
Walker, and there are millions more who will do exactly the same
thing." A woman in Oakland, California, wrote: "What people admired most about Woodrow Wilson was his fearless independence
and his disregard of consequences, and the same is true of Theodore
Roosevelt and all other men in public life of independent minds. The
case against Mayor Walker affords an excellent opportunity for you
to prove to the entire country that you are equal to the emergency
and can meet the test."

Answering Thomas Whitfield Davidson of Dallas, who had tact-
fully suggested that, if possible, he remove Mayor Walker prior to
the opening of the convention, Roosevelt addressed him "My dear
Governor," amiably agreed with his sentiments, and added, "It will
be absolutely impossible to go through the eight volumes of testimony before the end of this week. As you know, I have apppointed
two lawyers to read it and give me their slant and I am reading it
myself, but it is a tremendous task. Everything looks well for the
convention at Chicago."

What hurt Roosevelt—and encouraged Seabury—was the way
Walter Lippmann kept throwing barbs in his "Today and Tomorrow" column in the *New York Herald Tribune*. In a widely quoted
column written at the beginning of 1932, he had said Roosevelt was
merely "a pleasant man, who, without any important qualifications
for the office, would very much like to be President." The man who
wanted to run the country in the Depression was "no crusader," "no
enemy of entrenched privilege" and, indeed, "no dangerous enemy
of anything." These were the very things Seabury felt, but only
hinted at cautiously in public. If a hard-hitting crusader was needed
to lick the nation's economic crisis, wasn't there one at bat in New
York City?

Seabury's timing with the Walker charges had been perfect, and
his part in the movement to stop Roosevelt was well played. On the
eve of the convention, Lippmann could say that "Governor Roosevelt

has lost his moral freedom. He is so heavily mortgaged to Tammany that he must prove his independence of it. Yet at this late date there is no way of proving his independence except by a procedure which must outrage everyone's sense of justice. For to try James J. Walker before a man who stands to profit enormously by convicting him is a revolting spectacle." Lippmann would be proved wrong about Roosevelt's ties to the Tammany Hall leaders in the New York delegation. But Seabury's small camp of legal associates read what they wanted to and chuckled gleefully.

Although their average age was twenty-eight, Seabury's associates had acquired a lifetime of investigative and courtroom experience since the first of the three investigations had begun under Seabury in 1930. They had seen politics at work on the ward level and on the bench; they had seen deals for judgeships that crossed party lines; they had been encouraged to strike out on their own for—as Seabury liked to say—"the power of an ideal." Mistakes had been made in private and public hearings, accusations were not always proved, but their zeal and honesty were unquestioned. Seabury had complimented their abilities generously and stood up for them when they were attacked. And, late at night, in his mansion on East 63rd Street, or relaxing in East Hampton, he had impressed his assistants with his intellectual powers. In his library he liked to recite for them, particularly these inspirational lines from Browning:

> One who never turned his back, but marched breast forward;
> Never doubted clouds would break;
> Never dreamed, though right was worsted, wrong would triumph;
> Held, we fall to rise, are baffled to fight better;
> Sleep to wake.

Their loyalty to the gentleman crusader was great. Now they had an opportunity to show their devotion in a personal way. They decided that, at their own expense, they would show up at the convention and work for the cause: Seabury for President.

The campaign "manager" seemed to be the energetic Walter Chambers. His publisher, Roy Howard, was considered to be inclined to Newton Baker, but all Seabury's "boys" knew what the scheme was. *The World-Telegram* was especially friendly to Seabury. If McAdoo could hold the fort with Hearst on the West Coast, there would be good newspaper support.

"We've got to figure out a hell of a welcome in Chicago for the Judge when he gets there," Chambers told Bill Mulligan. "It's got to be big." Chambers and Mulligan flew out, looked over the situation in the headquarters that held the most attention, and decided that unless they could offer roving delegates whiskey they were sunk. Chambers began frantically to call Chicago bootleggers, but other Democratic camps had exhausted all supplies. "You've got to fly back to Buffalo and bring back a case, Bill," Chambers pleaded. "The stuff comes over the border from Canada, and there's plenty there." He gave Mulligan the money and the name of a Buffalo bootlegger; the next day Harvard Law's Mulligan carried out his assignment, and they were able to greet the well-oiled Democrats properly in their rooms at the Congress Hotel.

Four more Seabury stalwarts piled into Phil Haberman's Essex and took off for Chicago. "We remembered to go by way of Canada to get the Canadian Club," Louis Molloy said later. Together with Harold Melniker and George Levy, they went around to the various delegations and invited people up for a drink in their suite, all the while talking the case for Newton Baker and Sam Seabury. Phil Haberman was even welcomed at Al Smith's headquarters because of his friendship with Smith's adviser, Judge Joseph Proskauer. Oren Herwitz and his brother drove out with John Walsh, dropped off their bags with a relative in Chicago, and joined the others on lobby patrol at the Congress and Drake hotels. Bob Davidson went out to the convention with his father, Maurice, a prime mover in all the New York reform organizations.

"We had a terrific *esprit de corps,* even though we didn't know precisely what role to play," one of the assistant counsel later said. "We buttonholed delegates and told them we were New Yorkers for Baker of Ohio, that neither Smith nor Roosevelt would do, and that the only New Yorker respected in all parts of the country was Seabury. If they wavered, we invited them to our rooms for shots of Canadian. And, if they were considered important enough, we gave them free copies of the campaign biography. All of us passed around armloads of books about our noncandidate. Since we didn't have a formal campaign headquarters, we whirled around like tops from one state delegation to another in a most undignified way. We would have gone to the moon for Seabury."

Judge Seabury himself, in proper convention style, made it his business to be elsewhere. He accepted an invitation to address the members of the Jamestown Bar Association in western New York on the way to Chicago. In his party were his three nephews, his former law secretary, John Lowe, and Mrs. Seabury. It was not only timing, however, that took him to Jamestown but a sense of duty. As president of the New York State Bar Association, he was obliged to speak to lawyers and local bar groups. There was not a hint of his candidacy in the speech, which was mainly concerned with the need for a central judicial council to administer court rules and procedures. He reiterated a point made in his report to the First Department's appellate division: judges of the lower criminal courts should be appointed not by local political leaders (via the mayor) but by the justices of the appellate division. It was probably the least hortatory speech he had made all year.

The Seaburys checked into a large suite at the Drake, overlooking Lake Michigan. The sidewalks broiled in hundred-degree heat. He invited all his "boys" to join him for dinner at the hotel. They reported their activities on his behalf and he beamed in approval. But Mulligan could not help noticing, though, that Seabury also gave his enthusiasts looks of skepticism, as if to say, "I don't want you to think I'm taking any of this seriously." The powerhouse headquarters run by Smith and Roosevelt were getting the main play at the Congress Hotel; their representatives had been on the scene for weeks. It did not look too hopeful, on the surface. "Do you think Uncle Sam has any chance for the nomination?" one of his nephews asked Ray Moley, who replied, "Of course, the lightning might strike anybody, but you have to have a reasonable cause to support it."

Judge Seabury also spoke to Moley, who respected him for his work exposing Tammany's manipulation of the city government. "He was most uncomplimentary in his remarks to me about Roosevelt at the convention," Moley later recalled. Seabury paid his respects as an old Democratic campaigner to various state delegations where renegade Bull Moosers, Wilsonian Democrats, Western Progressives and congressional antimonopolists could be spotted. These were his kind of reformers; they spoke the language he had been

speaking for the first three decades of the twentieth century. Walter
Lippmann, who had friendly personal relations with Seabury, talked
to him at the convention, serving not just as a news source but as an
informal adviser. Seabury sought his ideas on what might happen in
case of a deadlock.

Ironically, the great anti-Tammany fighter found himself in league
with Tammany at the convention in the stop-Roosevelt movement.
Most of the New York City delegates were committed to Smith at
Chicago, with the exception of those from the Bronx, who were being held in line for Roosevelt by his Secretary of State, Edward J.
Flynn. Flynn himself was angry at Seabury because the investigative
staff had tried to find evidence of Bronx corruption. "The person
Seabury was really after was me," Flynn later said. "If he could
embarrass Roosevelt's Secretary of State, then he thought he could
use that as a springboard to the Presidency. He searched my records
from the time I was born, but he found nothing and he never would
admit that he found nothing." The Smith camp did not have enough
delegates before the balloting began, but they did have the big city
machines in New York, Jersey City, and Chicago—Boss John Curry,
Boss Frank Hague, and Boss Ed Kelly—and these combined forces
to try to lick Roosevelt on the first ballot.

As for Samuel Seabury, the professionals were aware of his moves
but discounted his strength. Sam Rosenman recognized that Seabury
dreamed of himself as a dark-horse candidate, but, he later recalled,
"I doubt whether he had more than a handful of delegates who
would have voted for him under any circumstances." Jim Farley, like
Roosevelt himself, had heard from supporters that the Walker situation was an embarrassment and a test of gubernatorial independence
from Tammany Hall. Seabury was a thorn to Roosevelt professionals
in Chicago.

Jim Farley's war map of the United States, blocked in with Roosevelt states in red crayon, claimed an impressive number of delegates
from thirty-four states and six territories. Farley figured he had a
majority—but not the necessary two-thirds. And now, before the
votes were to be cast, he and one of his many odd bedfellows, Huey
Long of Louisiana, made an effort to change the nominating rules
so that a simple majority would prevail. A howl went up from the
delegates, especially those from Southern states, who had learned to

use the wedge of their veto power. All the stop-Roosevelt forces recognized the danger of a majority rule, and Seabury spoke up vehemently to the press:

> Any candidate for the Presidency who changes the rules which pre-
> vailed at the time the delegates were elected in order to win the nomi-
> nation cannot, in my judgment, be elected. There are good reasons for
> adhering to the two-thirds rule. Like the principles upon which our
> government is established, it is designed to protect not only the rights
> of the majority but of the minority as well. If the two-thirds rule is to
> be abrogated, it would be possible for relatively few states to combine
> and nominate the candidate. . . . The rule is a tradition of the Democratic
> party and has been in force for a century. The maintenance of this tra-
> dition and the other reasons which support the rule are too important
> to be sacrificed to a rule-or-ruin policy in the personal interests of any
> candidate.

Farley was forced to back down, and Roosevelt, sensing that the
move had antagonized Southerners, repudiated the effort by his campaign manager. The Smith and Seabury camps felt they had a better
chance as the balloting began.

Roosevelt was still in Albany, guiding his managers by direct wire,
but Seabury, Smith, and Walker were all on the scene. Seabury had
obtained tickets for his "boys" in the convention hall. All but one of
the principal actors in the investigation were in Chicago. The Tammany men sat around Curry, who hated Roosevelt and Seabury and
whose affection for Smith was only by default. Curry was strictly
Walker's man; Smith considered him stubborn and slow-witted as a
politician.

For the first three ballots, the stop-Roosevelt forces succeeded.
Walker, a member of the committee on resolutions, deliberately
defied Roosevelt—destined to be his judge the following month at
Albany hearings—in what some considered an act of courage. When
the New York delegation was polled, he stood up and declared, "I
vote for Alfred E. Smith." The Smith forces applauded loudly, and
Smith himself exclaimed, "Good old Jimsie! Blood is thicker than
water."

Seabury was watching not New York, where he had no support in
the clash of the state's governor and ex-governor, but California.

Everything depended on the Westerners' holding the line. But un-known to Seabury cannier politicians than he were following the developments and computing the totals. A deal was on for the Cali-fornia and Texas delegations; the *quid pro quo* was the Vice Presi-dency. The pivot man was William Randolph Hearst, sitting in splendor at San Simeon, nursing his luxuries and hatreds. Farley reached the publisher and gave him the facts. Hearst disliked Smith and Baker, but they were liable to be compromise candidates unless Roosevelt could reach the necessary 770 votes on the fourth ballot. John N. Garner of Texas, Speaker of the House of Representatives, was Hearst's conservative choice; he would get the Vice Presidency if Hearst would swing California and Texas to Roosevelt. As a lagniappe, Roosevelt would throw in a cabinet post for McAdoo.

Now California was called on the fourth ballot. McAdoo got up and announced that his "sovereign state" (the sovereign being Hearst) had democratically decided to support Franklin Delano Roosevelt. Cheers and stamping broke out in the broiling convention hall. The Seabury lawyers, flushed with two years of municipal vic-tories, sat on their hands and glanced sideways at their hero. He wore that half-smiling, half-quizzical look on his face that his family al-ways said reminded them of the Bishop on the painting over the fireplace.

"That's it—it's all over," Seabury said to his nephew, Andy Oliver, the moment McAdoo switched his state. He sounded more resigned than angered.

Texas quickly fell in line when Garner released his delegation. Smith still was able to hold 190 delegates, but by now Roosevelt had attained 945 and victory. Curry's New Yorkers refused to make it unanimous or to join in the victory parade. Seabury and all his "boys" left the convention hall, and he invited them to dine with him. Some were bitter, muttering that "McAdoo was a liar," that once again "Hearst betrayed Seabury," that "if only California had held for one more ballot. . . ."

That evening, gathering in Seabury's suite, they listened to the nominating and acceptance speeches on a hotel radio and debated the campaign far into the night. They talked about Roosevelt's inertia in dealing with the Walker case and what effect that would have on Election Day if the Mayor remained in office. Seabury recalled an-

other political encounter—the gubernatorial campaign in 1916—
when Frank Roosevelt had been for him and Teddy Roosevelt had
reneged on his promise of support.

A war and a depression separated the two futile campaigns, the
two political disappointments. The young lawyers in the Seabury
camp were downhearted but Seabury said, "I never put any stock in
my chances." And good-humoredly, "There was never any danger of
my being nominated." Although he had taken only tentative steps
to secure the nomination, there was no question that he hoped to be
in the running in Chicago. Yet he had emerged with his personal
dignity unscathed. What Seabury did not realize then, as he and his
friends watched the dawn come up over Lake Michigan, was that
the future President would not forgive him for daring to dream.

CHAPTER **15**

Seabury vs. Walker Before "Judge" Roosevelt

The scene: Executive Chamber, Hall of Governors, the Capitol, Albany. The room opens off the Governor's private office on the second floor of the statehouse. On the cherry-paneled walls hang the portraits of all the governors of the Empire State, forgotten and famous, with the exception of the impeached Governor Sulzer. On the east side of the chamber, before cathedral windows, there is a great mahogany desk with a matching high-backed leather chair. A state trooper stands at either side of the Governor's chair. To the left, facing the desk, are the table and chairs for the accused and his defense counsel; to the right, a table and chairs for the accuser and his assistants. A waist-high brass rail separates those at stage center from the newspaper correspondents at the press tables and spectators on benches and standing against the walls.

The time: August 11 to September 1, 1932. During the late mornings and afternoons, sunlight streaks across the desks; during the night sessions, chandeliers cast a pale light over the room, intensifying the deep maroon in the carpeting.

The cast: Governor Franklin D. Roosevelt, sitting as a judge in the removal proceedings against Mayor James J. Walker brought by Samuel Seabury and others. The Governor is aided by two special counsel, M. Maldwin Fertig and Martin Conboy. The Mayor's chief counsel is John J. Curtin, aided by Reuben A. Lazarus, assistant corporation counsel of New York City. William J. Schieffelin and Maurice P. Davidson represent a citizens' group, the Committee of One Thousand. Surrounding Samuel Seabury, who has brought the charges, are six young assistants, headed by George Trosk—all lawyers who have been working toward this moment for two years.

The language of the theater seems not merely appropriate but necessary. Here was high drama, enacted before an audience of millions, which followed the events in this room every day and evening on the radio and in the newspapers. The three stars measured every move; all were nervous. Franklin Roosevelt, the Democratic nominee for President, was delaying his campaign in order to show the voters that he could maintain an unpolitical judicial mien suitable for one who sought to be Chief Executive. Jimmy Walker was trying to save his job as mayor and his carefree life in hard times. Samuel Seabury, in a public sense, had the least to lose. He had no office to hold or gain. He spoke now not as counsel but as citizen. The Joint Legislative Committee—which had not brought these charges against Walker—had recessed in June. Whether or not the proceedings for removal of the Mayor succeeded, the public recognized that Seabury had performed a selfless task for two years; the legal profession admired the skill with which he had presented evidence before the legislative committee. In a private sense, however, Seabury had a great stake here: he had devoted his life to a crusade against municipal corruption.

On the evening before the proceedings began, Judge Seabury and Maud stepped into the Lincoln in front of their house on East 63rd Street. Accompanying them on their drive to Albany were Trosk and Molloy. Long afterward, Trosk remembered that the Judge and Maud had held hands during most of the trip.

Seabury's assistants piled themselves and volumes of mimeographed testimony and records into Bill Mulligan's Marmon. To their chagrin, a motorcycle patrolman pulled them over to the side on Route 9W, not far from Hyde Park. He looked suspiciously at the bundles blocking their back window and poked them to see if they were a cover for some illicit operation. Although Trosk and Molloy had identification cards issued by the Governor for the Albany hearing, they did not show them. The patrolman waved them on with an admonition to keep their rear window clear. Actually, they were on their own. The state legislature was not paying their salaries; they, like Seabury, were contributing their services to the Walker case as private citizens. Judge Seabury, however, paid for their hotel expenses at the De Witt Clinton. He was never reimbursed by the state.

On the same day, at Grand Central Station, fifty policemen cleared a path to Track 34 for Mayor Walker. Thousands had come to see him off for his ordeal upstate. They cried, "Atta boy, Jimmy!" and "You show 'em, Jimmy!" Among those with whom he shook hands while waiting for the Albany train to pull out was Joe Jacobs, the suspended manager of the boxer Max Schmeling, who had lost the heavyweight title to Jack Sharkey on a close decision. When Jacobs wished him good luck, Walker retorted, "Thanks, Joe. I hope they don't hand me the same kind of decision you got." Walker was accompanied by his wife, Allie, to make it appear as if they were reconciled. No one was fooled by this, least of all, Roosevelt. After everything that had been printed about "the unnamed person," Betty Compton, the "reconciliation" struck many people as shameful hypocrisy.

When Judge Seabury arrived in Albany, there was no welcoming committee for him. He checked into the DeWitt Clinton without fanfare, and, as was his custom, read for an hour or two past midnight. This time, instead of political philosophy, he studied the Walker records.

Around 7 P.M., the same evening, there was the unexpected blare of a brass band, and the booming of aerial bombs, as thousands greeted Mayor Walker in Albany. They had turned out in force on orders of the Democratic overlord of the city of Albany, who was linked closely to Tammany. In front of the Hotel Ten Eyck, Walker announced, "I have no fear of removal," and clasped his hands overhead in the prize fighter's acknowledgment of the crowd.

At 1:30 P.M. on August 11, 1932, Mayor Walker entered the executive chamber. He was on time, and sartorially subdued. Judge Seabury and his staff were already seated at their long table. Seabury sat quietly, looking out across the elm-shaded lawns of the Capitol leading down toward the Hudson River. At 1:40 there was a rap on the door to the Governor's private office. A hush fell over the executive chamber as Roosevelt suddenly stood framed in the doorway.

Just behind him was his secretary, Guernsey Cross. The Governor looked around the room, his chin in the air, and then, on his secretary's arm, began what seemed an interminably long walk to his desk. As he moved forward through dead silence, the creak of his braces could be heard. Every step was a major effort. When he finally reached his desk, his powerful arms gripped the sides of his high-backed chair. He tried to lower himself inconspicuously, but finally dropped into the seat. The tension in the breathless room eased.

Oren Herwitz, the youngest member of the Seabury staff, sat nearest the Governor, and found himself both touched and embarrassed by what he had seen. Few in that room thereafter thought of Governor Roosevelt's infirmity. His voice trembled nervously in the first few moments of the proceedings, but he was soon in complete command of his courtroom. In his performance for the next two weeks as judge, he was self-assured, well briefed, tough, and, at the same time, impartial. He even knew his law and rules of evidence and he impressed, if not astounded, Judge Seabury.

"I think before proceeding with the hearing it will simplify matters and save time if I should read a little statement in regard to procedure and some of the matters that have come up during the preliminary stages before the hearing," Governor Roosevelt began. He pointed out that Section 122 of the New York City Charter provided that the mayor could be removed by the governor in the same manner as sheriffs. Since Governor Roosevelt had removed Sheriff Farley in this very room, the analogy was apt. Then he reviewed briefly the circumstances that had led to the hearing:

Judge Seabury addressed a communication to the Governor June 8 of this year containing certain charges designated as conclusions with respect to the conduct of the Mayor of the City of New York, and with them sent an analysis of the evidence presented before the Joint Legislative Committee. I examined these charges and on June 21 sent them to the Mayor to be answered. The Mayor's answer was received on July 28. To the answer there was attached as an argument in support of the contention that the Governor may not remove a public officer for acts or omissions occurring prior to his present term of office. I do not agree with this contention. It was raised at the trial of the charges against Governor Sulzer. I do not believe it is necessary for me to enter into a further discussion of the authorities on this question of law. The power

of removal must certainly be regarded as adequate to accomplish the
purpose for which the power was given, which is to purge the public
service of an unfit officer.

Governor Roosevelt made it clear that this was *his* hearing, and
not a higher court rehearing of all the evidence that had been accumulated by Judge Seabury and his staff. He had no intention of allowing
Mayor Walker's counsel to recall more than a hundred witnesses to
Albany for cross-examination, but made it clear that he would subpoena, "upon due consideration," any witness *he* felt necessary to
protect the Mayor's rights and in the "spirit of justice." The question
of witnesses caused the first dispute between John Curtin, the May-
or's counsel, and Governor Roosevelt. Curtin disliked Roosevelt
because he had defeated his good friend Al Smith in the struggle for
the Democratic presidential nomination. Furthermore, Curtin looked
upon the hearings as an opportunity to express his dislike for Samuel
Seabury, who had defaced the mottled image of Tammany.

Attempting to invalidate the results of two years of work, Curtin
told the Governor: "The testimony before the Hofstadter committee
has no better legal value than the story of Robinson Crusoe or
Grimm's fairy tales." Walker followed this up by condemning the
charges that Seabury had brought in his own name: "Seabury submitted his conclusions not to the legislative committee that engaged
him but gratuitously, voluntarily, to Your Excellency." When Governor Roosevelt asked Seabury if he had any comment to make at
the start of the hearing, he replied: "In view of my letter of June 8,
1932, the analysis of the evidence that accompanied it, and the evidence itself, the answer of the Mayor of the City of New York in
reply and his rejoinder, I feel that as to specific matters or details,
unless Your Excellency desires anything, I should not add anything
further to it."

This was to be Seabury's tactic for the next two weeks. Having
presented his evidence in writing, having examined Walker and
been often frustrated by the Mayor's evasions, he was more than
willing to let the Governor discover for himself whether or not honest answers were being given. Walker's written reply to Seabury's
conclusions, which had brought them both to the executive chamber
of the statehouse, had said that his accuser was motivated by either

"ignorance" or "malice." That Seabury's investigation was "conceived, born and fostered in politics." That the real attack was against "the strongest Democratic center in the country" and inspired by "the Republican organization, city, state and national." That the Seabury method was to project "suspicion and innuendo without proof and documents." Finally, after offering some contrary evidence, Walker declared that he was an elected official, and as such, "it is sound American doctrine that the will of the people as expressed by their votes is not to be brushed aside."

From his law office at 120 Broadway, Seabury had on August 2, 1932, countered Walker's answer by underscoring the points that the Mayor failed to mention or evaded by half-truths. "The personal abuse directed against me cannot divert attention from the Mayor's own acts of official dereliction, which are abundantly proved in this record." He added that he would ignore the "abuse and animadversions" and stick strictly to the record. "The Mayor's position may be summarized," he said, "as a claim of honest intentions based wholly upon unrecorded mental reservations, with a defiant challenge of prosecution for perjury and a plea that even if the facts be true and the conclusions justifiable, the acts may not be inquired into because they occurred in a prior term of office."

To this the Mayor had made a rejoinder on August 8, 1932, calling Seabury "a reckless and partisan prosecutor, and not the disinterested and impartial investigator he pretended to be," and adding that Seabury had presented charges "either in inexcusable ignorance of the law or in utter disregard of it." Addressing the Governor, Walker said: "Upon your decision depends my tenure of office as Mayor of New York City, to which I have been elected by the people."

Now Governor Roosevelt personally swore him in as witness, and immediately discovered that Walker intended to continue what he had done with Seabury: address himself to the people instead of the issues. While Seabury sat back in silence, Walker went into his soft-shoe routine. "Now I must have my twenty-three years in public office snuffed out without an opportunity of looking in the faces of the men who would tear up my past, present, and future," Walker said. "I can't be unlike every other human being in the world. I can't be so different than the rest of the human family." And he threw in the same red herring that he had used when Seabury had cross-examined him earlier in the year, saying, "I haven't been transported back to Russia."

Governor Roosevelt patiently said, "It is to give you a square deal, Mayor, that I am going to ask questions." Roosevelt did so, basing his questions on Judge Seabury's evidence and conclusions, and Seabury seldom interrupted. With almost every reply came a speech and a lecture by the Mayor's counsel, Curtin, who insisted that the Governor's hearing be conducted like an ordinary trial, including the right of cross-examination and confrontation of witnesses. Walker had warned his lawyer not to get "Frank's Dutch up," but Curtin did so when he patronized Roosevelt about his knowledge of the law. On the second day, there was an exchange between Roosevelt and Curtin that had the country laughing. Roosevelt had the last word, a wisecrack.

"May I add one more word, and I dislike in some ways to refer to this, but perhaps it won't be amiss," Curtin said. "The earliest recorded—so far as I know—instance of the value of cross-examination is contained in the Bible itself. You may recall one of the Apocryphal books, the story of Susanna and the Elders; Susanna, a beautiful lady, and two of the Elders enamored of her. She repulsed them, whereupon, to get square, they accused her of impropriety with some other third person. And these Elders were men of good standing in that community, and they swore definitely before the counsel that this lady committed this impropriety, and there was nobody to gainsay that, except the lady herself, who met it with tears and denial. There is nothing dramatic about a denial. And she was condemned to death, under the laws of Moses. And then Daniel arose and said, 'Not so fast'—I am not quoting accurately—'Not so fast. Let me examine these Elders.' And he put them both out, then brought in one of them, and said, 'You are sure this thing happened?' 'Yes.' 'Did you see this thing happen?' He said, 'Yes, and I am sure of it.' 'Where did it happen?' 'Under the mastic tree.' He was sent away. And the other fellow was brought in. 'You are sure this thing happened?' 'Yes.' 'You saw it with your own eyes?' 'Yes, and I couldn't be mistaken.' 'Where did it happen?' 'It happened under the yew tree.' Whereupon the committee put to death not Susanna but the accusers."

Curtin added, "I am talking thus bluntly to you as one lawyer to another, although I am not speaking to you in the capacity of a lawyer in your [*sic*] capacity."

After a suitable pause, Governor Roosevelt replied, "You have referred to the testimony before the legislative committee as 'minutes.' I consider it evidence. You have referred also to the interesting case of Susanna and the Elders. I think it is a very apt case. *You* are in the position of the Prophet Daniel. I will *not* say that His Honor," Roosevelt said, smiling, "is in the position of Susanna."

Seabury and his assistants joined the courtroom spectators in laughter. Curtin uttered a few words of protest, and Walker claimed he felt that he was indeed like the innocent Susanna. But the biblical tale had boomeranged, and Roosevelt pressed his own cross-examination of Walker. Later, the New Testament was referred to when Walker told newsmen, "This fellow Seabury would convict the Twelve Apostles if he could."

The Seabury evidence and analysis formed the basis of the Governor's hearing. Whenever Walker departed from the "script," or Curtin tried to upstage Roosevelt, Seabury would interrupt courteously and ask for permission to interpose the record of his own investigation. Sometimes he would call upon George Trosk, or one of his other assistants, to cite chapter and verse to contradict Walker's memory. If Roosevelt leaned in either direction, it was toward Seabury, for he, too, soon recognized the difficulty of trying to get straight answers from Walker. At one point, Seabury read a letter giving certain details about Walker's secret accounts in which he deposited the large sums he received from a friend who hoped to sell his product to the City of New York. The exchange that followed illustrated Seabury's respectful tone, Curtin's lecturing manner, and Roosevelt's judicial ability.

"One minute," Curtin protested. "I would like to know if that paper is in evidence that Judge Seabury is going to read."

"It is not in evidence," Seabury said.

"Well, then, it cannot be used, I am sure of that. I don't know what it says, but it can't be used."

"It can be marked for identification," Governor Roosevelt suggested.

"Yes, for identification," Seabury agreed.

Curtin objected, "Let someone say that they know something

about it, through his own knowledge, and testify about it under oath."

Governor Roosevelt stopped him. "Mr. Curtin, I happen to be a lawyer, and remarks of that kind are wholly unnecessary to the Governor of this state."

"I assume that you do know that," Curtin said. "Still, when a lawyer makes a statement as to what the——"

"All right," Roosevelt broke in. "Don't try to instruct me about the difference between putting a thing into evidence and marking it for identification."

Thereafter, Judge Seabury read, or had George Trosk read, from many of the records that had been introduced at their own legislative committee hearings. Legalisms were brushed aside by the Governor. "Perhaps you are right in not calling this law," Roosevelt told Curtin and Walker, "but you would also be right in calling it my public policy in regard to this state." As evidence or merely as "marked for identification," most of the main points made by Seabury in his charges got into the record of the Governor's hearing.

In the evenings, Seabury invited his young legal assistants to dinner. Then he and Maud went for a short drive into the country outside Albany. On the week end, when Governor Roosevelt adjourned his hearing, they returned to East Hampton. With the Seaburys were their nephews and some of the legal staff. Louis Molloy recalled walking around the farm, reviewing the facts with the Judge. "What answer can Jimmy come up with?" Seabury always asked. Week ends before and during the hearing in Albany were spent in strategy conferences.

On the other side of the fence, Walker and his attorneys knew they were having a difficult time. "The charges against Walker were couched in such clever, overlapping technical language that they were unanswerable," Reuben A. Lazarus later recalled. Walker had a high regard for Lazarus's ability as an assistant corporation counsel and had him assigned to Curtin. "The charges were the joint work of Judge Seabury and his highly competent staff. If one of the charges was denied, Walker was trapped into a confession on one of the others. My advice to Walker, under these circumstances, was to resign and resubmit himself to the electorate in the fall. His popularity at that time was so great that he probably would not have failed to be re-elected. The then leader of Tammany Hall, John Curry, overruled me."

To the Tammany and Walker camp, the terrifying enemy remained Judge Seabury. "The impression created by Seabury," Lazarus remembered, "was that of an avenging angel. His imposing physical bearing, his white hair and florid complexion, his reputation as a lawyer and former associate judge of the court of appeals, and his graphic day-by-day delineation of the shortcomings of the Walker administration, divided people into two groups: the vast majority of the public who were 'against sin' and the minor group of professional politicians who were sympathetic to any politician, in any political party, who was caught—all this latter group hated Seabury. He was their implacable enemy."

Meanwhile, the central character in the hearings, Governor Roosevelt, was feeling the pressure mounting on him as the Democratic party's candidate for President. Forthright as he was in the courtroom, he was extremely cautious about his political position. He was receiving all sorts of advice from the press, the politicians, and the public.

"The old gay Mayor, he ain't what he used to be," cracked F.P.A. in his column. But it was no joking matter to a national candidate. More soberly, Walter Lippmann wrote in his column, "I continue to believe that the problem before Governor Roosevelt is essentially the same: he must not only do justice as a judge but he must convince the people as a leader that justice has been done."

Harold L. Ickes introduced himself by mail to Governor Roosevelt, pointing out that he had been an active Progressive and the Chicago manager of Colonel Theodore Roosevelt's campaign in 1912, and quickly offered some advice: "I realize, of course, that there are two edges to your sword, but as one who wishes you success in this campaign I am hoping that on the issues the duty to remove Mayor Walker will be so clear as to convince even the doubtful." To which Roosevelt answered: "As to the charges against Mayor Walker, I am withholding judgment until after both sides have fully presented their case; and shall then proceed to do what is right regardless of any personal or political consideration."

Joseph P. Kennedy of Hyannisport, Massachusetts, kept in touch with Governor Roosevelt during the Walker hearings, supplying him with information to use in a speech on the causes of the stock market collapse and the Depression. Roosevelt invited Kennedy to Albany, adding, however, that "as long as the Walker hearings go on I am engaged at the Capitol until about 5 P.M., but after that I am usually reasonably free."

Father Charles E. Coughlin, the Fascist priest from Detroit with the huge radio audience, wrote Roosevelt that he should go to the limit to give Walker his day in court. Roosevelt trod gingerly with the powerful demagogue, extending himself in politeness: "It is good to have your letter and you may have seen that my old friend John Curtin, the Mayor's counsel, thought of the Book of Daniel. He used the story and I, perforce, turned it on him by accepting its application and suggesting that he occupy the place of Daniel and that I give him the same right to call the accusers who had testified against the Mayor. I think he will do so this coming week. I am, as you know, giving the defense every latitude and I am being scrupulously careful not to make up my mind in any way until their case is wholly in." He concluded the letter by expressing the hope that he would have "the privilege of seeing you again soon."

James A. Farley, Roosevelt's national campaign manager, served as one link between the Governor and the Mayor. Walker met privately with Farley and John F. Curry, presumably only to arrange for matters of procedure during the hearing. The case caused Farley much grief. "I had known and liked Walker for a great many years," he said later, "and his friends assumed that the only thing necessary was for me to call up Albany, tell the Governor to call off the hearings, give Jimmy a clean bill of health, and the whole thing would be over." Farley admitted that he brought the case to Roosevelt's attention personally on two occasions, once to try to get the hearings postponed. But the Walker case was too hot and too far out in the open for any tampering, regardless of friendship. One thing was certain: Farley did not like Seabury, calling him "dour but thorough."

Roosevelt's mail ran overwhelmingly in favor of a tough but fair trial. "Your friends in Dutchess County and throughout the United States are proud of you," he read in one letter. "You may lose a few Tammany votes but gain many independent votes." Another correspondent wrote him, "Your cousin Theodore Roosevelt would do the courageous thing." People west of the Hudson wanted a show of strength against New York corruption; a man of Roosevelt's keen sensibilities was aware of this.

Toward the end of August, the sessions in the executive chamber grew longer, some carrying over almost to midnight. Roosevelt, following the Seabury brief, pursued Walker's strange financial deals and odd code of public conduct. He questioned Walker about the "disappearance" of Russell Sherwood, his fiscal agent who had fled to Mexico. "I wish Sherwood were here today," Walker said, and the Governor answered, "So do I." What Roosevelt could not understand was why Walker made no effort to locate the man with whom he shared a safe-deposit box. Nor could Roosevelt understand how Walker received large sums from Paul Block without paying income taxes; Walker's statements that his taxes were paid "at the source" by Block from their joint account sounded like a course in nightmare accounting. "The most extraordinary business proposition I ever heard of," Roosevelt exclaimed about the Block–Walker transfers.

The Mayor's brother, Dr. William H. Walker, who served as a medical examiner to the Department of Education and the City Pension Retirement Board, made a fortune in split fees with a small group of doctors who monopolized the city's workmen's compensation cases. He received one-half the fee, to the fraction of a cent. The Mayor had told Judge Seabury in justification that "anyone who knows him knows that he is an earnest, plugging type who is lost in a situation like this." At the Governor's hearing, at first the Mayor said, "I had no knowledge whatsoever of the scope of his business, nor with whom he did business." Then, revealing his own standards, he said, "I don't know of itself that fee splitting is wrong. I have done it. I don't know whether Your Excellency has done it in your law practice or not, but most lawyers have." Roosevelt did not appreciate the remark. Walker got into deeper hot water: "If the city was not defrauded, the service was rendered and the bill was paid, and the doctors, because of some other arrangement between them, were paid off by splitting the check, or as many checks as there were, I don't see anything unethical about that."

Judge Seabury interjected some questions about Walker's payments to the "unnamed person," his mistress, when Walker became evasive in his replies to the Governor. Immediately, Walker stood on his dignity. He complained that Seabury was playing for "newspaper values" and that he was making "hourly summations" after "fourteen months of parading." When the Governor pointed out that a letter of credit had been issued to "this person" and asked the Mayor if he knew anything about it, Walker replied, "I do not." This, despite the fact that the Mayor had revealed the sex of the "unnamed person" by referring to her as "she." The Governor as well as Judge Seabury went along with the gentlemanly pretense by speaking of Miss Compton as "this person" or "the person." When one of the tabloids mentioned her name, the Governor lectured the press against doing so again. "It is contrary to the rules under which this hearing is being conducted," he declared, "and contrary to common decency."

Curtin applied to Justice Ellis J. Staley of the New York State Supreme Court for an order to halt the proceedings, on the ground that Roosevelt had no jurisdiction over Walker and, besides, had exceeded his powers as an examiner of the facts. Justice Staley played his decision down the middle, granting that the Governor was legally authorized to conduct a hearing to remove the Mayor, but setting up various objections. "The requirement for a fair trial," he wrote, "does not countenance the wholesale receipt and use of testimony taken by an investigating committee, where the accused officer has not been represented by counsel or afforded the opportunity of cross-examination." But, he added, courts have no power over the Governor: "He is responsible, not to the courts, but to the people, and to his own conscience." Roosevelt knew his legal rights; in his corner, briefing him as to facts and law, were M. Maldwin Fertig, his counsel, and Martin Conboy, a special counsel recommended by Raymond Moley as an able attorney and a prominent Catholic, whose appointment would stop short any hints of anti-Catholic taint in the hearings. Roosevelt did not forget Justice Staley's obiter dicta about the manner in which the Governor's hearing was conducted; later as President-elect, he strongly criticized Justice Staley for his "ill-advised" observations on the case.

The Mayor's attorney made an argument on his motion to dismiss by saying that Judge Seabury's "grueling investigation" had cost New York City and the state $750,000, with the only result being "a clean bill of health" for Walker's administration. "You have now the living testimony of the Mayor," Curtin said. "He has met each charge by a very clear, full—and I may say—by a very vigorous examination conducted by Your Excellency. Are you going to say, 'Because an answer was not given as might have been expected, as Judge Seabury charged that he was evasive'? Evasive in that manner means that Judge Seabury didn't trap, or otherwise get him into positions that he would regard as fatal, or hurtful to the Mayor."

Governor Roosevelt then turned to the man who had brought the Mayor of New York to the gubernatorial bar of justice. "Do you wish to be heard, Judge Seabury?" Seabury arose, bowed in courtly fashion to His Excellency, ignored the steady gaze of Walker and Curtin, and responded:

> I have listened for a day and a half to the eloquence of learned counsel in making a motion to dismiss these charges. It seems to me that there is nothing that he has said that can result in any mistake on the part of Your Excellency, who knows the facts of this case. The salient facts upon which each charge is based are really undisputed here. In almost every case, it's a question of an assertion of good intentions on the part of the Mayor. It's a question that involves the credibility of the Mayor, and those are questions which Your Excellency can determine in view of the manner in which he has testified, and in view of the other circumstances that exist in this case. Now, if there is any particular point in regard to any charge to which Your Excellency wants me to call your attention to any evidence, I will be glad to do that; but it seems to me that nothing that has been said here could result in the dismissal of any of these charges.
>
> This day and a half of oration that we have listened to here isn't proof. That isn't evidence. That's only an effort to explain away the facts that are established by this record. Unless Your Excellency particularly wishes it, I do not think that I ought to put upon you the burden of going over each of these particular charges in reference to the evidence that has been presented. Nothing has been shown which would justify the dismissal of a single one of these charges.

At 4:02 P.M., on August 26, 1932, the hearing was adjourned until Monday evening, August 29. On that day Governor Roosevelt announced that he had been informed of the death of Mayor Walker's brother, George, and the next hearing date was set, instead, for September 2.

Backstage, the three main actors went about their business. Presumably, more witnesses would be called, more evidence introduced, more charges and countercharges filed as the case continued into September. Roosevelt, Seabury, Walker—each stopped for a moment to catch his breath.

"I am confident that it is best I should not give them any chance to say that I am railroading the case," Roosevelt informed Professor Felix Frankfurter, of Harvard Law School, as the end was still not in sight. Frankfurter had been summoned to Hyde Park before the hearings and had discussed the legal problems involved. "I worked out with Roosevelt," he later recalled, "the legal theory on which Jimmy Walker had to go; the theory being that when a public official has acquired money during the time that he was in public office, the presumption of wrongdoing lies there unless he can explain why he suddenly came into money that he couldn't have got merely through his salary." But even before the Walker case, Roosevelt and Rosenman had applied a similar test in the hearing that resulted in the removal of Sheriff Tom Farley.

Roosevelt met with his closest political and judicial advisers, alone and in groups. Once he turned to Raymond Moley and said, half to himself, "How would it be if I let the little Mayor off with a hell of a reprimand?" And Moley remembered that Roosevelt answered himself, "No, that would be weak." Samuel Rosenman saw Roosevelt and later remarked, "I am sure that he was becoming persuaded that Walker should be removed, and that he was getting ready to do so." "As I remember it," Mrs. Franklin D. Roosevelt said, "he had made up his mind to remove Walker from office."

But some of the political professionals were still trying to save Walker. Friendship and the big city vote motivated them. Tammany Hall's frantic leaders conferred with Walker at the Plaza Hotel, after which one of them asked Farley to plead Walker's case with Roosevelt. Walker himself was downhearted. On September 1, he attended his brother's funeral services, and later told a friend, "I think Roosevelt is going to remove me." Walker asked Smith's advice, and the former Governor replied, "Jim, you're through. You must resign for the good of the party." Meanwhile, Farley was in Albany, doing his best to save Walker.

In the Governor's mansion that evening, Sam Rosenman recalled, a group of intimates sat around a table in Roosevelt's study, discussing the effects of the case nationally. Rosenman and Basil O'Connor were there; so were Frank Walker, Arthur Mullen, national committeeman from Nebraska, and Farley. The professional politicians felt that Roosevelt should not remove Walker but, instead, end the case with a severe reprimand. As the discussion grew hot, O'Connor lit a cigarette, flicked the match at Roosevelt, and angrily said, "So you'd rather be right than President!" And Roosevelt replied, "Well, there may be something in what you say."

Dramatically, the phone rang that evening in Roosevelt's study. Walker had resigned. He had sent an official message to City Clerk Michael J. Cruise: "I hereby resign as Mayor of the City of New York, the same to take effect immediately." Everybody in the Governor's study was relieved by the news; it solved a political dilemma.

Judge Seabury was in his house on East 63rd Street, preparing his material for the resumption of the hearings in Albany the following afternoon. After midnight, he heard the news from one of his associates. At three in the morning, Seabury called Trosk; at five, that morning of September 2, Trosk and Seabury sat in the kitchen of the Judge's house, drinking coffee, and discussing what moves, if any, came next. "We were about to go into Walker's finances," Trosk later said, "and the details would have completely destroyed him."

Early that morning the reporters called on Seabury for a statement, and he issued one from his kitchen:

> All I care to say tonight about the Mayor's resignation is: The charges against the Mayor were fully proved and corroborated in many instances by documentary evidence which was undisputed, and by the admission of the Mayor. The Mayor's resignation in the face of this record is equivalent to a confession of guilt. No intelligent person will be misled by the Mayor's attempt to substitute for a defense an assault upon the good faith and motives of the legally constituted authorities to review his acts while in office. It is highly significant that this excuse is availed of by the Mayor on the eve of the Governor's inquiry into relations between the Mayor and his fugitive agent, Sherwood.

At 1:30 on the afternoon of September 2, 1932, Governor Roosevelt sat at his desk in the executive chamber and read a statement that in view of the resignation of the Mayor, the proceedings before him were terminated and therefore the hearings were closed. What had begun as a liability and possible embarrassment for Roosevelt had turned into an asset and victory.

Walker was a tired and embittered man. His domestic life, as well as his political future, was confused. When he issued an angry statement calling Roosevelt "unfair" and his hearing "un-American," when he promised to take his case to the people and run again for mayor, he sounded pathetic. Nobody yelled "You tell 'em, Jimmy!" any more; never again would roses be strewn at his feet. More charmer than rogue, he was still beloved by many and disliked by few; yet he had learned, sadly, that December was not May; who knew better than the Mayor that he had written the lyrics of his own swan song?

Twice that summer the Seaburys had canceled their plans for a vacation abroad. Now they hastily packed their steamer trunks and booked passage on the French liner *Paris*. Accompanying them for a month in England and on the Continent were Henry Stevenson and Bill Northrop. They went aboard late in the afternoon of September 2, 1932, only hours after Governor Roosevelt had declared the hearings over. Reporters and newsreel photographers asked many questions for the papers and the cameras. Seabury refused to answer specific questions but read a statement that he had worked on in the midst of packing.

"I know the pressure to which Governor Roosevelt must have been subjected with a view to inducing him to save a guilty and recreant mayor at the expense of the public interests," he read on shipboard. "His firmness in standing up against this pressure, and the fair and thorough manner in which he conducted the hearing, have won for him the admiration of fair-minded people throughout the nation. Throughout these hearings, he proved himself a worthy successor in the governorship to Samuel J. Tilden and Grover Cleveland."

He then went into some details of Walker's defense, saying that the Mayor had enriched himself while in office. "When the Governor put pointed questions to him, he stammered and stuttered and made almost incoherent replies," Seabury said. "He made no explanation as to how his financial agent, Russell Sherwood, the $3,000-

a-year accountant, was able during the Mayor's term of office to deposit in his various accounts $1,000,000, three-quarters of which was in cash." Seabury enumerated other names and sums that had become part of the catechism of the Walker case.

"The elimination of Mr. Walker as mayor of this city is a distinct victory for higher standards of public life," he concluded, "and in the elevation of this standard Governor Roosevelt did much to contribute by reason of the manner in which he conducted the hearings."

Judge Seabury, no admirer of Roosevelt up to the time of the hearings in the executive chamber in Albany, had changed his opinion rather suddenly. "He thought Roosevelt was wonderful," Raymond Moley later said, recalling a meeting with Seabury while the Governor was bearing down on Walker. Seabury had been fighting Walker for two years; Roosevelt for two weeks. The investigation had dominated Seabury's every activity during that period. He had sacrificed several hundred thousand dollars by closing down his law practice. And his nervous habit of clearing his throat before speaking had grown more pronounced.

But the olive branch Seabury extended to Roosevelt on the eve of his departure for Europe and two months before the presidential election was acknowledged only by silence. Roosevelt did not forget that Seabury had wanted the Democratic presidential nomination.

Seabury and Roosevelt had damaged Tammany Hall beyond repair in the greatest investigation of political corruption in the city's history. Ironically, the two reformers remained respectful but cool toward each other. It was a pity.

CHAPTER 16

All Over but the Shouting?

THE deposed Mayor's financial agent was hiding out in Mexico and the ex-Mayor himself was on a slow boat to Europe. The resignation of Walker was a shattering blow to New Yorkers, who had already been rocked by the exposure of the parade of clowns called sheriffs, the magistrates, vice cops, district leaders, and Tammany officials on the take in every department. Something here ran deeper than mere corruption in the unmaking of the city; something would have to be done about the municipality's structure; and someone would have to come along to remove the cynicism and administer a new New York.

Samuel Seabury breathed easily for the first time in two years and went to London to find relaxation in the offices of archivists and genealogists in Chancery Lane. In the evening, after a roast beef dinner with Maud, he lit a cigar and took a stroll, swinging his walking stick. And since he could not sleep without a game of chess with his nephew or an hour or so of reading, he rediscovered the pleasures of literature. There were lecture invitations from leading American universities and a final report to make to the state legislative committee, a summing up and a formula for building high the walls against corruption in New York. For the moment, these could wait. Among his authors, as he contemplated the philosophy of government that had taken him this far, he could find Oliver Goldsmith, writing "The Bee" in 1759, not without current meaning:

What cities, as great as this, have . . . promised themselves immortality! Posterity can hardly trace the situation of some. The sorrowful traveller wanders over the awful ruins of others . . . here stood their citadel, but now grown over with weeds; there their senate-house, but now the haunt of every noxious reptile; temples and theatres stood here, now only an undistinguished heap of ruins.

From the ruins of New York City's government, Judge Seabury envisioned strong laws and strong men of a new kind arising. During the hearings a Tammany-oriented supreme court judge, John Ford, had denounced the committee and its counsel, saying that even during the Walker administration New York was a city of "sweetness and light." Going over some of his papers while vacationing in preparation for his final report, Seabury made a note that Justice Ford had displayed "a bitterness of feeling and an absurdity of expression rarely attained in judicial utterances." He did not intend to let off lightly those who had obstructed the investigation, but he now concentrated on something more positive—a new city charter.

When he returned from Europe on the *Berengaria* in mid-October, 1932, he began to go regularly to his law office at 120 Broadway. George Trosk was there, of course, overseeing the task of rebuilding a legal practice, and so were Bill Northrop, Henry Collins, and Bernard Richland. At times some had been on the state payroll. But the office staff had been kept on during the investigation; no one's salary was reduced. Seabury had seldom visited his office, except to conduct an interview away from press scrutiny. Now a number of would-be clients knocked at his door who, directly and indirectly, had business dealings with the City of New York. He turned them all down to avoid any questions of propriety. Gradually, other lawyers brought him appeal work, as they had done before the investigation.

Seabury felt an obligation to keep an eye on his "boys," and they reported their progress as lawyers regularly. Molloy, Levy, and Herwitz formed a partnership at 70 Pine Street, and Seabury steered a number of clients their way. Disgruntled citizens with grievances still considered Seabury the one to tell their troubles to, and while many of these citizens had only fanciful tales to tell, he was able from time to time to send some cases over to his former legal assistants. When Mulligan and Herwitz wrote a paper on the workings of legislative investigating committees for the *Columbia Law Review,* Judge Seabury contributed a foreword praising its "clarity and accuracy." Later, Seabury was instrumental in placing several of his "boys" in the office of the corporation counsel.

Tammany's mayor was out, but the tiger refused to roll over. In the fall of 1932, Tammany leaders, led by Boss Curry, struck back at Roosevelt and Seabury. On the eve of the Democratic state convention, Roosevelt sent a telegram to Curry: "Quite apart from local political aspect, in which I do not desire to interfere, I want to express to you my wholly personal hope that Rosenman will receive designation tonight." The Governor had given an interim supreme court appointment to Samuel I. Rosenman, and this nomination would assure a full term on the bench. Although Roosevelt was now the presidential nominee, he was defied by the hardheaded Curry. Roosevelt consoled Rosenman, "The fellow who is behind in the first quarter-mile is very likely to finish first. I am nevertheless terribly disappointed, but you will remember that I have a long memory and a long arm for my friends." Rosenman subsequently received an interim appointment from Governor Lehman and was duly elected.

What surprised Roosevelt, Seabury, the Bar Association, and the press was that Tammany was giving its bipartisan support to Republican State Senator Hofstadter in addition to Aron Steuer, a Democrat, who was the son of Max D. Steuer, Tammany's favorite lawyer. As chairman of the Joint Legislative Committee investigating Tammany, Senator Hofstadter had shown great judicial skill and been publicly commended by Seabury and members of the legislature. For two supreme court vacancies, now the Republicans and Democrats had agreed to back each other's candidates—and this startled the press, Seabury, and many lawyers.

"By a secret deal with the local Republican machine," wrote Walter Lippmann in a column called "Tammany at Bay" in the Republican *Herald Tribune,* "Tammany endorsed the chairman of the Seabury committee for a job as a judge. This removes from the campaign one of the principal persons in a position to expound to the voters the hideous mass of corruption unearthed by the Seabury committee. But that is not all. There is every probability that the deal is more far-reaching, and that it includes some understanding not to present the Seabury data for prosecution. . . . The local Republican machine differs from Tammany only in that it is more incompetent."

The accusation of a judicial deal was denied by both Tammany and the Republican county committee president, Samuel S. Koenig. At the time the storm broke Seabury was still vacationing abroad. Upon his return, he looked at the new problem more broadly than most of his colleagues at the bar. He recognized that any nomination for a supreme court post in New York had complex political origins and that bipartisan endorsements had been customary in the past. He was primarily interested in seeing to it that nothing would harm the Joint Legislative Committee, including its undeniably able chairman, before he filed his final report, with recommendations for changes in the city charter.

Nevertheless, Seabury spoke out strongly for the Bar Association's independent candidates, George W. Alger and Bernard S. Deutsch. He joined John W. Davis, Elihu Root, C. C. Burlingham, and Nicholas Murray Butler of Columbia in the campaign to defeat Hofstadter and Steuer. Addressing himself to the Bar Association, he declared: "Senator Hofstadter was nominated by Mr. Curry and Mr. Koenig for the purpose of embarrassing and crippling the work of the legislative committee of which Senator Hofstadter is chairman. It is perfectly clear to me, as I think it is to others who are familiar with the circumstances, that Senator Hofstadter should have refused to allow himself to be made a party to any such scheme."

As the November, 1932, election approached, Judge Seabury said that he was going to support Franklin D. Roosevelt. "He will be overwhelmingly elected and will make an excellent President," Seabury said, adding that he did not intend to campaign for the Governor because no effort was needed for his election. Locally, however, Seabury delivered a powerful political talk at Town Hall.

"Tammany Hall and the Republican party have agreed to make supreme court judges out of Senator Hofstadter and Mr. Aron Steuer. There can be no doubt that they were nominated as the result of a political bargain," he said. "In order to make sure that the bargain would be carried out, Senator Hofstadter was selected to fill the judicial place—the theory being that the Republican party could not denounce Tammany Hall for the corruption disclosed before the legislative committee while the chairman of that very committee was running for office with a Tammany nomination." He went on to say that the Democratic organization in New York County should have nominated Governor Roosevelt's appointee, Justice Rosenman. And he concluded, "The truth is that the Tammany Hall and Republican organizations in New York County are both corrupt. They exist for no public purpose, but only for the gain which they get through commercializing the processes of its government."

Election Day came. Despite Seabury's antipathy to Roosevelt before the presidential nomination, he admired the way the Governor had handled the Walker case and was pleased to see him defeat Hoover in 1932. Locally, it was evident that nothing short of a miracle could elect independent candidates against Hofstadter and Steuer. Nevertheless, the independent judges received nearly 300,000 votes and ran far ahead of the Republican candidates for any other office. The public could be aroused in large numbers; it was a fact that Fusionists did not forget in the mayoralty race the following year.

The Republicans on the legislative committee began to fight among themselves, demanding that Justice-elect Hofstadter resign as chairman. Led by Assemblyman Hamilton F. Potter, the vice chairman, they said that their fellow Republican would harm the committee's work if he remained on the job. With this stand, Judge Seabury strongly disagreed. He felt that Hofstadter should remain as chairman; he did not want interparty strife to divert attention from the committee's work; Hofstadter stayed. As for the eventual meaning to the bench of the bipartisan endorsement, Hofstadter and Steuer both turned out to be among the most respected justices of the supreme court.

Early in December, 1932, the committee entered its constructive phase. Here witnesses were asked to offer their opinions on how to improve the city's government. Former Governor Alfred E. Smith responded to Judge Seabury's call, and condemned the administrative organization of the city. He recommended that the Board of Estimate be replaced, and said he spoke as a former member of the board. He was willing to keep only one city-wide sheriff, and admitted that "I was sheriff myself and was busy looking for something to do." He called for combinations of various city departments to cut out waste, and he thought the mayor ought to have to handle less detail and have more administrative control.

Judge Seabury simply asked Smith to "go ahead" and never once interrupted him. When the witness said that "under the present system there is little the people can do about electing judges" and "they might as well be appointed," the spectators at the county courthouse applauded—and looked at Chairman Hofstadter. Smith continued: "No man sitting on the bench should feel that he owes anything to anybody. He should feel that he is answerable only to the people. Long ago we even elected treasurers, and we couldn't even remember their names." At this point Assembly Minority Leader Irwin Steingut interrupted, "Well, that applies now to the Vice President and Lieutenant Governor, doesn't it?" Smith wittily retorted, "According to *Of Thee I Sing.*" At the conclusion of Smith's presentation, Judge Seabury said, "I shouldn't like to mar what the Governor has said by asking a single question."

In succeeding sessions, Judge Seabury put a cross section of New York leaders in the "constructive" witness chair. Nicholas Murray Butler came up with the suggestion that Staten Island be given away to New Jersey. He then praised Governor Smith's reorganization plan. So did a representative from the League of Women Voters. Norman Thomas, Socialist candidate for President, enlivened the proceedings when he told the legislative committee that he had no hope for good government under the capitalistic system.

On December 27, 1932, Samuel Seabury, counsel, filed his last report "In the Matter of the Investigation of the Departments of the Government of the City of New York." His salutation simply read, "Sirs." Privately, he told his friend Walter B. Walker, who was assisting on the financial aspects of the report, that he would not address the legislators as "Gentlemen"—because it would be inaccurate. Again he praised George Trosk for his help throughout all the investigations. As a courtesy, he sent a copy to President-elect Roosevelt and added, "With kind personal regards and best wishes for a Happy New Year." When Roosevelt's personal counsel forwarded this copy, he noted the unusual cordiality of the close. Roosevelt did not return the compliment.

The Seabury report discussed the cost of Tammany domination. "No substantial improvement in the processes of our government can be anticipated unless a radical change be made in the legislative and money-spending agencies to insure full and open discussion of their activities," he declared. Although he admitted that the state had not designated him counsel to a charter revision committee, he said that it had become apparent that there were serious defects in the municipal structure, enabling a minority of the city's voters to keep one political organization in control. Therefore, he suggested these changes:

Election of a council to take over the powers of the Board of Estimate, the board of aldermen and the Sinking Fund Commission.

Election of council members by boroughs upon a nonpartisan ballot without party designation or emblems at the ratio of one council member to each 50,000 registered voters, creating a body of about twenty-eight members.

Election of the mayor and controller on a nonpartisan ballot, both officials to be nominated by petitions, thus eliminating the primaries.

Establishment of an executive budget like the one in the state constitution.

Abolition of the offices of the borough presidents and vesting of their duties in one commissioner of public works.

Creation of ten departments—executive, fire, health, inspection and licenses, law, police, public works, social welfare, taxes and assessments, and transportation and commerce; education would remain untouched.

Appointment by the council of a commissioner of inquiry, to be removable only on two-thirds vote, to exercise the powers now vested in the commissioner of accounts and to have other duties of investigation.

Creation of a nonpartisan municipal civil service commission of three members, to be appointed by the council from a list of ten nominees named by a board made up of the presidents of Columbia, New York University, Fordham, City College, Hunter College, and the Brooklyn Institute of Arts and Sciences.

Prohibition of those in the service of the city from taking part in municipal elections, or from making donations of any sort to any municipal party.

The charter changes proposed by Judge Seabury combined ideas outlined by Nicholas Murray Butler, former Governor Smith, and Acting Mayor Joseph V. McKee (who, as president of the board of aldermen, succeeded Walker), and included Seabury's own thinking on the subject, based on observations of government on and off the bench since the turn of the century. Two and a half years had passed since the summer of 1930, when he had been enlisted to investigate the magistrates' courts. In the conclusion of this final report by Seabury as counsel to the legislative committee, he did not forget those who had obstructed him.

Truth compels the statement that the evidence of waste and positive corruption which was adduced before the committee was presented in the face of the consistent opposition of the city authorities and of the leaders of the dominant political organization. There were some exceptions to this rule but they were few. Indeed, at one of the earliest meetings of the committee, Assemblyman Cuvillier moved that the committee adjourn without making any investigation at all on the ground that the committee was not constitutionally created. At the outset of the public hearings Mr. Curry took up the battle for Dr. Doyle and it appeared that his "heart and his sword" had been enlisted to test the constitutionality of the powers of the committee.

I should not be entirely frank if I did not point out the fact, attested by every page of the record, that all the minority members of the committee, whose duty it was, having accepted membership, to aid in the effort to obtain the facts, consistently obstructed that purpose. There was no witness who took the stand, no matter how depraved and corrupt he showed himself to be, who was not defended and championed. I venture to hope that such a course cannot reflect the normal standard which the legislature of the State of New York approves in the conduct of investigations which it directs. If I am in error in this, I commiserate with the people of the state.

At this time, Judge Seabury traveled around New York state, lectured at colleges in the East, and spoke to lawyers and civic groups about municipal reform and social legislation. He was serving as president of the New York State Bar Association. From that office he proposed that Benjamin Cardozo be appointed a United States Supreme Court justice. He admired his social views of the law. Indeed, Samuel Seabury spoke publicly like a premature New Dealer. This did not surprise those familiar with his record on the bench in the early 1900's.

"Much of our social welfare legislation the constitutionality of which is now taken for granted would, twenty-five years ago, have been declared unconstitutional, as subversive of the liberty of the individual whose conduct was sought to be regulated." So he spoke to the West Virginia Bar Association at the end of 1932. "We stand today confronted by the evils which have followed an economic depression unparalleled in its severity. The party going into power is confronted with great responsibilities to redeem pledges made to the American people. The task, if it is to be accomplished, will require much more than what we have been accustomed to refer to as social welfare legislation. We sincerely hope that no cramped and impractical conception of 'Liberty' will be permitted to nullify the efforts of legislative bodies to afford redress in these circumstances."

Statements such as these, together with Seabury's reputation as the country's most notable investigator, inspired a series of letters and telegrams addressed to President Roosevelt. All suggested that Seabury be named Attorney General of the United States. Roosevelt's appointee, Thomas J. Walsh, had suddenly died, and it occurred to many people that Seabury should replace him. "Samuel Seabury for Attorney General will make Franklin Roosevelt the greatest man since that babe born in Bethlehem nineteen hundred and thirty-three years ago"—so said a telegram from Louis De Rochemont. Others simply said, "Why not your friend Sam Seabury?" The assumption of friendship was optimistic. All the replies were identical. They were written by Louis Howe, acknowledging receipt thereof and adding that the President appreciated the letters about Judge Seabury. Homer Cummings, a professional politician, was chosen for the post.

There was only one more little detail to attend to and the Seabury investigation would be over. At 80 Centre Street, there were 61,000 pages of private testimony taken by Seabury and his assistants. Included were names and leads, statements bold and rash, proven and unproven. To publish these now, Seabury felt, would be to harm reputations merely by mention of the names. He ordered the records destroyed. Henry Collins and Bill Northrop helped to load a two-ton truck to near capacity, and the papers were carted away to an unknown destination—unknown at least so far as the curious newspapermen were concerned. Actually, the truck was driven to the Lawyers Press at 165 William Street. There, Seabury's men personally shredded all the pages on paper-cutting machines. The paper was dumped into a row of separate trash cans and disposed of as scrap to different dealers. The guarded private testimony of the Seabury investigation ended as confetti.

Not everybody thought that the information should have been destroyed. One of the organizers of the No-Deal Judiciary party, an anti-Tammany Democrat named James E. Finegan, said that Seabury should have continued in his reports about scandals in departments of the city that had not been touched—water supply, public markets, tax and auditing, and all the offices of the borough presidents. But most people in New York had had enough of the hearings, and the resignation of Mayor Walker had seemed a fitting climax to the proceedings. They were primed for a mayoralty campaign where a battling reformer would be running—and in Fiorello H. La Guardia, the approved candidate of Judge Seabury, they would get their man.

It came as a surprise to many people in New York to learn in 1933 that Judge Seabury had never been paid for his services (his staff had been paid by the state) while acting as referee for the appellate division's investigation of the magistrates and magistrates' courts. (He received $150,000 for his two years of work as counsel in the state hearings.) Now Presiding Justice Finch disclosed the correspondence between Seabury and himself. Finch had pressed Seabury, in writing and in person, to accept $75,000, telling him that he had lost at least that much in legal fees away from his personal practice. But Seabury refused any payment and would not boast about his refusal. It was Finch who revealed that Seabury said he preferred to give his services as a "contribution" from his honored profession of law to the City of New York.

In that same year, 1933, a name reappeared in the news which, somehow, put the Seabury investigation in perspective. The Reverend

Charles H. Parkhurst, who had exposed the vice scandals in the
Tenderloin from his pulpit in the Madison Avenue Presbyterian
Church, died from injuries caused by a fall while walking in his
sleep. From his political "exile" in Paris, London, Rome and the
Riviera, ex-Mayor Walker had a kind word for Parkhurst. "I always
had a liking for the Doctor," he said, "even though he took a few
telling shots at me and my administration. I admired him because he
did not seek to bring virtue by coercion, for he once said, 'You cannot legislate the human race into Heaven.'"

As a youth, Sam Seabury had heard his father decry Privilege and
Corruption, the Hydra of the reformers; had watched, from a small
desk in his father's library, as Dr. Seabury prepared sermons supporting Dr. Parkhurst. He did not believe that good government was
possible only in the next world. "Social reform can be secured by
the awakening of thought and the progress of ideas," Henry George
had told him, sitting in his study overlooking the Narrows. Now
Seabury, having contributed to that awakening with his driving investigation, felt the City of New York was ready for a government
to match its greatness.

BOOK III

Citizen Seabury of New York

1933-1958

If the people desire self-government, both in the political and industrial spheres, they must exert themselves to secure it. The work cannot be done by politicians, or by the political state.

Samuel Seabury, *The New Federalism*

Samuel Seabury lived a massive consistency, perhaps no sure qualification for great political success.

Raymond Moley, former professor of public law,
Columbia University

CHAPTER **17**

La Guardia for Mayor, or Else—

"*SAM*," asked Mrs. William Marston Seabury, Seabury's sister-in-law, "how did you possibly come to pick La Guardia to run for mayor?"

"Because," replied Seabury, "he's absolutely honest, he's a man of great courage, and he can win."

The selection of Fiorello H. La Guardia, the flamboyant half-Italian, half-Jewish ex-congressman from East Harlem, by Samuel Seabury, the direct descendant and namesake of the first Episcopal Bishop of the United States, who lived in the fashionable East 60's and East Hampton, puzzled many people, including Seabury's brother's wife, who was a Park Avenue society matron. There were half a dozen men of standing available who, on the basis of professional or business experience, reliability, dignity, and social acceptability, seemed to fit the role better than La Guardia. Yet, once Seabury had given the word that it was to be La Guardia, from East Harlem to Park Avenue and into the corners of the five boroughs people united behind the green four-leaf-clover emblem of the City Fusion party.

It revealed something perhaps, about the nature of this unsmiling man behind the pince-nez that he chose "the little Italian" instead of one of "his own kind." About his single-mindedness to destroy Tammany, which had once knifed him . . . about his consistently youthful ideas of social reform . . . about his almost religious fervor concerning a person's worth as an individual—about, to use a big word, "democracy."

A new spirit of government pervaded Washington in 1933; a municipal New Deal to parallel the Federal program of bringing the true beneficence of America closer to large numbers of people was demanded in the City of New York. From the arts and the professions, from bench, bar, and government an amazing motley of people enlisted under the City Fusion banner: Franklin P. Adams, Brooks Atkinson, Heywood Broun, A. A. Berle, Sr. and Jr., Nicholas Murray Butler, Frederic R. Coudert, Jr., John Foster Dulles, George and Ira Gershwin, Virginia Gildersleeve, Moss Hart, Charles Evans Hughes, Jr., Jacob Javits, William Travers Jerome, Walter Lippmann, Vito Marcantonio, Ogden L. Mills, Dorothy Parker, Ida M. Tarbell, Oswald Garrison Villard, Lillian Wald, and Alexander Woollcott. These and thousands more—people who had been associated in reform movements early in the century and those whose fame lay ahead—all joined the fun and the parade under the Fusion campaign committee. Samuel Seabury served as honorary chairman; the other leaders were Charles C. Burlingham, Maurice P. Davidson, and William M. Chadbourne. Once the decision was made to support La Guardia, these Republicans and Democrats and independents fused their great talents behind him.

But La Guardia was not the first choice. It was widely recognized among the reform organizations in the city that Sam Seabury himself had "first refusal rights." In the spring of 1933, various individuals began to sound out the possibilities of a Fusion candidate. Paul Windels, later the city's corporation counsel, went to see Seabury with the owners of the *Brooklyn Eagle* to urge him to run. Roy Howard, publisher of the Scripps-Howard newspapers and a long-time Seabury supporter, boosted the great investigator's stock regularly. "The very agreeable relationship between Judge Seabury and the *New York World-Telegram* continued as long as he was active in public life," Mr. Howard later said, "and the association was continued and intensified during the organization of the Fusion party and its successful election campaign." The Committee of One Thousand, composed of a cross section of disenchanted Democrats, liberal Republicans, Citizens Union members, City Club members, and many powerful lawyers and future Fusionists, had joined Seabury in his charges against Jimmy Walker before Governor Roosevelt in Albany. But Seabury had insisted, in response to inquiries, that he was not interested in the job of mayor. He had had to say so many times during the hearings when he was accused of attacking the Walker administration to further his own personal ambitions.

When meetings of the Fusion leadership to study the possible candidates were reported in the press, letters and calls came to Seabury from all over the city. With the investigation behind Seabury, no one could quite believe that he was not a candidate. Finally, he was forced to issue a statement turning down the nomination in positive language. On May 20, 1933, he declared:

> I am deeply appreciative of the multitude of communications, oral and written, which have come to me from Democrats, Republicans and Independents, urging me to accept the Fusion nomination for mayor and pledging me support and assistance in the campaign. Their view seems to be that inasmuch as I was instrumental in exposing the shocking conditions for which Tammany Hall is responsible, and because of which it should be driven from power, it is my duty to become a candidate for mayor. To my mind this conclusion does not follow. Indeed, I feel that I can be of greater service in the effort to rid the city of Tammany Hall's domination if I am not interested as a candidate in the outcome of the election.
>
> When I undertook to conduct the investigation into the affairs of the city, I determined that it would be as thorough, as fair and as nonpartisan as I could make it. Never had I any desire to capitalize the results of the investigation by election to office. To make that clear I announced that I would not accept any nomination for office in the municipality. I feel bound to adhere to that decision. When, during the investigation, I said I would not be a candidate for mayor, I meant what I said. I still mean it and my position in this respect will not change. I have neither desire nor inclination for the office, but I shall do all that lies within my power to aid in the election of a Fusion ticket worthy of support.
>
> We have in this city a situation where Tammany Hall can be beaten, and beaten under such circumstances that it will not be able to come back. The planning which must precede the execution of this service to the community makes it necessary that no precipitate action should be taken. It is now more than five months before Election Day. A city ticket composed of the three best qualified citizens of New York can be selected, and those interested in the Fusion movement should, I think,

direct their energies to that end. Such a ticket can, and I confidently believe will, be elected and carry the anti-Tammany cause to success.

The City Fusion leaders now had a clear field. They looked among themselves and shopped around the city. There were some outstanding men who did not want to run for Mayor of New York. Nathan Straus, Jr., a leading merchant and former state senator, reasoned that, with Governor Herbert H. Lehman in Albany, to have another Jew in City Hall might give bigots ammunition. With the rise of Hitlerism, he told Maurice Davidson, he did not want to contribute to any possible spread of anti-Semitism. John C. Knox, senior judge of the United States District Court, was asked in his daughter's presence if he would step down from the bench to run. "But, Daddy," his daughter said, "if you were mayor you could ride in your official car, turn the siren on full blast, and speed from the Battery to Harlem past every red light." A gleam came into the judge's eye at this enticing prospect, according to a Fusionist, but he preferred his own job. Several more names were brought up, to no avail.

Finally, it came down to three men. The front runner was General John F. O'Ryan, commander of the 27th Division during World War I, and later a member of the Transit Commission. Politically, he was considered an independent, but conservative, Democrat. Next came Robert Moses, former Secretary of State under Governor Smith and authority on the city and state's park system. Politically, even though he was a Republican, he was independent enough to have served under a Democratic governor. Finally, there was Fiorello.

Behind the scenes, now, a quiet move was made. Adolf A. Berle, Jr., professor of corporation law at Columbia, telephoned Seabury and asked if he might be able to see him to discuss the mayoralty nomination. Seabury invited him to his office. They did not know each other, but they had historic ties in common. Berle's father, like Seabury's, had been a clergyman and theological professor; both had helped to spread the gospel of Dr. Charles H. Parkhurst's anti-Tammany vice investigations in the 1890's. They could talk the same language.

"I've taken at face value that you don't want to be mayor yourself," Berle said.

"No, I'm not a candidate," Seabury replied. "The investigation was nonpolitical. I've even transferred my residence to Wyandanch Farm, my home in East Hampton."

"I want to put forward the name of Fiorello H. La Guardia," Berle said. "He's the best possible man for the office."

Berle explained that he was familiar with La Guardia's record. He had met him the year before through one of his former students, Paul H. Kern, who had helped to draft legislation for Congressman La Guardia. Although the Democratic presidential landslide in 1932 had made La Guardia a lame-duck congressman, he and Berle had worked together to introduce New Deal legislation on behalf of President-elect Roosevelt.

"Tell me," said Seabury. "You're in the new national Administration. What do they think of the candidates for mayor?"

"President Roosevelt has no obligations to Tammany here," Berle said. "Besides, La Guardia is in the Roosevelt camp on all his social legislation."

Seabury said nothing for a moment and then told Berle, "I haven't made up my mind yet. But I will give La Guardia every consideration."

Later, Seabury studied the La Guardia record more closely, arranged to meet him with Berle at the East 63rd Street house, and was impressed by La Guardia's sincerity and zeal.

In the spring of 1933, the Fusion leaders began to meet regularly. Sometimes Seabury was present, but, more often, he stood in the wings. They breakfasted at the Plaza Hotel or at one of their clubs. Sometimes they met at the home of William M. Chadbourne, a prominent Republican lawyer who had once been connected with the Bull Moosers and knew Seabury from those campaign years before the war. At first this inner circle leaned toward General O'Ryan but kept Moses as a possibility; La Guardia seemed out of the running. What these respected Fusionists had not yet realized was that Seabury had made up his mind to support La Guardia. He told them so. Nevertheless, La Guardia's name was rejected, and Seabury withdrew from further meetings, reserving his independence of action.

The Fusion inner group then decided upon Robert Moses as their candidate. Maurice Davidson and Seabury lunched at the Bankers Club the following day. When Davidson told Seabury that the nomination had been offered to Moses, Seabury reddened, brought his fist down on the table, and said he would have no further dealings with a group that was selling out to Tammany. Later Seabury admitted to C. C. Burlingham that his language had been too extreme. He declared that Moses was Al Smith's man and that no real anti-Tammany fight could ever be possible with him as mayor; furthermore, Seabury said he was against Moses because Moses opposed proportional representation. Privately, Smith admitted to Moses that he would have to back the Democratic party's nominee even if Moses got the Fusion nomination. Seabury, of course, did not know this, but it is doubtful if he would have supported Moses anyway. The stormy lunch broke up.

When the full Fusion group met, without Seabury present, and Davidson explained what had occurred, they, in turn, felt that Seabury was hurting the cause. Joseph M. Price of the City Club phoned Moses and told him what was happening; Moses, aware that no one could win without Seabury's backing, decided to decline. Then a proposal was made to nominate another impartial candidate, and General O'Ryan was designated. Former Governor Whitman led the conservative group backing O'Ryan. It was Whitman who had defeated Seabury for governor in 1916—an unforgotten fact. The Fusionists were feeling pleased about their new candidate when, suddenly, a reporter from *The World-Telegram* entered with a newspaper statement from the busy Seabury.

"The present effort which I am making is to prevent Tammany Hall from naming the Fusion candidate for mayor," Judge Seabury declared, in an outburst of indignant political prose. "Some of these Republican machine leaders for whom Governor Whitman speaks, and whose will he is registering, are and have long been the owned and operated chattels of Tammany Hall. I regret the dissensions and divisions which have existed in the Fusion ranks. I am still for Fusion, on condition that it is an honest Fusion, but I am against Tammany and its whole system. I think the action of the Whitman committee is a complete and disgraceful sellout to Tammany Hall."

Now there were two Fusion elements: Seabury, insisting on La Guardia; against, nearly everyone else. Either the two groups would be brought into harmony or Tammany would dominate the city again, despite the investigations. Some of the Fusionists asked Rollo

Ogden of *The Times* to write an editorial calling for unity, and he obliged. Roy Howard of *The World-Telegram,* recently returned from a trip to Japan, heard out both sides when they called upon him at his home. He sat cross-legged, like a Buddha, in his new Japanese pajamas. Then he ordered an editorial demanding a harmony committee. Seabury did not ignore Howard's efforts; the publisher had strongly supported him all during the investigations.

On August 3, 1933, C. C. Burlingham called together the Fusion leaders for a meeting at the Bar Association. Seabury, Berle, and Louis Molloy were present to advance La Guardia's cause. Molloy, head of the Knickerbocker Democrats, an anti-Tammany group, had been one of Seabury's assistants during the city-wide investigation, and was his close political adviser. First, they presented the case against General O'Ryan, maintaining that he was too mild and conservative for the election battle ahead. Then, they argued on behalf of La Guardia. Someone interrupted and said, "If it's La Guardia or bust, I say bust!"

At one point, Seabury grew so vehement that Burlingham shocked all present by saying, "Sit down, Sam, sit down!" No one had ever heard the Judge called by his first name in public before.

Slowly the facts of life became clear: harmony meant La Guardia; Seabury would not budge. Of all those present, Berle knew La Guardia's abilities best—and he brought his own growing prestige as a Roosevelt brain truster to the meeting. He spoke up to say that when he was trying to put through a piece of legislation to protect stockholders, he had asked leaders of both parties to suggest an active and able man in Congress to push it. "Finally," Berle related, "the Democrats said, 'There is only one man, although we feel ashamed to confess it, who could do it, if you can secure his interest. It is Fiorello H. La Guardia, Independent.' I gave the bill to La Guardia, who showed great interest. He mastered its provisions and took the matter up with the conservative Senate Judiciary Committee. The bill passed both houses and became law. Now a man like that is needed to clean up the New York situation."

Seabury echoed these sentiments, adding that La Guardia was a good vote getter. One by one the Fusion harmony group came around. O'Ryan was reached by telephone from the meeting and graciously consented to withdraw. "Tell La Guardia I'll support him with pleasure," O'Ryan said. In a little room outside sat La Guardia, waiting for the word. Louis Molloy, after many hours, finally was the bearer of the good tidings. "Congratulations, Major," he said, shaking his hand, "you've just been nominated."

The next day, Seabury issued a gleeful statement. "The selection of Fiorello H. La Guardia to head the Fusion ticket this fall presents to the voters of this city an opportunity to express their indignation and disgust of Tammany Hall and its methods by the election of an honest, fearless and capable anti-Tammany mayor; a sincere and militant opponent of graft, corruption and waste, who will put an end to the squandering and wasting of the people's money by Tammany Hall for the enrichment of the politicians and their friends and restore it to unemployment relief, schools, hospitals and the other purposes for which it was intended."

Between C. C. Burlingham and Maurice Richardson now passed an amusing note, which Burlingham marked "Secret." In it, he wrote: "You will be interested that *at last* S.S. referred to his outburst on the 'sellout' as too extreme in language and unfortunate! But he tells me that when he met La Guardia and Roy Howard that day they were so discouraged that they were ready to give up and it was then that he blew his trumpet blast."

La Guardia faced two opponents. The first was Mayor John P. O'Brien, Boss Curry's regular Democratic candidate. He was a prominent Catholic layman, a former New York surrogate, and an undistinguished gentleman whom his detractors called "The wild bull of the china shop." The second was Joseph V. McKee, the former president of the board of aldermen who had become acting mayor after Walker's resignation. McKee was running on the Recovery party ticket, a creation of Postmaster Farley and Boss Flynn of the Bronx. McKee was popular, had denounced Tammany rule, and was considered La Guardia's real rival. In the special election in November, 1932, McKee had received a surprising 260,000 write-in votes against O'Brien. The big question was whether Farley would be able to talk President Roosevelt into intervening for McKee in the New York City election.

Seabury threw himself into the campaign with characteristic zeal. He, as well as La Guardia, became the target of the opposing parties. Seabury was branded a "boss" for having dictated the choice of La

Guardia. La Guardia was called a "Communist at heart"—an accusation not unfamiliar to Seabury himself.

An anonymous broadside attacked Judge Seabury only half humorously for mingling his efforts and the blood of his ancestors with the wrong kind of people. One of the stories went: "The Samuel Seaburys will have as their grounds guests at East Hampton next week the East Harlem La Guardias. The Seaburys closed their home last week and went back to New York. The La Guardias—Fiorello is the chap who is always running for mayor—have hosts of warm friends *outside* East Hampton." Another story reminded Judge Seabury that his ancestor, Bishop Seabury, had been "driven from America because of his denunciation of the Revolutionary cause," and hinted that Judge Seabury's annual trips to England were un-American. Anyone with a long view of history could faintly detect the dormant echoes of the Society of Saint Tammany of the 1790's denouncing foreigners.

The campaign became still dirtier, and Judge Seabury was in the thick of it. Religion is always at least a tacit consideration in making up a political ticket in New York. Now it broke into the open, almost accidentally. Judge Seabury included Governor Lehman in a speech he made against Democrats in general and the manner in which relief funds were handled by the state and city in particular. The Fusion political command immediately realized that any derogatory remarks against Lehman might be construed unfavorably because of Lehman's great popularity in the city. McKee played this up, denouncing Seabury's remarks and demanding that La Guardia disavow Seabury. For a few anxious days, Fusion trembled.

"My God, Judge, you're ruining me," La Guardia told him privately. "Stop attacking Governor Lehman."

To answer McKee, who was trying to win on the popularity of Roosevelt and Lehman, La Guardia hastily drafted a reply clearing himself of any anti-Lehman sentiments. He showed it to Paul Windels, an old friend who was to become his corporation counsel. Windels tore up the draft. "You can't say this," he told La Guardia, "because it will drive a wedge between you and Seabury in the public's mind."

McKee persisted in his denunciation of Seabury. Doing so, he left himself wide open for a body blow to his own campaign. Paul Windels and Louis Molloy had been aware that, long in the past, McKee had written an article for the *Catholic World* pointing out that although the Jews made up only 25 per cent of the city's population, they made up 75 per cent of the high-school enrollment; that they were getting an extra educational advantage; behaving like Socialists, and so on. (At the time McKee was a high-school teacher, and, presumably, this was merely an educational report.)

The La Guardia counterattack, drafted by Windels and Molloy, asked McKee: "Are you trying to draw a red herring across the cowardly, contemptible and unjust attack that you have made and published against a great race gloriously represented by our governor? Answer that, Mr. McKee, and think twice before you send me another telegram." The embarrassed McKee offered denials, but it was too late. The spurious issue of anti-Semitism had boomeranged.

Judge Seabury, in the meantime, was campaigning all over the city. When funds ran short, La Guardia turned to William Chadbourne, the City Fusion campaign manager, and said, "If you can't go out and raise money, Judge Seabury and I will go out and ask for dimes and quarters from the back of trucks." On several occasions they did just that, Fiorello and Marie La Guardia and Sam and Maud Seabury going together to rallies in Brooklyn, or Richmond, then the sponsor and his candidate delivering a one-two punch on the platform.

Judge Seabury, still run down from the investigation, sometimes found it difficult to make public speeches. He cleared his throat constantly. Usually at his side during the drive to speaking engagements for La Guardia was one of his nephews, Andy Oliver, John Northrop, or Bill Northrop. Hidden beneath a blanket in the car, safe from the gaze of reporters, was an oxygen tank. Seabury's physician told him that if he inhaled the oxygen it would help him breathe and give him a lift. Seabury dashed to the platform, delivered his anti-Tammany, pro–La Guardia speech, then rushed back to the Lincoln. There, with gray shades drawn, he inhaled more oxygen on the way to the next political rally.

All of Seabury's "boys" were in there campaigning; and two were on the ballot themselves. Jacob Gould Schurman, Jr., was running for district attorney, George Trosk for supreme court justice.

"There is no result which Tammany fears more than the election of Mr. Schurman," Seabury told one rally. "Under him, action will replace inaction and aggressive pursuit of the criminal, whether a district leader or not, can be counted upon." In a mock trial conducted on top of a sound truck parked at Broad and Wall streets during the lunch hour, Bill Mulligan, another former Seabury assistant, cross-examined William Fellowes Morgan, Jr., a foe of the Fulton Street fish market racketeers, to show what a tough district attorney would do if elected.

Seabury helped Trosk's campaign as much as he could, but, in one situation, his sense of fairness brought no comfort to his closest legal associate. Seven candidates were running for two supreme court vacancies. Seabury had endorsed Trosk and Justice Samuel I. Rosenman, the choice of President Roosevelt and Governor Lehman. When La Guardia gave Trosk a letter written in Italian recommending his election and referring to Trosk's association with Judge Seabury, he showed the endorsement to Seabury before releasing it to the press. "I don't think you ought to use this," Seabury said. "It's unfair to your opponents to use a letter from the Major addressed to one special group of voters." Trosk was surprised, since there was nothing underhand about La Guardia's letter, but he abided by what he considered Seabury's too refined sense of correctness.

On the night of November 2, five days before the voters went to the polls, a huge rally was held in Madison Square Garden. From all over the city the green banner of the Fusion party was carried in torchlight parades toward the Garden. Voters had been alerted by newspaper advertisements, by telephone calls, and even by airplanes to come to the meeting. Every seat was taken inside, and crowds jammed Eighth Avenue for blocks around outside. And then it became known that Judge Seabury had just arrived. They cheered and whistled to the rafters and shouted, "We want Seabury!" Floodlights danced on the ceiling of the Garden. Then, in a moment of high drama the great investigator who had brought the campaign to this point appeared before the rally. Everyone arose in an ovation of respect. Finally the applause subsided, and the lights shone on the white hair of the reformer in pince-nez as he stood up to speak.

This campaign presents to the people of New York City the greatest opportunity that has been presented to them in many decades. This city has been ground beneath the heel of brutal political bosses for all too long a time. The attempt of Tammany and its allies, through the candidacies of Mayor O'Brien and Mr. McKee, to continue boss domination of New York City, is doomed to failure on Tuesday next.

The people of this city are ready to smash not only Tammany Hall but the whole Tammany system. They realize that the city and its people will be no better off whether the Tammany system is to be operated by Boss Curry or by Boss Flynn.

The election of Major La Guardia and the whole Fusion ticket will usher in for New York City a new era in municipal government, which will find expression in a humane, nonpartisan administration of the city's affairs. Charter changes will be made that will insure the permanent dissolution of the Tammany system of government in this city. A great victory, such as I believe you are to win next Tuesday, will be a message of encouragement and hope to the people of all the cities of America which have been afflicted with the same sort of misgovernment as that which has afflicted New York City.

Not only will this victory free New York from the waste, extravagance and corruption which political domination has introduced into our city government, but by placing Jacob Gould Schurman, Jr., in the district attorneyship of New York, you will prepare the way for a relentless warfare upon the gangster and racketeer. When we drive out the gangster and the racketeer, industry will be freed from the tolls and extortions now levied upon it, and the profits of industry will go where they belong —to the workers and employers, and not to political leaders and their gangster friends.

The whole country looks to New York City to promote the cause of good government. The hour is ripe for action. I ask you, by your votes, to strike the blow that will make the city free.

As speaker after speaker addressed the Garden crowd, climaxed by the fiery Fiorello himself, the savor of a feast on Election Day could almost be tasted. But there were some loose ends. McKee had attracted many independents who felt that the New Deal in Washington and the Recovery party in New York were somehow linked. Would Farley and Flynn be able to convince F.D.R. to come out against La Guardia, who with Adolf Berle had helped to draft New Deal legislation, in favor of the McKee ticket? They could not. Roosevelt continued his policy of silence; in effect, it was an endorsement of La Guardia.

In his column in the *New York Herald-Tribune,* Walter Lippmann came out for La Guardia. "The Seabury investigation which led to the forced resignation of Mayor Walker received, to state the case conservatively, no encouragement from any important element of the regular Democratic party in New York state," he said. "If the choice lay between O'Brien and McKee, there would be no question as to which man was preferable. But it happens that there is also La Guardia and Fusion, which, whatever may be its deficiencies, is in this campaign the only uncompromising enemy of the Tammany system. It would be a great mistake for the independent voters not to seize so great an opportunity to bring about a drastic change."

On November 7, 1933, the independent voters swung the balance to La Guardia. McKee received over 600,000, O'Brien nearly 600,000, and La Guardia nearly 900,000 votes. The key statistic was that almost half of Fiorello's vote came from the City Fusion party (the other half being Republican). For Seabury, there was personal disappointment in only one respect: Schurman and Trosk, his two faithful aides, had lost by small margins in their bid for office. La Guardia received the news of victory in Seabury's house and then both went to Fusion victory headquarters to take part in the celebration.

The following day it was Seabury who issued a victory statement. He commended the New York press, especially Roy Howard's *World-Telegram,* for its crusading spirit and support from the outset of the magistrates' courts investigation. He congratulated the people of the city for having defeated not just Tammany but the Recovery party. He deplored the "Federal group" led by Farley which had tried to interfere in the city election. And he reminded those who had been elected that they now owed an obligation to reform the city charter and the election law so that voting would be more truly representative of all the people.

Between the day after election and five minutes after midnight on January 1, 1934, when La Guardia was sworn in as mayor in Judge Seabury's home, once again Seabury had to pick up his neglected law practice. He and Trosk were back in the office, suite 1655 at 120 Broadway. One client Seabury dropped the moment that La Guardia was elected. He had represented the Brooklyn Ash Removal Company; now it seemed that the company's work would be taken over by the city sanitation department. He would have nothing to do with a company doing business with the city lest it appear that he was acting improperly.

The cases that were brought to his office involved major matters. In nearly every one it was the lawyer rather than the client who came to Seabury; he was still running his law office like a British barrister. He was one of the attorneys in a contest brought by others to set aside the will of Mrs. Florence Adelaide Pratt, Singer Sewing Machine heiress, in which an estate of $5,000,000 was involved. In this case,* Seabury's fee amounted to almost $100,000 for his successful defense of the will.

Cities and universities called upon him for words of guidance on municipal reform. At Yale and Columbia he described the Fusion campaign and what led up to it. At the University of Rochester he began to evolve a theory about "the New Federalism" that had begun in Washington. "Social changes all over the world attest to the fact that we are entering upon a new stage of social development," he declared. "As I see it, we are entering upon what I call a new federalism. The old federalism contemplated merely a division or apportionment of power upon a territorial basis among governmental units. The new federalism applied to industry visions the exercise of social power not merely in relation to territorial or governmental units, but to the industrial functions that are to be performed, and upon the proper discharge of which the prosperity and happiness of our whole people depend." And he interpreted this New Deal trend favorably: "As I see it, the Administration at Washington is endeavoring to give intelligent leadership to the great middle class of this nation, which, up to this time, have stood not only mute but unrepresented, while their interests have been ground between the upper and nether millstones of highly organized groups representing capital and labor. If we would achieve industrial democracy, the principle of representative government must be introduced into the great key industries of the nation."

A pleasant task confronted Samuel Seabury after Christmas, 1933. He asked La Guardia, "Where do you want to be sworn in?"

La Guardia answered, without hesitation, "In your library, Judge."

The Judge looked pleased, Adolf Berle later recalled.

"Whom do you want to swear you in?" Seabury continued.

* 246 A. D. 576.

"Puddinhead McCook," La Guardia replied, using the affectionate nickname of Supreme Court Justice Philip J. McCook, a distinguished member of the bench, who was a friend of both.

Friends of the La Guardias and Seaburys, leaders of the Fusion campaign and new city officials, gathered at the Seabury home on December 31, 1933, for the celebration. At the end of the constitutional oath, taken five minutes after midnight, the city's new chief executive said, "I do so solemnly swear." La Guardia turned to Marie and kissed her.

Maud Seabury exclaimed, "Now we have a Mayor of New York!" Seabury beamed.

A few moments later, speaking for the newsreels grouped in Judge Seabury's library on the second floor of the house at 154 East 63rd Street, Mayor La Guardia said: "I have just assumed the office of Mayor of the City of New York. The Fusion administration is now in charge of our city. Our theory of municipal government is an experiment, to try to show that a nonpartisan, nonpolitical local government is possible, and, if we succeed, I am sure success in other cities is possible."

The revolutionary keynote of what was about to take place on the sidewalks of New York was sounded by Bernard S. Deutsch, the new president of the board of aldermen. "As I see the hundreds of thousands of hungry people in this city, I wonder why the people of New York, and especially those of affluence, do not realize this condition cannot go on forever. Those people are not going to sit by idly while Rolls-Royces and other big cars roll comfortably down Fifth Avenue."

Even as his own chauffeur-driven limousine rolled down that symbolic avenue of aristocrats, Samuel Seabury was all for that revolution.

CHAPTER **18**

Futile Dreamer, III:
The Gubernatorial Nomination

IN the *East Hampton Star,* the local weekly newspaper whose quaintness was in keeping with the township of East Hampton, minor matters received major attention. At the end of January, 1934 —in the midst of such news items as the planting of another box hedge on Main Street by the Ladies' Village Improvement Society— there appeared an unusual political letter to the editor concerning an important citizen of the community. It was pseudonymously signed "Mr. Con Fusion."

The letter noted that the "Hon. Samuel A. Seabury" (the paper still added the nonexistent middle initial) had proved his love of East Hampton, "his desire to make civic governments of the people, by the people and for the people, plus his ability to make shyster politicians run like rats from a sinking ship." This being the case, said "Mr. Con Fusion," it was "possible that one term of office by Judge Seabury would bring to the surface certain conditions which have needed airing. Take heed, citizens and taxpayers—draft Samuel Seabury for Mayor of East Hampton."

Judge Seabury, who less than two years before had hoped to be drafted as the Democratic presidential candidate, who had run for Governor of New York in 1916 and had turned down the Fusion mayoralty nomination in New York City, managed to resist the blandishments of his neighbors in East Hampton.

Not that he had given up, at the age of sixty-one, his political ambitions. Mayor La Guardia had been sworn in at the Seabury town house; without holding any office in the new city administration, Seabury was considered the conscience if not the power behind the City Hall throne. He was consulted on major appointments, and the voluble Fiorello noticeably altered his tone in front of Seabury. In La Guardia, Seabury had at last found a man who could fight Tammany Hall's leaders with the proper skill and sarcasm. But Seabury still dreamed of high political office for himself. That dream never changed.

A gubernatorial election was coming up in November, 1934. Governor Herbert H. Lehman was expected to run again on the Democratic ticket. That left the tantalizing prospect of trying to achieve in the state what had just been achieved in the city: win with a combination of Republican, Fusion, and independent votes.

One evening in the spring of 1934, Louis Molloy was relaxing at the Judge's East 63rd Street house after dinner. As head of the Knickerbocker Democrats, an anti-Tammany movement that had sprung up in some Manhattan districts to support La Guardia, Molloy was extremely well informed about the power blocs that made or rejected candidates before the convention stage was reached. They discussed their favorite subject, politics; and they speculated about the choices available at the Republican state convention that September. They spoke the same language, so much so that when Seabury said, "Louis, don't you think . . . ?" Molloy replied, "Yes, Judge, I do," and he would go out to the kitchen and mix their Scotch highballs. Molloy remembered that Seabury said more than once that year: "Louis, if you're born with this disease called politics, there is no cure. You have the disease, and so have I."

The Republican convention was still half a year away, and changes were taking place too swiftly in Washington, Albany, and New York to seek delegate commitments in advance. President Roosevelt's recovery program affected the selection of candidates by both parties in every statehouse and city hall. Governor Lehman was a Roosevelt man; so was, in his own side-stepping Republican–Fusion way, Mayor La Guardia. Battling against Lehman, so popular in

New York and backed by the President, was at best foolhardy. And it was impossible to guess whether the mercurial La Guardia would throw his support, or a curve, at the Republicans' choice.

Judge Seabury had good reason to hope that he could be nominated. His voting residence was in Suffolk County, which was controlled by a fellow resident, W. Kingsland Macy. Macy was the Republican state chairman, and he and Seabury had met privately early in the year to discuss the gubernatorial nomination. Macy decided that Seabury was the man best able to come to the aid of the party. To his Republican colleagues he said: "I called on Judge Seabury and found that while he declared that under no circumstances would he make a move to obtain the nomination, and was strongly inclined against even accepting such an honor, he would as a matter of duty consider the suggestion more seriously if the Republican party really wished him to lead the fight for a sound state government." He added that with Seabury as a candidate, "several hundred thousand independent Democratic votes" could be obtained and his election would be assured.

With the Republican state chairman behind him, in the winter and spring of 1934 it looked as if Seabury would be the candidate. However, there were rumblings in the party. The Old Guard was still thinking like Hoover, while the younger Republicans were trying to live him down. In New York City they had a mayor—or did they? Anyway, the progressive-minded young Republicans who had fought for La Guardia alongside the Fusion forces had discovered that a Republican could be elected in New York if the independents were rallied. But the conservative Republicans fumed at the thought of Seabury.

In their anti-Roosevelt, anti–almost-everything new bimonthly magazine called *The Awakener,* they editorialized: "The juvenile suggestion that the Republican party should run away from the national issue in New York this November by nominating a Roosevelt Democrat in the person of Samuel Seabury is beneath discussion. Its consummation would be the death of the Republican party in the state. A candidate is needed who symbolizes the spirit of uncompromising, courageous opposition to the whole Roosevelt socialistic program." The *New York Herald Tribune* amplified the Old Guard position by saying that "while the admiration of the members of the

New York Young Republican Club for the achievements and capacities of Judge Samuel Seabury is readily understandable, the belief that a Fusion candidate for governor is desirable seems to show a lack of appreciation of the functions as well as the needs of the Republican party. What is needed in the state much more than a Fusion candidate is the reorganization and revivification of the Republican party."

Judge Seabury, meanwhile, made no open move for the nomination. But as a speaker at colleges and meetings of lawyers' organizations, he began to assail "evil and sinister forces" in the state. In a speech at the University Club in New York he predicted that "soon the work that has been done in towns and cities will be done throughout the state." The state legislature, in traditional form, had begun to throw roadblocks in the way of New York City's necessary expenditures, and this too caused Seabury to deplore those assemblymen who were defying La Guardia's legislative needs.

In the spring of 1934, he began to rationalize the possibility that he might run as a Republican. The words "candidate" and "nomination" never crossed his lips, yet he sounded, to close students of the Empire State political scene, like an advocate with a case—his own. Not that his words to the leaders of the City Fusion party did not have significance: "So many of our fellow citizens who think alike allow themselves in their political actions to be divided by party names and party titles. I venture to think that this is a mistake. Those who seek to use the powers of government for their selfish purposes do not divide in that way. In Republican districts they are Republicans; in Democratic districts they are Democrats." But, he added, there were independent citizens who allow themselves needlessly to be splintered into camps with empty party names and slogans. And he took a crack at Governor Lehman by indirection, noting that Governor Cleveland opposed the influence of Tammany Hall. "We have had many Democratic governors since Cleveland," Seabury said, "but I do not recall that any of them regarded the action of Cleveland as an example."

If there was any doubt about what this all meant to the City Fusion audience, it was erased when Maurice P. Davidson, La Guardia's commissioner of water supply, gas and electricity, introduced Seabury as "the next Governor of New York." The introduction was cheered; but Seabury made no reference to the compliment.

Nor did he make a play for the support of the Republican Old Guard. On the contrary: he continued to talk like a maverick New Dealer. While the Union League Club on Park Avenue called for a "justifiable war upon the New Deal theorists," Seabury was addressing the students at Rutgers University with revisionist capitalistic theories of his own. "The world has got to find methods which will bring about a just distribution of wealth," he stated. "Experience shows that under our system, which has sanctioned private monopolies, the production of wealth has not been equitably shared." The Old Guard, shuddering at such radical language, formed a committee headed by F. Trubee Davison, a former Assistant Secretary of War, and issued a resolution that they aimed to "promote the election of Republican candidates, who are actively interested in the restoration of Republican politics in the state." They meant Republican, not Fusion, and told Macy so in no uncertain terms.

The New York Young Republican Club, led by David W. Peck, endorsed Seabury for the nomination. "If he's orthodox enough for Macy, he ought to be orthodox enough for us," an officer of the club said. "Who has done the most for the Republican party in New York City? Samuel Seabury, the man who chased graft out of City Hall and put a Republican into the mayoralty." The Seabury strength extended upstate. A survey of the Association of New York State Republican Clubs showed sentiment overwhelmingly for Seabury against Robert Moses. "There is a growing realization that Mr. Seabury, if nominated," the survey said, "will stump the state for the Republican ticket and, if elected, serve the best interests of the Republican party and effectively aid the congressional candidates in their fight upon the undesirable and unsound aspects of the New Deal."

On one subject, Samuel Seabury did not maintain a judicious silence. It was a subject that touched fibers deep inside him—the principles that he had espoused all his life, especially one: human dignity. The occasion was a mass meeting of 20,000 people in Madison Square Garden, March 7, 1934, for a mock trial of Hitlerism and the Nazi government. It was sponsored by the American Jewish Congress, the American Federation of Labor, and fifty other liberal, anti-Nazi, educational and religious organizations. Most of the city's

fighting intellectuals were there, and the new La Guardia administration was well represented. The presentation of "The Case of
Civilization Against Hitlerism" was timed to take place during the
week of the first anniversary of the Third Reich.

The floodlights in the Garden gallery were played on the platform
as Bainbridge Colby, one of the founders of the Progressive party and
a former Secretary of State, stood up to make the opening indictment. William Green, president of the A.F. of L.; Chancellor Harry
Woodburn Chase of New York University; Senator Millard E. Ty-
dings of Maryland; Abraham Cahan of the *Jewish Daily Forward;*
John Haynes Holmes of the Community Church; former Governor
Alfred E. Smith and other leaders testified on behalf of American
public opinion. When Mayor La Guardia and Samuel Seabury entered the Garden together, they received a whistling and clapping
ovation. At the end of the evening, Seabury, "as an outstanding
member of the American bar," in the words of *The New York
Times,* "summed up the case for civilization." Even the fifty members of the Silver Shirts, an American Fascist organization, sitting in
the balcony, kept their silence as Seabury spoke:

> Those interested in the cause of civilization should beware of the ad-
> vance of barbarism, manifesting its approach through religious persecu-
> tion and race hatred. Yet these are the banners under which Hitlerism
> is seeking to make its advance. According to Hitler, the lines of other
> national states are to be eliminated by war and conquest and in less than
> a hundred years the continent of Europe is to be inhabited by 250,000,000
> Germans, actuated by the Hitler lust for power, accomplishing its pur-
> poses by the Hitlerized processes of violence and cruelty, until the Ger-
> man power shall have "subjugated the world" and become "the sole
> master of this earth." The policy of Germany has been to arm, and while
> it disguises the groups that it keeps equipped for battle, they include not
> only the regular army, but the Prussian Police, the Brown Shirts, the
> Black Coats, the Steel Helmets and others, a force of over a million men,
> ready, when their leader shall give the signal, to exterminate France and
> subjugate the world.

He exposed the plan that Hitler had set forth in *Mein Kampf* and
told the audience about the steps already taken to stifle liberty in the
New Germany. "In this Hitlerized state all intellectual and cultural

activities are formulated, standardized and co-ordinated so as to mislead the people with false propaganda. The publicity and the attempt to mold public opinion is made by the Ministry of Public Enlightenment and Propaganda. A black list is established for books and many are upon the Hitler Index. The government not only dictates to the libraries what they may collect, but upon occasion the Nazi state directs the burning of books." He was applauded strongly when he added, "You can no more stay the progress of truth by reducing to ashes the form in which it is expressed, than you can imprison it behind iron bars."

And then he addressed himself to the outrages of racial hatred:

> The Jewish people have been subjected to inhuman, uncivilized and barbarous methods. They constitute the majority of those who have been herded into concentration camps, where they have been subjected to every cruelty and indignity. Slavery without any mitigating circumstances must be the lot of the Jew who remains in Germany while the Nazi state is in power. And yet laws have been enacted which forbid the Jew to go elsewhere. Prisoners to the Hitler state, denied the right to expatriate themselves, they must continue to remain under the Hitler regime and suffer the persecutions and cruelties. They are the galley slaves in the Nazi ship of state. What can we say of such a state and the evils that it has produced except what Garrison said of slavery: that it is the "sum of all villainies." In the discrimination against the Jews, other people must not be so short-sighted as to conclude that they are not also affected. Persecution of one is an injury to all.

Judge Seabury concluded by saying that public opinion could be the force, and the boycott the weapon, to break the power of Hitlerism. He called for organized public opinion and action that would find its best expression in a boycott "as wide as civilization." Unfortunately, the rest of civilization was not yet willing to recognize the threat and resist the tyrant. Indeed, only two months later, in Madison Square Garden, another organization of Americans assembled who called themselves the "Friends of the New Germany." Nazi swastikas were carried side by side with the United States flag by American Bundists in Storm Trooper uniforms. George Sylvester Viereck was cheered and heiled as he spoke on "good business" reasons for supporting the Hitler government and opposing the boycott.

He said that a "reign of terror" had been foisted upon the United States and especially the City of New York by "certain professional Jews and their Bolshevist confederates."

Among those whose names were booed and hissed by the "Friends of the New Germany" was Samuel Seabury.

Seabury took a stand on other issues in a forthright manner. None occupied his attention more than the need to revise New York City's charter. On public platforms and in newspaper articles and interviews, he denounced the old charter as a "legalistic strait jacket." He said that the city-wide investigation and the election of a new city administration still left unfulfilled the third aspect of reform—a charter that would abolish the five county governments and make New York City a unified and more efficient municipality.

In the summer of 1934, Judge Seabury made a behind-the-scenes move to gain the nomination. He had the support of W. Kingsland Macy. Now he wanted to see where he stood with other political leaders, including La Guardia himself. Paul Windels, the corporation counsel, came to his house and briefed him on the general situation. When Seabury told him that he had the Republican state chairman behind his candidacy, Windels warned, "Don't go into that convention as the candidate of Macy. Some of the top rank-and-file leaders of the Republican party are trying to unhorse him." Seabury asked him what his best approach to the nomination should be, and Windels said, "The thing for you to do is to be your own candidate." The thought was that Seabury could gain the highest number of state delegates without affiliating himself with either of the warring party factions.

Macy began to broaden the base of his campaign for Seabury's nomination. He spoke to a number of upstate leaders and asked them to call on his candidate. They did so and came away impressed. Macy told various Republican committees that Seabury had promised to make a campaign that would rebuild the Republican party and return it to its once powerful position. This struck some Old Guard ears as overly optimistic. The Old Guard distrusted Seabury and condemned Macy's "rule or ruin" policy for the party. They preferred as candidate either former United States Senator James W. Wadsworth or Robert Moses, now the city's park commissioner. But upstate and in the city, Seabury was picking up independent support.

Among those coming out for Seabury were the anti-Tammany
Knickerbocker Democrats. But what would happen when the hard-
core Republicans met in Rochester at the end of September was extremely uncertain.

"The idea of carrying Fusion into the state ticket and taking out
of state politics issues which have no place there is intriguing to anyone interested in clean government," the "noncommitted" Seabury
declared, "but mid-July is no time to talk about candidates. Anyone
interested in clean government is interested in principles now rather
than candidates. When the issues are drawn, there is plenty of time
to talk about the captains and the leaders." There was no doubt in
anyone's mind in midsummer that Seabury, while playing the disinterested game in the usual political tradition, was ready to be a
"captain" for the Republicans. But, the regulars suspected, it would
have to be on his own terms. Seabury was no one's man. On the eve
of the nominating convention in Rochester at the end of September,
1934, he would tell the delegates so.

In spite of Macy's position, the feeling had grown among the Republicans in the state that only a Republican should be nominated.
Now Moses was considered in the lead, the choice of the anti-Macy
group, followed by Queens Borough President George U. Harvey,
Seabury, and the Mayor of Syracuse, Rolland B. Marvin. Yet Macy
declared that "Mr. Seabury will be nominated on the first ballot."
There was no headquarters, no place for Seabury delegates to rally.
It looked like just another hopeful structure without solid political
underpinning.

Where did La Guardia stand? At the last moment, he backed
Seabury. He called on Corporation Counsel Windels to go to the convention on the day it began and to make it clear that the city administration favored Seabury's nomination. The Mayor's decision placed
him in the position of pledging the city's support to Seabury at a
time when a member of his own cabinet was the leading contender.
At a private meeting a few days before, La Guardia had resisted
Seabury's inquiry about help, saying he did not think it was right for
the Fusion Mayor of New York to get involved in the Republican
state convention. Even when he did come out for Seabury, it was
through another person. The Mayor, that day, "had a cold."

Nevertheless, the announcement gave a lift to the Seabury candidacy. A headquarters was opened at the Hotel Sagamore. The first Seabury posters came forth. On them was the slogan "Success With Seabury." The Seabury headquarters was run by William Grant Brown, a Bull Mooser who with Teddy Roosevelt had defected from the Old Guard in 1912. Campaign literature stressed that Seabury was "a real fighter for true Republicanism" and the "bitterest foe of Tammany since the days of Tweed." But being a fighter *for* "Republicanism" was not exactly the same thing as being a "Republican."

Former State Senator Clayton R. Lusk, a Macy adherent, put the question to Seabury in a telegram. The delegates wanted to know where he stood on national and state issues; also, whether he would be sympathetic with the principles of the Republican party if he were made the choice of the convention. Seabury might have been suitably vague to satisfy the delegates. Instead, his response was anything but reassuring—even to his supporters at the convention. He refused to change his stance, even for a gubernatorial nomination.

While the Republicans in Rochester were jumping all over the New Deal in speech after speech, Seabury's reply was much more judicious. "Some of the New Deal proposals have been good," he declared, "such as the closing of the banks on Inauguration Day and keeping them closed until proper inquiry could be made into their solvency. The practice of distributing emergency relief has been necessary and should not be abated while the need exists." Having said these complimentary words, he added that he was not in sympathy with any policy that would drive the small businessman out of business or would not protect the consumer against unduly high prices. His complaints sounded faint, indeed, to Republicans at the convention. "I am not in sympathy with a wholesale attack upon the New Deal, or upon any other genuine effort to promote national recovery."

Only when he mentioned his lifelong foe, Tammany Hall, did he warm up. "While Tammany Hall was in power in New York City, Governor Lehman acquiesced in its rule and never ventured even a protest against the shameful conditions for which it was responsible. Mr. Farley, as chief spoilsman of the Federal Administration, falsely claims to have established a reformed Tammany Hall. He has merely put in power in that organization those who will do his bidding rather than the bidding of the former deposed leader. Mr. Farley's activities have given the country an exhibition of a most disgusting attempt to influence nominations and elections in this state and in its cities by the use of Federal patronage."

But he gave the Republicans no comfort when he said, "If the views expressed by certain critics of some of the proposals of the New Deal are sound, much of the social welfare legislation of the last generation would be unconstitutional, whereas it has already been declared constitutional by the Supreme Court of the United States. I favor a short work day under present conditions, and the establishment of a minimum wage large enough to enable men to live in accordance with American standards of life. I also favor unemployment insurance." Was this a speech designed to win a *Republican* nomination? Or was it an attack upon the very things that the state Republicans considered sacred? "There should be an administration at Albany free from any connection with the utility and power interests of this state, and aggressive steps should be taken to drive any representatives of these interests from legislative halls. The liberty of the monopolists and the exploiters of the people, whatever form the method of exploitation may take, must be restricted."

His conclusion was no more consoling to his supporters shopping for delegates. "I do not know whether my views will find favor with the convention, but I would be unwilling to accept leadership unless it is definitely understood that I should lead along these and similar lines. While I am leader of a party it will not wear the livery of privilege; it will be the outspoken champion of the interests of the people of this state against special interests, which have been treated with undue tolerance by the representatives of government. If I become the nominee of the Republican party, and that party stands for the principles in which I believe, I will devote myself unreservedly to the advancement of its success, to the end that it may become a useful instrument of service to the people. Should the party depart from those principles, it could not command my support."

This was not an appeal; it was a lecture: Seabury was telling them, not asking them. And his message was that if he received the Republican nomination, he would play not ball but havoc with the Grand Old Party. Whatever chance he had to rally independent support in the split Republican ranks disappeared after this principled statement.

Unknown to his Republican supporters, Seabury had called upon Louis Molloy to run up to Rochester and give him the plain facts. "I took a room in a fleabag there to remain anonymous," Molloy later recalled. "After surveying the situation among the delegations, I called Seabury and told him, 'There isn't any possibility of your getting the nomination.' And he replied, 'Well, Louis, I know you have given me an accurate report. Others have given me false hopes or tried to soften the real news.' The Judge took the news in stride."

Nevertheless, he was placed in nomination by former State Senator Frank L. Wiswall. "What he has done for the party in the city, he can do for the state. You must have a fearless, two-fisted, courageous fighting leader for this campaign. There is one man whose name carries the greatest threat to the democracy of this state. Every Democrat wants us to nominate someone else. That hope is our recommendation. Men and women delegates, let's be big. Let's stand up on our two legs and give the people of New York Samuel Seabury."

The convention applauded mildly, a band broke out in a short march, and it was all over. Moses received the nomination by a large majority. He was an "Al Smith Republican," an ambiguity to both parties. It was obvious to the regular Republicans that Seabury squirmed uncomfortably on the elephant's back. He looked like, but was not, the political cartoonist's image of the Old Guard Republican; he was not their kind.

Back in New York City after the convention, Seabury continued to look over La Guardia's shoulder. At the end of his own business day, he called upon the Mayor and the two often went off together for an evening drive and conference. La Guardia stated, "I'll vote for Bob Moses," but Seabury made no such affirmation. He was still trying to hack his own path, hoping that the voters would follow. A week before Election Day, he predicted that progressive Republicans and progressive Democrats would join "at a time not far distant" under an independent banner to curb "the monopoly elements."

In his only campaign talk, before the City Fusion party on November 2, 1934, he urged the election of Controller Joseph D. McGoldrick but said that the public would be the loser regardless of whether Lehman or Moses was elected governor. "Draw, if you can, any fine distinction between Governor Tweedledee on one side and Commissioner Tweedledum on the other, and then, if you find any advantage in either candidate, vote for that candidate." La Guardia sat on the same platform at the Hotel Astor but made no appeal for either of the gubernatorial candidates. In this contest, where Governor Lehman was overwhelmingly re-elected, La Guardia played the supporting and Seabury the silent role.

In the mayoralty election of 1933, Seabury had given the La Guardia campaign a steadiness and conservatism which had helped to balance the public's idea of the fiery Fiorello. Because of La Guardia's sense of loyalty to Seabury, he had backed him—though rather quietly—at the Rochester convention. But Seabury, who had rallied voters in both parties for La Guardia, attacked both parties when he himself was a candidate. He sneered at the Old Guard Republicans. And he was beginning to ruffle the feathers of the New Deal's Blue Eagle.

He had a great following of Fusionists, catch-all reformers and sentimental Progressives and Bull Moosers, in the city, state, and country. But what did principle matter if the voters could not find his name on the ballot on Election Day? "Seabury was a great fighter," Paul Windels said, long afterward, "but he was inclined to put his head down politically—and charge." So ended another Seabury dream of a mandate from the public to chart a course above politics.

CHAPTER

The Mayor's "Bishop"

THEY were a strange, unlikely pair: Seabury, whose ancestors were proud names in old New York, and La Guardia, whose immigrant parents were among the millions of non–Anglo-Saxons efflorescent in new New York. La Guardia, Mayor of New York from 1934 to 1945, gave the city an honest and exciting government through the years of a depression and a war; all this time Seabury stood behind him as a private citizen, not telling La Guardia what to do but serving as his conscience and his guide.

Seabury called La Guardia "Major," his World War I rank that had stuck as a *nom de guerre* in his political life; La Guardia usually called Seabury "Judge," but sometimes, when speaking of him to mutual friends, La Guardia referred to him as "the Bishop."

"Fiorello considered Seabury dignified and learned," Mrs. La Guardia recalled. "They disagreed on political matters from time to time, but there was never any rift between them. When I first met the Judge he seemed cold and stiff, yet he was very kindly and courtly. But he relaxed around Fiorello. We would have cocktails and dinner with the Judge and Maud—she was very sweet. Fiorello would josh the Judge a little, and the Judge had quite a sense of humor, in his gentlemanly way."

"La Guardia and Seabury had the same basic views on major issues concerning the City of New York," Edward Corsi, a former United

States Commissioner of Immigration, remembered. "Theirs was essentially a liberal approach. If Judge Seabury called La Guardia on the phone, La Guardia would jump. That was rare. La Guardia could be very rough with his friends, but he was always controlled with Seabury."

"La Guardia talked to Seabury as if to a father," said Adolf A. Berle, Jr., former city chamberlain and United States Assistant Secretary of State. "La Guardia never blew his top with Seabury. Whenever La Guardia attacked the courts and lawyers generally, Seabury would say, 'But you're not the one to say so from your position as mayor. You have an obligation to uphold the dignity of the courts and the law.' Sometimes the Judge would cheer us up when we were trying to effect changes and get things done, especially in unifying the transit system. I remember the Judge saying, 'Everything that's good counts. If our plan is good and helps things, there are people who will come along later and put the good ideas into effect.'"

While staying with the Seaburys one week end at East Hampton, La Guardia answered the phone, then quickly remembered that he was hiding from the cares of office, briefly. "Seabury residence," La Guardia said. "Is Mayor La Guardia there?" a voice on the city end persisted. "No," said La Guardia. "Who is this I am speaking to?" demanded the voice. "This," said La Guardia, suddenly mimicking a British accent, "is Judge Seabury's butler." And he quickly hung up.

Judge Seabury found this amusing. "Actually," Seabury told an office associate, "La Guardia is a very urbane gentleman. He has a great sense of what's right. One day he was being driven up a one-way street the wrong way and he insisted that his chauffeur turn around, saying, 'Do you want me to get a ticket?' This showed the proper example for a city official. La Guardia knew how to be correct."

In the course of a harangue against the newspapers for failing to be as incensed as himself about a piece of legislation, La Guardia made a disparaging remark about Lee Wood, an important *New York World-Telegram* editor. When this got back to the newspaper, an editorial storm began to brew. La Guardia called in Seabury to smooth matters over, but found him unsympathetic. Seabury said, "Major, *The World-Telegram* supported the investigations and your candidacy most strongly. I would urge you to apologize—or I will be forced to issue a statement." La Guardia backed down.

Seabury often dropped into City Hall at the end of the day, and with La Guardia drove for an hour around the boroughs, looking over new construction projects. Both were interested in the city's transportation system. Before going home, La Guardia would stop off for a predinner drink at the Seabury town house. In the summer, they met on Monday mornings at a gasoline station in the center of Long Island, near Commack, Seabury driving in from East Hampton and La Guardia driving down from Northport. Then La Guardia stepped into Seabury's limousine, and they talked over municipal matters on the rest of the drive into the city.

Seabury recognized that La Guardia's outbursts were a part of his nature. When La Guardia bawled out one of the lawyers (who, incidentally had worked as a Seabury assistant during the city-wide investigation) in the corporation counsel's office, Seabury stood up for the young attorney. Yet having done so in front of La Guardia, Seabury later defended La Guardia's behavior. "Don't let the Major bother you," Seabury said. "It is part of his temperament to blow up —and he does have a most difficult job. But he really doesn't mean it personally."

A number of Seabury's associate and assistant counsel from the investigations joined the La Guardia administration. Irving Ben Cooper became a special counsel in the Department of Accounts and eventually a magistrate and chief justice of the court of special sessions. William B. Northrop also became a magistrate and special sessions judge. Jacob Gould Schurman, Jr., served as a judge in general sessions. Philip W. Haberman, Jr., William G. Mulligan, Oren Herwitz, Joseph G. Miller, and W. Bernard Richland all served as assistant corporation counsel. J. G. Louis Molloy became Mayor La Guardia's law secretary, and others who had worked on the three investigations were encouraged by Seabury to join the new city government.

Seabury, himself, refused to take any position for pay in La Guardia's administration, but he did accept the job, without compensation, of special counsel to the Board of Estimate to solve the problem of unifying the city's rapid-transit system. This enormous undertaking was closest to La Guardia's heart; in later years the Mayor said it was the outstanding achievement of his administration.

Seabury, City Chamberlain Berle, Corporation Counsel Windels, and his assistant, Bill Mulligan, took on the job of "buying" all the private subways and elevated railways and combining them into one city-owned nickel-fare system.

Few people recalled at the time that Seabury had been one of the moving forces for public ownership not only of transportation but other utilities; that he had worked with William Randolph Hearst, during the latter's reform period in 1905, in the Municipal Ownership League; that Seabury's 1905 book, *Municipal Ownership and Operation of Public Utilities in New York City,* had served to arouse city reformers all over the country. As a young radical on the bench, Seabury had stood for municipal ownership to protect the people from monopolists, trusts, and swindlers, and, now, more than three decades later, he would see a visionary idea come into existence.

"Seabury and Berle struggled night and day for two years with all the divergent interests of stockholders and bondholders and noteholders and lawyers representing the traction companies," Mulligan, who did much of the legal groundwork at their side, recalled. "Finally in 1936 they obtained an agreement for a unification plan— the first plan where all interested parties agreed. Under the Seabury-Berle plan the city would have acquired privately owned properties and brought about cancellation of inequitable subway contracts at a cost forty million dollars less than had ever before been proposed. The total price in their plan was four hundred and sixteen million dollars for the combined BMT, IRT, and elevated systems."

But the State Transit Commission blocked the Seabury–Berle plan in 1937. A familiar name turned up, John J. Curtin, the commission's counsel, who had defended Mayor Walker during the hearings before Governor Roosevelt. An editorial in the *New York Herald Tribune* pointed out that the "whole transit affair has degenerated under Curtin's handling from a serious consideration of the one unification agreement ever achieved into a cheap political controversy." And *The World-Telegram* added, "The long-abused public should realize that Tammany action through the Transit Commission is out to wreck unification. The victims of all this Tammany assault are the same millions who have been the victims of this political kicking about of unification—the millions who ride down to the city on straps and go home the same way."

As if to prove the contention that the Seabury–Berle plan was held up for political reasons, ex-Mayor Walker was appointed to a post as assistant counsel to the State Transit Commission. His specific job was to eliminate grade crossings—"a $12,000 flagman," said a City Fusion party wag. This was something of a comedown for the former Mayor, returning from several years of enforced retirement on the Riviera and elsewhere in Europe. The appointment was an obvious slap in the face for those who had labored to unify the transit system. Nothing ever aroused Seabury more than the reinstatement of Walker in this city post.

In a sarcastic open letter to the Transit Commission, Seabury referred to Walker as "the captain of the Tin Box Brigade" and suggested that Russell T. Sherwood, Walker's onetime financial agent who had fled to Mexico during the investigation, be given "an equally comfortable place" on the payroll. In his well-publicized letter, Seabury reviewed the circumstances of Walker's partnership with Sherwood in the joint safe-deposit box and his various "beneficences" from people doing business with the city. "Of course, there may be those detractors who will say that your honorable Transit Commission is acting like one of the few remaining strongholds of the Tammany plunderbund. While I cannot congratulate you upon your appointment of Mr. Walker, I do wish to press for your very serious consideration the suggestion of the appointment of Mr. Sherwood. I feel satisfied that such public confidence in your honorable commission as may now exist would in no way be impaired by adding to your staff both of these Gold Dust Twins." And Seabury explained that the real aim of the appointment was that it came within two weeks of Walker's pension deadline from the City of New York.

"Mr. Seabury is now a politician and I am not," Walker retorted, having lost none of his glibness after five years out of public office. "He is a political boss and I am out of politics. So I have to make some allowance for the fact that as a political boss he must be expected to make statements for political campaign purposes. There never was a statement made by Mr. Seabury under circumstances that would permit the answer to go along with the charge at the same time. I've had a good deal of experience with that. He is still using me to get into the papers. His old style is innuendo and half-truth and misrepresentation."

The crusade for transit unification dogged the La Guardia administration year after year. The Mayor attempted to get the Transit Commission abolished by the state legislature, unsuccessfully. The Seabury–Berle plan was scrutinized and belittled by the state commissioners; also, there were some doubts raised by the Citizens Budget Commission about its cost to the city. In November, 1938, voters approved an amendment authorizing a $315,000,000 debt exemption for the purchase of the private lines. Finally, in June, 1940, the BMT and IRT systems were purchased by the city (though some surface lines remained privately owned). The push given to transit unification by the Seabury–Berle plan paved the way for the long-dreamed-of municipal ownership.

Another nonpaying job that occupied Seabury's attention was charter reform. In the constructive phase of his city-wide investigation, after Jimmy Walker's resignation, Seabury had put Al Smith and other experts in the witness chair to testify on how to improve municipal government. Now he was given the chance to change the structure of the old charter and, at the same time, introduce one of his own pet ideas—voting by proportional representation for the city's councilmen. Governor Lehman and Mayor La Guardia both saw the need for a streamlined charter. It looked easy.

No sooner did the New York City Charter Commission meet in 1934 than Smith and Seabury, the chairman and vice chairman, resigned. Ex-Governor Smith explained why picturesquely: "The people I couldn't get along with were the stowaways who were put on board with monkey wrenches to throw into the machinery and scuttle the ship." And Seabury found an old enemy present: "It became evident that the Charter Commission had been so packed that the Tammany element, which were opposed to any real reform, were in a majority on the commission." Mayor La Guardia contributed a futile note: "The poor Charter Commission is in the position of a girl in a country town that has something whispered about her behavior. She may be innocent and lily-white but the fact remains that if the idea gets around, she can never get away from it and it will ruin her reputation for years to come. With what's been said about the commission, I'm afraid that the only thing to do is to begin again."

That was what happened next. Smith and Seabury applied pressure on Governor Lehman and the state legislature. A new law was approved for a more compact Charter Revision Commission appointed by Mayor La Guardia. Thomas D. Thacher was named chairman, but Smith and Seabury decided not to be on the commission this time. However, invisible support was given by Seabury for the new charter. When it appeared on the ballot in the fall of 1936, Seabury took to the air to urge voters to support the charter and the proportional representation (PR) system.

"Personally, I should have liked to see the charter go further in some respects," Judge Seabury said, "but we can make progress step by step." He noted that home rule was granted; the power of the borough presidents was limited; a city planning commission was established, and the cumbersome board of aldermen was replaced by a city council. Seabury especially urged voters to support the independent plan for PR. "Unless you carry proportional representation, the new council which takes the place of the board of aldermen will be an unrepresentative body."

Both the new charter and PR were approved. The badge of liberalism was to favor PR, of conservatism to oppose it. The idea was to give fair representation to opposition and minority political parties. Seabury championed PR before it came into existence, in 1937, and after it was abolished, in 1947, in favor of district voting (thereby insuring the Democrats overwhelming majorities in the city council). Some civic officials, such as Robert Moses, felt that all PR did was allow Communists and other minority parties into the city council, teaming councilmen who could not work together effectively.

But Seabury's deeper reasons for advocating PR were twofold. First, "our duty in America's great cities is to establish truly representative government." He saw it as an answer to Hitler, Mussolini, and other tyrants "when democracy is on trial all over the world today." Second, "proportional representation will do much to destroy the partisan Tammany domination under which New York City has suffered in years past." As an independent Democrat, he was willing to see minority parties—Republicans, Socialists and others—represented in the city council, "otherwise it is disfranchisement of their citizenship."

When the Mayor ran for a second term in 1937, Seabury again was a factor in the selection of the ticket and throughout the campaign.

The anti–New-Deal Republicans in the city wanted to drop La Guardia in favor of someone more "regular." Seabury worked to persuade his influential friends in the downtown law offices to continue their support of the Fusion mayor. The newly formed American Labor party, which had helped President Roosevelt in New York state the year before, swung behind La Guardia, but Seabury and Berle worked furiously to preserve the balance of Fusion supporters from the 1933 campaign ranks.

An interesting side development involved the selection of Thomas E. Dewey as candidate for district attorney on the La Guardia ticket. Dewey had served as special prosecutor in the investigation of organized crime from 1935 to 1937, and La Guardia and Seabury felt he would strengthen their slate before the more conservative voters. "I was assigned to get the support of the Labor party group for Dewey," Berle stated. "It was I who first interviewed him. He immediately laid down conditions—a guarantee of a large sum of money for campaigning, three weeks of clamor for him in the press, and the right to campaign independently." His self-centered demands were not appreciated by the idealistic Fusion nominating group, Chairman Seabury's Citizens Non-Partisan Committee, yet they were met. "Judge Seabury was not happy about Dewey's behavior afterwards," Berle said. "He thought, rightly, that Dewey was making a grandstand play for the Presidency."

In the fall of 1937, Judge Seabury campaigned all over the city, stumping for La Guardia's re-election. Again, the oxygen tank was hidden under a blanket in the back of his limousine, the shades were drawn, and he inhaled the revivifying air between speaking engagements. Dorothy Benner, his secretary, diligently filled a small volume later that contained his speeches and press clippings. It was labeled *Municipal Campaign of 1937*.

The La Guardia–Seabury team delivered their one-two punch on several occasions. When the Mayor formally accepted the nomination of the American Labor party at a packed rally in Carnegie Hall, he characterized Seabury as "the greatest exterminator of crooks in the history of this country, and founder of good government in New York City." Although the Judge, with Maud, had come to the meeting simply as a guest, he was persuaded to speak by Sidney Hillman president of the Amalgamated Clothing Workers of America. As the labor leaders in the audience cheered, Seabury ridiculed the "Red issue" raised by Jeremiah T. Mahoney, the Democratic candidate, and styled Tammany as "the Amalgamated Order of Grafters and Crooks."

In Madison Square Garden, Mayor La Guardia repeated his praise of Seabury in front of a huge turnout of trade unionists. He reminded his audience of 18,000 that during his unsuccessful mayoralty campaign in 1929, he had attacked Tammany Hall for its graft and dishonesty, but the people were not yet ready to believe him. "Then along came one man, who called witness after witness, and before he was through some went to Canada, some went to Cuba, others went to England, and I went to City Hall. That man, to whom we all are indebted for our being here tonight under these conditions, is Judge Samuel Seabury." And Seabury responded: "Let me say this. New York City has had a long procession of misfit mayors. For years we longed for a man who would appreciate the human elements in government, a mayor whose great heart could be in harmony with the needs and aspirations of the people. But he never appeared until La Guardia came along."

New Yorkers rose early and voted, the lucky ones escorted by the bagpipe band of the "Irish Nonpartisan Committee for La Guardia," possibly singing the parodied words of "Tammany" which they had heard Sigmund Spaeth lead at rallies of Republicans:

> *Tammany, Tammany, better stay in your tepee,*
> *Watch a Fusion victory,*
> *Tammany, Tammany*
> *Crack 'em, smack 'em, rock 'em, sock 'em,*
> *Tammany!*

The day after La Guardia had swamped 'em, with the American Labor party more than making the difference between victory and defeat, a *New York Times* editorial called it "Judge Seabury's victory."

The name of Judge Samuel Seabury was not flashed in lights or shouted in top headlines this week. He was not running for any office. Yet without the cornerstone which he so well and truly laid, the edifice of good government which we now see rearing its sturdy walls might not have been built. It was Samuel Seabury who, by the patient accumulation and courageous presentation of damning evidence against the Tammany regime in 1932, not only forced the retirement of Mayor Walker and of other officials but aroused public opinion to a point where it demanded the further investigations of Special Prosecutor Dewey. More than any other man Judge Seabury deserves credit for the charter revision movement. He exposed dishonesty and made honesty seem something more than a glittering dream.

Although the "Major" and the "Bishop" were close political allies, respectful of each other's talents and cordial in their personal association, they were not intimates. Few of Seabury's friends claimed that privilege. His life during the period in the late 1930's and mid-1940's, when his law practice dwindled, revolved around Maud, his nephews, and others in the family; he met small groups of friends at Sunday teas in town. Whenever possible, however, week ends were reserved for the relaxed life at the farm in East Hampton, where Maud could cultivate her English garden and the Judge could putt at the Maidstone Club, go for a sail in Three Mile Harbor, play chess with his nephews, and pursue his studies in his library.

When the Bishop of Aberdeen came to the United States for a visit, he and his wife found the Seaburys sympathetic friends. They stayed with them at the town house and at the farm. After the bishop returned to Scotland, Judge Seabury sent him a gift of a small Ford. Here was a clergyman who represented a link with the British Isles and his ancestors. That, more than religion, counted with him.

Maud was more active in religious and social affairs in East Hampton. She worked with Episcopal women's groups to help poor children and was active in church organizations. The war threat from Europe enlisted the efforts of both. The Seaburys turned over to the Red Cross a house owned by them located on Main Street, and Maud was on the Suffolk Council of the American Red Cross. The English-Speaking Union of the United States, helping to promote Anglo-American unity, found their services useful and Maud received the King's Medal during the war.

Hitler's barbarism, especially the bombing of London, aroused Seabury to write a letter to the United States Navy offering them his thirty-two-foot sailboat, the *Maud S,* and he was amused by the form reply: If he would deliver the boat from its mooring at the Devon

Yacht Club to 90 Church Street, the Navy would accept it. Sure enough, one day a young sailor walked into his office at 40 Wall Street and stood at attention before Bernard Richland. Richland walked into the Judge's office and announced, "Yeoman Ginsberg is here to take delivery on the yacht." The Judge invited him in, signed the necessary papers, and "delivery" was made in Manhattan. "The yeoman insisted that I take a dollar for it for the duration," the Judge informed his friends.

As president of the Bar Association for 1940-41, Seabury helped to create a new committee on national defense. During his term, the committee on foreign law was encouraged to take part in the newly organized Inter-American Bar Association. Between President Roosevelt of the United States and President Seabury of the Bar Association passed a formal though almost cordial letter, reflecting their cool but respectful relationship. "As a member of the Association," Roosevelt wrote, reminding the members that he had once practiced in New York, "I am glad to hear of a committee on National Defense, because the organized Bar has a peculiar responsibility to the community." A few more letters came from Roosevelt to Seabury, commending the Bar Association for its dinner to Justice William O. Douglas on one occasion and its encouragement of the cause of arbitration on another, but the two men who, as governor and counsel, a decade before, had overturned New York City's government, kept a distance between them.

Although Seabury deplored Roosevelt's running for a third term and campaigned for Wendell Willkie, he was all in favor of Roosevelt's program of early aid to England. "When the news reached us of the bombing of the Middle Temple by the Germans," he told his colleagues in the Bar Association, "our committee sent a message of sympathy and an expression of hope that there had been no serious destruction of the books in their library. It is unthinkable that any human beings, even those so savage and inhumane as these Germans have proven themselves to be, could deliberately wreck the instrumentalities of civilization and its facilities, as has happened to the Middle Temple buildings. All of us here vaunt ourselves anew, on our heritage from England and on our kinship with the glorious English, even though that kinship be more remote than we would wish."

When Judge Seabury learned that the collection of American Reports had escaped damage when *Luftwaffe* bombs hit the Middle Temple, he said to his fellow lawyers good-humoredly: "Can it be that the weightiness of the decisions contained therein form such a solid foundation of justice as to render them immune from disturbance, even by the most powerful weapons of international lawlessness?"

At the time Judge Seabury was president of the Bar Association, several lawyers were disbarred, some as a result of links with the senior member of the circuit court of appeals, Judge Martin Manton, who had been tried and convicted of selling justice. Thomas E. Dewey, the district attorney, followed the Seabury method in tracking down the bank deposits, and the tin boxes, of suspected bribers and officials taking graft. One afternoon early in 1941, Judge Seabury and Bernard Richland of his office staff were returning from lunch at the Bankers Club when, suddenly, Seabury excused himself and walked across the street. He stopped a lawyer who, unfortunately, had recently been disbarred as a result of an involvement with ex-Judge Manton. Seabury spoke to him for a few moments, patted him on the shoulder, and then returned to where Richland waited, surprised. He wondered why aloud, and the Judge replied, "I comforted that misguided man because it's easy to be pleasant to someone when he is up. But it is more important to show friendship to someone when he is down on his luck."

After serving as president of the Bar Association for two years, Judge Seabury continued his interest in the affairs of lawyers as professionals and members of the community. Knowing of Seabury's democratic ideas, William Dean Embree, president of the New York County Lawyers Association, appointed him chairman of a special committee to investigate the charges that the American Bar Association discriminated against Negro lawyers. The matter was touched off when the A.B.A. failed to admit Francis E. Rivers, an assistant district attorney in New York County. Seabury's distinguished committee included Henry W. Taft, Charles E. Hughes, Jr., Joseph M. Proskauer, and Basil O'Connor, and they uncovered the fact that A.B.A. applicants had been required to say whether they were "white, Negro, Indian or Mongolian."

Several years later, in his own private practice, Judge Seabury, representing the Metropolitan Life Insurance Company, took what appeared to be the opposite position when he defended housing discrimination by private owners. He argued that there were many legal precedents that allowed the landlord to choose his own tenants. Having handled many important cases and negotiations for Metropolitan Life over a period of years in the 1940's, Seabury thus found himself in the sticky position of defending a client's property rights going counter to his own long-held ideas of human rights.

With Lee McCanliss, a former partner of John W. Davis, Seabury was involved in a number of important cases and appeals, representing the Guaranty Trust Company and other major clients. "When he represented clients on appeals," McCanliss said, "Judge Seabury's fees ran from $10,000 to $50,000. The reason was, he did them well. He, John W. Davis, and Nathan Miller were the big appeals men." By the end of the war, however, Seabury's practice had begun to fall off, and his name was used on briefs only for the name value.

McCanliss, whose respect for the Judge grew into a close friendship, was responsible for the final futile political dream by Seabury: the nomination for the Presidency in 1940. Actually, Seabury himself made no effort this time to get the nomination, though he was aware that a few of his friends were sounding out political leaders opposed to Roosevelt's third term. By then he was sixty-seven. "The independent Democrats had an idea that Roosevelt would run in 1940," McCanliss said. "A few of us considered the possibility that Seabury might be able to obtain the nomination. I talked with Judge John Mack of Poughkeepsie, who had nominated FDR twice. When FDR attempted to purge Senator Walter George of Georgia, I raised money for him and helped to get the vote out. Another Senator I spoke to about Seabury was Wild Bill Langer from Dakota, a close friend of mine from law-school days. We had soured on Roosevelt, as had Judge Seabury, and wanted to stop him. But nothing at all came of our attempt to put forward Seabury's name quietly."

Since Seabury had never put any stock in his chances, he did not feel the keen disappointment of 1932 when he had actively tried for the nomination. No open moves had been made. "I did not know that there was any convention activity in Seabury's behalf in 1940," Sam Rosenman later stated.

The 1940 presidential race found Seabury thrilled by the apparent independence of Wendell L. Willkie. "You were not the choice of machine politicians or a controlled convention but of the plain people of this country," Seabury wired him. "Your nomination justifies the hope that under your Presidency order and equality of opportunity may supplant the present bureaucratic chaos." Willkie voiced his appreciation and characterized Seabury as "the most distinguished man in the country in cleaning up corrupt political machines."

For Seabury, the presidential and mayoralty campaigns for third terms suddenly became related because of the return of an old Tammany foe: Jimmy Walker. Roosevelt and La Guardia, allies in governmental change, maintained an unwritten truce between themselves regarding New York City. The President refused to intervene on behalf of a Democratic candidate for mayor running against La Guardia. And La Guardia would, in spite of the half of him that was a Republican, make it perfectly clear that he favored "That Man in the White House." Seabury and La Guardia's mutual respect and friendship withstood their differing attitudes toward Roosevelt.

But Mayor La Guardia's selection of Walker as impartial chairman of the dress industry in New York strained his relationship with Seabury almost to the breaking point. Jim Farley had arranged for Walker to pay a social call on Roosevelt at the White House a few years before, and this had amounted to an imprimatur for the tarnished ex-Mayor. Shortly thereafter he received an invitation to City Hall for a talk with La Guardia, and he wisecracked as he emerged to reporters, "We were trying to find out if Diogenes was on the level." Nor was Walker's popularity diminished when he introduced La Guardia at a music festival in Carnegie Hall as "the greatest mayor New York ever had." A year later La Guardia named Walker to the $20,000-a-year job as the impartial chairman of the garment industry in New York, settling labor disputes.

In the midst of a speech for Willkie, Seabury blamed the President for inducing La Guardia "to forget his obligations as the reform, nonpartisan Mayor of New York City, and to stultify himself by the designation of Walker, the shocking character of whose administration had enabled the Mayor to win his present place." He interpreted the Mayor's appointment as an attempt to gain votes for Roosevelt among New Yorkers who still liked Walker. To La Guardia's denial that the President had anything to do with the appointment, Seabury replied that it did "credit to the Mayor's sense of humor." He accused La Guardia of "stepping down from his position of leadership among those who are striving for decent municipal government in the United States." Sorrowfully, he said that La Guardia had acted like Browning's "Lost Leader":

> *Just for a handful of silver he left us,*
> *Just for a riband to stick in his coat.*

When La Guardia heard Seabury utter these words over radio station WJZ, he was unhappy but fairly restrained. "The Walker selection by the dress industry is not an issue in this presidential campaign," he said. "Judge Seabury is on one side of this presidential campaign and I on the other. A statement like his, coming from one I admire so much and am so fond of—it hurts me personally."

Only months after President Roosevelt's re-election to a third term, the differences between Seabury and La Guardia had been repaired. Despite faltering by some of the conservative Republicans, in the spring of 1941 Seabury again spearheaded a Fusion drive to support a third term for La Guardia. Seabury's business friends in the Republican ranks reminded him that La Guardia had gone a little too far in supporting Roosevelt and in calling Willkie the candidate of the "utilities gangsters." But at many private conferences, Seabury said that there were two overwhelming reasons for supporting La Guardia again: First, he had committed fewer blunders than any mayor the city had had in more than a generation; second, there was no other candidate who could defeat a Tammany combination of the New York, Bronx, and Brooklyn machines.

In November, 1941, Seabury stood up before a Fusion party rally in Madison Square Garden and spoke to the people of New York for La Guardia. He reviewed the record of Tammany and the reforms under La Guardia. He praised La Guardia, ironically, for some of the reasons that he used against Roosevelt. "The government of the City of New York has been converted into an agency for social service," Seabury told the Fusion audience. "The improvements that have taken place have effected not only the financial rehabilitation of the city, but have served the material, cultural and social needs of the people." This time, Seabury pointed out, even President Roosevelt was backing Mayor La Guardia openly, a statement which brought applause and cheers. In his effort to convince the voters, Seabury marshaled every forceful argument in his brief for La Guardia's election. What counted with him, as always, was to defeat Tammany Hall.

On Election Day La Guardia won by a plurality of 132,000 votes, the closest mayoralty race in three decades. The Democrats had falsely raised issues that Seabury and La Guardia had been accused of before—Communist ideology and support. And they had come up with a temporarily popular candidate, William O'Dwyer, the Brooklyn district attorney, riding high on his record as the prosecutor of Murder, Inc. A disappointed political columnist in the *Brooklyn Eagle,* attacking Seabury, said that La Guardia was now dominated by "Saint Sam-any" instead of Tammany.

Seabury urged La Guardia to run for a fourth term in 1945, but the Mayor's mind was elsewhere all during the war. Like many other World War I officers, the "Major" was trying to get overseas in an important post; few public officials had his record in or knowledge of the Mediterranean area. La Guardia expected to be commissioned a brigadier general in charge of military government in Italy (a job held, instead, by Colonel Charles Poletti, former Lieutenant Governor of New York). According to Robert Moses, Seabury and C. C. Burlingham persuaded their old friend, Secretary of War Henry L. Stimson, not to approve La Guardia because the Mayor was irreplaceable in New York City. There was, undoubtedly, opposition among the military in Washington and Europe to having such a temperamental and politically important man as La Guardia in an Allied Military Government post calling for diplomacy.

When La Guardia declined to run again, declaring that he believed in rotation in office (though some held he withdrew because he could not win), Seabury refused to back either the Democratic or Republican candidates. "I shall not support the sham Fusion ticket nominated by the Republican party. We now have two Tammany Hall tickets in the field," he said. "One is headed by William O'Dwyer and the other unworthy one is headed by Jonah Goldstein." He accused Goldstein of being a "lifelong Tammanyite" in spite of his acceptance by the Republicans. After saying that New Yorkers would be insured a return to the corruption and demoralization which prevailed before Mayor La Guardia if either major-party candidate won, he urged the election of an independent, Newbold Morris, on a "No-Deal" ticket, which La Guardia supported. Without Fusion's own machine behind him, Morris did not stand a chance. O'Dwyer became mayor.

Thus ended the great Fusion movement. The friendship of La Guardia and Seabury, the "Father of Fusion," continued in the final months of life left for the former Mayor. On September 20, 1947, at the age of sixty-four, La Guardia died of cancer. The next day, over Station WJZ, Judge Seabury, who had spoken often on the same station exhorting the people to vote for La Guardia, led a memorial program.

"No man who has ever been Mayor of New York City did more for its people than did Mayor La Guardia," Seabury declared. "He did not spare himself. His boundless energy was always in action to promote the welfare and happiness of the whole people of New York. He was a great character. Few cities have ever been favored with such a dynamic personality. The truth is, Mayor La Guardia loved the people and had no other wish or purpose except to serve their interests. This he did in a remarkable manner. He stands at the head of the great men who have been Mayors of New York City. As time goes on his great reputation for achievement will be increased."

"I am reasonably certain of one thing," La Guardia had declared. "When it's time for me to step down, the people will say, 'Well, the little fellow played square.'"

The "Major" had been the "Bishop's" outstanding political accomplishment.

Seldom had righteousness found such an armorer.

CHAPTER 20

A Citizen of New York

THE wheel of life had come almost full circle. In three-quarters of a century, Seabury's moments of greatness overbalanced his lesser moments. In law, he had reached the bench at an earlier age and earlier in his career than most judges; he had practiced as he desired, as a barrister; his investigative assignment had given him the chance to do more than settle old political scores; and, as the conscience for the Fusion movement and its outstanding mayor, he had become the first citizen of reform in New York, setting an example for future municipal reformers in the United States.

That evaluation, measured not in public but in personal terms, included shortcomings rather in manner than in character. Beyond his circle of intimates, he could be sanctimonious, humorless, and unforgiving of human failings. Although his aloofness was merely a way of showing respect for the privacy of others, nevertheless he did maintain some distance between his associates and himself; he could be a most generous friend but not a companion. The same unbending will that stiffened his personal relations was the force behind his public achievement. He was born to be admired, not loved.

On his birthday in 1950, he sat in a high-backed leather chair behind the huge oak desk in his small law office at 31 Nassau Street talking with a caller. His mien was still judicial, his blue suit, starched white shirt, and gray, figured tie still gave him a look of elegance and authority; but old age had changed his probing glance into a vague and questioning stare. On his desk lay two large albums of clippings from the investigation days. One headline read: "SEABURY CALLS TAMMANY MENACE TO NATION." He puffed on his pipe and, almost matter of factly, said, "It still is." More to himself than to the caller, he added, "I don't want to go through it all again. I don't want to talk about myself. One only hopes to be obscurely good. I have no particular story to tell—it's all ancient history."

The law practice dwindled, and Seabury shortened his day. The ritual of going to the office, reading the mail, dictating answers, lunching with friends, attending meetings of lawyers' groups replaced work. His now-married secretary, Dorothy Benner Whitbeck, stood by faithfully, guarding the confidential files for the last remaining writing projects that occupied him.

Nearly every day Seabury lunched with Lee McCanliss, discussing old cases they had shared, legal education, and the country's political currents. From time to time Seabury's "boys" would drop in; they were always welcomed. To them he remained the reformer of the early 1930's and not an aging antagonist of the New Deal. He took one of them to lunch at the Bankers Club. Looking around at some of the captains of Wall Street, Seabury suddenly said, "I have nothing against capitalists—it's capitalism which must go."

The remark was not so far out of character as it sounded. This was a Henry George disciple talking, a radical and reformer of the 1890's. On the one hundredth anniversary of George's birth, Seabury had stood up and declared his lasting faith: "Although men have not as yet adopted specific remedies which he proposed, they have, nevertheless, absorbed much of his philosophy, and that fact has, of itself, enriched the thought of those throughout the world who believe in democracy. . . . As we look at the complications of our social and economic system, no fair-minded student can avoid the conclusion that many of the principles which Henry George expressed are applicable to it." When Anna George de Mille, the daughter of Henry George, died, Seabury and Harry Emerson Fosdick spoke at a service at Riverside Church, with Seabury praising the single taxer and recounting how he had campaigned for George's mayoralty bid in 1897. At a dinner party in 1950, Seabury showed little interest in the conversation until George's name was mentioned. Flushed and excited, Seabury demanded, "Has anyone ever disproved Henry George's single-tax theory?"

His own principal investment had been land, and now Seabury was forced to sell out, acre by acre, to maintain his way of life. When he decided to sell the house on East 63rd Street, appraisers came to set a replacement price and insurable value on every rug, painting, piece of silver, and stick of furniture—personal objects whose market value decreased on the market while their sentimental value increased. How could an impersonal appraisal firm judge the worth of the possessions he and Maud had collected over the years? The value of the paintings of distinguished historical personages by Raeburn, Romney, and Reynolds did not decrease, but the value of the prized books did. "Some of the books on North of Ireland history and events in India are absurdly valued," Seabury informed his nephew, John Northrop. "I paid much more for them and made extensive searches in order to get them." He invited the New York Genealogical and Biographical Society to examine the library, hoping they would buy it, but they did not because they already had most of the books.

The town house was sold, and the Seaburys moved into an apartment on Park Avenue, but their real home, more than ever, remained the farmhouse in East Hampton. They stayed there for longer week ends; the trips to and from the city were a burden. Their health was affected by their age. Judge Seabury recognized an infirmity in his hearing and joked about it in the office. "This business of getting old is no fun," he said to Floyd Tomkins, Jr., who worked for him. But there were still a few dreams to pursue which required his presence in the city and, of these, the most important was the publication of his book *The New Federalism,* expounding his ideals of government.

He began the book with studied leisure in the 1920's, dictating whenever he could, and putting it aside altogether during the investigation. By the late 1940's the work had grown to three volumes. His friends and nephews tried to interest book publishers, with no success. Finally, a group of them, led by John Northrop, arranged to subsidize the original printing by E. P. Dutton & Company in 1950. Tomkins rearranged the manuscript, eliminating some repetition. "The book derived from his Henry George ideas," Tomkins said, "and I found much of it interesting but verbose." At first the Judge did not know the book was subsidized, but he was, nevertheless, pleased when he found out at contract-signing time what his friends had done. When the book appeared, with a photograph of Seabury by Edward Steichen on the jacket, Maud gave a party for all the backers. It was a sentimental occasion. The book was dedicated "To My Wife, Maud Richey Seabury."

The New Federalism was subtitled "An inquiry into the means by which social power may be so distributed between state and people as to insure prosperity and progress." It was all this and more, a diffuse attempt to blend some of the leading European and American economic and political theories to provide a coherent solution of problems that had vexed geopoliticians and government planners for thousands of years. The task was obviously an impossible one, and Judge Seabury had reached an age where he could not apply to it his once keen analytical sense. But he bravely began his work with a quotation from George's *Progress and Poverty.*

A theme he set forth was that Man, in the United States and elsewhere, must have bread, butter, and justice from governmental and nonstate sources. "The masses are not asking for favors," he wrote, "but insisting upon equality of opportunity and the full measure of freedom which permits them to receive or suffer the consequences of their own actions." He pointed out that we are living under a monopolistic economy that must be restrained by the state until replaced by a voluntary economic order. An anti–New-Deal undertone was present, but he saw a hopeful sign on the horizon in the consumers' co-operative movement that envisioned a form of guild socialism. And quoting from Ortega y Gasset's *The Revolt of the Masses,* he warned against state intervention so powerful that it would suck out the marrow of society. The book abounded in scholarly citations.

In the *Columbia Law Review,* Herbert Agar interpreted Seabury's effort as a cogent expression of traditional American hatred for the encroaching state and a plea for an old Calhoun form of constitutional government. Most of the reviewers in the newspapers and periodicals were hard put, with justification, to summarize the contents of *The New Federalism,* but they were respectful.

No publisher could be found, however, for a book of autobiographical jottings—notes, clippings, and speeches. Mrs. Whitbeck bound the papers in loose-leaf books and, from time to time, the Judge went over the typed pages, adding a few words. He had dictated to begin with, "As I take my pen in hand to sketch the outline of my life, I am reminded of the admonition on the sun dial that, 'Time stays, we go.' It would seem, therefore, that if the task is to be undertaken, it cannot be longer deferred. I was born. . . ." The pages and clippings were detailed up until the political blow when he was defeated for governor in 1916.

The notes for an autobiography were fragmentary, with many omissions of fact, and they revealed no intimate thoughts or psychological insights. For Judge Seabury, even when he wanted to place himself in the history of his times, characteristically was unable to invade even his own privacy. No mention was made, for example, of his deliberate efforts to obtain the Democratic nomination for President or Vice President in 1932. However, the title did describe the role he chose to play in his city: "Samuel Seabury, Citizen of New York."

In the middle of July, 1950, the Seaburys were at their home in East Hampton. The Judge sat in an old wicker chair on the back patio, puffing his pipe in the shade of a gnarled apple tree. He could see Maud walking in the English garden, "Aunt Maud's side" of the back of the farm. She was clipping a hedge, when she suddenly complained of indigestion. A doctor was summoned, and it was discovered that she had suffered a heart attack. Less than a week later, on July 21, 1950, she died, at the age of seventy-two.

Services were held at St. Luke's Church on James Lane in East Hampton. The rector, Samuel Davis, spoke of her activity as a devoted and wonderful churchwoman, of her work for the American Red Cross, the Garden Club of America, and the English-Speaking Union of the United States; she had received the King's Medal "for service in the cause of freedom" during World War II. She was buried in the Seabury plot in Trinity Church's cemetery in upper Manhattan.

The sparkle left the Judge's life. "How I wish I could do or say something to S.S. that would be 'comfortable' (to quote the Prophet Isaiah)," C. C. Burlingham, the old civic reformer, wrote Bill Northrop. "I had never thought it possible that our so dearly beloved Maud could die first and leave him alone and desolate." The Judge remained at the farm; his nephews looked in from time to time. A faithful housekeeper, Elizabeth Smith, who had been with the family for many years, assumed the responsibility of caring for him. To Dudley Tooth in London, an art dealer who had become a friend of the Seaburys during their many trips abroad, he wrote of his grief. "You and Mrs. Tooth will be sorry I know to hear of Mrs. Seabury's death quite suddenly last summer. You can imagine how great a blow her going has been to me."

Toward the end of the year, Seabury began to wind up his affairs. He changed his will after Maud's death so that his three nephews were the principal beneficiaries of his estate, mainly the farm and hundreds of acres of East Hampton property. Several thousands of dollars each were listed for other relatives and employees, including his secretary, gardener, and housekeeper. The Brueghel and the Hogarth were bequeathed to John and William Northrop, respectively. As executors, he named "my nephew," Andrew Oliver, and the "nephew of my late wife," John Northrop.

His own health was, in the kind phrase of friends, "beginning to slip." He was suffering from senile dementia caused by a constriction of the blood vessels to the brain. "The heart went out of him after Maud's death," friends said, attributing his decline to sorrow. In 1950, he had moments of lucidity that alternated with longer moments of blankness. When he left his apartment for a walk in Manhattan, he carried a card in his pocket with his name and address so that he could be helped home in case he lost his way. He gave up his New York apartment in 1951, and moved out to East Hampton permanently.

The terrible present meant nothing to him, and he often repeated himself, but, strangely, on matters of the past his memory was nearly perfect: the great past was the only reality. Lee McCanliss came by regularly, and Seabury's face would light up. "Mac," the Judge said, "have we anything on today in court?" McCanliss would say no, and Seabury would continue with one of his favorite remarks, "How many possibilities are open to us?"

The farm in East Hampton was safer for him than the city. Old friends and old employees were near by. His former chauffeur, Nick Livingston, lived in the village and stopped in at the farm to take the Judge for a drive. They drove around Three Mile Harbor, The

Springs, and Amagansett. Seabury, who had always been five minutes early leaving for court or the investigation chambers, periodically asked, "What time is it?" And, afterward, when he was helped out of the back seat, he always said, "A very lovely ride, Nicholas, a very lovely ride."

In March of 1955, he suffered a fracture of the hip while preparing to go to bed. A few years before he had broken his shoulder. Dr. David Edwards placed him in the Southampton Hospital. He could no longer remain at the farm; he was eighty-two years old and an invalid, and professional nurses were constantly needed.

After Dr. Edwards had pinned his hip, the Judge was moved to Hand's Nursing Home, a private old mansion in East Hampton. The beloved farm and most of the land was sold to pay for his final years. He was unable to walk by himself. Most of his days were spent in bed, but in good weather he sat up in a wheelchair. Sometimes he looked at the television screen. Some friends and relatives visited him. His former secretary came with her husband, and light came to his eyes briefly when he saw her. Even though he could barely talk, he motioned toward her and raised his hands up and down. John Whitbeck said, "The Judge's eyes tried to tell the nurse that Dorothy was a friend from a time when things were different." When his brother's widow, Mrs. William Marston Seabury, visited him, he recognized her and whispered, "Kitty, Kitty," the name he called her when both were young. . . .

Later in the year, as quietly as court procedures allowed, his nephews, Andrew Oliver and John Northrop, made application in Suffolk County for their appointment as a committee in charge of "the Person and Property of Samuel Seabury, an Alleged Incompetent Person." Dr. Edwards testified that his patient's speech was wholly incoherent and that his senile dementia, caused by arteriosclerotic changes, made him unfit to care for himself or his affairs.

A psychiatrist, Dr. Arthur E. Soper, testified that he was unable to obtain any intelligent responses from Judge Seabury. "I asked him questions about former Mayor La Guardia, recalling his public life," Dr. Soper declared. And he said that Seabury responded by mumbling over and over, "We'll get them, we'll get them."

Justice Peter M. Daly of the supreme court in his charge recalled Judge Seabury's years of greatness and then, as required by statute, turned the matter over to the jury. In a few minutes they returned with the only possible verdict. On November 9, 1955, former Judge Samuel Seabury was officially declared an incompetent person in the eyes of the law.

Judge Seabury died at the age of eighty-five, on May 7, 1958, at 1:30 in the morning. Many people were surprised to discover from their newspapers that day that he had still been alive. For the quarter of a century that had passed since his famous investigations, he had remained in the background, "obscurely good."

Two hundred and fifty people came to the funeral service at Trinity Church. Besides his relatives, all his "boys" from the investigation years were there; now they were leading attorneys and judges and public officials. Others paying tribute were United States Attorney General William P. Rogers; former Governor Dewey; Roy Howard of *The World-Telegram;* Mrs. Fiorello H. La Guardia; many state supreme court justices and the presidents of the Association of the Bar of the City of New York, the New York County Lawyers Association, the New York State Bar Association, and the New York Law Institute, all of which he had presided over at one time or another.

Although the Judge had attended church only occasionally, the leading dignitaries of the Episcopal Church were present: The Right Reverend Horace W. B. Donegan, the Bishop of New York, conducted the service, assisted by the Very Reverend Lawrence Rose, dean of the General Theological Seminary, the Reverend Canon Bernard C. Newman, vicar of Trinity Church, and the Reverend Dr. Samuel Davis, the rector of St. Luke's in East Hampton. The sermons were short; there was little else to say other than that this Samuel Seabury, like his revered ancestor, had added new glory to the name and moments of greatness to his times. The choir sang *The Strife Is O'er, the Battle Done* and *Once to Every Man and Nation.* Hearing the hymns, those present thought of the man who was the most inspired investigator of municipal corruption in the first half of the twentieth century. If an awareness of other historic eras survived, Plato's "ministers of political corruption" would always produce courageous antagonists in a republic.

Seabury's former assistants that morning heard again his admonitions to them: *Old heads for counsel, young heads for war. There is more eloquence in the testimony of a single illiterate witness telling of oppression suffered from legal processes than in the greatest sermon or editorial. Let's attack this subject man-fashion. Do not be discouraged—the facts we brought out are going to sink into the public's mind long after the wisecracks are forgotten.*

On the Seabury family crest the Latin motto read: *Supera Alta Tenere* (Hold to the Most High). The life force that boiled in his veins, making him the crusading reformer and uncompromising man of principle, caused him to honor the venerable words. An Anglo-Saxon idea of justice and the ethics of a long tradition had caught fire in a young mind long ago and glowed through changing years.

An old friend, walking past Trinity's weather-beaten headstones after the service, said simply: "Seabury really cared for New York."

The Publications of Samuel Seabury

PAMPHLETS AND BOOKS

Law Syllabus on Corporation Law. (In collaboration with S. Sherman Pickford, LL.B.) 36 pp. New York. 1894.

A Review of the Labor Laws Relative to the Rate of Wages and the Hours of Labor in the State of New York. 53 pp. New York: E. R. Mantz, printer. 1901.

Municipal Ownership and Operation of Public Utilities in New York City. 202 pp. New York: Municipal Ownership Publishing Co. 1905.

The Law and Practice of the City Court of the City of New York. 1,317 pp. New York: Baker, Voorhis Co. 1907.

Two Hundred and Seventy-five Years of East Hampton. A historical sketch. 140 pp. Published for the community, East Hampton, L.I., by Bartlett Orr Press, New York. 1926.

Captain Henry Martin Beare (1760–1828), Life, Ancestry and Descendants. 275 pp. Printed by Lawyers Press, New York, for private distribution. 1938.

The New Federalism. An inquiry into the means by which social power may be so distributed between state and people as to insure prosperity and progress. 311 pp. New York: E. P. Dutton & Co., Inc. 1950.

OFFICIAL SEABURY INVESTIGATION REPORTS

In the Matter of the Investigation, Under Commission Issued by the Governor of the State of New York, of Charges Made Against Honorable Thomas C. T. Crain, District Attorney of New York County. 85 pp. Aug. 31, 1931.

In the Matter of the Investigation of the Magistrates' Courts in the First Judicial Department and the Magistrates Thereof, and of Attorneys-at-Law Practicing in Said Courts. Supreme Court, Appellate Division, First Judicial Department. Final report. 256 pp. Mar. 28, 1932.

In the Matter of the Investigation of the Departments of the Government of the City of New York, Pursuant to Joint Resolution Adopted by the Legislature of the State of New York, Mar. 23, 1931. Intermediate report. 198 pp. Jan. 25, 1932.

In the Matter of the Investigation of the Departments of the Government of the City of New York, Pursuant to Joint Resolutions Adopted by the Legislature of the State of New York. Second intermediate report. 140 pp., plus 10 appendices. 219 pp. Dec. 19, 1932.

In the Matter of the Investigation of the Departments of the Government of the City of New York, Pursuant to Joint Resolutions Adopted by the Legislature of the State of New York. Final report, 143 pp., plus exhibits. Dec. 27, 1932.

MINUTES OF PUBLIC HEARINGS

Magistrates' courts investigation. Transcript of testimony, 299 witnesses examined. From Sept. 29, 1930, to May 14, 1931, covering 4,596 mimeographed pages.

Joint Legislative Committee to Investigate the Departments of the City of New York. Transcript of testimony, 320 witnesses examined. From July 21, 1931, to June 1, 1932. In 16 volumes, covering 10,620 mimeographed pages.

Hearing before Governor Franklin D. Roosevelt, in the matter of the charges against Mayor James J. Walker, brought by Samuel Seabury, William J. Schieffelin, as chairman, on behalf of the Committee of One Thousand, James E. Finegan, and others. Transcript of testimony of 34 witnesses, led by Mayor Walker. Aug. 11, 1932, to Sept. 2, 1932. In 5 volumes, covering 2,000 mimeographed pages.

BOOKS ABOUT SAMUEL SEABURY

Samuel Seabury: A Challenge. By Walter Chambers. 389 pp. New York: The Century Co. 1932.

The Insolence of Office: The Story of the Seabury Investigations. By William B. Northrop and John B. Northrop. 306 pp. New York: G. P. Putnam's Sons. 1932.

Index